MARIE CURIE
A Portrait Made in 19??

MADAME CURIE

BY

EVE CURIE

TRANSLATED BY VINCENT SHEEAN

WILLIAM HEINEMANN LTD
LONDON :: TORONTO

104.

FIRST PUBLISHED FEBRUARY 1938
REPRINTED FEBRUARY, APRIL, JUNE 1938
CHEAP EDITION (8s 6d) OCTOBER 1938
REPRINTED NOVEMBER, DECEMBER 1938
FEBRUARY, SEPTEMBER 1939
JANUARY 1940
JANUARY, MAY, JUNE, NOVEMBER 1941
MARCH, AUGUST, DECEMBER 1942
APRIL 1943, OCTOBER 1947

MANUFACTURED IN THE NETHERLANDS

INTRODUCTION

THE LIFE OF MARIE CURIE contains prodigies in such number that one would like to tell her story like a legend.

She was a woman, she belonged to an oppressed nation; she was poor; she was beautiful. A powerful vocation summoned her from her motherland, Poland, to study in Paris, where she lived through years of poverty and solitude. There she met a man whose genius was akin to hers. She married him; their happiness was unique. By the most desperate and arid effort they discovered a magic element, radium. This discovery not only gave birth to a new science and a new philosophy: it provided mankind with the means of treating a dreadful disease.

At the moment when the fame of the two scientists and benefactors was spreading through the world, grief overtook Marie: her husband, her wonderful companion, was taken from her by death in an instant. But in spite of distress and physical illness, she continued alone the work that had been begun with him and brilliantly developed the science they had created together.

The rest of her life resolves itself into a kind of perpetual giving. To the war wounded she gave her devotion and her health. Later on she gave her advice, her wisdom and all the hours of her time to her pupils, to future scientists who came to her from all parts of the world.

When her mission was accomplished she died exhausted, having refused wealth and endured her honours with indifference.

It would have been a crime to add the slightest ornament to this story, so like a myth. I have not related a single anecdote of which I am not sure. I have not deformed a single essential phrase or so much as invented the colour of a dress. The facts are as stated; the quoted words were actually pronounced.

I am indebted to my Polish family, charming and cultivated, and above all to my mother's eldest sister, Mme Dluska, who was her dearest friend, for precious letters and direct evidence on the

v

youth of the scientist. From the personal papers and short biographical notes left by Marie Curie, from innumerable official documents, the narratives and letters of French and Polish friends whom I cannot thank enough, and from the recollections of my sister Irène Joliot-Curie, of my brother-in-law, Frederic Joliot and my own, I have been able to evoke her more recent years

I hope that the reader may constantly feel, across the ephemeral movement of one existence, what in Marie Curie was even more rare than her work or her life: the immovable structure of a character; the stubborn effort of an intelligence; the free immolation of a being that could give all and take nothing, could even receive nothing; and above all the quality of a soul in which neither fame nor adversity could change the exceptional purity.

Because she had that soul, without the slightest sacrifice Marie Curie rejected money, comfort and the thousand advantages that genuinely great men may obtain from immense fame. She suffered from the part the world wished her to play; her nature was so susceptible and exacting that among all the attitudes suggested by fame she could choose none: neither familiarity nor mechanical friendliness, deliberate austerity nor showy modesty.

She did not know how to be famous.

My mother was thirty-seven years old when I was born. When I was big enough to know her well, she was already an ageing woman who had passed the summit of renown. And yet it is the celebrated scientist who is strangest to me—probably because the idea that she was a "celebrated scientist" did not occupy the mind of Marie Curie. It seems to me, rather, that I have always lived near the poor student, haunted by dreams, who was Marya Sklodovska long before I came into the world.

And to this young girl Marie Curie still bore a resemblance on the day of her death. A hard and long and dazzling career had not succeeded in making her greater or less, in sanctifying or debasing her. She was on that last day just as gentle, stubborn, timid and curious about all things as in the days of her obscure beginnings.

It was impossible to inflict on her, without sacrilege, the pompous obsequies which governments give their great men.

In a country graveyard, among summer flowers, she had the simplest and quietest burial, as if the life just ended had been like that of a thousand others.

I should have liked the gifts of a writer to tell of this eternal student—of whom Einstein said: "Marie Curie is, of all celebrated beings, the only one whom fame has not corrupted"—passing like a stranger across her own life, intact, natural and very nearly unaware of her astonishing destiny.

EVE CURIE.

CONTENTS

PART ONE

PART TWO

PART THREE

ILLUSTRATIONS

PART ONE

CHAPTER I

Manya

DEEP silence invaded the school building in Novolipki Street on
Sundays. Beneath the stone pediment, carved in Russian letters
with the words "High School for Boys," the principal door was
bolted and the columned vestibule looked like an abandoned
temple Life had retired from the single storey of the long, low
structure, from its light-filled rooms where the desks of black wood
were aligned, scratched by pen-knives and cut with initials. Nothing could be heard but the bells of the Church of the Virgin,
ringing for vespers, and, now and then, coming from the street,
the rattle of a cart or the lazily trotting horse of a droshky. Behind
the railing which bordered the court-yard the school's four lilac
trees bloomed, dusty and meagre, and passers-by in their Sunday
best turned with surprise to catch a breath of the sugary scent It
was hot, even though May was hardly ended. In Warsaw the sun
is as tyrannous and intense as the frost.

But something had disturbed this sabbatical peace. From the
left wing of the building, on the ground floor, where dwelt
M. Vladislav Sklodovski, professor of physics and under-inspector
of the school, there came the muffled echo of mysterious activity.
It sounded like hammer-strokes, without order or cadence; then
the rumble of a structure falling to pieces, saluted by sharp yells;
then blows again. And brief orders shouted in Polish:

"Hela, I've run out of munitions!"

"The tower, Joseph! Aim at the tower!"

"Manya, get out of the way!"

"Why? I'm bringing you some cubes!"

3

"O-oh-oh!"

A crash, the thunder of wooden blocks across the polished floor, and the tower was gone. The noise was doubled; projectiles flew, alighted.

The battlefield was a huge square room with windows giving on an inside court-yard of the Gymnasium Four children's beds occupied its corners, and, between them, four children from five to nine years of age played their game of war with shrieks and yells. The peaceful uncle, a lover of whist and patience, who had given the small Sklodovskis a building game for Christmas, had certainly not foreseen the use to which his present would be put. For some days Joseph, Bronya, Hela and Manya had obediently built castles, bridges and churches according to the models they found in the big wooden box; but the blocks and beams soon found their true destiny: short columns of oak formed an artillery, the small squares were bullets, and the young architects had become field-marshals.

Crawling on his belly across the floor, Joseph was gaining ground, and moved his cannon methodically forward toward the adversary. Even at the height of the battle his healthy child's face, with its firm features underneath fair hair, kept the seriousness proper to an army commander. He was the eldest and the most learned of the four; he was also the only man Around him were girls, nothing but girls, all dressed alike and all wearing, over their Sunday clothes, little frilled collars and dark beribboned aprons.

But, to be just, the girls fought well. The eyes of Hela, Joseph's ally, blazed with savage ardour. Hela was mad with rage at her six and a half years; she wanted to fling her blocks farther and harder; she envied Bronya her eight years—Bronya the dimpled and dazzling creature whose blonde hair whipped the air as she pranced about defending her troops, drawn up between the two windows.

At Bronya's side a tiny aide-de-camp in a fancy apron gathered up munitions, galloped from one battalion to another, and busied herself mightily, her face aflame, her lips dry from having cried and laughed too much   ,

"Manya!"

The child stopped in full flight and allowed her apron, which she held clutched to her breast, to fall; a consignment of blocks clattered to the floor.

"What's the matter?"

Zosia, the eldest of the young Sklodovskis, had just come into the room. Although she was not yet twelve she appeared, beside her younger brother and sisters, to be a grown person. Her long, ash-blonde hair was thrown back to fall loosely on her shoulders. She had a lovely, animated face and dreaming eyes of exquisite grey.

"Mother says you've been playing too long. You must stop now."

"But Bronya needs me . . . I'm the one that brings her blocks!"

"Mamma says you're to come now."

After a moment's hesitation Manya took her sister's hand and made a dignified exit. It is hard to fight a war at the age of five, and the little girl, at the end of her strength, was not altogether unhappy to abandon the battle. From the next room a gentle voice was calling her by names like caresses: "Manya . . . Manyusya . . . my Anciupecio . . ."

In Poland, diminutives and nicknames are very common. The Sklodovskis had never called Sophie, their eldest daughter, anything but "Zosia." "Bronya" had taken the place of Bronislava, Helen became "Hela," and Joseph "Jozio." But none of them had received as many nicknames as Marya, the youngest and best-loved in the house. "Manya" was her ordinary diminutive, "Manyusya" a name of affection, and "Anciupecio" a comic nickname dating from her earliest infancy.

"My Anciupecio, how mussed your hair is! And how red you are!"

Delicate hands, too pale and too thin, tied the undone ribbons of the apron and smoothed the short curls from the stubborn face of the future scientist. Little by little, the child relaxed and was at peace.

Manya had an infinite love for her mother. It seemed to her that no other creature on earth could be so graceful, so good or so wise.

Mme Sklodovska was the eldest daughter in a family of country squires. Her father, Felix Boguski, belonged to that small land-owning nobility which has so many representatives in Poland. Too poor to live on his own estate, he had to administer the property of families more powerful than his own. His marriage was romantic: he fell in love with an aristocratic young girl with no fortune but of nobler birth than his, and carried her off to a secret marriage in spite of the protests of the beauty's parents. Years rolled on: the seducer became a timid, shivering old man and his beloved a peevish grandmother. . . .

Of their six children Mme Sklodovska was certainly the most balanced and the most intelligent She received a very good education in a private school in Warsaw, and, having decided to devote herself to teaching, became a professor in the same school and finally director of the institution When, in 1860, Professor Vladislav Sklodovski asked her hand in marriage, he was choosing a very accomplished wife. She had no money; but she was well-born, she was pious and she was active. She had an assured career ahead of her. Moreover, she was a musician: she could play the piano and sing the ballads of the day in a ravishing languid voice.

Last of all, she was very beautiful. An exquisite photograph shows her to us at the time of her marriage, with her perfectly drawn face; her smooth and heavily plaited hair, the marvellous arch of her brows, and the peaceful, secret look of her grey eyes lengthened like the eyes of Egypt.

It was what people called a "very suitable" marriage; the Sklodovskis were also part of that minor nobility which the mis-fortunes of Poland had ruined. The cradle of the clan, Sklody, was an agglomeration of farms about a hundred kilometres north of Warsaw. Several families, allied among themselves and originating at Sklody, bore the name of Sklodovski: according to a widespread custom, the lord of the manor at some time in the past was supposed to have bestowed on his tenants the right to adopt his coat of arms.

The natural vocation of these families was to cultivate the earth; but in times of trouble the estates grew poorer and were frittered away. Though in the eighteenth century the direct ancestor of Vladislav Sklodovski possessed several hundred acres and could lead a comfortable life, and even his descendants lived like well-to-do farmers, the same was not true of Joseph, the young professor's father. In his desire to improve his own condition and to honour the name of which he was so proud, that Sklodovski turned toward study; and after a career made dramatic by wars and revolutions, he is to be found directing the boys' school in an important town, Lublin. He was the first intellectual in the family.

The Boguski and the Sklodovski formed numerous households: six children here, seven there. Farmers, school-teachers, a notary, a nun. . . . And then a few eccentric shadows appear: one of Mme Sklodovska's brothers, Henryk Boguski, was an incurable dilettante who believed himself to be gifted for the most perilous enterprises of genius. And as for the reckless Zdzislav Sklodovski —the professor's brother—that jolly fellow who was successively a lawyer in Petersburg, a soldier in the Polish insurrection, and an exile, a Provençal poet and doctor of law at Toulouse, wavered perpetually between ruin and riches.

On both sides of the family hotheads and peaceable characters occur at once; men of judgment rub shoulders with knights-errant.

The parents of Marie Curie were among the judicious. Her father, following his own father's example, went far in his scientific studies at the University of Petersburg, and returned to Warsaw to teach mathematics and physics. Her mother successfully conducted a school to which the best families of the town sent their daughters. During eight years the family lived at her school in Freta Street, on the first floor. Every morning, as the schoolmaster left the conjugal lodging—which gave on the court-yard with balconies light as garlands from window to window—the rooms at the front of the house echoed with the chatter of young girls waiting for their first class.

But when, in 1868, Vladislav Sklodovski left the school where he had been teaching to become professor and under-inspector at the high school in Novolipki Street, his wife had to adapt herself to the new existence. It would have been impossible for her to live in the apartment allotted them by her husband's new position, keep her place as principal of the girls' school, and at the same time bring up the five children she had brought into the world. Not without regret Mme Sklodovska gave up her work at the boarding school and left the Freta Street house where, some months before (November 7th, 1867), she had given birth to Marie Curie, little Manya.

"Now then, Anciupecio, are you asleep?"

Manya, doubled up on a little hassock at her mother's feet, shook her head.

"No, Mamma. I'm all right."

Once again Mme Sklodovska ran her light fingers over the forehead of her youngest child. That familiar gesture was the sweetest Manya knew. As far back as Manya could remember she had never been kissed by her mother. She could imagine no greater happiness than to crouch near-by, as close as possible to the pensive and charming figure, and to feel confusedly, by almost imperceptible signs—a word, a smile, an affectionate look—what immense tenderness watched over her young destiny

She did not yet understand the cruel origin of these rites and of the isolation to which her mother was condemned: Mme Sklodovska was seriously ill. The first signs of tuberculosis had appeared when Manya was born, and in the five years since then, in spite of care and consultation, the disease had made certain progress. But Mme Sklodovska, a courageous Christian, was determined that nobody at home should notice her suffering more than she could help. Dressed with neatness, ever high-spirited, she continued the life of a busy housewife and gave the illusion of being well even though she imposed strict rules on herself; she would use only dishes reserved for herself, and would never embrace her son or her daughters. The little Sklodovskis knew very little about her dreadful disease: short attacks of dry coughing, which they heard from one room to the next; a desolate shadow on their father's face; and the short phrase, "Restore our mother's health," which, for some time past, had been added to their evening prayer. . . .

The young woman rose and gently put aside the childish hands that clung to her.

"Let me go, Manyusya . . . I have things to do."

"May I stay here?—I—may I read?"

"I wish you would go into the garden instead. It's so beautiful to-day!"

A very special timidity reddened Manya's cheeks when she broached the subject of reading: the year before, in the country, Bronya, finding it extremely boring to have to learn the whole alphabet by herself, had taken it into her head to make her sister an experiment in education, to "play teacher" to her. For several weeks the little girls had amused themselves by arranging, in what was often enough an arbitrary order, their letters cut out of cardboard. Then, one morning, while Bronya was faltering out a very simple reading lesson to her parents, Manya grew impatient, took the opened book from her hands, and read aloud the opening sentence on the page. At first, flattered by the silence that surrounded her, she continued this fascinating game, but suddenly panic seized her. One look at the stupefied faces of M. and Mme Sklodovski, another at Bronya's sulky stare, a few unintelligible stammers, an irrepressible sob—and instead of the infant prodigy there was only a baby of four, crying in a doleful voice through her tears:

"Beg—pardon! Pardon! I didn't do it on purpose. It's not my fault—it's not Bronya's fault! It's only because it was so easy!"

Manya had suddenly conceived, with despair, that she might perhaps never be forgiven for having learned to read.

After that memorable session the child had grown familiar with her letters; and if she did not make remarkable progress it was owing to the adroit diplomacy of her parents, who constantly avoided giving books to her. Like prudent pedagogues, they were afraid of the precocity of their little girl, and every time she put out her hand toward one of the big-lettered albums that abounded in the house, a voice suggested: "You'd better play with your blocks. . . . Where is your doll? . . . Sing us a song, Manya." Or else, as to-day: "I wish you would go into the garden instead."

Manya cast a speculative eye in the direction of the door through which she had entered a while before. The rumble of blocks on the floor and the cries that came almost unmuffled through the partition proved that she had small chance of finding a walking companion there. There was no hope in the direction of the kitchen, either: a steady chatter and the crash of poker and stove-lid announced that the servants were preparing the evening meal.

"I'll look for Zosia."

"If you like."

"Zosia . . . *Zosia!*"

Hand in hand the two sisters went, through the narrow yard where, every day, they had played hide-and-seek and blind-man's buff. Passing the school buildings they reached a big level garden guarded by its gate of worm-eaten wood.

A faint smell of the earth, of countryside, was exhaled from the meagre grass and walled-in trees.

"Zosia, are we going to Zwola pretty soon?"

"Not yet—not until July But can you remember Zwola?"

Manya, with her astonishing memory, could recollect it all: the stream in which she and her sisters had paddled for hours at a time last summer. . . . The mud-cakes they had secretly kneaded, spattering their dresses and aprons with blackish spots, and as secretly put out to dry in the sun on a board known only to themselves. . . . The old lime-tree which was sometimes climbed by as many as seven or eight conspirators at a time, cousins and friends; they used to lift her, too, the "little one" whose arms and legs were not long enough. . . . The main branches were padded with cabbage leaves, cold and crackling; in other cabbage leaves among the smaller branches they cooled their provisions of gooseberries, of tender raw carrots, of cherries . . .

And at Marki, the torrid granary where Joseph used to go to learn his multiplication tables, and where they tried to bury Manya under the moving grain. . . . And old Father Skrzypovski, who made his whip crack so brilliantly when he drove the "break"! And Uncle Xavier's horses . . .

Every year the children had intoxicating holidays in the country. The fact was that in this vast family only one branch had become city dwellers; the Sklodovskis had numerous relations on the land. In each province there were some Sklodovskis and some Boguskis who cultivated a little of the Polish earth, and even though their houses were not sumptuous, they all had room enough to take in the professor and his family during the fine weather. In spite of her family's modest revenue, Manya was saved knowledge of the dull holiday-making of the cheap "summer resorts" frequented by the inhabitants of Warsaw. In summer this daughter of intellectuals became—or perhaps became again, in accordance with the deepest instinct of her race—a hardy little peasant.

"Let's run. I'll bet I can get to the end of the garden before you!" Zosia cried, taking her role as "mother" with becoming seriousness.

"I don't want to run. I want you to tell me a story."

Nobody—not even the professor or his wife—could tell a story like Zosia. Her imagination added extraordinary touches, like the brilliant variations of a virtuoso, to every anecdote or fairy tale. She also composed short comedies, which she performed with spirit in front of her astonished sisters and brother. Zosia's gifts as author and actress had quite subjugated Manya, who giggled and shuddered by turns as she listened to adventures so fantastic that their thread was not always easy for a baby of five to follow.

The girls turned back toward the house. As they drew nearer to the high school the elder instinctively slowed down and lowered her voice. The story she was making up and declaiming was not finished: even so, Zosia cut it short. The children walked silently past the windows in the right wing of the school all veiled by the same stiff lace curtains.

Behind those windows lived the person whom the Sklodovski family most feared and detested: M. Ivanov, director of the Gymnasium, the man who represented, within the walls of that school, the government of the Tsar.

It was a cruel fate, in the year 1872, to be a Pole, a "Russian subject," and to belong to that vibrant intelligentsia whose nerves were so near the surface; among them revolt was ever brooding, and they suffered more painfully than any other class in society from the servitude imposed upon them.

Exactly a century before, greedy sovereigns, the powerful neighbours of a greatly weakened State, had decided Poland's ruin. Three successive partitions had dismembered it into fragments which became officially German, Russian and Austrian. On several occasions the Poles rose against their oppressors: they succeeded only in strengthening the bonds that held them prisoners. After the failure of the heroic revolution of 1831 the Tsar Nicholas dictated severe measures of reprisal in Russian Poland The patriots were imprisoned and deported in a body; their property was confiscated. . . .

In 1863 another attempt and another catastrophe: the rebels had nothing but spades, scythes and clubs to oppose to the Tsarist rifles. Eighteen months of desperate struggle—and in the end the bodies of the insurgent leaders swung from five gibbets on the ramparts of Warsaw.

Since then everything had been done to enforce the obedience of a Poland that refused to die. While the convoys of chained rebels made their way toward the snows of Siberia, a flood of policemen, professors and minor functionaries was let loose over the countryside. Their mission? To keep watch over the Poles, to wear down their religion, suppress suspicious books and newspapers, and abolish the use of the national language little by little—in a word, to kill the soul of a people.

But in the other camp resistance was quick to organise. Disastrous experience had proved to the Poles that they had no chance of reconquering their liberty by force, at least for the moment. Their task was, therefore, to wait—and to thwart the dangers of those who wait, cowardice and discouragement.

The battle, therefore, had changed ground Its heroes were no longer those warriors armed with scythes who charged the Cossacks and died saying (like the celebrated Louis Narbutt): "What happiness to die for my country!" The new heroes were the intellectuals, the artists, priests, school-teachers—those upon whom the mind of the new generation depended. Their courage consisted in forcing themselves to be hypocrites, and in supporting any humiliation rather than lose the places in which the Tsar still tolerated them—and from which they could secretly influence Polish youth and guide their compatriots.

Thus beneath the affectations of politeness a profound antagonism existed between conqueror and conquered throughout the Polish schools—between the harassed teachers and the spying principals, the Sklodovskis and the Ivanovs.

The Ivanov who reigned over the school in Novolipki Street was particularly detestable. Without pity for the fate of his subordinates who had been forced to teach the children of their own country *in the Russian language*, he would pass with them from honeyed compliments to the coarsest reproof. In his zeal, Ivanov, who was an ignorant man, would review the compositions of day pupils, looking for the "Polish-isms" which occasionally slipped out in the work of little boys. His relations with Professor Sklodovski had grown singularly cold after the day when the latter, in defence of one of his pupils, had calmly replied:

"M. Ivanov, if that child made a mistake, it was certainly only a slip. . . . It happens that you, too, write Russian incorrectly at times—and indeed fairly often. I am convinced that you do not do it deliberately, any more than the child does."

The professor was talking to his wife of this same Ivanov when Zosia and Manya, returning from their walk, slipped into their father's study.

"Do you remember the Mass that the second-year boys had celebrated at church last week 'for the granting of their most ardent prayer'? They had got up a collection among themselves to pay the cost, and they wouldn't tell the priest what this extraordinary prayer was. Well, little Barzynski confessed the whole thing to me yesterday: they had learned that Ivanov's little girl had typhoid fever, and in their hatred for the principal, they had a Mass said to bring about his child's death! If the poor priest had known that, he would be in despair at having taken such a responsibility in spite of himself!"

M. Sklodovski was delighted with the incident; but his wife, a more fervent Catholic than he, would not laugh at it. She bent over her work, which was singularly rough: with shoemaker's knife and awl Mme Sklodovska was making shoes. One of her special characteristics was to find no task unworthy of her. Since her pregnancies and her illness had obliged her to stay indoors she had learned the cobbler's trade, and thereafter the shoes that the children wore out so quickly cost no more than the price of the leather in them. It was not so easy to get along. . . .

"This pair is for you, Manyusya. See how fine your feet are going to look in them!"

Manya watched the long hands cutting out a sole and managing the sticky string. Near-by, her father had just settled himself comfortably in his favourite arm-chair. It would have been pleasant to climb up on his knees and make a mess of his big necktie, knotted with such care; or to pull the nut-brown beard that framed his rather heavy face and his kind smile.

But the talk of the grown-ups was too boring: "Ivanov . . . the police . . . the Tsar . . . deportation . . . a plot . . . Siberia . . ." Every day since she had come into the world Manya had heard the same phrases to which she obscurely attached some sort of fearful significance. By instinct she withdrew from them, holding off the moment when she would have to understand.

Isolating herself in deep childish dreams, the infant turned away from her parents and the murmur of their affectionate conversation, cut now and then by the sharp noise of the hammer on a nail, the squeak of the scissors on leather. With her nose in the air Manya wandered about the room and stopped, like a boulevard idler, to admire the objects which were especially dear to her.

This workroom was the finest room in the family lodging—or at any rate the most interesting to Manya. The big French mahogany desk, the Restoration arm-chairs covered by an indestructible red velvet, filled her with respect. How clean and shining the furniture was! One day, when Manya grew older and went to school, she would have a place at one end of the long ministerial desk with many drawers, Professor Sklodovski's desk around which the children assembled in the afternoon to do their work.

Manya was not attracted by the majestic portrait of a bishop—framed in heavy gold and attributed in the family, but only in the family, to Titian—which decorated the wall at the end. Her admiration was reserved for the bright green malachite clock, fat and brilliant, which stood on the desk, and for the round table one of their cousins had brought from Palermo the year before. Its top represented a checkerboard, and each square on it was made of a different kind of veined marble.

The little girl avoided the stand which held a blue cup and saucer of Sèvres china ornamented by a medallion of Louis XVIII's good-natured face—she had been told a thousand times not to touch it, and in consequence regarded it with terror—and finally stopped before the dearest of her treasures.

One, hung on the wall, was a precision barometer mounted in oak, with its long gilt pointers glittering against the white dial; on certain days the professor regulated and cleaned it minutely in front of his attentive children.

The other was a glass case with several shelves laden with surprising and graceful instruments, glass tubes, small scales, specimens of minerals and even a gold-leaf electroscope. . . . Professor Sklodovski used to take these objects into his class-room, but since the government had reduced the hours devoted to science, the glass case was always shut.

Manya could not imagine what these fascinating trinkets were. One day, straining on the tips of her toes, she was contemplating them with bliss when her father simply told her their name: "Phy-sics app-a-ra-tus."

A funny name.

She did not forget it—she never forgot anything—and, as she was in high spirits, she sang the words in tune.

CHAPTER II

Dark Days

"MARYA SKLODOVSKA."

"Present"

"Tell us about Stanislas Augustus."

"Stanislas Augustus Poniatovski was elected King of Poland in 1764. He was intelligent and very cultivated, the friend of artists and writers He understood the defects that were weakening the kingdom and tried to remedy the disorders of the State. Unfortunately, he was a man without courage . "

The schoolgirl who stood up in her place—in the third row it was, near one of the big windows that looked out over the snow-covered lawns of the Saxony Garden—looked much the same as her comrades as she recited her lesson in a clear, assured voice. Boarding-school uniform of navy-blue serge with steel buttons and a well-starched white collar imprisoned the figure of the ten-year-old child. And Anciupecio's short curls, always in disorder, where were they now? A tight braid, tied with narrow ribbon, pulled the curly hair back behind the tiny, perfect ears and made the wilful little face seem almost ordinary. Another braid, thicker and darker, had replaced Hela's ringlets. Hela sat at the next desk. Strict costume, severe coiffure: that was the rule in Mlle Sikorska's "private school."

The teacher in the chair had no frivolous demeanour, either. Her black silk corsage and whalebone collar had never been fashionable, and Mlle Antonina Tupalska had not the slightest pretension to beauty. She had a heavy, brutal, ugly face, which nevertheless appealed to the sympathies. Mlle Tupalska—

16

currently nicknamed "Tupsia"—was not only teacher of arithmetic and history, but also exercised the functions of sturdy superintendent; in that capacity she had been obliged to act with vigour, sometimes, against the independent spirit and stubborn character of the little Sklodovska.

However, there was much affectionate kindness in the look she bent on Manya. How could she not be proud of this brilliant pupil, two years younger than her classmates, who seemed to find nothing difficult and was invariably first in ciphering, first in history, first in literature, German, French and catechism?

Silence reigned in the classroom—and even something a bit more than silence. These history lessons took place in an atmosphere of passionate fervour. The eyes of twenty-five motionless, exalted little patriots and the rough countenance of Tupsia reflected their earnest enthusiasm. And, speaking of a sovereign dead many years ago, it was with singular fire that Manya stated in her chanting voice:

"Unfortunately he was a man without courage . . ."

The unattractive schoolmistress and her too serious pupils, to whom she was actually teaching the history of Poland *in Polish*, had the mysterious look of accomplices in conspiracy.

And suddenly, like accomplices, they were all startled into silence: the faint clatter of an electric bell had been heard from the landing.

Two long rings, two short ones.

The signal set up an instant agitation, mute but violent. Tupsia, on the alert, hastily gathered up the books spread out on the chair; swift hands had piled up the Polish books and papers from the desks and dumped them into the aprons of four lively schoolgirls who disappeared with their load through the little door that led to the dormitory of the boarders. A sound of chairs being moved, of desk-lids opened and stealthily closed . . . The four schoolgirls, breathless, returned to their places. And the door to the vestibule opened slowly.

On the threshold, laced into his fine uniform—yellow pantaloons and a blue tunic with shiny buttons—appeared M. Hornberg, inspector of private boarding-schools in the city of Warsaw. He was a thick-set fellow, sheared in German fashion; his face was plump and his eyes piercing behind their gold-rimmed glasses.

Without saying a word, the inspector looked at the pupils. And near him, apparently unmoved, the director who accompanied him, Mlle Sikorska, looked at them too—but with secret anxiety. The delay had been so short to-day. The porter had just had time to sound the agreed signal when Hornberg, going ahead of his guide, reached the landing and plunged into the classroom. Was everything in order?

Everything was in order. Twenty-five little girls bent over their work, thimble on finger, making impeccable buttonholes in squares of stuff unravelled at the edges. Scissors and spools of thread lay about on the empty desks. And Tupsia, with purple face and veins which showed in her forehead, held on the table in front of her a volume propeily printed in orthodox letters. . . .

"These children have two hours of sewing each week, Mr. Inspector," the directress said calmly.

Hornberg had advanced toward the teacher.

"You were reading aloud. What is the book, mademoiselle?"

"Krylov's *Fairy Tales*. We began them to-day."

Tupsia had answered with perfect calm. Bit by bit her cheeks were regaining their natural colour.

As if absent-mindedly, Hornberg opened the lid of the nearest desk. Nothing. Not a paper, not a book.

After having carefully finished off the stitch and fastened their needles in the cloth, the girls interrupted their sewing. They sat motionless with crossed arms, all alike in their dark dresses and white collars; and the twenty-five childish faces, suddenly grown older, wore a forbidding expression which concealed fear, cunning and hatred.

M. Hornberg, accepting the chair offered him by Mlle Tupalska, seated himself heavily.

"Please call on one of these young people."

In the third row Marya Sklodovska instinctively turned her frightened little face toward the window. A prayer rose in her: "Please God, make it somebody else. . . . Not me. . . . Not me."

But she knew very well that the choice would fall upon her. She knew that she was almost always chosen for the government inspector's questioning, since she was the most knowledgeable and since she spoke Russian perfectly.

At the sound of her name she straightened up. She felt very warm—no, she felt cold. A dreadful shame seized her by the throat.

"Your prayer," snapped M. Hornberg, whose attitude showed his indifference and boredom.

Manya recited "Our Father" correctly, in a voice without colour or expression. One of the subtlest humiliations the Tsar had discovered was to make the Polish children say their Catholic prayers every day *in Russian*. Thus, while pretending to respect their faith, he was able to profane what they reverenced.

Again silence.

"Name the Tsars who have reigned over our Holy Russia since Catherine II."

"Catherine II, Paul I, Alexander I, Nicholas I, Alexander II."

The inspector was satisfied. This child had a good memory. And what a marvellous accent! She might have been born in St. Petersburg.

"Tell me the names and titles of the members of the Imperial family."

"Her Majesty the Empress, His Imperial Highness the Cesarevitch Alexander, His Imperial Highness the Grand Duke . . ."

At the end of the enumeration, which was long, Hornberg smiled faintly. This was excellent, he thought. The man could not see, or did not wish to see, Manya's suffering, her features hardened by the effort she made to dissimulate her rebellion.

"What is the title of the Tsar in the scale of dignities?"

"*Vielichestvo.*"

"And my title—what is it?"

"*Vysokorodye.*"

The inspector took pleasure in these hierarchic details, more important to his way of thinking than arithmetic or spelling. For his own simple pleasure he asked again:

"Who rules over us?"

To conceal the fire of their eyes, the directress and the superintendent stared hard at the registers they held before them. As the answer did not come quickly enough, Hornberg, annoyed, asked again in louder tones:

"Who rules over us?"

"His Majesty Alexander II, Tsar of All the Russias," Manya articulated painfully. Her face had gone white.

The session was over. The functionary rose from his chair, and after a brief nod, moved off to the next room, followed by Mlle Sikorska.

Then Tupsia raised her head.

"Come here, my little soul"

Manya left her place and came up to the schoolmistress, who, without saying a word, kissed her on the forehead And suddenly, in the classroom that was coming to life again, the Polish child, her nerves at an end, burst into tears.

"The inspector came to-day! The inspector came!"

The excited children gave the news to their mothers and their *nyanyas* who were waiting for them when school was over. Groups of muffled-up little girls and grown persons thickened by their fur coats scattered rapidly on the pavements covered by the year's first snow. They spoke in undertones: any idle passer-by, any loiterer staring at a show window might perhaps be an informer for the police.

Hela was telling the story of the morning to Mme Michalovska —Aunt Lucia—who had come to meet the two sisters.

"Hornberg questioned Manya, and she answered very well, but then she cried. It seems that the inspector had no criticism to make in any class."

The exuberant Hela whispered and chattered away, but Manya walked along beside her aunt silently. Even though several hours had passed since her examination by the inspector, the little girl was still troubled by it. She hated these sudden panics, these humiliating exhibitions in which one had to tell lies, always lies. . . . Because of Hornberg's visit she felt the sadness of her life more heavily to-day. Could she even remember having been a care-free baby? Successive catastrophes had stricken the Sklodovski household, and the last four years seemed to Manya like a bad dream.

First there was the departure of Mme Sklodovska, with Zosia, for Nice. It was explained to Manya that "after her cure Mamma will be quite well." When the child saw her mother again, a year later, she could hardly recognise the ageing woman already marked by fate. . . .

Then, in the autumn of 1873, there had been the dramatic day of their return from the holidays. Arriving with his family, M. Sklodovski had found an official envelope on his desk: by order of the authorities his salary was reduced and his lodging as a functionary taken away from him, along with his title of under-inspector. It was official disgrace. Principal Ivanov was avenging himself cruelly on a subordinate who was not servile enough. He had won the battle.

Thereafter the Sklodovskis moved several times, to find themselves finally installed in a corner apartment at the crossing of Novolipki and Carmelite streets; and their existence, once so peaceful and sweet, gradually suffered the changes brought about by straitened circumstances. The professor took two or three boarders at first—then five, eight, ten. He gave lodging, food and private instruction to these young boys, chosen from among his pupils. The house was transformed into a noisy barracks and intimacy vanished from the family life.

This arrangement had become necessary not only because of M. Sklodovski's lowered position and the sacrifices he had to make to pay for his wife's treatment on the Riviera, but being led into risky speculation by a wretched brother-in-law—who was financing a "marvellous" steam mill—the poor man, ordinarily so prudent, had lost the thirty thousand roubles which represented his savings; and ever after, tormented by regret and troubled for the future, he mourned over them; in an excess of scruple he accused himself constantly of having made his family poor and deprived his daughters of their marriage portions.

But it was in January 1876, just two years earlier, that Manya had made sudden brutal acquaintance with unhappiness. One of the boarders had contaminated Bronya and Zosia with typhus. What horrible weeks! In one room the mother tried to control her spasms of coughing; in another, the two little girls shook and moaned with fever.

One Wednesday the professor came to take Joseph, Hela and Manya to their eldest sister for the last time. Zosia, dressed in white, was stretched out on the bier, her face bloodless and as if smiling, her hands folded, marvellously beautiful in spite of her close-cropped head.

It was Manya's first encounter with death. It was the first funeral she ever followed, dressed in a drab little black coat, while Bronya, convalescent, was weeping into her pillow, and Mme Sklodovska, too weak to go out, dragged herself from window to window to pursue with her eyes the coffin of her child as it slowly passed down Carmelite Street.

"We're going to have a little walk, children. I must go and buy some apples before the worst of the cold begins."

The excellent Aunt Lucia led her nieces at a brisk pace across the Saxony Garden, nearly deserted on this November afternoon. She seized any pretext to press her nieces into taking the air, away from the confined quarters where their consumptive mother lay. If the contagion touched them——! Hela looked healthy, but Manya was so pale and so depressed

Leaving the Garden, the trio entered the old quarter of Warsaw, in which Manya had been born. Here the streets were much more diverting than in the new town. Under great sloping roofs, white-covered, the houses in Stare Miasto Square showed their grey fronts covered with a thousand sculptured ornaments: cornices, saints' faces, the figures of animals serving as signs for inns or shops.

In the icy air the church bells answered one another on several tones. These churches awoke the whole departed childhood of Marya Sklodovska. Her baptism had taken place in that of St. Mary, her first communion in that of the Dominicans—a memorable day, dominated by the oath Manya and her cousin Henrietta had sworn not to touch the Host with their teeth. . . . The girls came often to St. Paul's Church, to listen to the Sunday sermons in German.

Nove Miasto Square, empty and windswept, was also familiar to Manya: her family had lived there for a year after leaving the Gymnasium. Every day the child went with her mother and

sisters to the Chapel of Our Lady, a strange and ravishing church
whose square tower and main body, all stairs of red stone worn
away by the centuries, twisted crookedly up the crest which over-
looked the river.

On a signal from Aunt Lucia the girls went in again to-day. A
few steps into the shadows beyond the narrow Gothic doorway
and Manya was on her knees, trembling. It was bitter for her to
come here without Zosia, who had gone for ever, and without her
mystic mother, tortured by suffering, on whom God seemed to
have no pity.

Once again Manya's prayer rose to the God in which she
believed. She asked Jesus with passion and despair to grant life
to the being she loved most in the world. She offered to the Lord
her own existence: in order to save Mme Sklodovska, she was
ready to die. Bent down near her, Aunt Lucia and Hela prayed
in low voices.

They met again outside the church and began the descent of the
uneven steps which led down to the water. The Vistula, spreading
enormously before them, did not seem to be in good humour. Its
yellowish water swept round the sandbanks which formed pale
islets in the middle of the river and beat against the irregular shore
encumbered with floating baths and rafts for washing clothes. The
long grey paddle-boats on which happy crowds of young people
used to go in summer lay there motionless and disarmed. The
river's animation was concentrated about the "galleys" with
apples. There were two of them: two great pinnaces, narrow and
pointed, weighted down almost to the water's edge.

The master, buried in his sheepskins, pushed aside armfuls of
straw to show his merchandise. Under this soft litter, which
protected them from the frost, the hard red shining apples made
a brilliant cargo. There were hundreds, thousands, piled up even
with the hull. They came from the upper Vistula, from the fine
town of Kazmierz, and it took them days and days to come down
this far.

"I want to pick out our apples!" Hela cried; and, quickly
imitated by Manya, she put down her muff and wriggled her
schoolgirl's bag from her shoulder.

Nothing was more sure to enliven the girls than this expedition, every bit of which they adored. They took the apples one by one, turning them back and forth carefully; those which passed inspection were thrown into a big wicker basket. If there were any rotten ones, you threw them with all your might into the Vistula, and you watched their little round vermilion wreck go down. When the basket was full you left the boat, holding in your hand a finer apple than any of the others. It was cold and crackly under the teeth, and it was exquisite to crunch it while Aunt Lucia debated over the payment and pointed out, among the spotty-faced urchins who hung about the neighbourhood, those whom she judged worthy to carry the precious provision home.

Five o'clock. After tea the servants cleared the long table in the dining-room and lighted the petroleum suspension lamp. The hour of work had come. The board pupils grouped themselves by twos and threes in the rooms where they lived. The son and daughters of the professor remained in the dining-room, transformed into a study, and opened their papers and books. After a few minutes there arose, from everywhere and nowhere, the obsessing chant which for years remained the leitmotiv of life in that house

It was always the same children who could not keep from drawling aloud their Latin verses, their history dates or the statements of their problems. In every corner somebody was grumbling, somebody was struggling hard How difficult everything was! Many a time the professor was obliged to calm the despair of some hopeful scholar who understood a demonstration perfectly when it was made in his own language, but who, in spite of every effort, was incapable of understanding it in Russian, the official language—and even more incapable of repeating it.

Little Manya knew none of this anguish. Her memory was such that her comrades, hearing her faultless recitation of a poem they had seen her read no more than twice, thought at once of a trick, and accused her of learning verses secretly. She finished her tasks long before the others, and often, out of natural kindliness or lack of something else to do, she would extricate one of her companions from the embarrassment and difficulty of a theorem.

But what she preferred was to install herself with a book at the big table, as she did to-night—well propped up on her elbows, her hands on her forehead, her thumbs closing her ears as protection from Hela, who had never been able to run through a lesson without shouting at the top of her voice. The precaution was superfluous, for after a bit the little girl, fascinated by her reading, completely lost consciousness of what was happening around her.

This gift of absorption, the only oddity in a healthy child, afforded great amusement to her sisters and friends. A dozen times, with the boarders for accomplices, Bronya and Hela had organised a terrific hubbub around their avidly reading sister without even getting her to raise her eyes.

To-day they wanted to try something really good; the presence of Henrietta Michalovska, Aunt Lucia's daughter, had aroused their evil demons. They crept forward on their toes and began to build a scaffolding of chairs about the motionless Manya, lost in her reading. Two chairs on each side, one behind, two others on top of the first three, and one at the summit crowning the edifice. . . . They retired in silence, and pretended to work. Then they waited.

They had to wait a long time. The child noticed nothing: neither the whispers nor the stifled laughter nor the shadow of the chairs above her head. For half an hour she remained like that, threatened, without knowing it, by the unstable pyramid. When her chapter was finished, she closed her book, lifted her head—and everything collapsed with the noise of a cataclysm. Chairs danced across the floor; Hela shrieked with joy; Bronya and Henrietta leaped nimbly into defensive positions, for a counter-attack was to be feared.

But Manya remained unmoved. She did not know how to be angry, but neither could she be amused at a trick which had frightened her. Her ash-grey eyes expressed the stupor of a sleepwalker suddenly jerked out of her dream. She rubbed her left shoulder, which a chair had struck a bit roughly, picked up her book and took it into the next room. Passing in front of the "big girls" she said just two words:

"That's stupid!"

A calm verdict, with which the "big girls" were not very satisfied.

These moments of total absent-mindedness were perhaps the

only ones in which Manya found again the wonder-struck quality of her earliest childhood. She read, pell-mell, poetry and scholastic manuals, adventure stories and technical works borrowed from her father's library.

And thus she put away from her, for brief moments at a time, the dark phantoms: she forgot Russian spies and the visits of Hornberg. She forgot her father's face, crushed by his miserable tasks, and the perpetual tumult of the house, and the black dawns when, still half asleep, she had to get up from her moleskin divan so that the boarders could have their breakfast in the dining-room, which was also a dormitory for the Sklodovski children.

She forgot her terrors: terror of the oppressor, religious terrors, terror of illness and death. Instinctively she tried to escape from a "climate" too heavy for her.

They were fleeting respites. As soon as she regained conscious-ness everything came back to her at once—and first of all the dull, constant sadness created in the house by the illness of her mother. The patient, once so beautiful, was now hardly more than a shadow. And in spite of the comforting words with which the grown-ups attempted to deceive her, Manya felt clearly that her ecstatic admiration, her great love and the ardour of her prayers would not be strong enough to prevent the horrible thing that was drawing near.

Mme Sklodovska, too, thought of the inevitable. She took care to see that the event found her ready without upsetting the existence of the house. On May 9th, 1878, she asked the doctor to make way for the priest. The priest alone was to know the final anguish of her Christian soul, her grief at leaving her beloved husband to care for four children, her anxiety for the future of the youthful beings she must now abandon, for little Manyusya who was only ten. . . .

In front of her family she allowed herself to show only a face of peace, to which the last hours had restored an extreme gracious-ness. She died as she had wanted to die, without delirium or disorder. Her husband, her son and her daughters watched beside her bed in the tidy room. And her long, pathetic grey eyes, already dulled by death, fixed themselves in turn on each of the five ravaged faces, as if the dying woman wished to ask their pardon for causing them so much pain.

She found energy enough to say farewell to each one. Weakness was slowly overcoming her. The spark of life that remained permitted only one more gesture and one more speech. The gesture was a sign of the cross; seized with a terrible trembling, her hand sketched it in the air to bless them all. The words—her last—she murmured in one breath, looking at the husband and children from whom she took her leave: "I love you."

Dressed in black once more, Manya, worn with grief, wandered miserably about the apartment in Carmelite Street. She could not get used to the fact that Bronya occupied the dead woman's room; that only Hela and herself now slept on the moleskin divans; that a housekeeper, hastily engaged by the professor, came every day to give orders to the servants, decide on the food for the boarders, and vaguely oversee the children's dressing. M. Sklodovski devoted all his free hours to his orphaned children. But he could care for them only in an awkward, touching way— the care of a man.

Manya learned that life was cruel. Cruel for the race, cruel for the individual. . . .

Zosia was dead. Mme Sklodovska was dead. Deprived of her mother's tenderness and the protection of her eldest sister, the child grew older, without once complaining, in partial abandonment. She was proud but she was not resigned. And when she knelt in the Catholic church where she was used to going with her mother, she experienced the secret stir of revolt within her. She no longer invoked with the same love that God who had unjustly inflicted such terrible blows, who had slain what was gay or fanciful or sweet around her.

CHAPTER III

Adolescence

THERE appears to be a moment of expansion, a sort of maximum, in the history of every family. Mysterious reasons force a generation to distinguish itself from others by abundance of gifts, magnificent excess of vitality, beauty, success.

This moment had arrived for the Sklodovski family, in spite of the tribute it had just paid to unhappiness. Death, carrying off Zosia, had taken a hostage from among five ardent and intelligent children. But the others, the four young people born of a consumptive mother and an intellectual worn out by work, carried an invincible force within them. They were to conquer adversity, to disdain all obstacles and to become, all four, exceptional human beings.

They were a superb spectacle, this sunny morning in the spring of 1882, gathered for breakfast around the table. Hela was sixteen, tall and graceful, incontestably the "beauty of the family." Bronya had golden hair and the face of an opened flower; Joseph, the eldest, displayed the lines of a Nordic athlete in his student's uniform.

And as for Manya. . . . It must be admitted that she had taken on weight and that her well-fitted uniform outlined a figure which was not exactly thin. Since she was the youngest, she was also, for the moment, the least beautiful. But she had an animated and pleasing face, and had the light, clear eyes and hair and skin of Polish women.

Only the two younger girls wore uniform now: Hela was still in blue, like a faithful child of the Sikorska school, but Manya was dressed in maroon, since she had become, at fourteen years of age, one of the most brilliant pupils of a government Gymnasium —the same Gymnasium where Bronya, the eldest of the three sisters, had finished her studies last year by winning a gold medal and a great deal of glory.

Bronya was no longer a schoolgirl—she was a "young lady." She had taken over the management of the house, replacing the housekeepers who had often been unpleasant. She kept the books, watched over the boarders—those eternal boarders who changed only their faces and names—and wore her hair up and her skirts long like a grown person, with a bustle and a train and a multitude of little buttons.

Joseph had been awarded a gold medal like Bronya's when he left the boys' high school. Envied and admired by his sisters, the young man was studying at the Faculty of Medicine. How lucky they thought him! Already tormented by intellectual ambition, the three Sklodovski girls grumbled at the rule forbidding women to enter the University of Warsaw; and they listened in rapt attention to their brother's stories of student life in the "Tsar's University"—mediocre though it was—where the teachers were ambitious Russians and subservient Poles.

But the conversation never made them lose a mouthful. Bread, butter, cream and jam disappeared as if by magic.

"Joseph, to-night is dancing school and we need you to be our escort," said Hela, mindful of serious things. "Do you think my dress will do, Bronya, if it's well ironed?"

"As you have no other one, it'll have to do," said Bronya philosophically. "We'll look it over at three o'clock, when you come home."

"Your dresses are very pretty," Manya affirmed.

"Oh, you don't know anything about it. You're too young."

The quartet was breaking up. Bronya cleared the table, Joseph vanished with his papers under his arm, and Hela and Manya made off for the kitchen helter-skelter.

"My bread and butter, please. . . . My *serdelki*. . . . Where has the butter got to?"

In spite of their copious breakfast the young ladies were still preoccupied with food. The lunch they were to eat at school at the eleven-o'clock recess went into cloth bags: bread, an apple, and a pair of those wonderful Polish sausages called *serdelki*.

Manya tied up her lunch and flung her schoolbag over her shoulder.

"Hurry up! You'll be late for your appointment!"

Hela scoffed, getting ready in her turn.

"No, no, it's only half-past eight. Good-bye!"

On the stairs she passed two of her father's boarders who, although with less haste than herself, were making their way also to school.

Gymnasium, boarding school, day school . . . the youth of Manya Sklodovska was completely obsessed by such words. M. Sklodovski taught in a Gymnasium, Bronya had just left the Gymnasium, Manya was going to a Gymnasium, Joseph to the university, Hela to Mlle Sikorska's boarding school. Even their home was, in its way, a sort of school. Manya must have grown to imagine the universe as an immense school where there were only teachers and pupils and where only one ideal reigned: to learn.

The boarders had become a little more bearable after the family left dreary Carmelite Street and installed itself in Leschen Street. The building was charming; the façade had style, there was a tranquil courtyard where grey pigeons cooed, and there were balconies hung with Virginia creeper. And the apartment of the first floor was spacious enough for the Sklodovskis to have four rooms of their own, away from the boys.

Its broad pavements bordered by substantial houses made Leschen Street very "respectable." That is to say, it was guiltless of Slavic picturesqueness. On the contrary, in the near-elegance of the quarter everything evoked the West, from the Calvinist church opposite the house to the columned French building in Rymanska Street, evidence of the adoration Napoleon had inspired in Poland—an adoration which endures to the present time.

Her bag on her back, Manya hastened to reach the "Blue Palace," the residence of the Counts Zamoyski. Avoiding the grille and the principal entrance she went through to an oldish courtyard guarded by a bronze lion. Then she stopped short; the courtyard was empty.

An affectionate voice hailed her.

"Don't run off, Manyusya dear . . . Kazia is coming down."

"Oh, thanks, madame! Good morning, madame!"

From one of the windows on the lower floor Mme Przyborovska, wife of Count Zamoyski's librarian, her dark hair smoothly drawn back under a thick crown of braids, looked with friendly eyes on the round-cheeked and lively young Sklodovska who had been her daughter's best friend for two years.

"You must come and have tea with us this afternoon. I'll make you some *paczki* and that chocolate ice that you love!"

"Of course you've got to come to tea!" Kazia cried, bolting down the stairs and seizing her friend by the arm. "We must hurry, Manya, we're late."

"Yes. I was just about to lift the lion's ring!"

Manya came to pick Kazia up every morning under the porch of her house. When Manya found nobody at the meeting-place she lifted the heavy ring which the bronze lion bore in his maw and turned it back over the animal's nose before going on to school. Kazia, seeing the ring, learned that Manya had already been and gone, and that she would have to hurry if she wanted to catch up.

Kazia was very charming; cheerful and high-spirited, she was a happy little creature whose excellent parents did their best to spoil her. M. and Mme Przyborovski did likewise by Manya, whom they treated as one of their own daughters in an effort to make her forget that she was motherless. But by many little details in the appearance of the two girls in brown dresses it was easy to tell that one was a petted child, whose attentive mother brushed her hair and tied her ribbons every morning, while the other, at fourteen and a half years of age, was growing up in a house where nobody had time to bother about her.

Arm in arm the girls passed along narrow Zabia Street. They had not seen each other since tea on the day before, and they had a thousand urgent matters to discuss. Their thousand bits of gossip nearly all had to do with their Gymnasium in Krakovsky Boulevard—a Russian school which, having been destined at first for the children of Germans in government service, kept its Germanic discipline and traditions.

It had been a great change, after Mlle Sikorska's profoundly Polish seminary for young ladies, to become the pupil of an official institution governed by the Russifying spirit. It was a necessary change—since the imperial Gymnasia were the only ones which bestowed recognised diplomas—but Manya and Kazia avenged themselves on it by making all manner of fun of their teachers from Russia, as well as of the boring Pastor Meding, their German teacher, and above all of Mlle Mayer, the detested and detestable superintendent of studies.

Mayer, a tiny, dark woman with greasy hair, who wore silent spy's slippers, was the declared enemy of Manya Sklodovska. She reproached Manya with everything: her stubborn character and the "scornful smile" with which, according to Mayer's story, Manya received the most wounding criticism.

"That Sklodovska! It's no use talking to her—it's just like throwing peas against a wall!" the superintendent groaned. She was particularly annoyed by Manya's curly hair, which she declared "disordered and ridiculous"; with many a heavy stroke of the brush she tried to straighten out the rebellious locks and transform the Pole into a Gretchen with tight braids. Useless! After a few minutes the light, capricious curls would break out again about the young face, and Manya's too innocent gaze was fixed with singular insistence upon the superintendent's shining braids.

"I forbid you to look at me like that!" Mayer sputtered. "You mustn't look down at me!"

In a fit of impertinence one day Manya, who was a head taller than Mayer, replied: "The fact is that I can't do anything else."

War went on, day after day, between the sour old maid and the fractious pupil. The worst of the storms had taken place the year before. Mlle Mayer, coming into the classroom unexpectedly, had found Manya and Kazia dancing with joy among the desks to celebrate the assassination of Tsar Alexander II, whose sudden death had just plunged the empire into mourning.

One of the most melancholy results of political constraint is the spontaneous ferocity it develops among the oppressed. Manya and Kazia felt such rancours as free human beings never know. Even though they were by nature tender and generous, they lived in accordance with a particular morality—the slave morality—which turns hatred into a virtue and obedience into cowardice.

By reaction, the adolescents threw themselves with passion into whatever they were permitted to love. They reverenced handsome young M. Glass, who taught them mathematics, and M. Slosarski, professor of natural sciences. They were Poles—accomplices. Even with regard to the Russians there were shades of feeling. What was one to think, for example, of the mysterious M. Mikieszin, who, wishing to recompense a pupil who had made great progress, silently handed her a copy of the poems of Nekrasov, a revolutionary writer? The surprised students perceived brief movements from the enemy's camp, signals of solidarity. In Holy Russia all were not faithful to the Tsar. . . .

In Manya's class Polish, Jewish, Russian and German girls sat side by side without serious disagreement. Their common youth and the excitement of school rivalry smoothed out, for the time being, their differences of race and thought. To see them help each other in their work and play together during recesses one might even have believed that they enjoyed perfect mutual understanding.

But as soon as school was over each one returned to her language, her patriotism and her religion. The Polish girls, more arrogant than the others because they were the persecuted, went off in tight little groups and met one another afterwards at tea parties to which it would have been impossible to ask a Russian or a German.

Their intransigence was not without secret troubles. Everything seemed guilty to them, from the involuntary friendship they might feel for a foreign girl to the pleasure they experienced in spite of themselves at hearing lessons in science or philosophy from the mouth of the oppressor—at receiving that "official" education which they thought worthy of hatred.

The summer before, Manya had written to Kazia a moving and timid confession filled with shame:

"Do you know, Kazia, in spite of everything, I like school. Perhaps you will make fun of me, but nevertheless I must tell you that I like it, and even that I love it. I can realise that now. Don't go imagining that I miss it! Oh no; not at all. But the idea that I am going back soon does not depress me, and the two years I have left to spend there don't seem as dreadful, as painful and long as they once did. . . ."

The Saxony Garden—along with Lazienki Park, where she passed many of her leisure hours—was one of Manya's favourite spots in that city which she was to call, for years to come, "my beloved little Warsaw."

Passing the iron grille, Manya and Kazia followed the avenue which led to the palace. Up to two months ago they had played the ancient game of trailing their rubbers in the large mud-puddles along the way: enough, that is, to get them wet up to the edges, but not enough to immerse them altogether and dampen their shoes. When springtime came, they went back to other games which, in spite of their simplicity, caused uproarious amusement. Example: the game of "green."

"My French copy-book is nearly finished," Manya would begin in placid tones. "Would you like to come with me to buy a new one? I saw some very pretty ones with *green* covers . . ."

But Kazia was on guard. At the word "green" she suddenly thrust at Manya a little piece of green velvet she had hidden in her pocket, and thus avoided paying a forfeit. Manya, vexed, seemed to abandon the game and turned the conversation towards the history lesson one of their teachers had dictated to them yesterday, in which it was mentioned that Poland was a province and the Polish language a dialect, and that the Poles had caused the Tsar Nicholas I, who loved them so much, to die of grief over their ingratitude. . . .

"Just the same, the poor man was embarrassed when he told us such horrors. Did you notice how he looked away, and that awful face of his?"

"Yes. He went absolutely *green*," Kazia ventured, trying to look as if she was thinking of something else. But at once she saw a young chestnut leaf of tender green shaken under her nose.

Groups of children made mud-pies or chased their hoops. Manya and Kazia, choking with laughter over their game, passed on beneath the slender columns of the Palace of Saxony and almost ran across the great square. Suddenly Manya cried:

"But we've passed the monument. We must go back at once!"

Kazia turned without a word. The giddy pair had just committed an unpardonable offence. In the middle of the Saxony

Square was a pompous obelisk surrounded by four lions and bearing, in orthodox letters, the words: "To the Poles faithful to their Sovereign." This tribute from the Tsar to those Poles who had betrayed their country and made themselves allies of the oppressor was an object of disgust to the patriots, and their tradition was to spit every time they passed the monument. If, by inadvertence, one failed to observe this custom, one had to go back and make good the omission.

With their duty in this respect duly accomplished, the two girls returned to their talk.

"They're dancing at home this evening," Manya said. "Are you coming to watch them?"

"Yes. Oh, Manyusya, when shall we have the right to dance, too? We're such good waltzers already!" Kazia complained impatiently.

When? Not until school was over and the girls had "come out." They were only allowed to practise among themselves and to learn the lancers, the polka, the mazurka and the oberek from the school ballet master. Relegated to little chairs at the side, they were also present when the young people of a few friendly families gathered for dancing lessons once a week in the Sklodovskis' house.

But before they could expect their turn to come, they must pass more months in the Gymnasium which now rose before them in the avenue; the great, bald, three-storeyed building stood over against the exquisite Chapel of the Visitation, twisted and ornate, a fragment of the Italian Renaissance lost among severer edifices. Their comrades were already plunging into the archway. There was the little blue-eyed Wulf girl, and Anya Rottert, the flat-nosed German who was the best in the class after Manya; and Léonie Kunicka. . . .

But what was the matter with Kunicka? Her eyes were swollen with tears; and she, who was always so neatly dressed, seemed to have had her clothes thrown at her to-day.

Manya and Kazia ceased smiling and ran toward their friend.

"What's the matter? What has happened to you, Kunicka?"

Kunicka's delicate face was colourless. The words passed her lips with difficulty.

"It's my brother. . . . He was in a plot. . . . He was denounced. . . . We haven't known where he was for three days."

Stifled by sobs, she added:

"They are going to hang him to-morrow."

The other two girls, horror-struck, surrounded the unlucky one with their questions and their support; but the sharp voice of Mlle Mayer broke in with brief orders:

"Come, come, young ladies, enough of your chatter. Hurry up."

Stunned with shock, Manya made her way slowly toward her place. Just now she had been dreaming of music and dances. Now, while the first phrases of a geography lesson to which she was not attending rumbled in her ears, she saw the ardent young face of the condemned boy—and the scaffold, the hangman, the rope. . . .

That night, instead of going to the dancing lesson, six girls of fifteen kept silent watch in Léonie Kunicka's narrow room. Manya, Hela and Bronya came with Kazia and her sister Ula to wait for the dawn with their comrade.

They mingled their rebellion and their tears. They took humble and tender care of their friend, convulsed as she was with grief; they bathed her swollen eyes, obliged her to drink a little hot tea. · The hours passed somehow, so fast, so slow, for the six children of whom four still wore their school uniform. When the pallor of dawn, accentuating their own pallor, came to mark the moment of the end, they fell on their knees and said a last prayer, their hands concealing their young faces full of terror.

One gold medal, two gold medals, three gold medals in the Sklodovski family. . . . The third was for Manya and marked the end of her secondary studies on June 12th, 1883.

In stifling heat the list of rewards was read. Speeches and the flourish of trumpets, the congratulations of the teachers; a limp shake of the hand from M. Apushtin, grand master of education in Russian Poland, answered by a last curtsy from Manya. In her black dress of ceremony with a bunch of tea roses pinned at the waist, little Sklodovska said her farewells and swore she would write to her friends every week; then, laden with Russian prize books which she loudly declared to be "horrible" (as it was her last day, what did she risk?), she left the school in Krakovsky Boulevard for ever, escorted by her father whom her success had overwhelmed with pride.

Manya had worked very hard—and very well. M. Sklodovski decided that she was to go to the country for a year before choosing her means of livelihood.

A year's holiday! . . . One might be tempted to imagine the child of genius, obsessed by an early vocation, studying scientific books in secret. But such was not the case. In the course of the mysterious passage called adolescence, while her body was transformed and her face grew finer, Manya suddenly became lazy. Abandoning the school books, she tasted, for the first and last time in her life, the intoxication of idleness.

A rural interlude occurs here in the story of the professor's daughter. "I can't believe geometry or algebra ever existed," she writes to Kazia. "I have completely forgotten them." She was staying far from Warsaw and school, with relations in the country who welcomed her for weeks at a time in exchange for vague lessons to be given to their children, or for a tiny payment of board; and she gave herself up to the sweetness of being alive.

How care-free she was! How young and happy, suddenly—so much younger than in the dark days of her childhood! Between an excursion and a nap she barely had energy enough to describe her beatitude in letters beginning "My dear little devil" or "Kazia, my heart":

Manya to Kazia:

I may say that aside from an hour's French lesson with a little boy I don't do a thing, positively not a thing—for I have even abandoned the piece of embroidery that I had started . . . I have no schedule. I get up sometimes at ten o'clock, sometimes at four or five (morning, not evening!). I read no serious books, only harmless and absurd little novels. . . . Thus, in spite of the diploma conferring on me the dignity and maturity of a person who has finished her studies, I feel incredibly stupid. Sometimes

I laugh all by myself, and I contemplate my state of total stupidity with genuine satisfaction.

We go out in a band to walk in the woods, we roll hoops, we play battledore and shuttlecock (at which I am very bad!), cross-tag, the game of Goose, and many equally childish things. There have been so many wild strawberries here that one could buy a really sufficient amount for a few *groszy*—and by that I mean a big plateful heaped high. Alas, the season is over! . . . But I am afraid that when I get back my appetite will be unlimited and my voracity alarming.

We swing a lot, swinging ourselves hard and high; we bathe, we go fishing with torches for shrimps. . . . Every Sunday the horses are harnessed for the trip in to Mass, and afterward we pay a visit to the vicarage. The two priests are clever and very witty, and we get enormous amusement from their company.

I was at Zwola for a few days. There was an actor there, M. Kotarbinski, who delighted us. He sang so many songs and recited so many verses, concocted so many jokes and picked so many gooseberries for us, that on the day of his departure we made him a great wreath of poppies, wild pinks and cornflowers; and just as the carriage was starting off we flung it at him with shouts of "*Vivat! Vivat!* M. Kotarbinski!" He put the wreath on his head immediately, and it seems that afterward he carried it in a suitcase all the way to Warsaw. Ah, how gay life is at Zwola! There are always a great many people, and a freedom, equality and independence such as you can hardly imagine. . . . On our journey back Lancet barked so much that we didn't know what was to become of us. . . .

Lancet played an important part in the lives of the Sklodovskis. If he had been properly trained the brown pointer might have become a respectable hunting dog. But Manya, her two sisters, and Joseph had given him a disastrous upbringing. Cuddled, kissed and over-fed, Lancet became an enormous beast whose dictatorship weighed on the whole family. He spoiled the furniture, upset vases of flowers, devoured food that was not intended for him, leaped upon every guest in sign of welcome, and then tore to bits whatever hats or gloves had been imprudently left about

MME SKŁODOWSKA
Marie Curie's Mother

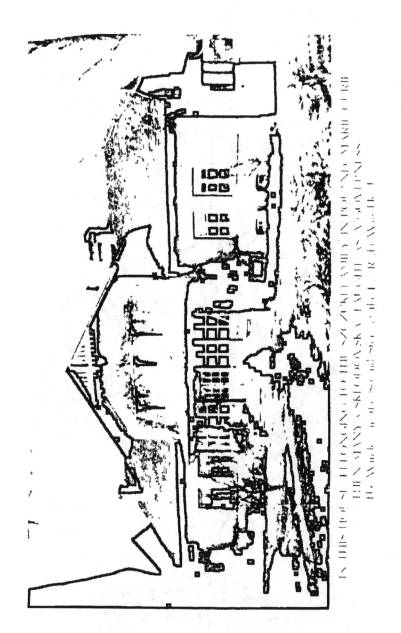

IN THIS FIRST OF THE ONENS TO THE HERO, SOME FAMILY IS FORWARD ABOUT OTHERS
BEEN MANY SHOOAKYA TAUGHT AS AGONIENS
HE... With in the South Side Place of R. H. Mitchell

M. SKLODOVSKI AND HIS THREE DAUGHTERS
From a Photograph Taken in 1890 From Left to Right Manya, Bronya and Hela

in the hall. So many virtues had earned him the adoration of his owners, who disputed the privilege of taking their despot on holiday every summer.

During her year of laziness, during which Manya's intellectual ardour seemed to drowse, the young girl was seized by a passion which was to last as long as her life: the passion for the country. Observing the changes of the seasons, first in one province and then in another, she was constantly discovering new beauties in that Polish earth over which her family was scattered. At Zwola it was peaceable country where nothing arrested the gaze, nothing but the round horizon which seemed farther away than anywhere else in the world. At Zawieprzyce, where Uncle Xavier lived, there were about fifty thoroughbred horses in the fields around the estate—a regular stock farm. Dressed in breeches of doubtful elegance, borrowed from her cousins, Manya learned to gallop and trot beautifully, and became a horse-woman.

But nothing exceeded her enchantment when she saw the Carpathians. Like a true child of the plains she was struck with wondering stupor at the snowy glittering summits and the stiff black firs. She was never to forget those ascents by footpaths carpeted with bilberries, or the mountaineers' cottages where every object was a masterpiece of sculptured wood, or the pure and icy little lake hemmed in by peaks at the top, with its exquisite name "The Eye of the Sea."

It was not far from there, on the frontier of Galicia, that Manya was to pass the winter in the noisy family of her Uncle Zdzislav, a notary at Skalbmierz. The master of the house was a jovial fellow, his wife was beautiful, and their three daughters lived for laughter. How could Manya be bored in such company? Every week the arrival of a new guest or the approach of a feast-day gave the signal for a burst of commotion. The grown people dressed game for the feast and the young girls made cakes, or else, in the seclusion of their rooms, hastily sewed ribbons on to the motley costumes that would serve to disguise them at the next *kulig*.

The *kulig* was by no means only a ball. It was a dizzying, magic journey in the full excitement of carnival. Two sleighs went off in the evening over the snow with Manya Sklodovska and her three cousins, masked and dressed as Cracow peasant girls, huddled under the covers. Young men in picturesque rustic dress escorted them on horseback, brandishing torches. Other torches twinkled through the fir-trees, and the cold night was filled with rhythm, the musicians' sleigh came up, bringing four little Jews from the village, mad and charming creatures who for the next two nights and days would wring from their fiddles the intoxicating tunes of the waltz, the krakoviak and the mazurka, tunes caught up in chorus by the whole crowd. The little Jews would play until three, five, ten other sleighs, answering their call, had found them in the night. In spite of jolting and sliding down dizzy slopes of ice they never missed a stroke of the bow, and they would lead the fantastic night dance in triumph to the first stop.

The shouting crowd then left the sleighs to pound on the door of a sleeping house, where the master duly pretended to be surprised. A few minutes later the musicians were perched on a table and the ball began, lighted by torches and lanterns while the food—prepared long in advance—emerged on the sideboard. Then, at a given signal, the place was emptied, emptied of masques, inhabitants, food, horses, sleighs, everything, and the farandole, longer and thicker than before, slid across the forest toward another house, and another and still another, acquiring new recruits at each stop. The sun rose and set. The fiddlers had just time enough to get their breath and to sleep a little in any convenient barn, mixed pell-mell with the exhausted dancers. But nevertheless when the army of sleighs stopped on the second night, jingling and clanking and pawing, in front of the largest house of the neighbourhood, where the *real* ball was to be held, the little Jews attacked their first krakoviak with a conquering fortissimo while the others took their places for the marvellous figure dance.

It was then that a young man dressed in embroidered white wool made haste to invite the best of the dancers, a vigorous girl of sixteen called Manya Sklodovska, who, in her velvet jacket, puffed sleeves of lawn and long ribbons of every colour falling from her coronet of young wheat, looked like a mountain lass in festival raiment.

Naturally Manya shared her enthusiasm with Kazia.

I have been to a *kulig*. You can't imagine how delightful it is, especially when the clothes are beautiful and the boys are well dressed. My costume was very pretty. . . . After this first *kulig* there was another, at which I had a marvellous time. There were a great many young men from Cracow, very handsome boys who danced so well! It is altogether exceptional to find such good dancers. At eight o'clock in the morning we danced the last dance—a white mazurka.

A climax had to come to this enchanted leisure.

In July 1884, just after Manya's return to the apartment in Warsaw, a lady came to see M Sklodovski It was the Comtesse de Fleury, a Polish woman married to a Frenchman and once a pupil of Mme Sklodovska. Since the professor's younger daughters had no plans for their holidays, she suggested, why should they not come to spend two months at her house in the country?

This happened on Sunday [Manya wrote to Kazia], and on Monday evening we were gone, Hela and I: we had been notified by telegraph that the carriage would meet us at the station. We have now been at Kempa for several weeks and I ought to give you an account of our existence here—but as I haven't the courage, I shall only say that it is marvellous. Kempa is at the junction of the Narev and Biebrza rivers—which is to say that there is plenty of water for swimming and boating, which delights me. I am learning to row—I am getting on quite well—and the bathing is ideal. We do everything that comes into our heads, we sleep sometimes at night and sometimes by day, we dance, and we run to such follies that sometimes we deserve to be locked up in an asylum for the insane. . . .

Manya hardly exaggerated. A breeze of innocent madness stirred all summer long over that beautiful house set between the curves of two smooth, shining rivers. From the window of their room the little Sklodovskis could see greenery and water without limit, and the gentle banks, bordered with poplar and willow, over which the swollen current so often rose to fill the fields with an immense sheet of water where the sun was reflected.

Hela and Manya had quickly taken command of the troop of

boys and girls who lived at Kempa. The masters of the house had adopted a most original attitude: when they were together they sermonised, censured and pretended to be acting with vigour against the excessive spirits of the young; but separately husband and wife had both become the secret accomplices of the guilty ones, to whom they contributed active co-operation and complete indulgence.

What were they to do to-day, for instance? Go riding? Walk in the woods, gather mushrooms or whortleberries? Too tame by far! Manya asked Jan Moniuszko, Mme de Fleury's brother, to go on an errand to the neighbouring town. In his absence, helped by the others, she would succeed in hanging everything the young man's room contained from the big rafters in the ceiling: the bed, the table, the chairs, his luggage, his clothes and all Then poor Moniuszko would have to struggle, on his return, against his aerial furniture in the dark. . . . And what sort of wonderful tea was this, prepared for guests of distinction? A tea party from which the "children" were excluded? Intolerable! Seizing the moment when the visitors were exploring the garden, the "children" devoured the pastries and good things, carried off what they could not stuff into themselves, placed before the devastated table a hastily constructed straw man representing the Count de Fleury when he had eaten well, and took flight. . . .

Where were the delinquents to be found, that day or any other day during the summer? Every time they committed a crime they vanished like phantoms. When they were supposed to be in their rooms they were stretched out on the grass in the depths of the park; when they were supposed to be out walking they were in the cellar, emptying a basket of big gooseberries stolen from the kitchen; and if there seemed to be an unusual amount of order at five in the morning, it was because the house was deserted; Manya, Hela and their followers had chosen sunrise as the time to bathe in the river. There was only one means of collecting them together, and that was to announce a celebration, charades or a dance. The Comtesse de Fleury employed this means as often as possible: in eight weeks she organised three balls, two garden parties, excursions and boating trips.

Her husband and she found their recompense for such liberal

hospitality. They had the adoration of the wild young creatures, their comradeship and confidence, and the spectacle of their marvellous joy—a joy which, in its wildest extravagance, remained singularly pure.

They also experienced the surprises prepared for them by the young people: for the fourteenth anniversary of their marriage, two delegates presented them with an enormous decorative crown of vegetables weighing forty pounds and invited them to sit under a cleverly draped canopy. In solemn silence the youngest of the girls gravely recited a poem written for the occasion.

The poem was Manya's work. She composed it striding up and down her room, in the fire of inspiration. It ended as follows:

> *For St. Louis' Day*
> *We expect a picnic,*
> *Ask some boys for us,*
> *One boy for each of us,*
> *So that, following your example,*
> *We may climb as soon as possible—*
> *As soon as possible—*
> *Up the steps of the altar.*

The prayer was not unanswered. The Fleurys immediately announced a grand ball. The mistress of the house gave her orders for cakes, candles and garlands of flowers, and Manya and Hela worked upon their dresses for the night of nights.

It was not easy for the poor girls to be exquisite: they had only two dresses a year, one for dancing and one for ordinary wear, made for them by a little daily dressmaker. The two sisters reckoned up their combined fortunes and made their decisions. Even though the tulle which covered Manya's dress was frayed, the foundation of blue satin was still in good condition. They must go into the town and buy the cheapest blue tarlatan they could find, to take the place of the defaulting tulle; it had to be draped on that indestructible foundation. And then, what with a ribbon here and a knot there, and some new shoes of russet leather, there was nothing left to do but pick flowers from the garden for their waists and roses for their hair.

On St. Louis' night, while the musicians were tuning their instruments and Hela, astonishingly beautiful, was already fluttering about the festive house, Manya took one last look at herself in the glass. All was well!—the stiff, smart tarlatan, the fresh flowers near her face, and those fine new shoes; those shoes which she was to throw in a corner at dawn because she had danced too much and their soles had ceased to exist. . . .

Many years later my mother sometimes evoked those happy days for me. I looked at her tired face, worn out by nearly half a century of care and immense toil. And I thanked the destiny which, before it dictated this woman's austere and inexorable summons, had allowed her to follow by sleigh after the wildest *kuligs*, and to use up her shoes of russet leather in one night of dancing.

CHAPTER IV

Vocation

I HAVE attempted to show Manya Sklodovska, child and adolescent, in her studies and at play. She was healthy, honest, sensitive
and gay. She had a loving heart. She was, as her teachers said,
"remarkably gifted"; she was a brilliant student But on the whole
no startling characteristic distinguished her from the children who
grew up with her: nothing had yet indicated her genius.

Here is another portrait: that of the young girl. It is a graver
one. Some beloved figures had vanished from Manya's life, to be
kept alive only by her tender memory for years to come. Her
friendships, too, were changing little by little; the boarding school,
the high school had ceased to exist—as had the bonds of comradeship, so strong in appearance, which fell away with the daily
familiarity that had maintained them. Manya's destiny was to
define itself between two persons whom she valued and admired,
two beings full of kindness, understanding and honour, who happened to be her nearest relations—her father and her elder sister.

Now I should like to show Manya, between these two friends,
building the future in her sturdy head. But whereas most humans
do their wishing on a scale altogether disproportionate, how very
humble—even in its apparent audacity—was the dream of the girl
who was to become Marie Curie!

In September, still giddy from a whole year's roaming, Manya
took the road to Warsaw again, to the family's new lodging near
the Gymnasium where she had lived in her childhood.

The desertion of Leszno Street for Novolipki was justified by
a notable change in the living conditions of the Sklodovskis. As

45

age drew on, the professor, without giving up his teaching at the high school, decided to take no more board pupils. Manya and her family were installed in a smaller apartment now, more intimate and also poorer. The surroundings and the company were made for reflection and work.

Those who met M. Sklodovski for the first time found him severe in manner. Thirty years of teaching in secondary schools had given the plump little man a certain solemnity, and a thousand details of his appearance revealed the perfect government official: his dark clothes, always most carefully brushed, his precise gestures and his sententious speech. Every action of his life was performed with method. If he composed a letter its sentences were logical and its handwriting orderly. If he took the children on an excursion during the holidays nothing was left to chance. An itinerary worked out in advance led them punctually to the places most deserving of their attention, and, as they walked, the professor commented eloquently upon the charm of a landscape or the historic interest of a monument.

Manya never even noticed these small peculiarities of the pedagogue. She loved her father tenderly: he was her protector, her master. And she was not far from believing that he possessed universal knowledge.

It was true that M. Sklodovski knew everything, or nearly everything. In what country of Europe nowadays could one find an obscure schoolmaster with such erudition? The poor man, father of a family, balancing his budget with the greatest difficulty, had found leisure to develop his scientific knowledge by going through publications which he procured by considerable effort. It seemed to him quite natural to keep up with the progress of chemistry and physics, just as it was natural to know Greek and Latin and to speak English, French and German (as well as, of course, Polish and Russian); to translate the finest works of foreign authors into his native language in prose or verse; and, in his idle moments, to compose poetry which he carefully transcribed into his student's notebook with the black and green cover: "To my friends," "Toast for a marriage," "To my former pupils." . . .

Every Saturday for years past M. Sklodovski, his son and his three daughters had passed the whole evening together in the pursuit of literature. They chattered around the steaming tea in an otherwise silent house. The old man recited poetry or read aloud, and his children listened to him with rapture: the professor with his receding hair, his thick, placid face lengthened by a neat little grey beard, had a remarkable talent for speech. Saturday after Saturday the masterpieces of the past were brought to Manya in this way by a familiar voice. In the old days that voice had told fairy tales, read stories of travel, or initiated her into *David Copperfield*, which M. Sklodovski translated into Polish without a hitch as he read from the English text. Now, in the same voice, a little broken by innumerable hours of teaching in the high school, he interpreted for the four attentive young people the finest writings of those romantic authors who were the poets of servitude and revolt in Poland: Slovacki, Krasinski, Mickiewicz. Turning the pages of worn volumes, some of which—forbidden by the Tsar—had been printed secretly, the reader scanned the heroic outbursts of *Messer Thaddeus* or the mournful verses of *Kordyan*.

Manya was never to forget those evenings. Thanks to her father she lived in an intellectual atmosphere of rare quality known to few girls of her age. She was attached by powerful bonds to the man who made such touching efforts to render her life interesting and attractive. In her anxious affection she could guess the inner torments beneath M. Sklodovski's apparent serenity: the sadness of a widower who had never consoled himself, the gloom of a harassed official condemned to subordinate kinds of work, and the remorse of a scrupulous creature who could never forgive himself for that risky speculation which had swallowed up his modest fortune.

Sometimes, when his self-control failed, the poor man allowed a complaint to escape him.

"How could I have lost that money? I, who wanted to give you all the most brilliant educations, to send you abroad and let you travel! I have ruined it all I have no money and I can't help you Before long I shall be on your hands myself. What is to become of you?"

The professor would sigh with anguish and turn toward his children, unconsciously asking them for those happy protests and assertions by which they were wont to comfort him. They were all grouped beneath the high oil lamp in the little study enlivened by affectionately tended green plants. Four stubborn heads, four courageous smiles looked back at him, and in all those shining eyes, which ranged from periwinkle-blue to ashen-grey, could be seen the same ardour and the same hope:

"We are young. We are strong. We will succeed."

M. Sklodovski's terrors are easy to understand. That year, upon which their whole future depended, the situation of the young people was far from brilliant.

The problem was simple: the head of the family was barely able to pay for rent, food and a servant on his slender salary, which was soon to be succeeded by an even slenderer pension. Joseph, Bronya, Hela and Manya would have to earn their living.

The first idea that came to these children of two teachers was naturally that of giving lessons "Medical student will do private tutoring." Or (another advertisement)· "Lessons in arithmetic, geometry, French, by young lady with diploma. Moderate fees." The Sklodovskis entered the ranks of the hundreds of young intellectuals who were looking for work in Warsaw.

It was an ungrateful job. Before she was seventeen Manya had learned to know the fatigues and humiliations that attended it: the long walks across town, in rain and cold; the refractory or lazy pupils; the parents who made one wait for ever in draughty halls ("Tell Mlle Sklodovska to wait; my daughter will be there in a quarter of an hour!"), or who, out of sheer giddiness, forgot to pay the few roubles they owed one at the end of the month—those roubles so anxiously expected, that one had counted on having that very morning!

The winter advanced. In Novolipki Street life was dull and each day resembled the one before.

Nothing new at home [Manya wrote]. The plants are healthy, the azaleas are in flower, Lancet sleeps on the carpet. Gucia, the seamstress, is making over my dress, which I have dyed; it will be suitable and very pretty. Bronya's dress is finished and looks very nice. I have written to nobody; I have so little time, and even less money. A person who knew of us through friends came to inquire about lessons; Bronya told her a half-rouble an hour, and the visitor ran away as if the house had caught fire. . . .

It might be supposed that Manya was at this time a young lady without a dowry, active and sensible, whose only interest was in building up her list of pupils. The supposition would be untrue. She had bravely accepted the toilsome life of giving private lessons, by necessity; but she had another life, passionate and secret. Like every Pole of her place and time she was exalted by dreams.

There was one dream common to all the youths: the dream of nationhood. In their projects for the future, the desire to serve Poland took precedence of personal ambition, of marriage and of love. One would dream of violent struggle and would organise conspiracies at the risk of his life, another would dream of action by means of controversy; still another would take refuge in mystic dreaming—for the Catholic religion was also a resource, a force of resistance against the Orthodox oppressor.

The mystic dream no longer dwelt in Manya. By tradition and convention she remained a practising Christian, but her faith had been shaken by Mme Sklodovska's death: little by little it had now evaporated. She had felt the dominion of her pious mother profoundly, but for six or seven years she had been living under the influence of her father, a lukewarm Catholic, a free thinker without acknowledging it. From the devoutness of her childhood there remained only vague aspirations, the unconscious wish to adore something very high and very great

And even though she had among her friends some revolutionary patriots, to whom she lent her passport in time of danger, Manya did not indulge the alternative dream of taking part in assassinations, throwing bombs at the Tsar's carriage or at the governor of Warsaw. There was a powerful movement just starting, among the intelligentsia to which the young girl belonged, to discard and forget all vain chimeras—sterile regrets and disordered impulses toward independence. For them only one thing counted: to work, to build up a magnificent intellectual capital for Poland, and to develop the education of the poor, whom the authorities deliberately maintained in darkness.

The philosophical doctrines of the period gave this national progressionism a special direction. For some years past the positivism of Comte and Spencer had instigated new ways of thinking in Europe. At the same time the work of Pasteur, Darwin and Claude Bernard had endowed the exact sciences with immense prestige. At Warsaw as elsewhere—even more than elsewhere—intellectual fashion grew away from the romantic spirit; it disdained the world of art and sensibility for a while; and the young people, inclined by their age to downright judgments, suddenly placed chemistry and biology above literature and deserted the writer's cult for that of the scientist.

In free countries this current of ideas was allowed to develop publicly; but such was not the case in Poland, where every manifestation of independence of mind was regarded with suspicion. The new theories made their way and spread by underground routes.

It was soon after her return to Warsaw that Manya Sklodovska allied herself with some ardent positivists. A woman, Mlle Piasecka, assumed great influence over her. She was a high-school teacher of twenty-six or twenty-seven, thin and fair, of an appealing ugliness: she was in love with a student named Norblin, lately expelled from the university for his political activity, and she was passionately interested in the modern doctrines.

At first timid and untrusting, before long Manya was conquered by her friend's bold ideas. Along with her sister Bronya and the latter's good friend Marya Rakovska, she was admitted to sessions of the "Floating University"; which is to say, to lessons in anatomy, natural history and sociology, given by benevolent teachers to young people who wished to extend their culture. The sittings took place in secret, at Mlle Piasecka's house or in some other private dwelling. The disciples gathered to the number of eight or ten at a time and took notes: they passed pamphlets and articles from one to the other; at the slightest noise they trembled, for if they had been discovered by the police it would have meant prison for all of them. '

I have a lively memory of that sympathetic atmosphere of social and intellectual comradeship [Marie Curie was to write forty years later]. The means of action were poor and the results obtained could not be very considerable; and yet I persist in believing that the ideas that then guided us are the only ones which can lead to true social progress. We cannot hope to build a better world without improving the individual. Toward this end, each of us must work toward his own highest development, accepting at the same time his share of responsibility in the general life of humanity —our particular duty being to help those to whom we feel we can be most useful.

The aim of the Floating University was not only to carry on the instruction of young people just out of the secondary schools. In their turn the students were to become educators. Stimulated by Mlle Piasecka, Manya was to give lessons to women of the poor. She began by reading aloud to the employees of a dressmaking establishment and got together a little library of books in Polish, volume by volume, for the use of the working women.

How is one to imagine the fervour of this girl of seventeen? Her childhood had been passed before mysterious divinities, the physics apparatus in her father's study; even before the sciences had been made "fashionable" M. Sklodovski had transmitted his passionate curiosity to her. But that world was not enough for impetuous Manya; she plunged eagerly into other sections of the the world's knowledge; she grasped at Auguste Comte and social evolution; she dreamed no longer of mathematics or chemistry alone, but wished to reform the established order and enlighten the masses of the people. . . . With her advanced ideas and her generous soul she was, in the pure sense of the word, a Socialist; but at the same time she did not join the group of Socialist students which existed in Poland. Her liberty of judgment made her fear the party spirit, and her love of country kept her out of Marxian internationalism. Before everything and above everything she wanted to serve her country.

She did not yet know that the time would come when she must choose between these dreams. She had confounded, in the same exaltation, her patriotic feeling, her humanitarian ideas and her intellectual aspirations.

By some miracle she remained charming in the midst of such

doctrines and such excitements. The strict, high-minded education she had received, the example of the modest creatures who had watched over her youth, protected her from excess. There was a cool and moderate dignity in her nature, an innate gravity that accompanied her enthusiasm—not to say her passion. We shall never see her affect any snobbishness of revolt or bad manners. She will never even have the wish to light an innocent cigarette.

When her tutoring in the town and her clandestine courses in anatomy left her some respite she locked herself in her room. But the day of the "harmless and absurd little novels" had passed. Now she was devouring Dostoevsky and Goncharov and Boleslav Prus' *The Emancipated*, in which she found the portrait of her kind, of all the little Polish girls who had gone mad for culture. Her notebook reflects the inner life of an over-eager young being, bewildered by the diversity of her gifts: for ten pages we find pencil drawings which painstakingly illustrate La Fontaine's *Fables;* then German and Polish poetry, a fragment of Max Nordau on "The Conventional Lie"; Krasinski, Slovacki, Heine. Three pages from Renan's *Life of Jesus;* "Nobody ever made the interest of Humanity predominate in his life over worldly vanity as He did . . ."; Russian philosophical essays; a passage from Louis Blanc, a page of Brandes, and again drawings, flowers, animals; then Heine again; and Musset, Sully Prudhomme and François Coppée, translated by Manya into Polish verse

For—what contradictions!—the "emancipated girl" who in her disdain for frivolity had just cut her fair hair almost to the roots, sighed in secret and copied verses at great length, charming and more than a little dim:

> If I told you, dark one with blue eyes, that I love you,
> Who knows what you would say?

Manya took good care, one imagines, to keep her stern comrades from knowing that she appreciated *Adieu Suzon* or *The Broken Vase*. She barely admitted it to herself Severely dressed, her face made strangely childish by the short curls which, instead of accentuating her personality, had transformed her into a little girl, she hurried from meeting to meeting, she argued and glowed.

If she recited poetry in front of her friends she chose the exhortations of Asnyk, who was not a great artist but had written works inspired by such sympathetic fire that they became the Credo of the group:

> Look for the clear light of Truth;
> Look for unknown new roads . . .
> Even when man's sight is keener far than now,
> Divine wonder will never fail him . . .
> Every age has its own dreams,
> Leave, then, the dreams of yesterday;
> You—take the torch of knowledge,
> Perform a new work among the labours of the centuries
> And build the palace of the future. . . .

Even when she presented Marya Rakovska with her photograph, standing beside Bronya in an affectionate attitude, she did not fail to make the gift a sort of profession of faith by writing across the picture this definite statement:

"To an ideal positivist—from two positive idealists."

Our two "positive idealists" passed many hours together attempting to draw up a plan of their future lives. Unfortunately, neither Asnyk nor Brandes could point out a means of obtaining higher education for them in a city where the university was closed to women; nor could those authors supply a magic formula for getting rich quickly on lessons at half a rouble an hour.

And Manya's generous heart grieved There was the instinct of a Newfoundland dog in the child, youngest of her family; she felt responsible for her father's future, for the future of her elders. Joseph and Hela, luckily, gave her no cause for worry; the young man was going to be a doctor, and the lovely, stormy Hela, hesitating between a teacher's profession and a career as a singer, sang at the top of her voice and acquired diplomas and refused offers of marriage all at the same time.

But Bronya! How could Bronya be helped? Ever since she had left school four years ago all the cares of the household had fallen upon her. By dint of buying food, inventing menus and presiding at the preparation of preserves, she had become a remarkable housekeeper—and she was in despair at being only that. Manya understood the torments of her elder sister, whose great secret wish was to go to Paris and study medicine, then to return to Poland and practise in the country. The poor girl had saved a little money, but it cost so much to go abroad! How many months or years would she have to wait?

Manya was so made that her sister's visible anxiety and discouragement became her constant preoccupation, in which her own ambition was forgotten. She forgot that she, too, fascinated by the promised land, had often dreamed of traversing the thousands of miles that separated her from the Sorbonne, there to quench the thirst for knowledge that was her essential characteristic, and of bringing back the precious learning to her work as an educator in Warsaw, among her beloved Poles.

If she took Bronya's career so to heart, it was because finer bonds than those of blood attached her to the girl whose exquisite affection had given her maternal support since the death of Mme Sklodovska. In a very united family these two had chosen to prefer each other. Their natures were singularly complementary; the elder, by her experience and her practical sense, overawed Manya, who submitted to her all the little problems of daily life; the younger, at once more fiery and more timid, was for Bronya a marvellous young companion in whom love was enriched by a feeling of gratitude, by the vague notion of an indebtedness.

One day when Bronya was scribbling away at a piece of paper, counting how much money she had—or rather how much she lacked—Manya made a direct attack.

"I have reflected a lot just lately. I have also talked to Father. And I think I've found out a way."

"A way——?"

Manya came nearer to her sister; what she had to say and get accepted was delicate; she would have to weigh her words with prudence.

"Let's see. With what you have saved, how many months could you live in Paris?"

"I have enough to pay my journey and one year's expenses at

the Faculty," Bronya answered quickly. "But the medical course lasts five years, you know very well."

"Yes. But you understand, Bronya, that with lessons at half a rouble a time we shall never be able to do it."

"Well?"

"Well, we could make an alliance. If we keep on struggling separately, each on her own account, neither of us can ever get away. Whereas on my system you can take the train in the autumn—in a few months."

"Manya, you are mad!"

"No. To start with, you will spend your own money. After that I'll arrange to send you some; Father too. And at the same time I'll be piling up money for my own future studies. When you are a doctor, it will be my turn to go. And then you will help me."

Bronya's eyes filled with tears. She felt the greatness of the offer; but one point remained obscure in Manya's programme.

"I don't understand. You don't hope to make enough money for your own support and part of mine and then still more to save, do you?"

"Exactly that," said Manya casually. "That's where my system comes in. I am going to get a job as governess in a family. With board, lodging and laundry all free, I shall have four hundred roubles a year in wages, perhaps more. You see how that will settle everything."

"Manya . . . little Manyusya . . ."

It was not the choice of position that moved Bronya: like a good idealist she shared her sister's scorn for social prejudices. No; it was the idea that Manya could condemn herself for years to cruel waiting in an unattractive profession so that she, Bronya, could begin her studies immediately. She resisted.

"Why should I be the first to go? Why not the other way round? You are so gifted—probably more gifted than I am. You would succeed very quickly. Why should I go?"

"Oh, Bronya, don't be stupid! Because you are twenty and I'm seventeen. Because you've been waiting for hundreds of years and I've got lots of time. That's what Father thinks too; it is only natural that the elder should go first. When you have your practice you can bury me in gold—in fact, I count on it.

We're doing something intelligent at last, something that will work . . ."

One morning in September, 1885, a silent young girl was awaiting her turn in the reception room of an employment agency. She had put on the severer of her two dresses. Her fair curls, which she had allowed to grow again for several months, were pinned in place more or less firmly under her black hat. A governess—even a positivist!—ought not to wear her hair short: a governess had to be correct, commonplace, and look like everybody else. . . .

The door opened A thin woman with a discouraged face passed through the vestibule and gave Manya a farewell gesture as she went out. A colleague. They had fallen into talk a while ago, seated side by side on the cane-bottomed chairs which formed the only furniture in the place, and they had wished each other good luck.

Manya got up. She felt timid suddenly Her hand tightened mechanically over a thin bundle of papers and letters In the next room a fat lady was seated behind a tiny desk.

"What is your business, mademoiselle?"

"I am looking for a place as governess."

"You have references?"

"Yes. I have already given lessons. Here are some recommendations from the parents of my pupils Here is my diploma "

The directress of the agency examined Manya's documents with a professional eye. Her attention was caught; she raised her head and considered the girl with a little more interest.

"You have a perfect command of German, Russian, French, Polish and English?"

"Yes, madame. English not so well as the others. . . . But I can teach the material required on the official school lists. I left my high school with the gold medal."

"Ah! And how much money do you require?"

"Four hundred roubles a year, and my living."

"Four hundred," the lady repeated without expression. "Who are your parents?"

"My father is a teacher in the secondary schools."

"Very weii. I shall make the usual inquiries. I may have something for you. But how old are you, by the way?"

"Seventeen," said Manya; then she blushed and added very quickly, with an encouraging smile: "But I shall be eighteen soon "

The lady drew up the applicant's form in an impeccable "English" script:

Marya Sklodovska, good references, capable, wants place as governess. Salary: four hundred roubles a year.

She returned Manya's papers.

"Thank you, mademoiselle. I shall write to you if anything turns up."

CHAPTER V

Governess

"Dear Henrietta," Manya wrote to her cousin Michalovska on December 10th, 1885, "since we separated my existence has been that of a prisoner. As you know, I found a place with the B——'s, a family of lawyers. I shouldn't like my worst enemy to live in such a hell. In the end, my relations with Mme B—— had become so icy that I could not endure it any longer and told her so. Since she was exactly as enthusiastic about me as I was about her, we understood each other marvellously well

"It was one of those rich houses where they speak French when there is company—a chimney-sweeper's kind of French—where they don't pay their bills for six months, and where they fling money out of the window even though they economise pettily on oil for the lamps. They have five servants. They pose as liberals and, in reality, they are sunk in the darkest stupidity. And last of all, although they speak in the most sugary tones, slander and scandal rage through their talk—slander which leaves not a rag on anybody. . . . I learned to know the human race a little better by being there. I learned that the characters described in novels really do exist, and that one must not enter into contact with people who have been demoralised by wealth."

The picture is without indulgence. Coming from a creature so devoid of malice, it suggests how naïve and full of illusions was Manya. In placing herself with a well-to-do Polish family chosen by hazard she had had the hope of finding pleasant children and understanding parents. She was ready to attach herself and to love. Her disappointment was severe.

58

The letters the young governess was to write make us feel, indirectly, the distinction of the environment she had been obliged to leave. In her circle of intellectuals Manya had met people of small ability, but she had scarcely ever seen any of low or calculating spirit, any without honour. She had never heard an ugly or vulgar word at home. Family quarrels or spiteful chatter would have inspired horror in the Sklodovski household. Every time the girl met with stupidity, pettiness or vulgarity, we can perceive her astonishment and revolt.

Strange paradox: the high quality of Manya's youthful companions and their lively intelligence may be taken as explaining the secret of a haunting enigma. How was it that nobody discovered the extraordinary vocation, the genius, of this young girl? Why had she not been sent to study in Paris, instead of being allowed to seek employment as a governess?

Living among exceptional beings, with three young people who carried off diplomas and medals, who were brilliant, ambitious and ardent for work like herself, the future Marie Curie did not seem remarkable. In an intellectually narrow circle, surprising gifts are soon shown; they provoke astonishment and comment; but here, under the same roof, Joseph, Bronya, Hela and Manya were all growing up, rivalling one another in aptitude for knowledge. Thus it came about that nobody—neither the old nor the young—recognised in one of these children the signs of a great mind; nobody was touched by its first radiations. There was no suspicion that Manya might be of a different essence from her brother and sisters, and she had no idea of it herself.

When she compared herself to her relatives her modesty approached humility. But in the middle-class families to which her new profession introduced her there was no disguising her superiority. This was evident even to Manya's own eyes, and she became aware of it with some pleasure. The girl counted the privileges of birth and wealth as nothing; envy was never to touch her; but she was proud of her origin and of the training she had received. Through the judgments which we shall see her pass upon her employers there pierces the point of scorn and of an innocent pride.

Philosophical instruction on the human race, or upon "people demoralised by wealth," was not the only sort Manya received from her first experience. She learned that the plan, once explained to Bronya needed serious revision.

Manya had hoped, by taking a place in Warsaw, to earn respectable sums of money without condemning herself to painful exile. To remain in the city was a mitigation of the sentence: it meant staying near home and being able to go every day and talk for a bit with her father. It meant keeping up contact with her friends of the Floating University and being able—perhaps—to attend a few evening courses.

But those who have the taste for sacrifice within them cannot stop at half-immolations. The lot the young girl had chosen was still not arid enough: she could not earn enough money, and above all she spent too much. Her salary, frittered away in little daily purchases, left her with insignificant savings at the end of the month. She had yet to prepare herself to subsidise Bronya, who had gone to Paris with Marya Rakovska and was living in poverty in the Latin Quarter. And then, too, M Sklodovski's retirement was drawing near. Soon the old man would need help. What was she to do?

Manya did not hesitate for long. She had heard of a good post as governess in the country two or three weeks ago. No sooner said than done. She would accept the distant province, the leap into the unknown. It would be years of separation from those she loved, total isolation. What did that matter? The salary was good, and in that forgotten village the expenses were reduced practically to nothing.

"And I love the open air so much!" Manya told herself. "Why didn't I think of it sooner?"

She informed her cousin of her decision:

I shall not be free long, for I have decided, after some hesitation, to accept a place in the country to-morrow to begin in January. It is in the Government of Plock, and pays five hundred roubles a year dating from the first of January. It is the same post that was suggested to me some time ago, which I let slip. The family are not satisfied with their governess and now they are asking for me. It is quite possible, for that matter, that I shall please them no better than the other one.

The first of January, 1886, the day of her departure for the journey in the dreary cold, was to remain one of the cruellest dates of Manya's existence. She had bravely said good-bye to her father. She had repeated her new address for him:

Mlle Marya Sklodovska,
In Care of M. and Mme Z.,
Szczuki,
Near Przasnysz.

She had climbed into the railway carriage. For one more moment she could see the stocky outline of the professor, for one more moment she smiled. Then suddenly, as she sat down on the bench in the carriage, she felt the pressure of solitude. Alone—she was all alone, for the first time in her life.

The girl of eighteen was abruptly seized by panic. In the train which was carrying her heavily toward a strange house and family Manya shivered with shyness and terror. Supposing her new employers were like the old ones? Suppose M. Sklodovski were to fall ill in her absence? Would she ever see him again? Had she not done a thoroughly foolish thing? Torturing questions assailed the girl as she crouched near the window of the compartment looking out through her tears—she dried them with her hand, but they always came back—at vast plains hushed beneath the snow in the falling day.

Three hours in the train were followed by four hours in a sleigh over very straight roads in the majestic silence of winter night M. and Mme Z., estate administrators, farmed part of the lands of the Princes Czartoryski, one hundred kilometres north of Warsaw. When she arrived at the door of their house on an icy night Manya, broken with fatigue, could barely see, as in a dream, the great stature of the master of the household, his wife's dim face, and the intense stares of the children fixed upon her with sparkling curiosity.

The governess was received with hot tea and friendly words. Then, going up to the first floor, Mme Z showed Mayna her room and left her there in the company of her poor luggage.

Manya to her cousin Henrietta, February 3rd, 1886:

I have now been with M. and Mme Z. for one month; so I have had time to acclimatise myself in the new post. Up to now all has gone well. The Z.s are excellent people. I have made friends with their eldest daughter, Bronka, which contributes to the pleasantness of my life. As for my pupil, Andzia, who will soon be ten, she is an obedient child, but very disorderly and spoiled. Still, one can't require perfection. . . .

In this part of the country nobody works; people think only of amusing themselves; and since we in this house keep a little apart from the general dance, we are the talk of the countryside. One week after my arrival they were already speaking of me unfavourably because, as I didn't know anybody, I refused to go to a ball at Karvacz, the gossip centre of the region. I was not sorry, for M. and Mme Z. came back from that ball at one o'clock the next afternoon. I was glad to have escaped such a test of endurance, especially as I am not feeling at all strong just now.

There was a ball here on Twelfth Night. I was treated to the sight of a certain number of guests worthy of the caricaturist's pencil, and enjoyed myself hugely. The young people here are most uninteresting. Some of the girls are so many geese who never open their mouths, the others are highly provocative. It appears that there are some others, more intelligent. But up to now my Bronka (Mlle Z.) seems to me a rare pearl both in her good sense and in her understanding of life.

I have seven hours of work a day: four with Andzia, three with Bronka. This is rather a lot, but it doesn't matter. My room is upstairs. It is big, quiet and agreeable. There is a whole collection of children in the Z. family: three sons in Warsaw (one at the university, two in boarding schools). In the house there are Bronka (eighteen years old), Andzia (ten), Stas who is three, and Maryshna, a little girl of six months. Stas is very funny. His nyanya told him God was everywhere. And he, with his little face agonised, asked: "Is He going to catch me? Will He bite me?" He amuses us all enormously.

Manya interrupted her letter, put her pen down on the writing-desk she had installed near the long window, and braving the cold in her woollen dress, went out on the balcony. The view offered her there still had the gift of making her laugh. Wasn't it comic to set out for an isolated country house, imagining rural landscapes in advance, with prairies and forests, and then, on opening the casement of her room for the first time, to perceive a tall, aggressive factory chimney which, shutting off and dirtying the sky, spat opaque plumes of black smoke?

There was not a field or a coppice for miles around: nothing but sugar beet and again sugar beet, filling the great monotonous plain. In the autumn these pale earthy beetroots, piled up in bullock carts, slowly converged on the factory to be made into sugar. The peasants sowed, hoed and reaped for the factory. The huts of the little village of Krasiniec were crowded near these dreary red brick buildings. And the river itself was the slave of the factory, entering limpid and departing soiled, its surface charged with a dark, sticky scum.

Monsieur Z., an agriculturist of repute, familiar with new techniques, controlled the farming of two hundred acres of beet-root. He was a wealthy man: he owned a great part of the shares in the sugar factory. And in his house, as in the others, the factory was the object of preoccupation.

There was nothing on the grand scale about this. The factory, however absorbing it seemed, was only an enterprise of average importance like dozens of others in the provinces. The Szczuki estate was small: two hundred acres, in that country of vast estates, are nothing. The Z.s were well off but not rich. And although their house was more attractive than the neighbouring farms, it would be impossible, with the best will in the world, to call it a château. It was a rather old-fashioned villa, one of those great low buildings with sloped roofs overhanging walls of dull stucco, pergolas covered with Virginia creeper and verandas all glassed in and full of draughts.

One concession only was made to beauty: the pleasure garden, which became very pretty in summer with its lawn, its shrubbery and its croquet ground sheltered by a row of well-cut ash-trees. On the other side of the house there was an orchard, and farther on the four red roofs of the barns, stables and cattle sheds where forty horses and sixty cows were lodged. Beyond that, as far as the horizon, was nothing but loam for beetroot.

"Well, I haven't done so badly," Manya told herself as she shut the window. "The factory isn't beautiful, certainly. But just the same it's because of it that this provincial hole is a little more animated than some others. People often come from Warsaw and others go there. There are engineers and directors at the sugar factory; that is pleasant enough. One can borrow books and reviews there. Mme Z. has a bad temper; but she is not at all a bad woman. If she doesn't always treat me, the governess, with tact, that's no doubt because she was once a governess herself, and fortune came to her a bit too quickly. Her husband is charming, her elder daughter is an angel, her children are tolerable. I ought to think myself very lucky."

After warming her hands before the immense stove in shining porcelain which filled one of the alcoves of the room from floor to ceiling, Manya went back to her correspondence—until such time as an imperious call, "Mademoiselle Marya!" might inform her, through walls and doors, that her employers had need of her.

A governess all alone might be expected to write many letters, if only to receive answers with news from the town. As the weeks and months went by, at regular intervals Manya gave her relatives an account of the various events of her existence, in which humble tasks alternated with hours of "company" and pleasures which were part of her work. She wrote to her father, to Joseph and to Hela; to her dear Bronya; to Kazia Przyborovska, her school friend. To her cousin Henrietta, who was now married and living in Lvov but had remained a fierce positivist, she freely confided some graver reflections: her discouragement and her hope:

Manya to Henrietta, April 5th, 1886:
I am living as it is customary to live in my position. I give my lessons and I read a little, but it isn't easy, for the arrival of new guests constantly upsets the normal employment of my time. Sometimes this irritates me a great deal, since my Andzia is one of those children who profit enthusiastically by every interruption of work, and there is no way of bringing her back to reason afterwards. To-day we had another scene because she did not want to get up at the usual hour. In the end I was obliged to take her

calmly by the hand and pull her out of bed. I was boiling inside·
You can't imagine what such little things do to me: such a piece of
nonsense can make me ill for several hours. But I had to get the
better of her. . . .

. . . Conversation in company? Gossip and then more gossip.
The only subjects of discussion are the neighbours, dances and
parties. So far as dancing is concerned, you could look far before
you would find better dancers than the young girls of this region.
They all dance perfectly. They are not bad creatures, for that
matter, and certain ones are even intelligent but their education
has done nothing to develop their minds, and the stupid, incessant
parties here have ended by frittering their wits away. As for the
young men, there are few nice ones who are even a bit intelligent.
. . . For the girls and boys alike, such words as "positivism" or
"the labour question" are objects of aversion—supposing they
have ever heard the words, which is unusual. The Z. household is
relatively cultivated. M. Z. is an old-fashioned man, but full of
good sense, sympathetic and reasonable. His wife is rather
difficult to live with, but when one knows how to take her she is
quite nice. I think she likes me well enough.

If you could only see my exemplary conduct! I go to church
every Sunday and holiday, without ever pleading a headache or a
cold to get out of it. I hardly ever speak of higher education for
women. In a general way I observe, in my talk, the decorum
suitable to my position.

At Easter I am going to Warsaw for a few days. Everything
inside me so leaps with joy at the thought that I have difficulty
restraining wild cries of happiness   . .

It was all very well for ironic Manya to describe her "exemplary
conduct," but there was a daring and original character in her
which could not long tolerate the conventional life. The "positive
idealist" was always there, eager to be useful, to fight.

One day when she met some little peasants in the muddy road,
boys and girls miserably dressed, with bold faces under their
hempen hair, Manya conceived a plan. Why should she not put
into practice, in this small world of Szczuki, those progressive
ideas which were so dear to her? Last year she had dreamed of

"enlightening the people." Here was an excellent opportunity. The village children were for the most part illiterate. If any of them had been to school at any time, they had only learned the Russian alphabet there. How fine it would be to create a secret course in Polish, to awaken these young brains to the beauty of the national language and history!

The governess submitted her idea to Mlle Z., who was immediately taken with it and decided to assist.

"Think it over carefully," said Manya, to calm her enthusiasm. "You know that if we are denounced we shall be sent to Siberia."

But nothing is more contagious than courage: in the eyes of Bronka Z., Manya saw ardour and resolution. There was only the authorisation of the head of the family to be obtained, and they could begin their discreet propaganda in the peasant huts.

Manya to Henrietta, September 3rd, 1886:

. . . I could have had a holiday this summer, but I didn't know where to go, so I stayed at Szczuki. I did not want to spend the money to go to the Carpathians. I have many hours of lessons with Andzia, I read with Bronka, and I work an hour a day with the son of a workman here, whom I am preparing for school. Besides this, Bronka and I give lessons to some peasant children for two hours a day. It is a class, really, for we have ten pupils. They work with a very good will, but just the same our task is sometimes difficult. What consoles me is that the results get better gradually, or even quite quickly. Thus I have pretty full days—and I also teach myself a little or a lot, working alone. . . .

Manya to Henrietta, December, 1886:

. . . The number of my peasant pupils is now eighteen. Naturally they don't all come together, as I couldn't manage it, but even as it is they take two hours a day. On Wednesdays and Saturdays I am with them a little longer—as many as five hours consecutively. Of course this is only possible because my room is on the first floor and has a separate entrance on the stairway to the court-yard—thus, since this work doesn't keep me from my obligations to the Z.s, I disturb nobody. Great joys and great consolations come to me from these little children. . . .

Thus it was not enough for Manya to listen to Andzia droning out her lessons, to work with Bronka and to keep Julek—who was back from Warsaw and had been turned over to her—from going to sleep over his books. When all that was done, the dauntless girl went up to her room and waited until a noise of boots on the stairs, mingling with the shuffle of bare feet, announced the arrival of her disciples. She had borrowed a pine table and some chairs so that they could practise their writing comfortably. She had taken enough from her savings to buy them some copybooks and the pens which the numbed little fingers managed with such difficulty. When seven or eight young peasants were installed in the big room with chalked walls, Manya and Bronka Z. were barely able to maintain order and rescue the unhappy pupils who, sniffling and snorting with anguish, could not spell a difficult word.

These sons and daughters of servants, farmers and factory workers, who pressed round Manya's dark dress and fair hair, were not always well washed. They did not smell nice. Some of them were inattentive and sullen. But in most of their bright eyes appeared a naive and violent desire to accomplish, some day, those fabulous acts: reading and writing. And when this humble end was achieved, when the big black letters on white paper suddenly took on meaning, the young girl's heart contracted at the noisy, prideful triumph of the children and the wondering admiration of their illiterate parents who sometimes stationed themselves at the end of the room to watch the lessons. She thought of all this good will wasted, and of the gifts that perhaps lay hidden in these baulked and defrauded creatures. Before their sea of ignorance she felt disarmed and feeble.

CHAPTER VI

The Long Wait

THE little peasants never suspected that "Mlle Marya" often meditated darkly upon her own ignorance. They did not know that their young teacher's dream was to become a pupil again, and that she would like to be learning instead of teaching.

To think that at this very minute, when Manya at her window was once more contemplating the carts that brought beetroot to the factory, there were thousands and thousands of young people in Berlin, Vienna, Petersburg and London who were listening to lessons and lectures, who were working in laboratories, museums and hospitals! To think, above all, that inside the famous Sorbonne they were teaching biology, mathematics, sociology, chemistry and physics!

Marya Sklodovska wanted to study in France more than in any other country. The prestige of France dazzled her. In Berlin and Petersburg the oppressors of Poland reigned; but in France liberty was cherished, all feelings and all beliefs were respected, and there was a welcome for the unhappy and the hunted, no matter whence they came. Was it true, was it even possible, that some day she might take the train for Paris—that this great happiness might be given her?

She had lost all hope of it. The first twelve months of a stifling provincial life had undermined the illusions of a girl who, in spite of her intellectual passions and her dreams, was by no means given to the pursuit of phantoms When she stopped to consider, Manya saw before her a clear situation which was apparently without issue. In Warsaw there was her father, who would soon have need of her. In Paris there was Bronya, who must be helped for years more before she could earn a penny. And on the estate of Szczuki there was herself, Manya Sklodovska, governess. The project of amassing a capital, which once had seemed practical to her, now made her smile. It was a childish plan. One does not escape from a place like Szczuki.

It is fine to see, in the despondency of this creature of genius, that she was not invulnerable—that, far from preserving an in-human confidence, she suffered and grew discouraged like any other girl of nineteen. It is fine to see her contradict herself and, in the very moment when she claims to have renounced everything, struggle with ferocious heroism against her own burial. It was indeed an all-powerful instinct that made her sit every night at her desk, reading volumes of sociology and physics borrowed from the factory library, or perfecting her knowledge of mathematics by correspondence with her father.

The task was so ungrateful that it is astonishing to see Manya persevere in it. All alone in that country house, she was without direction or advice. She felt her way, almost by sheer chance, through the mazes of the knowledge she wanted to acquire, as summarily explained to her by out-of-date handbooks. In her moments of dismay she resembled her little peasants when they despaired of ever learning to read and threw their alphabets away; but nevertheless, with a peasant's stubbornness, she pursued her effort.

Literature interested me as much as sociology and science [she was to write forty years later]. Still, during these years of work, as I tried gradually to discover my true preferences, I finally turned toward mathematics and physics.

These solitary studies were encompassed with difficulty. The scientific education I had received at school was very incomplete— much inferior to the programme for the baccalaureate in France. I tried to complete it in my own way, with the help of books got together by sheer chance. The method was not efficacious, but I acquired the habit of independent work and I learned a certain number of things which were to be useful to me later. . . .

She described one of these days in a letter from Szczuki.

Manya to Henrietta, December, 1886:

. . . With all I have to do, there are days when I am occupied from eight to half-past eleven and from two to half-past seven without a moment's rest. From half-past eleven to two there are a walk and lunch. After tea, I read with Andzia if she has been good, and if not we talk, or else I take my sewing, which by the way I also have by me during the lessons. At nine in the evening I take my books and go to work, if something unexpected does not prevent it . . . I have even acquired the habit of getting up at six so that I work more—but I can't always do it. A very nice old man, Andzia's godfather, is staying here just now, and Mme Z. asked me to ask him to teach me how to play checkers—to amuse him. I also have to make a fourth at cards, and that drags me away from my books.

At the moment I am reading:

(1) Daniel's *Physics*, of which I have finished the first volume;
(2) Spencer's *Sociology*, in French;
(3) Paul Bers' *Lessons on Anatomy and Physiology*, in Russian.

I read several things at a time: the consecutive study of a single subject would wear out my poor little head, which is already much overworked. When I feel myself quite unable to read with profit, I work problems of algebra or trigonometry, which allow no lapses of attention and get me back into the right road.

My poor Bronya writes from Paris that they are giving her a lot of difficulty with her examinations, that she is working hard, and that her health is causing a certain amount of worry.

. . . My plans for the future? I have none, or rather they are so commonplace and simple that they are not worth talking about. I mean to get through as well as I can, and when I can do no more, say farewell to this base world. The loss will be small, and regret for me will be short—as short as for so many others.

These are my only plans now. Some people pretend that in spite of everything I am obliged to pass through the kind of fever called love. This absolutely does not enter into my plans. If I ever had any others, they have gone up in smoke; I have buried them; locked them up; sealed and forgotten them—for you know that walls are always stronger than the heads which try to demolish them. . . .

These vague thoughts of suicide, this disappointed and sceptical sentence about love, call for explanation.

The explanation is simple and very ordinary. It could be called "the romance of a poor young girl." Numerous sentimental novels have recounted stories exactly like it

The beginning of the story is that Manya Sklodovska had grown pretty. She did not yet possess the exquisite unreality revealed by her portraits of a few years later; but the chubby adolescent had changed into a fresh, graceful girl, with lovely skin and hair, fine wrists and slender ankles Although her face was neither regular nor perfect, it attracted attention by the wilful curve of the mouth and by her ash grey eyes, sunk deep under her brows, and made bigger by the surprising intensity of her gaze.

When the eldest son of M. and Mme Z., Casimir, came back from Warsaw to Szczuki for his holidays, he found in the house a governess who could dance marvellously, row and skate; who was witty and had nice manners; who could make up verses as easily as she rode a horse or drove a carriage; who was different—how totally, mysteriously different!—from all the young ladies of his acquaintance. He fell in love with her. And Manya, Manya who hid a vulnerable heart beneath her revolutionary doctrines, was enamoured of him, the handsome, agreeable student.

She was not yet nineteen. He was only a little older. They made their plans to marry. . . .

There seemed to be nothing against this union It was true that Manya was, at Szczuki, only "Mlle Marya," the children's governess. But everybody there regarded her with affection: Monsieur Z took long walks with her across the fields, Mme Z mothered her and Bronka adored her. The Z s had always treated her with particular courtesy: on several occasions they had invited her father, brother and sisters to stay with them. On her birthday they gave her flowers and presents.

It was therefore without too much apprehension, indeed almost with confidence, that Casimir Z. asked his parents if they approved of his engagement.

The answer was not slow in coming. Father fell into a rage, Mother almost fainted. He, Casimir, their favourite child, to marry this girl who hadn't a penny, who was obliged to work "in other people's houses"? He who could marry the richest and best-born girl of the neighbourhood to-morrow? Had he gone mad?

In one instant the social barriers went up, insurmountable, in a house where it had been a point of pride to treat Manya as a friend. The fact that the girl was of good family, that she was cultivated, brilliant and of irreproachable reputation, the fact that her father was honourably known in Warsaw—none of this counted against six implacable little words. one does not marry a governess

Apostrophised, shaken and preached at, the student felt his resolutions melt within him. He had little character. He was afraid of reproaches and anger. And Manya, lacerated by the scorn of creatures inferior to herself, withdrew into awkward coldness and a nervous silence. She had made up her mind, she would never again give a thought to the vanished idyll.

But love is like ambition: a decree of death will not kill it.

Manya could not take the step—cruel but clear—of leaving Szczuki She did not want to worry her father, and above all she could not afford the luxury of giving up such a good post, now that Bronya's savings were a mere memory it was she, Manya, who had to help her father pay her elder sister's expenses at the Faculty of Medicine She sent her sister fifteen roubles every month and sometimes twenty—nearly half her salary. Where could she find another such salary? There had been no direct explanation between the Z s and herself, no painful discussion It was better to swallow her pride and stay at Szczuki, as if nothing had happened

Life resumed its way thereafter just as it had been before. Manya gave her lessons, scolded Andzia, shook Julek—who was put to sleep by the slightest intellectual work—and continued her work among the little peasants. She studied chemistry as always, making fun of herself and shrugging her shoulders at her own useless perseverance. She played draughts and rhyming games, went to dances, took walks in the open air. . . .

In winter [she was to write later], the vast snow-covered plains were not without charm, and we made long trips in the sleigh. At times we could hardly make out the road.

"Don't lose the trail!" I cried to the driver. He answered: "We are in the exact middle of it," or "Don't be afraid!"—and then we turned over. Such catastrophes only added to the gaiety of our excursions.

. . . I remember also the marvellous snowhouse we built one year when the snow was very high in the field. We could sit down in it and from there contemplate the immense white expanse, tinted with rose. . . .

Unhappy in love, disappointed in her intellectual dream and materially very hard up—for by the time she had helped this one and that there was nothing left—Manya attempted to forget her fate, the rut in which she felt herself stuck for ever. She turned toward her family, not to ask their help and not even to express her bitterness: in each of her letters she poured out advice and offered her support. She wanted them to have full lives.

Manya to Joseph, March 9th, 1887:
. . . I think that if you borrowed a few hundred roubles you could remain in Warsaw instead of burying yourself in the provinces. First of all, my dear little brother, don't be angry if I write something stupid; remember that I am telling you sincerely what I think, as we have always agreed. . . . You see, darling, everybody says that to work in a small town would prevent you from developing your culture and doing research. You would be thrust into a hole and would have no career at all. Without a pharmacy, without a hospital or books, one gets very dull, in spite of the best resolutions. And if that happened to you, darling, you will not be surprised to hear that I should suffer enormously, for now that I have lost the hope of ever becoming anybody, all my ambition has been transferred to Bronya and you. You two, at least, must direct your lives according to your gifts. These gifts which, without any doubt, do exist in our family must not disappear; they must come out through one of us. The more regret I have for myself the more hope I have for you. . . .

Perhaps you will make fun of me, or else shrug your shoulders at such a lecture. I am not in the habit of speaking or writing to you in such a tone. But this comes from the depths of my heart and I have thought it for a long time, since you first began your studies

And think, too, what a joy it will be for Father to have you near him! He loves you so much—he loves you more than all of the rest of us. Imagine, if Hela married M. B. and you went away from Warsaw, what would become of our poor father all alone! He would be very sad. Whereas this way you would live together, and it would be perfect. Only, just in the spirit of economy, don't forget to save a little corner for the rest of us in case we should come back.

Manya to Henrietta [who had just given birth to a dead child]. April 4th, 1887:

. . . What suffering it must be for a mother to go through so many trials for nothing! If one could only say, with Christian resignation: "God willed it and His will be done!" half of the terrible bitterness would be gone. Alas, that consolation is not for everybody. I see how happy are the people who admit such explanations. But, strangely enough, the more I recognise how lucky they are the less I can understand their faith, and the less I feel capable of sharing their happiness

. . . Forgive me these philosophical reflections: they are caused by your complaint against the backward and conservative spirit of the town where you live. Do not judge it too hardly, for social and political conservatism usually comes from religious conservatism, and the latter is a happiness—even though for us it has become incomprehensible So far as I am concerned, I should never voluntarily contribute toward anybody's loss of faith Let everybody keep his own faith, so long as it is sincere. Only hypocrisy irritates me—and it is as wide-spread as true faith is rare. . . . I hate hypocrisy. But I respect sincere religious feelings when I meet them, even if they go with a limited state of mind. . . .

Manya to Joseph, May 20th, 1887·

. . . I still don't know if my pupil, Andzia, is going to take her examinations, but I am in torment over them already. Her attentiveness and memory are so uncertain. . . . It is the same thing with Julek. To try teaching them is truly to build on sand, b cause when they learn one thing they have already forgotten what one taught them the day before At times this is a sort of torture. Also I am very much afraid for myself· it seems to me all the time that I am getting terribly stupid—the days pass so quickly and I make no noticeable progress Even with the village children I had to interrupt my lessons because of the Masses of the month of Mary. Still, it seems to me that I don't require a great deal to be content: I only want to get the conviction that I am being of some use. . . .

Later on she says of Hela, whose engagement to marry had just been broken:

I can imagine how Hela's self respect must have suffered. Truly, it gives one a good opinion of men! If they don't want to marry poor young girls, let them go to the devil! Nobody is asking them for anything. But why do they offend by troubling the peace of an innocent creature?

. . . If something consoling could only come through you! I often ask myself how your business is going, and if you don't regret having remained in Warsaw. To tell the truth, I oughtn't to torment myself over it, as you will certainly come out all right: I firmly believe that. There are always more petty annoyances with the *babas**—but I, even I, keep a sort of hope that I shall not disappear completely into nothingness. . . .

Manya to Henrietta, December 10th, 1887:
. . . Don't believe the report of my approaching marriage; it is unfounded. This tale has been spread about the countryside and even at Warsaw; and though this is not my fault, I am afraid it may bring me trouble. My plans for the future are modest indeed. my dream, for the moment, is to have a corner of my own where I can live with my father. The poor man misses me a lot; he would like to have me at home; he longs for me! To get my independence again, and a place to live, I would give half my life. Therefore, if the thing is at all possible, I shall leave Szczuki—which can't be

---

**Babas:* In Polish, a mocking word for women.

done, in any case, for some time—I shall install myself in Warsaw, take a post as teacher in a girls' school and make up the rest of the money I need by giving lessons. It is all I want. Life does not deserve to be worried over . . .

Manya to Joseph, March 18th, 1888:

Dear little Jozio, I am going to stick the last stamp I possess on this letter, and since I have literally not a penny—not one!—I shall probably not write to you again until the holidays, unless by some chance a stamp should fall into my hands

The real purpose of this letter was to wish you a happy birthday, but if I am late it is only because of the lack of money and stamps which afflicts me dreadfully—and I've never yet learned to ask for them.

. . . My darling Jozio, if you only knew how I sigh and long to go to Warsaw for only a few days! I say nothing of my clothes, which are worn out and need care—but my soul, too, is worn out. Ah, if I could extract myself for just a few days from this icy atmosphere of criticism, from the perpetual guard over my own words, the expression in my face, my gestures! . . . I need that as one needs a cool bath on a torrid day. I have many reasons, besides, for wanting such a change

It has been a long time since Bronya wrote to me. No doubt she, too, has no stamp . . . If you can manage to sacrifice one, I beg you to write to me. Write to me, well and long, everything that happens at home; for in Father's and Hela's letters there are nothing but laments, and I ask myself if everything really is so bad; and I am in torment; and to these worries there are added quantities of worries I have here, of which I could speak—but I don't want to. If I only didn't have to think of Bronya I should present my resignation to the Z.s this very instant and look for another post, even though this one is so well paid.

Manya to her friend Kazia [who had just announced her engagement, and with whom Manya was soon going to stay for a few days]. October 25th, 1888:

. . . Nothing you could ever confide in me could ever seem excessive or ridiculous. How could I, your chosen little sister, not take to heart everything that concerns you, as if it were my own?

As for me, I am very gay—and often I hide my deep lack of gaiety under laughter. This is something I learned to do when I found out that creatures who feel as keenly as I do, and are unable to change this characteristic of their nature, have to dissimulate it at least as much as possible But do you think it is efficacious, or good for anything? Not at all! Most often the vivacity of my temperament runs away with me gradually, and then—well, one says things that one regrets, and with more ardour than is necessary

I write with some bitterness, Kazia, but you see . . . You tell me you have just lived through the happiest week of your life, and I, during these holidays, have been through such weeks as you will never know. There were some very hard days, and the only thing that softens the memory of them is that in spite of everything I came through it all honestly, with my head high (As you see, I have not yet renounced, in life, that carriage which brought me Mlle Mayer's hatred of old)

. . You will say, Kazia, that I am growing sentimental. Don't be afraid. I shall not fall into a sin so foreign to my nature—only, I have become very nervous recently Some people have done all they could to bring this about Nevertheless I shall be as gay and free as ever when I come to you. What a lot of things we have to say to each other! I shall bring along some chains for our mouths, as otherwise we should never get to bed until dawn. Will your mother give us lemonade and chocolate ices as she used to do?

Marya to Joseph, October, 1888:
I look sadly at my calendar: this day has cost me five stamps, not counting letter paper. Thus I shall soon have nothing to say to you!

Think of it: I am learning chemistry from a book. You can imagine how little I get out of that, but what can I do, as I have no place to make experiments or do practical work?

Bronya has sent me a little album from Paris It is very elegant.

Manya to Henrietta, November 25th, 1888:
I have fallen into black melancholy because our daily companions are dreadful west winds, with embellishments of rain

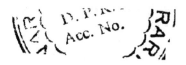

flood and mud. To-day the sky is a little more clement, but the wind roars in the chimney. There isn't a trace of ice, and the skates hang sadly in the cupboard. You are probably unaware that in our provincial hole the frost and the advantages it brings us are at least as important as a discussion between conservatives and progressives in your Galicia. . . . Don't conclude from this that your stories bore me: on the contrary, it is a real satisfacton for me to learn that there exist some regions and some geographic areas in which people move and even think. While you are living at the centre of the movement, my existence strangely resembles that of one of those slugs which haunt the dirty water of our river. Luckily I hope to get out of this lethargy soon.

I wonder if, when you see me, you will judge that the years I have just passed among humans have done me good or not. Everybody says that I have changed a great deal, physically and spiritually, during my stay at Szczuki. This is not surprising. I was barely eighteen when I came here, and what have I not been through! There have been moments which I shall certainly count among the most cruel of my life . . . I feel everything very violently, with a physical violence, and then I give myself a shaking, the vigour of my nature conquers, and it seems to me that I am coming out of a nightmare. . . . First principle: never to let one's self be beaten down by persons or by events.

I count the hours and days that separate me from the holidays and my departure to my own people. There is also the need of new impressions; the need of change, of movement and life, which seizes me sometimes with such force that I want to fling myself into the greatest follies, if only to keep my life from being eternally the same. Fortunately, I have so much work to do that these attacks seize me pretty rarely. It is my last year here; and I must therefore work all the harder, so that the children's examinations will go well. . . .

CHAPTER VII

The Escape

THREE years had passed since "Mlle Marya" became a governess. Three monotonous years they were: much work and no money, some few little pleasures, one grief But now, by small imperceptible stages, the tragic immobility of the young girl's existence was beginning to stir. In Paris, in Warsaw and at Szczuki certain events, small in appearance, modified the play of the mysterious game in which Manya's lot was decided.

M. Sklodovski, having obtained his pension, started out in search of lucrative employment He wanted to try to help his daughters In April, 1888, he accepted the most arduous and ungrateful of posts: the directorship of a reform school at Studzieniec, not far from Warsaw. The atmosphere, the surroundings, everything was unpleasant there—everything but the comparatively high salary, from which the good man instantly set aside a monthly sum for Bronya.

The first thing Bronya did was to direct Manya not to send her any more money. The second was to ask her father to hold eight roubles out of the forty roubles he gave her every month—eight roubles destined to repay, little by little, the sums she had received from her little sister. From that moment Manya's fortune, starting from zero, began to increase.

The medical student's letters brought other news from Paris. She was working. She was passing her examinations with success. And she was in love: in love with a Pole, Casimir Dluski, her comrade in study, brilliant with charm and good qualities, whose only awkward peculiarity was that he was forbidden to live in

Russian Poland and was threatened with deportation to Siberia if he returned there.

At Szczuki, Manya's task was approaching its end. After St. John's Day in 1889 the Z s would no longer need her services Naturally, she would have to find another place. The young governess already had one in view, with some rich industrialists of Warsaw, the F.s. It would be a change, at any rate—the change that Manya called for so eagerly.

Manya to Kazia, March 13th, 1889:
In five weeks it will be Easter. . . . For me it is a very important date, as my future will be decided then. Besides the post with the F.s, I am offered another. I am hesitating between the two and don't know what to do

. . . I think only of Easter! My head is so full of plans that it seems aflame. I don't know what is to become of me You see, your Manya will be, to the end of her days, a flighty-head of flighty-heads. . . .

Good-bye to Szczuki and the beet fields! With friendly smiles— a bit too friendly on both sides—Manya took her leave of the Z s. Liberated, she reached Warsaw and breathed the air of her native town with delight. Then she was off again, on the train to Zoppot, a dismal Baltic beach where she would join her new employers.

Manya to Kazia, July 14th, 1889:
. . . My journey went off all right, in spite of my tragic presentiments. . . . Nobody robbed me, or even tried to; I did not take the wrong train at any of my five changes, and I ate up all my *serdelki:* only the rolls and the caramels were too much for me. Along the way I had benevolent protectors who made everything easy for me. For fear that they would carry their amiability so far as to eat my provisions, I didn't show them my *serdelki.*

M. and Mme F. were waiting at the station for me. They are very nice, and I have been attracted to the children. Everything will therefore be all right—as indeed it must be.

Life was not very amusing in the Schultz Hotel at that summer resort wnere, Manya wrote, "one sees the same people all the time, around the Kurhaus, where they speak only of dresses and other equally interesting things. It is cold, everybody stays at home: Mme F., her husband, her mother—and they are in such temper that I should like to hide in a mousehole, if I could."

But soon afterward employers, children and governess returned to Warsaw, where they installed themselves for the winter.

The year to come was to be a comparatively pleasing interval for the young girl Mme F was very beautiful, very elegant, very rich. She had furs and jewels. There were some dresses by Worth in her wardrobe, and her portrait in evening dress hung in the salon During this time Manya became acquainted, as a spectator, with the frivolous and charming things wealth can offer a spoiled woman—things that she was never to possess First and last meeting with luxury! It was made agreeable by Mme F 's graciousness; that lady, attracted by the "exquisite Mlle Sklodovska," sang Manya's praises and required her to be present at all the tea parties, all the dances

Suddenly, one day, the thunderbolt: the postman brought a letter from Paris It was a hurried letter on squared paper, which Bronya had scribbled between two sessions in the operating theatre; therein the generous girl offered Manya hospitality in her new home—for the coming year.

Bronya to Manya, March, 1890:

. . . If everything goes as we hope, I shall surely be able to marry when the holidays begin. My fiancé will be a doctor by then, and I shall have only my last examination to pass. We shall stay another year in Paris, during which time I shall finish my examinations, and then we shall come back to Poland. I see nothing in our plans that is not reasonable Tell me if you think I am not right. Remember that I am twenty-four—which is nothing—but he is thirty-four, which is more serious. It would be absurd to wait any longer.

. . . And now, you my little Manya· you must make something of your life sometime. If you can get together a few hundred roubles this year you can come to Paris next year and live with us, where you will find board and lodging. It is absolutely necessary to have a few hundred roubles for your fees at the Sorbonne. The first year you will live with us For the second and third, when we are no longer there, I swear Father will help you in spite of the devil. You must take this decision; you have been waiting too long. I guarantee that in two years you will have your master's degree. Think about it, get the money together, put it in a safe place, and *don't lend* it. Perhaps it would be better to change it into francs right away, for the exchange is good just now, and later it might fall. . . .

One might think that the enthusiastic Manya would have answered her sister at once to say that she was exultant with happiness and was coming; but not at all Years of exile and loneliness, instead of souring this extraordinary girl, had made her over-scrupulous Her sacrificial demon could make her capable of deliberately missing her destiny. Because she had promised to live with her father; because she wanted to help her sister Hela and her brother Joseph, Manya no longer wished to go. And this is how she answered Bronya's invitation:

Manya to Bronya, March 12th, 1890 [*from Warsaw*]:
Dear Bronya, I have been stupid, I am stupid and I shall remain stupid all the days of my life, or rather, to translate into the current style: I have never been, am not and shall never be lucky. I dreamed of Paris as of redemption, but the hope of going there left me a long time ago. And now that the possibility is offered me, I do not know what to do. . . . I am afraid to speak of it to Father: I believe our plan of living together next year is close to his heart, and he clings to it; I want to give him a little happiness in his old age. On the other hand, my heart breaks when I think of ruining my abilities, which must have been worth, anyhow, something There is also the fact that I promised Hela to take her back home in a year, and to find her a post in Warsaw. You have no idea how sorry I felt for her! She will always be the minor child of the family, and I feel it is my duty to watch over her—the poor little thing needs it so. . . .
But you, Bronya, I beg of you, take charge of Joseph's interests with all your energy, and, even if it seems to you that it is not your

part to solicit help from that Mme S., who can extricate him, conquer the feeling. After all, the Bible says literally: "Knock and it shall be opened to you " Even if you are forced to sacrifice a little of your self-esteem, what does that matter? An affectionate request can offend nobody. How well I should know how to write that letter! You must explain to the lady that there is no question of a large sum, only of a few hundred roubles, so that Joseph can live in Warsaw and study and practise; that his future depends on it, that without this help such wonderful abilities will be ruine l. . . In a word, you must write all that, and at length; for, darling Bronczka, if you simply ask her to lend the money, she will not take the business to heart: that is not the way to succeed. And even if you have the feeling of being a nuisance, what of it? What's the difference, so long as the end is achieved? And besides, is it such a big request? Aren't people often greater nuisances than that? With this help Joseph can become useful to society, whereas if he leaves for the provinces he is lost

I bore you with Hela, Joseph and Father, and with my own wrecked future. My heart is so black, so sad, that I feel how wrong I am to speak of all this to you and to poison your happiness, for you are the only one of us all who has had what they call luck. Forgive me, but, you see, so many things hurt me that it is hard for me to finish this letter gaily.

I embrace you tenderly. The next time I shall write more cheerfully and at greater length—but to-day I am exceptionally unhappy in this world. Think of me with tenderness—perhaps I shall be able to feel it even here.

Bronya insisted, argued. Unfortunately, she lacked the decisive argument: she was too poor to pay the travelling expenses of her young sister and to put her authoritatively into the train. Finally it was decided that when Manya had finished her engagement with Mme F. she would remain still another year in Warsaw. She would live with her father, recently freed from his work at Studzieniec; she would complete her savings by giving lessons; and thereafter she would go.

After the torpor of the provinces and the agitated gaieties of the F.'s, Manya returned to the climate that was dear to her: a lodging of her own, the presence of old Professor Sklodovski and conversations interesting enough to stimulate her mind. The Floating University again opened its mysterious doors to her. And —incomparable pleasure, major event!—Manya, for the first time in her life, penetrated into a laboratory.

It was at 66 Krakovsky Boulevard, at the end of a court-yard planted with lilacs: a tiny building on one floor receiving light from Lilliputian windows. One of Manya's cousins, Joseph Boguski, there directed what was pompously called "The Museum of Industry and Agriculture." This title, wilfully pretentious and vague, was only a front to present to the Russian authorities. A museum would not arouse suspicion. Nothing prevented the teaching of science to young Poles behind the windows of a museum.

I had little time for work in this laboratory [Marie Curie was to write]. I could generally get there only in the evening after dinner, or on Sunday, and I was left to myself. I tried to reproduce various experiments described in the treatises on physics or chemistry, and the results were sometimes unexpected. From time to time a little unhoped-for success would come to encourage me, and at other times I sank into despair because of the accidents or failures due to my inexperience. But on the whole, even though I learned, to my cost, that progress in such matters is neither rapid nor easy, I developed my taste for experimental research during these first trials.

Coming home late at night, regretfully leaving electrometers, test-tubes and accurate balances, Manya undressed and lay down on her narrow bed. But she could not sleep. An exaltation different from all those she had known kept her from sleep. Her vocation, for so long uncertain, had flashed into life. She was summoned to obey a secret order. She was suddenly in a hurry, whipped onward. When she took the test-tubes of the Museum of Industry and Agriculture into her fine, clever hands Manya returned, as if by magic, to the absorbing memories of her childhood, to her father's physics apparatus, motionless in its glass case, with which, in the old days, she had always wanted to play. She had taken up the thread of her life again.

Though her nights were feverish her days were peaceful in

appearance. Manya concealed the furious impatience that possessed
her. She wished her father to be happy and at peace during these
last months of intimacy. She busied herself with her brother's
marriage; she looked for a position for Hela. And then, too,
perhaps a more selfish care kept her from fixing the date of her
departure: she thought she still loved Casimir Z. Even though she
felt herself driven toward Paris by an imperious power, she could
not contemplate an exile of several years without anguish.

In September 1891, while Manya was on holiday at Zakopane
in the Carpathians where she was to meet Casimir Z, M.
Sklodovski explained the situation to Bronya:

Manya had to stay at Zakopane and will not return until the
15th, because of a bad cough and influenza which, the local doctor
says, might drag along all winter if she does not get rid of it there.
The little rascal! It must be partly her fault, as she has always made
fun of all precautions and has never deigned to adapt her raiment
to the atmospheric conditions. She has written me that she was
very gloomy; I am afraid her grief, and the uncertainty of her
situation, may undermine her. Moreover, she has a secret about
her future, of which she is to speak to me at length, but only on
her return. To tell the truth, I can well imagine what it has to do
with, and I don't myself know whether I should be glad or sorry.
If my foresight is accurate, the same disappointments, coming
from the same persons who have already caused them to her, are
awaiting Manya. And yet if it is a question of building a life
according to her own feeling, and of making two people happy,
that is worth the trouble of facing them, perhaps. But the fact
is that I know nothing. . . .

Your invitation to Paris, which fell upon her in such unexpected
fashion, has given her a fever and added to her disorder. I feel the
power with which she wills to approach that source of science,
towards which she aspires so much. But the present conditions
are less favourable, and, above all, if Manya does not come back
to me completely cured, I should oppose her departure, because
of the hard conditions she would find herself in during the winter
in Paris—without speaking of all the rest of it, and without even
taking account of the fact that it would be very painful to me to

separate from her, for this last consideration is obviously secondary. I wrote to her yesterday, and tried to raise her spirits. If she remained in Warsaw, even if she could find no lessons, I should certainly have a bit of bread for her and for myself for a year.

I learned with great joy that your Casimir is doing well. How funny it would be if each of you had a Casimir!

Dear M. Sklodovski! In his heart of hearts he had no desire to see his Manya, his favourite, depart for the adventure of the great world. He would vaguely have preferred something to keep her in Poland· a marriage with Casimir Z , for instance

But at Zakopane, between two walks in the mountains, an explanation took place between the two young people As the student confided his hesitations and fears to her for the hundredth time, Manya, unable to bear any more, pronounced the sentence that burned her bridges:

"If you can't see a way to clear up our situation, it is not for me to teach it to you "

During this long but somewhat tepid idyll Manya showed herself, as Professor Sklodovski was to say later, "proud and haughty."

The girl had broken the feeble link that still held her. She stopped trying to control her hurry. She counted up all the hard years of boiling patience through which she had just lived It was eight years since she had left the Gymnasium, six years since she had gone out as a governess She was no longer the adolescent who saw her whole life before her. In a few weeks she would be twenty-four.

Suddenly she cried out: she called to Bronya for help.

Manya to Bronya, September 23rd, 1891:

. . . Now, Bronya, I ask you for a definite answer. Decide if you can really take me in at your house, for I can come now. I have enough to pay all my expenses If, therefore, without depriving yourself of a great deal, you could give me my food, write to me and say so. It would be a great happiness, as that would restore me spiritually after the cruel trials I have been through this summer, which will have an influence on my whole life—but, on the other hand, I do not wish to impose myself on you.

Since you are expecting a child, perhaps I might be useful to you. In any case, write and let me know. If my coming is just possible, tell me, and tell me what entrance examinations I must pass, and what is the latest date at which I can register as a student. I am so nervous at the prospect of my departure that I can't speak of anything else until I get your answer. I beg of you, then, write to me at once, and I send all my love to both of you You can put me up anywhere; I shall not bother you; I promise that I shall not be a bore or create disorder. I implore you to answer me, but very frankly.

If Bronya did not reply by telegram it was because telegrams were a ruinous luxury If Manya did not fling herself into the first train it was because she had to organise the great departure first, with parsimonious economy. She spread out on the table all the roubles she possessed, and to them her father, at the last moment, added a little sum which for him was an important one. And she began her calculations.

So much for the passport, so much for the railway. It would be sheer flightiness to take a third-class ticket from Warsaw to Paris—the cheapest way in Russia and France. There existed in Germany—thank God!—railway carriages of the fourth class, without compartments, almost as bare as freight cars: a bench on each of the four sides and an empty space in the middle where, seated on a folding chair, one was not badly off.

Practical Bronya's recommendation was not forgotten: to take along everything necessary to life, so as to have no unforeseen expenses in Paris Manya's mattress, her bedclothes, her sheets and towels, would leave long in advance, by freight. Her linen, made of strong cloth, her clothes, her shoes and her two hats were collected on a couch near which—unique and gorgeous purchase! —gaped the big wooden trunk, brown and bulging, very rustic but very solid, on which the girl had lovingly had painted her initials in broad black letters: M.S.

With the mattress gone and the trunk registered, there remained all sorts of awkward packets for the traveller, her companions on the journey: food and drink for three days on the train, the folding chair for the German carriage, books, a little bag of caramels, a quilt . . .

It was only after she had lodged these burdens in the net of the compartment and reserved her place on the narrow, hard bench that Manya stepped down to the platform again   How young she looked in her big threadbare coat, with her fresh cheeks and grey eyes which sparkled to-day with unwonted fever!

Suddenly moved, tormented again by scruples, she kissed her father and overwhelmed him with tender, timid words which were almost excuses:

"I shall not be away long . . . Two years, three years at the longest. As soon as I have finished my studies, and passed a few examinations, I'll come back, and we shall live together and never be separated again.   . . Isn't that right?"

"Yes, my little Manyusya," the professor murmured in a rather hoarse voice, clasping the girl in his arms. "Come back quickly Work hard Good luck!"

In the night pierced with whistles and the clank of old iron the fourth-class carriage was passing across Germany. Crouched down on her folding chair, her legs muffled up, her luggage—which she carefully counted from time to time—piled close around her, Manya tasted her divine joy. She mused upon the past, upon this magic departure for which she had waited so long. She tried to imagine the future. In her humility she thought that she would soon be back again in her native town, that she would find a snug little place as teacher there. . . .

She was far, very far, from thinking that when she entered this train she had at last chosen between obscurity and a blazing light, between the pettiness of equal days and an immense life.

PART TWO

CHAPTER VIII

Paris

THE finest quarters of Paris were not those between La Villette and the Sorbonne, and the journey was neither rapid nor comfortable. From the Rue d'Allemagne,* where Bronya and her husband lived, a double-decked omnibus drawn by three horses, and equipped with a little corkscrew staircase by which one mounted to the dizzy "imperial" on top, led to the Gare de l'Est. From the Gare de l'Est to the Rue des Ecoles there was another omnibus.

Naturally it was on to the "imperial," exposed to all weathers—so much more economical and amusing!—that Manya climbed, holding the old portfolio of worn leather which she had already carried to the Floating University. The young girl craned her neck and stared eagerly from her perch on this moving observatory, where the winter wind hardened her cheeks. What did she care about the commonplaceness of the interminable Rue Lafayette or the dismal succession of shops on the Boulevard Sébastopol? These little shops, these stripped elm-trees, this crowd, this smell of dust—all this was Paris: Paris at last.

How young one felt in Paris, how powerful, trembling and swelling with hope! And, for a little Polish girl, what a wonderful feeling of liberation!

At the moment when Manya, dulled by the tiresome journey, descended from the train to the smoky platform of the Gare du Nord, the familiar grip of servitude was suddenly loosened, her shoulders straightened, her lungs and heart felt at ease. For the

* Now the Avenue Jean-Jaurès

first time she was breathing the air of a free country, and in her
enthusiasm everything seemed miraculous: miraculous that the
passers-by who loitered along the pavement spoke the language
they wanted to speak, miraculous that the book-sellers sold works
from the whole world without restraint. . . . Before and above
everything else, it was miraculous that these straight avenues,
inclined in a gentle slope toward the heart of the city, were
leading her, Manya Sklodovska, to the wide-open doors of a
university. And what a university! The most famous, the one
described centuries ago as "an abridgement of the Universe", the
very one of which Luther had said: "It is in Paris that we find
the most celebrated and most excellent of schools: it is called
the Sorbonne." The adventure was fit for a fairy tale. This slow,
icy, disorderly omnibus was the enchanted carriage which took
the poor fair princess from her modest lodging to the palace of
her dreams.

The carriage crossed the Seine and everything around Manya
became delightful· the two arms of the misty river, the majestic
islands full of grace, the monuments, the squares, and down there,
on the left, the towers of Notre-Dame. . . . To get up the
Boulevard Saint-Michel the horses slowed down to a walking
pace. It was there—there—she had arrived!

The student seized her portfolio and gathered up the folds of
her heavy woollen skirt. In her haste she carelessly bumped into
one of her neighbours, and excused herself timidly, in hesitating
French. Then, having leaped down the steps from the "imperial,"
she was in the street, with intense face, running toward the iron
gate of the palace.

This palace of wisdom offered a rather unexpected picture in
1891: the Sorbonne, which had been under reconstruction for six
years, resembled some great python changing its skin. Behind
the long new façade, still quite white, the worn buildings of
Richelieu's day rubbed shoulders with builders' shanties resound-
ing with the noise of the pick and shovel. This general hubbub
put a picturesque disorder into student life. The courses migrated
from one hall to another as the work advanced. Some temporary
laboratories had to be installed in the unused old houses of the
Rue Saint-Jacques. But what did such things matter? This year,

as in other years, you could read on the white poster stuck on the wall near the porter's lodge:

FRENCH REPUBLIC

FACULTY OF SCIENCES—FIRST QUARTER

COURSES WILL BEGIN AT THE SORBONNE ON NOVEMBER 3, 1891.

The magic, sparkling words!

With the small amount of money she had saved, rouble by rouble, the girl had won the right to listen to such lessons, among the innumerable ones listed in the complicated schedule on the poster, as it would please her to choose. She had her place in the experimental laboratories, where, guided and advised, she could handle apparatus without fumbling and succeed in some simple experiments. Manya was now—oh, delight!—a student in the Faculty of Science.

In fact she was no longer called Manya, or even Marya: on her registration card she had written, in the French style, "Marie Sklodovska." But as her fellow-students could not succeed in pronouncing the barbarous syllables of "Sklodovska," and the little Polish girl gave nobody the right to call her Marie, she kept a sort of mysterious anonymity. Often in the echoing galleries young men would encounter this shy and stubborn-faced girl with soft, light hair, who dressed with an austere and poverty-stricken distinction, and would turn to each other in surprise, asking: "Who is it?" But the answer, if there were one, was vague. "It's a foreigner with an impossible name. She is always in the first row at the physics courses. Doesn't talk much." The boys' eyes would follow her graceful outline as it disappeared down the corridor, and then they would conclude: "Fine hair!" The ash-blonde hair and the little Slavic head were, for a long time to come, the only identification the students at the Sorbonne had for their timid comrade.

But young men were what interested this girl least at the moment. She was entirely fascinated by certain grave gentlemen from whom she wished to extract their secrets, named "professors" of superior instruction." According to the honourable rule of the period, they gave their courses dressed in white ties and evening clothes eternally spotted with chalk Marie lived in contemplation of these solemn garments and grey beards

On the day before yesterday it was M. Lippmann's course, so weighty and logical Yesterday she had heard M Bouty, whose extraordinary simian head concealed treasures of science. Marie would have liked to hear all the lessons and know all the twenty-three professors whose names were inscribed on the white poster. It seemed to her that she could never appease the great thirst within her.

Unforeseen obstacles had suddenly raised themselves before her during the first weeks. She had thought that she knew French perfectly; she had been wrong Some entire sentences, when said too rapidly, escaped her. She thought she had had sufficient scientific preparation to pursue the courses of the university. But her solitary work in the country, in the governess's room at "Szczuki, near Przasnysz," the knowledge she had acquired by correspondence with M. Sklodovski, and the experiments attempted by hook or crook in the Museum of Industry and Agriculture, did not take the place of the solid baccalaureate training of the Paris schools. In mathematics and physics Marie discovered enormous holes in her "culture" How she would have to work to win the enviable, magnificent title, which she coveted every instant·Master of Science!*

Paul Appell was lecturing to-day: clarity of exposition and picturesque style. Marie was one of the first to arrive; in the graded amphitheatre, stingily lighted by the December day, she had chosen her place down near the chair. She methodically arranged her penholder and the grey-covered copybook in which she would take notes before long in her fine regular writing. She became absorbed in advance, concentrating her attention, without even hearing the mounting roar of chatter which the professor's entrance brutally interrupted.

How surprising was the tense silence which certain masters knew how to create without a word! Appell was speaking now. Stoop-shouldered young men with fine faces worn by intellectual

* Licenciée ès Sciences.

work wrote down the equations which the professor's hand traced on the blackboard. There were none but the most passionate students. Make way for mathematics!

In his stiff tail coat, with his square beard, Appell was a superb figure. He developed the exposition in his calm voice, weighted by his slight Alsatian accent, which articulated each syllable so well. His demonstrations were always so clear and elegant that they seemed to juggle perils away and put the world at his mercy. Powerful and tranquil, he ventured into the most tenuous regions of knowledge, he played with numbers, with the stars, and as he was not afraid of imagery he pronounced in the most natural tones, accompanying the words with the easy gesture of a great property owner:

"I take the sun, and I throw it . . ."

The Polish girl on her bench smiled with ecstasy. Under her great swelling forehead her grey eyes, so pale, were illuminated with happiness. How could anybody find science dry? Was there anything more enthralling than the unchangeable rules which governed the universe, or more marvellous than the human intelligence which could discover them? How empty all novels seemed, and how fairy tales lacked imagination alongside these extraordinary phenomena, related among themselves by harmonious principles—this order in apparent disorder! An impulse comparable only to love sprang up from the soul of the girl toward the infinite of knowledge, toward things and their laws.

"I take the sun, and I throw it . . ."

It was worth while struggling and suffering far away during all these years to hear that little phrase pronounced by the peaceful and majestic scientist

Marie was perfectly happy.

Casimir Dluski [Bronya's husband] to his father-in-law, M. Sklodovski
92 rue d'Allemagne.
Consulting hours from one to three.
Free consultations Mondays and Thursdays from 7 to 8.

DEAR AND HONOURED SIR,

. . . Everything is going very well with us. Mademoiselle

Marie is working seriously; she passes nearly all her time at the Sorbonne and we meet only at the evening meal. She is a very independent young person, and in spite of the formal power of attorney by which you placed her under my protection, she not only shows me no respect or obedience, but does not care about my authority and my seriousness at all. I hope to reduce her to reason, but up to now my pedagogical talents have not proved efficacious. In spite of all this we understand each other very well and live in the most perfect agreement.

I await Bronya's arrival with impatience. My young lady does not seem to be in a hurry to get home, where her presence would nevertheless be very useful and where she is much in demand.

I may add that Mlle Marie is perfectly well and looks it.

With all my respect.

Such were the first tidings Dr Dluski gave of his little sister-in-law, whom he had installed in the Rue d'Allemagne in the absence of Bronya, detained for a few weeks in Poland. It need hardly be said that Marie had received a charming welcome from this sarcastic young man. Among all the Polish exiles who kept life and soul together in Paris, Bronya had quite simply chosen the most handsome, the most brilliant and the wittiest. And what devouring activity! Casimir Dluski had been a student at Petersburg Odessa and Warsaw. Obliged to flee from Russia because he was suspected of complicity in the assassination of Alexander II, he became a revolutionary publicist in Geneva, than a student at the School of Political Science in Paris, then medical student and finally a doctor. He had a rich family somewhere in Poland; and in France, in the files of the Ministry of Foreign Affairs, a lamentable document inspired by the reports of the Tsar's police— a document which would always keep him from obtaining his naturalisation and settling in Paris.

On her return to their lodging Bronya was greeted by the acclamations of her husband and her sister. As Casimir's letter indicated, the experienced housekeeper was urgently required to take over the management of the house. A few hours after her arrival order reigned again, as if by miracle, in the little flat on

the second floor, with its big balcony giving on the trees of the
Rue d'Allemagne. The cooking became full of taste again, the
dust disappeared, and flowers bought in the market ornamented
the vases. Bronya had a genius for organisation.

It was she who had had the idea of leaving the centre of Paris
to take lodging near the park of Buttes-Chaumont in La Villette.
Having borrowed a little money, she made mysterious visits to
the auction rooms, and one fine morning the flat was found to be
equipped with gracefully curved Venetian furniture, an upright
piano, some prettily draped curtains The atmosphere was made.
With the same ingenuity the young wife arranged the employment
of everybody's time. At certain hours the doctor's office
belonged to Casimir, who there received his first clients from
among the butchers at the slaughter-houses; at other times
Bronya used it for her first consultations in women's diseases.
The couple worked hard, hurrying from house to house to visit
their patients.

But when evening came and the lamps were lighted they threw
their worries aside. Casimir Dluski loved amusements The most
painful effort or the most complete poverty could not make him
lose his animation and wit After long, laborious days he would
organise an evening at the theatre in the cheapest seats, or if
money was lacking he would sit down at the piano, for he played
marvellously well As time passed, friends would ring at the
door—young couples from the Polish colony, who knew that
"one could always go to the Dluskis'" Bronya disappeared and
appeared again. The tea was steaming, and there appeared on
the table, between the syrup and the fresh water, some cakes which
the doctor-wife had just had time to make, that very afternoon,
between two consultations

One evening when Marie, bent over a book in her little room
at the end of the apartment, was preparing to work in solitude
for part of the night, her brother-in-law made an irruption.

"Your coat and hat, quick! I have free tickets, and we're all
three going to a concert."

"But . . ."

"No 'buts'! It's the Polish pianist I told you about. There are
very few seats taken, and we've absolutely got to help the poor

boy out by filling the hall. I've already recruited a whole crowd, and we'll applaud until our hands crack, so it'll seem to be a success anyhow. . . . And if you only knew how well he plays!"

It was impossible to resist the compelling force of Dluski, the big dark-bearded devil whose black eyes were electric with gaiety. Marie closed her book. The door of the apartment slammed, the three young people tumbled down the stairs and ran as fast as they could to catch their omnibus, just pulling up with the trot of its heavy horses.

A little later, seated in the Salle Érard—which was three-quarters empty—Marie saw a long, thin young man appear on the platform, his hair in a halo of red and copper colours, full of flames, about his extraordinary face. He sat down at the black piano. Under his subtle fingers Liszt, Schumann and Chopin came to life. His face was imperious and noble, his inspired eyes looked far away. . . . The girl listened with intoxication to this strange performer who, in his threadbare coat, before the almost deserted rows of seats, seemed, not at all a poor artist making his first appearance but an emperor or a god.

The musician was to come to the Rue d'Allemagne sometimes in the evenings, accompanied by the exquisite young woman, Mme Gorska, whom he had fallen in love with and was afterwards to marry. He spoke without bitterness of his miserable life, of his disappointments, of his struggles. Bronya and Marie recalled with Mme Gorska the distant period when she, then aged sixteen, had accompanied their mother Mme Sklodovska on a journey to take the cure. "When she came back to Warsaw," Bronya remembered, laughing, "Mamma said she would never dare take you to a watering-place again, because you were too beautiful!"

Seized by a hunger for music, the young man with the fiery mane would interrupt all talk to strike some chords. Then, by a stroke of magic, the poor upright piano at the Dluskis' instantly turned into a sublime instrument.

That pianist was half-starved and charming. He was in love, nervous, happy, unhappy. He was to be a virtuoso of genius and, one day, prime minister of a Poland reconstructed and set free.

His name was Ignace Paderewski.

Marie flung herself ardently into whatever her new existence offered. She worked as if in a fever. She also discovered the joys of comradeship, of that solidarity which university work creates. But, still too shy to make friends with the French she took refuge among her compatriots: two mathematicians, Mlles Kraskovska and Dydynska, Dr. Motz, the biologist Danysz, Stanislav Szalay, who was to enter the Sklodovski family later by marrying Hela, the young Wojciechovski—a future president of the Polish Republic—became her friends in that colony which formed a little island of free Poland in the Latin Quarter.

These poor students organised Christmas suppers for which benevolent cooks prepared the special Warsaw dishes· burning *barszez*, the colour of amaranth, cabbage with mushrooms, stuffed pike, cakes with poppy-seed, a little vodka and floods of tea. Theatrical performances took place in which Polish amateur actors interpreted comedy and drama. The programme of these evenings —printed in Polish, of course—was illuminated by symbolic pictures· at the top, in a snow-covered plain, was a hut; lower down a garret where a dreaming boy bent over his books. A Father Christmas, too, who poured scientific manuals down the chimney into a laboratory. In the foreground an empty purse, nibbled at by rats... .

Marie participated in these revels. She had not the leisure to learn parts and play them, but at a patriotic party given by the sculptor Waszinkovski it was she who was chosen to incarnate the chief character in the living pictures: "Poland breaking her bonds."

The severe little student became an unknown woman that night: dressed in a tunic in antique style she wore long veils in the national colours draped round her, and her loosened hair fell on her shoulders. In folds of pomegranate cloth, with her transparent skin, her blonde hair and her resolute face with its Slavic cheek-bones, she presented to these exiles the picture of their race.

It may be seen that neither Marie nor her sister had left Warsaw, in spite of exile and distance. By instinct they had chosen to live

in the Rue d'Allemagne, on the edge of the great city into which
they still did not dare penetrate, near the Gare du Nord and the
trains which had brought them to France Their fatherland was
with them, holding them by a thousand bonds—of which the
letters they exchanged with their father were not the weakest.
These well-brought-up and deferential young ladies, who still
wrote to M. Sklodovski in the third person* and ended each letter
by "I kiss my little father's hands," gave the old man long accounts
of their picturesque lives and charged him with all sorts of com-
missions. It never occurred to them that one could buy tea anywhere but in Warsaw, or that in case of strict necessity it might be
possible to find a reasonably priced pressing iron in France. . . .

Bronya to M. Sklodovski:
. . . I should be very grateful to my dear little father if he could
send me two pounds of ordinary tea, at two roubles twenty Aside
from that we don't need a thing; nor does Manya.
We are very well Manya looks very well and it seems to me
that the laborious life she leads does not tire her at all. . . .

M Sklodovski to Bronya:
Dear Bronya, I am very glad the pressing iron is all right. I
had to choose it myself, and I feared that it was not altogether what
you wanted. I didn't know who to get to make this purchase, any
more than the others. Even though they were within the feminine
domain, I had to busy myself with them.

Naturally, Marie gave her father an account of the evening at
the sculptor's studio, and of her personal triumph as Polonia. But
this time the professor was not enthusiastic:

M. Sklodovski to Marie, January 31st, 1892:
Dear Manya, your last letter saddened me. I deplore your taking
such active part in the organisation of this theatrical representation.
Even though it be a thing done in all innocence, it attracts attention to its organisers, and you certainly know that there are persons
in Paris who inspect your behaviour with the greatest care, who

* In Polish the the polite or formal mode of address is in the third person.

take note of the names of those who are in the forefront and who send information about them here, to be used as might be useful This can be the source of very great annoyance, and even forbid such persons access to certain professions Thus, those who wish to earn their bread in Warsaw in the future without being exposed to various dangers will find it to their interest to keep quiet, in a retreat where they may remain unknown. Events such as concerts, balls, etc , are described by certain correspondents for newspapers, who mention names. It would be a great grief to me if your name were mentioned one day. This is why, in my previous letters, I have made a few criticisms, and have begged you to keep to yourself as much as possible. . . .

Was it M. Sklodovski's firm authority or was it rather Manya's good sense that rebelled against such sterile agitation? The girl very soon observed that these harmless diversions kept her from working in peace. She drew away from them She had not come to France to figure in living pictures, and every minute she did not consecrate to study was a minute lost

Another problem presented itself. In the Rue d'Allemagne, life was charming and sweet; but Marie could not find perfect concentration there. She could not stop Casimir from playing the piano, receiving friends, or coming into her room while she was solving a difficult equation; she could not stop the young doctor's patients from breaking into the house. At night she was abruptly wakened by the ring of the bell and the footsteps of messengers who came to get Bronya for the confinement of some butcher's wife.

Above all, it was terribly inconvenient to live in La Villette: one hour's journey to the Sorbonne! And the price of two omnibus fares was, in the long run, exorbitant. After a family council of war, it was decided that Marie should go to live in the Latin Quarter, near the university, the laboratories and the libraries. The Dluskis insisted on lending the girl the few francs that her moving would cost, and on the next morning Marie started her campaign, visiting attics to let.

It was not without regret that she left the little flat in the neighbourhood of the slaughter-house, lost in prosaic surroundings but filled as it was with tenderness, courage and good temper.

Between Marie and Casimir Dluski a fraternal affection had been formed which was to last out their lives. Between Marie and Bronya a magnificent romance had been unfolding for years past: the romance of sacrifice and devotion, of mutual help

Weighed down by her pregnancy, Bronya supervised the packing of her younger sister's poor belongings, which were piled up on a handcart for the short journey. And, taking the famous omnibus once again, passing from "imperial" to "imperial," Casimir and his young wife solemnly accompanied the "little one" as far as her student's lodging.

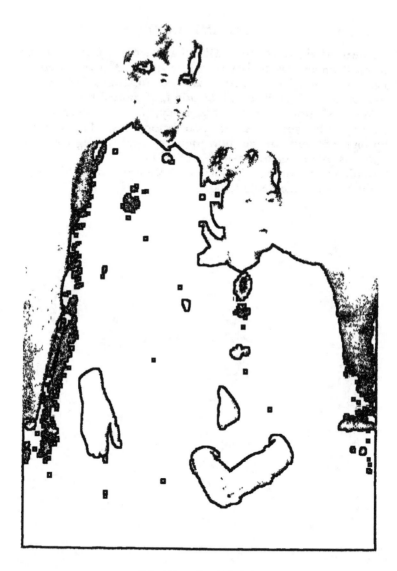

THE TWO POSITIVISTS
Manya and Bronya Sklodovska, 1886

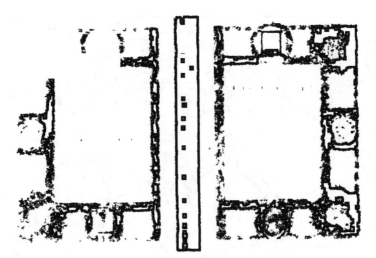

OLD DITCH OF LA STRADA DEI PILO.
M. (FROM THE ILLUSTRAZIONE.)

THE CURIE FAMILY

Standing Are Jacques and Pierre Curie. Seated, their Mother,
Mme Curie, and Father, Dr Eugene Curie

PIERRE CURIE

He Appeared Costume to the Glass in 1906

CHAPTER IX

Forty Roubles a Month

YES, Marie's existence had still further to be despoiled and made bare. The few months she had lived in the Rue d'Allemagne had been a stage in acclimatisation. Now the girl sank slowly into solitude. The beings she rubbed shoulders with existed for her no more than the walls she touched in passing, and conversation hardly cut in upon the silence in which she enveloped her hours. For more than three solid years she was to lead a life devoted to study alone: a life in conformity with her dreams, a "perfect" life in the sense in which that of the monk or the missionary is perfect.

Her life had to be of monastic simplicity in any case: for since Marie had voluntarily deprived herself of the board and lodging she had had at the Dluskis', she had to meet her expenses herself. And her income— made up by her own savings, divided into slices, and the small sums her father could send her—resolved itself into forty roubles a month.

How could a woman, a foreigner, live decently in Paris in 1892 with forty roubles a month, *three francs* a day, paying for her own room, meals, clothes, paper and books, as well as her fees at the university? Such was the problem the young student had urgently to solve. But Marie never failed to find the solution of a problem.

Manya to her brother Joseph, March 17th, 1892:
You have no doubt learned from Father that I decided to live nearer to the schools, as it had become necessary for several reasons, above all for the present quarter. The plan is now realised: I am writing to you, in fact, from my new lodging, 3 Rue Flatters.

It is a little room, very suitable, and also very cheap. In a quarter of an hour I can be in the chemistry laboratory, in twenty minutes at the Sorbonne. Naturally, without the Dluskis' help I should never have been able to arrange things like this.

I am working a thousand times as hard as at the beginning of my stay: in the Rue d'Allemagne my little brother-in-law had the habit of disturbing me endlessly. He absolutely could not endure having me do anything but engage in agreeable chatter with him when I was at home. I had to declare war on him on this subject After a few days Bronya and he began to feel badly about me, and they came to see me. We drank tea, bachelor fashion, and then we went downstairs to see the S.s, who also live here.

Is your wife taking care of Father, as she promised me? Let her take care, just the same, not to cut me out altogether at home! Father is beginning to speak of her a little too tenderly, and I am afraid that he will be forgetting me soon. . . .

Marie was not the only student who lived on a hundred francs a month in the Latin Quarter: most of her Polish comrades were as poor as she was. Some lived by threes or fours in the same lodging and took their meals together; others, who lived alone, devoted several hours a day to housekeeping, cooking and sewing, and by sheer ingenuity ate as much as they wanted, shod and clothed themselves in greater or lesser elegance. This was the method adopted earlier by Bronya, whose talents as a prize cook had been celebrated among her comrades.

Marie disdained to follow such wise examples. she was too fond of her tranquillity to share her lodging with a friend or two and too haunted by work to bother about her own comfort Even if she had wished to do so, for that matter, she would have been incapable of it: the girl who had been a governess in strange families at seventeen, giving seven or eight hours of lessons a day, had never found time or occasion for learning how to keep house. Everything that Bronya had learned when she was mistress of her father's house was unknown to Marie. And rumour had it, in the Polish colony, that "Mademoiselle Sklodovska doesn't know what you use to make soup."

She did not know, and she did not want to know. Why should

she pass a morning initiating herself into the mysteries of a broth'
when she might have been learning several pages of physics or
making an interesting analysis in the laboratory?

By deliberate intention she had suppressed diversions from her
schedule, as well as friendly meetings and contact with human
beings. In the same way she decided that material life had no
importance; that it did not exist. And, fortified by this principle,
she made for herself a Spartan existence, strange and inhuman.

Rue Flatters, Boulevard Port-Royal, Rue des Feuillantines. . . .
All the rooms Marie was to inhabit were alike in discomfort and
cheapness of rent. The first was situated in a poorly furnished
house where students, doctors and officers of the neighbouring
garrison lived. Later on the girl, in search of absolute calm, was
to take an attic like a servant's room at the top of a middle-class
house. For fifteen or twenty francs a month she found a tiny nook
which was lit from a loop-hole giving directly on the slope of the
roof. Through this skylight appeared a small square of the sky.
There was no heat, no lighting, no water.

Marie furnished this place with all the objects she possessed: an
iron folding bed, the mattress she had brought from Poland, a
stove, a white wooden table, a kitchen chair, a wash-basin; a
petroleum oil lamp, covered by a twopenny shade; a pitcher which
she had to fill at the tap on the landing; an alcohol heater about as
big as a saucer, which was to cook her meals for the next three
years; two plates, a knife, a fork, a spoon, a cup, a stewpan; and
finally a kettle and three glasses into which, according to Polish
custom, the student would pour tea when the Dluskis came to see
her. On the occasions—very rare at present—when Marie
received visitors, the rights of hospitality were asserted: the girl
lighted the little stove, whose zigzag pipe described complicated
angles in the room, and for a seat she pulled out of its corner the
bulging brown trunk which served her as wardrobe and chest of
drawers.

No service, of course: even one hour of cleaning a day would
have overweighted the expense side of the budget. Transportation
costs were suppressed: Marie went to the Sorbonne on foot in all
weathers. Coal was kept down to a minimum: one or two sacks
of "lumps" for the winter, which the girl bought from the

merchant on the corner and hoisted up the steep stairs herself to the sixth floor, bucketful by bucketful, stopping at each floor to breathe. Lights were at a minimum: as soon as night fell, the student took refuge in that blessed asylum called the Library of Sainte-Geneviève, where the gas was lighted and it was warm. Seated at one of the big rectangular tables with her head in her hands, a poor Polish girl could work until they closed the doors at ten o'clock. From then on all that was needed was enough oil to keep the light going in her room until two in the morning Then, with her eyes reddened by fatigue, Marie left her books and threw herself on the bed

The only thing she knew how to do, in the humble practical domain, was to sew—a memory of the "manual training" at the Sikorski boarding school and of the long days in Szczuki when the governess, as she supervised the children's study, took up her sewing. . . It would be rash to conclude from this that the exile ever, by chance, bought a bit of stuff at a low price and made herself a new blouse She seems to have sworn, on the contrary, never to give up her Warsaw dresses, and wore them, shiny, old-fashioned and threadbare, for ever But she took great care of her clothes, cleaned them and mended them. She also condescended to wash her linen in a basin when she was too tired to work and needed relaxation

Marie did not admit that she could be cold or hungry. In order not to buy coal—and through sheer carelessness too—she often neglected to light the little stove with the twisted pipe, and wrote figures and equations without noticing that her fingers were getting numb and her shoulders shaking Hot soup or a bit of meat would have comforted her; but Marie did not know how to make soup. Marie could not spend a franc and lose half an hour to cook herself a chop. She hardly ever entered the butcher's shop, much less the restaurant: it was too dear. For weeks at a time she ate nothing but buttered bread and tea When she wanted to eat, she went into a creamery in the Latin Quarter and ate two eggs, or else bought herself a piece of chocolate or some fruit.

On this diet the fresh, solid girl who had left Warsaw a few months before rapidly grew anæmic. Often, as she was getting up from her table, her head would go round. She had just time to get to her bed when she would lose consciousness. Coming back to herself, she would ask why she had fainted, she would think herself ill and disdain her illness as she did everything else. It never occurred to her that she was dropping with weakness and that her only disease was that of starvation.

Naturally, she did not boast of this superb organisation of existence to the Dluskis. Every time she went to see them she replied in monosyllables to their questions on her progress as a cook, or on her daily menus. If her brother-in law said she did not look well, she affirmed that she was overworked—which was, in fact, in her eyes, the only reason for her fatigue. And then, dismissing such worries with a gesture of indifference, she would begin to play with her niece, Bronya's baby, for whom she had great affection.

But one day, when Marie fainted in front of one of her comrades, the latter hurried to the Rue d'Allemagne to warn the pair of young doctors. Two hours later Casimir was leaping up the six flights of stairs to the attic where the girl, a little pale, was already studying to-morrow's lesson. He examined his sister-in law. He examined even more carefully the clean plates, the empty stewpan, and the whole room, in which he could discover only one comestible, a packet of tea. All at once he understood—and the questioning began.

"What have you eaten to-day?"

"To-day? I don't know. I lunched a while ago."

"What did you eat?" Casimir's voice took her up implacably.

"Some cherries and . . . and all sorts of things."

In the end Marie was obliged to confess: since the evening before she had nibbled at a bundle of radishes and half a pound of cherries. She had worked until three that morning and had slept four hours. Then she had gone to the Sorbonne. On her return she had finished the radishes. Then she had fainted.

The doctor made no long speeches. He was furious—furious against Marie, whose ash grey eyes looked at him with profound fatigue and innocent mirth, furious at himself, for he accused himself of not watching attentively enough over "the little one" who had been confided to him by M. Sklodovski. Without listening to his sister-in-law's protests he handed her her hat and coat, and ordered her to take the books and papers she would need for the coming week. Then, silent, dissatisfied, unhappy, he carried her off to La Villette; from the threshold of the flat he hailed Bronya, who dashed for the kitchen.

Twenty minutes passed, and Marie swallowed, mouthful by mouthful, the medicines ordered for her by Casimir: an enormous underdone beefsteak and a plateful of crackling fried potatoes. As if by a miracle, the colour came back to her cheeks. On the same evening Bronya herself came at eleven o'clock to put the light out in the narrow room where she had set up a bed for her sister. For several days Marie, well fed and cared for, "took the cure" and regained her strength. Then, obsessed by the approaching examinations, she returned to her attic, promising to be reasonable in the future.

And the next day she began again to live on air!

Work! . . . Work! Plunged altogether into study, intoxicated by her progress, Marie felt herself equal to learning everything mankind had ever discovered. She attended courses in mathematics, physics and chemistry. Manual technique and the minute precision of scientific experiment became familiar to her, little by little; soon she was to have the joy of being charged by Professor Lippmann with researches of no great importance, which nevertheless permitted her to show her deftness and the originality of her mind. In the physics laboratory of the Sorbonne, a high and wide room queerly ornamented by two little staircases which led to an interior gallery, Marie Sklodovska timidly tried her strength.

She had a passionate love for that atmosphere of attention and silence, the "climate" of the laboratory, which she was to prefer to any other up to her last day. She was on her feet, always on her feet, in front of an oak table supporting precision instruments, or else in front of the chemical hood where some material infusion bubbled away, worried at by the fierce blow-pipe. . She was hardly to be distinguished, in her big smock of wrinkled linen, from the thoughtful young men who bent beside her over other blowpipes and other instruments. Like them, she respected the concentration of the place. She made no noise, she pronounced no useless word.

One master's degree was not enough: Marie decided to obtain

two: one in physics and one in mathematics Her plans, once so humble, increased and grew richer so rapidly that she had not the time—and above all not the audacity—to confide them to M. Sklodovski, who, as she knew, impatiently awaited her return to Poland. As usual, the excellent man offered his help But it could be felt that he was vaguely worried at having hatched this independent creature who had taken to flying with her own wings after so many years of submission and sacrifice.

M. Sklodovski to Bronya, March 5th, 1893:
. . . Your last letter mentions for the first time that Manya intends to take her examinations for the master's. She has never spoken to me about it in her letters, even though I have questioned her on the subject Write me exactly when these examinations will take place, at what date Manya can hope to pass them, what are the fees for them and how much the diploma will cost I must think of all this in advance so as to be able to send some money to Manya, and on this my personal plans will depend

. . . I intend to keep the lodging I now occupy for next year: for myself and for Manya—if she comes back—it is perfectly suitable. . . . Little by little Manya will work up a list of pupils, and in any case I am ready to share what I have with her. We shall manage without trouble. . . .

Marie, however shy she might be, could not avoid meeting human beings every day Some of the students were cordial and friendly with her. Foreign women were highly regarded at the Sorbonne These poor girls, generally gifted, coming from far away to the university which the Goncourts called "the nursing mother of study," inspired sympathy among young Frenchmen. The Polish girl was tamed. She discovered that her companions, who were "grinds" for the most part, esteemed her and wished to show her kindness—sometimes more than kindness Marie must have been very pretty. her friend, Mlle Dydynska, a charming and somewhat over-excited young woman who had appointed herself as bodyguard, one day threatened to beat off a group of too eager admirers with her umbrella.

Allowing Mlle Dydynska to repel advances which left her

indifferent, the girl drew nearer to men who did not pay court to her and with whom she could talk about her work Between a physics lesson and a laboratory hour she would chatter with Paul Painlevé, who was already a professor; with Charles Maurain or Jean Perrin—future leaders of French science These were distant comradeships Marie had no time to give to friendship or to love. She loved mathematics and physics

Her brain was so precise, her intelligence so marvellously clear, that no Slavic disorder intruded to corrupt her effort. She was supported by a will of iron, by a maniacal taste for perfection, and by an incredible stubbornness. Systematically, patiently, she attained each of the ends she had set for herself. she passed first in the master's examination in physics in 1893* and second in the master's in mathematics in 1894 †

She had decided to learn the French language perfectly, as it was indispensable to her; and instead of cooing incorrect, sing-song sentences for years, as many Poles do, she learned her spelling and syntax with infallible sureness, and hounded down the very last traces of her accent. Only a very slight rolling of the "r" was to remain ever afterward as one of the graces of her rather muted voice, so sweet and charming

With her forty roubles a month she succeeded in living, and even, by depriving herself of the indispensable, achieved some-times a certain amount of luxury· an evening at the theatre, a journey to the suburbs, whence she brought back flowers picked in the woods to glow for several days on her table. The little peasant of other days was not dead, lost in the great city, she lay in wait for the birth of the leaves, and as soon as she had a little time and money she hurried to the woods.

Marie to M. Sklodovski, April 16th, 1893:
The other Sunday I went to Le Raincy, near Paris, in a pretty and agreeable neighbourhood. The lilacs and the fruit trees, even the apples, were in full bloom and the air was filled with the scent of flowers.

In Paris the trees get green as early as the beginning of April.

* Licenciée ès Sciences physiques
† Licenciée ès Sciences mathématiques

Now the leaves have sprung out and the chestnuts are blooming. It is as hot as in summer. everything is green. In my room it is beginning to be torrid Luckily in July, when I shall be working for my examinations, I shall not be here any more, for I have taken the lodging only to the eighth of July

The neaier the examinations come, the more I am afraid of not being ready. At the worst, I shall wait until November, but that will make me lose my summer, which doesn't appeal to me. For that matter, we must wait and see . . .

July: Fever, haste, agonising trials, crashing mornings when, shut in with thirty students in the examination hall, Marie was so nervous that the letters danced before her eyes and she could not even read the fateful paper for several minutes, with its statement of the problem and the "questions on the course" When the composition was turned in, there came days of waiting until the solemn moment of publication of the results Marie slipped in among the contestants and their families, crowded into the amphitheatre where the names of the elect would be read aloud, in order of merit Pushed and shoved about as she was, she waited for the entrance of the examiner. And in a sudden silence she heard him pronounce first of all her own name: *Marie Sklodvska*

Nobody was to guess her emotion. She tore herself away from the congratulations of her comrades, escaped from the crowd and made off. The time for holidays had come now—for the departure to Poland and home

Such homecomings among the poor Poles had their rites, which Marie scrupulously observed. She moved her furniture—bed, stove and utensils—into safety with a compatriot rich enough to keep her Paris lodging during the summer months. She took leave of her garret· before quitting it for ever, she cleaned it thoroughly. She said good bye to the *concierge*, whom she would not see again, and bought some provisions for her journey. Having counted up what she had left, she went into a big shop and did what she had not done for a year: she looked for trinkets, for scarves. . . .

It was accounted a shame to return to one's native land with money in the pocket. Grand style, supreme elegance, custom, required one to spend literally everything on presents for one's family and get into the train at the Gare du Nord without a sou. Was this not a wise course? Two thousand kilometres away, at the other end of the rails, there were M. Sklodovski and Joseph and Hela, a familiar roof to sleep under, as much food as one could eat, and a seamstress who, for a few *grosz y*, could cut out and sew linen and big woollen dresses: the dresses which Marie would wear when she came back to the Sorbonne again in November.

She was to reappear there cheerful and a bit too fat, having been stuffed with food for three months in all the houses of all the Sklodovskis in Poland, indignant as they were at her thinness. And again she faced a scholastic year in which she would work, learn, prepare an examination, grow thin.

But each time autumn returned the same anxiety assailed Marie: how could she go back to Paris? Where was she to find money? Forty roubles at a time—her savings were being exhausted; and she thought with shame of the little pleasures her father deprived himself of to come to her help. In 1893 the situation seemed desperate and the girl was on the point of giving up the journey when a miracle took place. That same Mlle Dydynska who had defended her with an umbrella the year before now extended even more opportune protection. Certain that Marie was destined to a great future, she moved heaven and earth in Warsaw to have the Alexandrovitch Scholarship assigned to her—a scholarship for students of merit who wished to pursue their efforts abroad.

Six hundred roubles! Enough to live on for fifteen months! Marie, who knew so well how to ask favours for other people, would never have thought of soliciting this help, and above all could never have had the boldness to make the necessary approaches. Dazzled and enchanted, she took flight for France.

Marie to her brother Joseph, September 15th, 1893:

. . . I have already rented my room, on the sixth floor in a clean and decent street which suits me very well. Tell Father that in that place where I was going to take a room there was nothing free, and that I am very satisfied with this room: it has a window that shuts tight, and when I have arranged it properly it should not be cold here, especially as the floor is of wood and not tiles. Compared to my last year's room it is a veritable palace. It costs one hundred and eighty francs a year, and is therefore sixty francs cheaper than the one Father spoke to me about.

I hardly need say that I am delighted to be back in Paris. It was very hard for me to separate again from Father, but I could see that he was well, very lively, and that he could do without me—especially as you are living in Warsaw. And as for me, it is my whole life that is at stake. It seemed to me, therefore, that I could stay on here without having remorse on my conscience.

Just now I am studying mathematics unceasingly, so as to be up to date when the courses begin. I have three mornings a week taken by lessons with one of my French comrades who is preparing for the examination I have just passed. Tell Father that I am getting used to this work, that it does not tire me as much as before, and that I do not intend to abandon it.

To-day I begin the installation of my little corner for this year—very poorly, but what am I to do? I have to do everything myself; otherwise it's all too dear. I must get my furniture into shape—or rather what I pompously call my furniture, for the whole thing isn't worth more than twenty francs.

I shall write soon to Joseph Boguski and ask him for information about his laboratory. My future occupation depends on this.

Marie to her brother, March 18th, 1894:

. . . It is difficult for me to tell you about my life in detail; it is so monotonous and, in fact, so uninteresting. Nevertheless I have no feeling of uniformity and I regret only one thing, which is that the days are so short and that they pass so quickly. One never notices what has been done; one can only see what remains to be done, and if one didn't like the work it would be very discouraging.

I want you to pass your doctor's thesis. . . . It seems that life is not easy for any of us. But what of that? We must have perseverance and above all confidence in ourselves. We must believe that we are gifted for something, and that this thing, at whatever cost, must be attained. Perhaps everything will turn out very well, at the moment when we least expect it. . . .

The Alexandrovitch Scholarship was providential. With passionate avarice Marie tried to string out her six hundred roubles, so as to remain a little longer in the paradise of lecture halls and laboratories. Some years later, with the same passionate avarice, she was to save six hundred roubles out of her first earnings—a technical study ordered from her by the Society for the Encouragement of National Industry—and was to take them to the secretary of the Alexandrovitch Foundation, stupefied though he was at a restitution without precedent in the annals of the committee. Marie had accepted this scholarship as testimony of confidence in her, a debt of honour. In her uncompromising soul she would have adjudged herself dishonest if she had kept for one unnecessary moment the money which now could serve as lifebuoy to another poor young girl.

Re-reading a little poem of my mother's, written in Polish, on this time of her life, and remembering the accounts of it that she sometimes gave me, with many a smile and humorous remark, looking at the only portrait of herself which she dearly cherished: the small photograph of a student girl with daring eyes and determined chin, I have felt that she never ceased to prefer these hard, fervent days to all others.

> *Ah! how harshly the youth of the student passes,*
> *While all around her, with passions ever fresh,*
> *Other youths search eagerly for easy pleasures!*
> *And yet in solitude*
> *She lives, obscure and blessed,*
> *For in her cell she finds the ardour*
> *That makes her heart immense.*

> *But the blessed time is effaced.*
> *She must leave the land of Science*
> *To go out and struggle for her bread*
> *On the grey roads of life.*
> *Often and often then, her weary spirit*
> *Returns beneath the roofs*
> *To the corner ever dear to her heart*

Where silent labour dwelled
And where a world of memory has rested.

No doubt Marie knew other joys later. But even in her hours of infinite tenderness, even in the hour of triumph and fame, the eternal student was never so content with herself, so proud, as in the poverty and fire of this integral effort. She was proud of her poverty; proud of living alone and independent in a foreign city. Working beneath the lamp in her poor room of an evening she felt that her destiny, still insignificant, mysteriously related itself to the high existences she most admired and that she became the humble unknown companion of those great scientists of the past, who were, like her, shut into their ill-lighted cells, like her detached from their time, and, like her, spurred their minds to pass beyond the sum of acquired knowledge.

Yes, these four heroic years were, not the happiest of Marie Curie's life, but the most perfect in her eyes, the nearest to those summits of the human mission toward which her gaze had been trained. When one is young and solitary and swallowed up in study, one can "not have enough to live on"—and yet live to the fullest. An immense enthusiasm gave this girl of twenty-six the power to ignore the trials and privations she endured: to magnify her sordid existence into magic. Later on, love, maternity, the worries of a wife and mother, the complexities of crushingly hard work, were to restore the visionary to real life. But in the enchanted moment when she was poorer than she was ever to be again, she was as reckless as a child. She floated lightly in another world, that which her thought was to regard always as the only pure and true one.

Each day could not be altogether excellent in an adventure like this. There were unforeseen accidents which suddenly upset everything and seemed irremediable: a fatigue impossible to surmount, a short illness requiring care. Still other, and terrifying catastrophes: the one pair of shoes, with leaky soles, gave out finally, and the purchase of new shoes became necessary. This meant a budget upside down for weeks, and the enormous expense had to be made up at all costs, on meals or on oil for the lamp.

Or else the winter was longer than usual and the sixth-floor garret was icy. It was so cold that Marie could no longer sleep; she shivered and chattered with it. Her supply of coal was exhausted. . . . But what of that? Could a Polish girl be conquered by a Parisian winter? Marie lighted her lamp again and looked about her. She opened the fat trunk and gathered together all the garments she possessed. She put on all she could, then, having slipped into bed, she piled the rest, her other dress, her linen, on top of the single coverlet. But it was still too cold. Marie stretched out her arm, pulled the one chair over to her, raised it and piled it, too, on top of the amassed garments, giving herself some sort of illusion of weight and heat.

All she had to do now was to wait for sleep, without moving, so as to preserve the scaffolding of which she was the living base. Meanwhile, a layer of ice was slowly forming in the water pitcher.

CHAPTER X

Pierre Curie

MARIE had ruled love and marriage out of her life's programme.

There was nothing extremely original in that. The poor girl, disappointed and humiliated in the failure of her first idyll, swore to love no more; still more, the Slavic student, exalted by intellectual ambitions, easily decided to renounce the things that make the servitude, happiness and unhappiness of other women, in order to follow her vocation. In all ages women who burn to become great painters or great musicians have disdained the norm, love and motherhood. Most often they are converted to family life when their dreams of glory come to nothing; or else, when they do make careers, it is in fact at the sacrifice of their sentimental life.

Marie had built for herself a secret universe of implacable rigour, dominated by the passion for science. Family affection and the attachment to an oppressed fatherland also had their place in it: but this was all. Nothing else counted, nothing else existed. Thus had she decreed, the beautiful creature of twenty-six who lived alone in Paris and met young men every day at the Sorbonne and in the laboratory.

Marie was obsessed by her dreams, harassed by poverty, overdriven by intensive work. She did not know leisure and its dangers. Her pride and timidity protected her, as did her distrust: ever since the Z.s had rejected her as a daughter-in-law she had had the vague conviction that poor girls found no devotion or tender-n ss among men. Stiffened by fine theories and bitter reflections, she clung fiercely to her independence.

No, it is not surprising that a Polish girl of genius, isolated by her arid existence, should have preserved herself for her work. But it is surprising, indeed wonderful, that a scientist of genius, a Frenchman, should have kept himself for that Polish girl, should have unconsciously waited for her. It is wonderful that at the time when Marie, still almost a child in the narrow apartment of Novolipki Street, dreamed of coming to study some day at the Sorbonne, Pierre Curie, returning home from that same Sorbonne, where he was already making important discoveries in physics, should have written down in his diary these melancholy lines:

. . . Woman loves life for the living of it far more than we do: women of genius are rare. Thus, when we, driven by some mystic love, wish to enter upon some anti-natural path, when we give all our thoughts to some work which estranges us from the humanity nearest us, we have to struggle against women. The mother wants the love of her child above all things, even if it should make an imbecile of him. The mistress also wishes to possess her lover, and would find it quite natural to sacrifice the rarest genius in the world for an hour of love. The struggle almost always is unequal, for women have the good side of it: it is in the name of life and nature that they try to bring us back. . . .

Years had passed. Pierre Curie, devoting body and soul to scientific research, had married none of the insignificant or nice little girls who had come his way. He was thirty-five years old He loved nobody.

When he was idly running through his diary, abandoned long ago, and re-read the notes once made in ink that was already growing pale, a few words full of regret and dull nostalgia caught his attention:

" . . . women of genius are rare . . ."

When I came in, Pierre Curie was standing in the window recess near a door leading to the balcony. He seemed very young to me, although he was then aged thirty-five. I was struck by the expression of his clear gaze and by a slight appearance of carelessness in his lofty stature. His rather slow, reflective words, his simplicity, and his smile, at once grave and young, inspired confidence. A con versation began between us and became friendly; its object was some questions of science upon which I was happy to ask his opinion.

Such were the words Marie was to use to describe their first meeting, which took place at the beginning of 1894.

A Pole, M. Kovalski, professor of physics in the University of Fribourg, was visiting Paris with his young wife, whom Marie had met at Szczuki. It was their honeymoon, but a scientific expedition as well. M. Kovalski gave some lectures in Paris, and attended the sessions of the Physics Society. On his arrival he had enquired after Marie and had asked her how she was. Marie had confided in him her worries of the moment: the Society for the Encouragement of National Industry had ordered a study from her on the magnetic properties of various steels. She had begun the researches in Professor Lippmann's laboratory; but she had to analyse minerals and group samples of metal, which required a cumbersome equipment—too cumbersome for the already crowded laboratory. And Marie did not know what to do, where to conduct her experiments.

"I have an idea," Joseph Kovalski said to her after some moments of reflection. "I know a scientist of great merit who works in the School of Physics and Chemistry in the Rue Lhomond. Perhaps he might have a workroom available. In any case he could give you some advice. Come and have tea to-morrow evening, after dinner, with my wife and me. I will ask the young man to come. You probably know his name: it is Pierre Curie."

In the course of the calm evening passed in the young couple's room in a quiet boarding-house, immediate sympathy brought the French physicist and the Polish student together.

Pierre Curie had a very individual charm made up of gravity and careless grace. He was tall. His clothes, cut on ample, old-fashioned lines, hung a bit loosely about his body, but they became him: he had much natural elegance. His hands were long and sensitive. His regular, almost motionless face, lengthened by a rough beard, was made beautiful by his peaceful eyes, with their incomparable look, deep and serene, detached from all things.

Although this man maintained a constant reserve and never

lifted his voice, it was impossible not to notice his expression of rare intelligence and distinction. In a civilisation in which intellectual superiority is seldom allied to moral worth, Pierre Curie was an almost unique specimen of humanity: his mind was both powerful and noble.

The attraction he felt from the first moment for the foreign girl who spoke so little was doubled by intense curiosity. This Mlle Sklodovska was truly a rather astonishing person. . . . She was Polish, come from Warsaw to study at the Sorbonne, had passed first in the physics examination last year, would pass her mathematics examination in a few months. . . . And if between her ashen-grey eyes a little preoccupied wrinkle appeared, was it not because she didn't know where to install her apparatus for the study of magnetism in steel?

The conversation, at first general, was soon reduced to a scientific dialogue between Pierre Curie and Marie Sklodovska. Marie, with a shade of timidity and deference, asked questions and listened to Pierre's suggestions. He in turn explained his plans, and described the phenomena of crystallography which fascinated him and upon which he was now engaged in research. How strange it was, the physicist thought, to talk to a woman of the work one loves, using technical terms, complicated formulæ, and to see that woman, charming and young, become animated, understand, even discuss certain details with an infallible clear-sightedness. . . . How sweet it was!

He looked at Marie's hair, at her high, curved forehead and her hands already stained by the acids of the laboratory and roughened by housework. He was disconcerted by her grace, which the absence of all coquetry made more surprising. He dug from his memory all that his host had told him about the girl when he had invited them together: she had worked for years before being able to take the train for Paris, she had no money, she lived alone in a garret. . . .

"Are you going to remain in France always?" he asked Mlle Sklodovska, without knowing why.

A shadow passed over Marie's face, and she replied in her singing accent:

"Certainly not. This summer, if I succeed in my master's

examination, I shall go back to Warsaw. I should like to come back here in the autumn, but I don't know whether I shall have the means to do so. Later on I shall be a teacher in Poland; I shall try to be useful. Poles have no right to abandon their country."

The conversation, in which the Kovalskis joined, turned toward the painful subject of Russian oppression. The three exiles evoked memories of their native land and exchanged news of their families and friends. Astonished, vaguely dissatisfied, Pierre Curie listened to Marie speak of her patriotic and social duties.

A physicist obsessed by physics, he could not imagine how this amazingly gifted girl could devote even one thought to anything outside of science, and that her plan for the future should be to use her strength in a struggle against Tsarism.

He wanted to see her again.

Who was Pierre Curie?

He was a French scientist of genius, very nearly unknown in his own country, but already highly esteemed by his foreign colleagues.

He was born in Paris, in the Rue Cuvier, on May 15th, 1859. He was the second son of a physician, Dr. Eugène Curie, who was himself the son of a doctor. The family was of Alsatian origin, and Protestant. The Curies, once of the lower bourgeoisie, had, through generations, become intellectuals and scientists. Pierre's father had to practise medicine to earn his living; but he was devoted to research. He had been for some time a worker in the laboratory of the Museum of Natural History in Paris, and he was the author of works on tubercular infection.

His two sons, Jacques and Pierre, were drawn by science from their infancy. Pierre, with his independent and dreamy mind, was unable to adapt himself to systematic work and discipline. He had never been to school. Dr. Curie, understanding that the boy was too original to be a brilliant pupil, had at first instructed him himself, and afterward had confided him to a remarkable teacher, M. Bazille. This liberal education had borne fruit: Pierre Curie was a Bachelor of Science* at sixteen and had a master's degree in physics† at eighteen. At nineteen he was appointed laboratory

* Bachelier ès Science.
† Licencié ès Physique.

assistant to Professor Desains in the Faculty of Science—a position he occupied for five years. He was engaged in research with his brother Jacques, who also had his degree and was a laboratory worker at the Sorbonne. The two young physicists soon announced the discovery of the important phenomenon of "piezo-electricity," and their experimental work led them to invent a new apparatus with many practical uses: *piezoelectric* quartz, which measures small quantities of electricity with precision.

In 1883 the two brothers separated with regret: Jacques was appointed professor at Montpellier, and Pierre became chief of laboratory at the School of Physics and Chemistry of the City of Paris. Even though he devoted much time to demonstrations for the pupils, he pursued his theoretical work on crystalline physics. This work led to the formulation of the principle of symmetry, which was to become one of the bases of modern science.

Taking up his experimental study again, Pierre Curie invented and built an ultra-sensitive scientific scale, the "Curie scale." Then he undertook research on magnetism and obtained a result of capital importance: the discovery of a fundamental law. "Curie's law."

For these efforts, crowned by dazzling success, and for the constant care he lavished on the thirty students confided to him, Pierre Curie was receiving from the French State, in 1894, after fifteen years of work, a salary of three hundred francs a month— just about what a specialised worker would receive in a factory.

But when the illustrious English scientist, Lord Kelvin, came to Paris, he was not satisfied with going to hear Pierre Curie's reports to the Physics Society. In spite of his great age and position, he wrote to the young physicist, spoke of his work, and asked for a meeting.

Lord Kelvin to Pierre Curie, August, 1893:

DEAR MONSIEUR CURIE,—

I thank you very much for having taken the trouble to obtain for me an apparatus by which I can so conveniently observe the magnificent experimental discovery of piezoelectric quartz, made by you and your brother.

I have written a note for the *Philosophical Magazine,* making it clear that your work preceded mine. This note should arrive in time to appear in the October number, but, if not, it will certainly appear in November. . . .

October 3rd, 1893.
DEAR MONSIEUR CURIE,—

I hope to arrive in Paris to-morrow evening; I should be very grateful if you could let me know when, between now and the end of the week, it would be convenient for you to let me come and see you in your laboratory.

In the course of these visits, when the two physicists discussed scientific questions for hours, the English scientist must have been astonished to observe that Pierre Curie was working without assistants in a pitiable place, that he devoted most of his time to poorly paid trudgery, and that hardly anybody in Paris knew the name of this man whom he, Lord Kelvin, considered a master.

Pierre Curie was even more than a remarkable physicist. He was a man who, when asked to offer himself as candidate for a post which would improve his material condition, replied:

They tell me one of the professors may perhaps resign and that in case he does I should submit my candidature as his successor. It is a nasty job being a candidate for any place at all, and I am not accustomed to this sort of exercise, demoralising in the highest degree. I am sorry I spoke of it to you. I believe there is nothing more unhealthy for the mind than to allow oneself to be pre-occupied with such matters.

When proposed by the director of the School of Physics for a decoration: *les Palmes académiques*, he refused in these terms:

MR. DIRECTOR,—

M. Muzet has told me that you intend to propose me to the Prefect again for decoration

I write to beg you to do no such thing. If you obtain this distinction for me, you will put me under the obligation of refusing it, for I have quite decided never to accept any decoration of any sort. I hope you will be good enough to spare me the necessity of a step which would make me rather ridiculous in the eyes of many people.

If it is your intention to give me an evidence of interest, you have already done so and in more efficacious fashion—by which I have been much touched—in allowing me the means of working at my ease.

He was also, or at least could have been, a writer. This man, whose education had been so fantastic, was possessed of an original, strong and graceful style:

"To stun with clatter a mind that wishes to think "*

Weak as I am, in order not to let my mind fly away on every wind that blows, yielding to the slightest breath it encounters, it would be necessary either to have everything motionless around me, or else, speeding on like a humming-top, in movement itself to be rendered impervious to external things.

Whenever, rotating slowly on myself, I attempt to speed up, the merest nothing—a word, a story, a newspaper, a visit—stops me, prevents my becoming a gyroscope or top, and can postpone or for ever delay the instant when, equipped with sufficient speed, I might be able to concentrate within myself in spite of what is around me.

We are obliged to eat, drink, sleep, laze, love; that is to say, to touch the sweetest things in this life, and yet not succumb in doing all that, to make the anti-natural thought to which one has devoted one's self remain dominant and continue its impassable course in one's poor head. One must make of life a dream, and of that dream a reality.

Finally, he had the sensibility and imagination of a poet or an artist, with their discouragements and anguish.

What shall I be later on? [he wrote in his diary in 1881]. I am very rarely all under command at once; ordinarily a portion of my

* *Étourdir de grelots l'esprit qui veut penser.* (Victor Hugo: *Le Rois' amuse.*)

being is asleep. It seems to me that my mind gets clumsier every day. Before, I flung myself into scientific or other divagations; to-day I barely touch on subjects and do not allow myself to be absorbed by them any more. And I have so many, many things to do! Is my poor mind then, so feeble that it cannot act upon my body? Is thought itself unable to move my poor mind? Then it is worth very little! And Pride, Ambition—couldn't they at least propel me, or will they let me live like this? In my imagination I shall find most confidence to pull myself out of the rut. Imagination may perhaps entice my mind and carry it away. But I am very much afraid that imagination, too, may be dead . . .

The poet had been immediately captivated by Marie Sklodovska, as had the physicist, and had understood what was unique in her. Pierre Curie, with gentle tenacity, endeavoured to get on friendly terms with the girl. He saw her again two or three times at the sessions of the Physics Society, where she was listening to the reports of scientists on new research. He sent her, by way of compliment, a reprint of his latest publication, *On Symmetry in Physical Phenomena: Symmetry of an Electric Field and of a Magnetic Field;* and on the first page he wrote in his awkward hand: "To Mlle Sklodovska, with the respect and friendship of the author, P. Curie." He had seen her in Lippmann's laboratory, in her big linen smock, bent silently over her apparatus.

And then he asked if he could visit her. Marie gave him her address, 11 Rue des Feuillantines. Friendly but reserved, she received him in her little room, and Pierre, his heart constricted by so much poverty, nevertheless appreciated, in the depths of his spirit, the subtle agreement between the character and the setting. In an almost empty attic, with her threadbare dress and her ardent, stubborn features, Marie had never seemed more beautiful to him. Her young face, thin and worn from the effort of an ascetic life, could not have found a more perfect frame than this denuded garret.

A few months passed. Their friendship strengthened, their intimacy increased, in proportion as their reciprocal esteem, admiration and confidence grew greater. Pierre Curie was already the captive of the too intelligent, too lucid Polish girl. He obeyed her and followed her advice. He was soon urged and stimulated by her, to shake off his indolence, write out his experiments on magnetism, and pass a brilliant thesis for the doctor's degree.

Marie still believed herself to be free. She did not seem disposed to listen to the final words which the scientist did not dare to pronounce.

This evening, for perhaps the tenth time, they were together in the room in the Rue des Feuillantines. It was warm: it was the end of an afternoon in June. On the table, near the mathematics books with the help of which Marie was preparing her approaching examination, there were some white daisies in a glass, brought back from an excursion Pierre and Marie had made together. The girl poured out tea, made on her faithful little spirit lamp.

The physicist had just been speaking at length about a piece of work that preoccupied him. Then, without transition:

"I wish you would come to know my parents. I live with them, in a little house at Sceaux. They are charming."

He described his father for her: a tall, ungainly old man with lively blue eyes, very intelligent, hasty and impetuous, apt to boil over like a quick soup, but extremely kind—and his mother, weighed down by infirmities, but still an expert housekeeper, brave, gay and courageous. He recalled his fantastic childhood, his interminable jaunts in the woods with his brother Jacques. . . .

Marie listened with surprise. What mysterious likenesses and coincidences! By changing a few details, transporting the little house at Sceaux to a street in Warsaw, you could turn the Curies into the Sklodovski family. Apart from religion—Dr. Curie, an Anticlerical freethinker, had not had his children baptized—it was the same sort of circle, wise and honourable, with the same respect for culture, the same love of science, the same affectionate alliance between parents and children, the same passionate liking for nature. Smiling and more at her ease, Marie told the tale of her merry holidays in the Polish countryside—that countryside which she was going to see again in a few weeks.

"But you're coming back in October? Promise me that you will come back! If you stay in Poland you can't possibly continue your studies. You have no right to abandon science now . . ."

These commonplace words of solicitude betrayed profound

anxiety. And Marie felt that when Pierre said: "You have no right to abandon science," he meant, above all, "You have no right to abandon me."

They were silent for a time. Then Marie, lifting her ash-grey eyes to Pierre, answered gently, in a voice that still hesitated:

"I believe you are right. I should like to come back—very much."

Pierre spoke of the future several times again. He had asked Marie to be his wife; but the answer was not a happy one. To marry a Frenchman and leave her family for ever, to renounce all political activity and abandon Poland, seemed to Mlle Sklodovska like so many dreadful acts of betrayal. She could not and must not. She had passed her examination brilliantly; and now she must go back to Warsaw for the summer at least, perhaps for ever. She offered the discouraged young scientist a friendship which was no longer enough for him, and took her train, having promised nothing.

He followed her in thought; he would have liked to join her in Switzerland, where she was passing a few weeks with her father who had come to meet her, or else in Poland—in that Poland of which he was jealous. But it could not be. . . .

So, from afar, he continued to urge his suit. Wherever Marie went, during the summer months, to Ciettaz, Lemberg, Cracow or Warsaw, letters in uncertain and rather childish handwriting followed, on inexpensive paper headed by the name of the School of Physics, attempting to convince her and bring her back: to remind her that Pierre Curie was waiting for her.

Pierre Curie to Marie Sklodovska, August 10th, 1894:
Nothing could have given me greater pleasure than to get news of you. The prospect of remaining two months without hearing about you had been extremely disagreeable to me: that is to say, your little note was more than welcome.

I hope you are laying up a stock of good air and that you will come back to us in October. As for me, I think I shall not go anywhere; I shall stay in the country, where I spend the whole day in front of my open window or in the garden.

We have promised each other—haven't we?—to be at least great friends. If you will only not change your mind! For there are no promises that are binding; such things cannot be ordered at will. It would be a fine thing, just the same, in which I hardly dare believe, to pass our lives near each other, hypnotised by our dreams: *your* patriotic dream, *our* humanitarian dream, and *our* scientific dream.

Of all those dreams the last is, I believe, the only legitimate one. I mean by that that we are powerless to change the social order and, even if we were not, we should not know what to do; in taking action, no matter in what direction, we should never be sure of not doing more harm than good, by retarding some inevitable evolution. From the scientific point of view, on the contrary, we may hope to do something; the ground is solider here, and any discovery that we may make, however small, will remain acquired knowledge

See how it works out: it is agreed that we shall be great friends, but if you leave France in a year it would be an altogether too platonic friendship, that of two creatures who would never see each other again. Wouldn't it be better for you to stay with me? I know that this question angers you, and that you don't want to speak of it again—and then, too, I feel so thoroughly unworthy of you from every point of view.

I thought of asking your permission to meet you *by chance* in Fribourg. But you are staying there, unless I am mistaken, only one day, and on that day you will of course belong to our friends the Kovalskis.

> Believe me your very devoted
> PIERRE CURIE.

I should be happy if you would write to me and give me the assurance that you intend to come back in October. If you write direct to Sceaux the letters would get to me quicker: Pierre Curie, 13 Rue des Sablons, Sceaux (Seine).

Pierre Curie to Marie Sklodovska, August 14th, 1894:

I couldn't decide to come and meet you; I hesitated all through one day, only to come to this negative result in the end. The first impression I received in reading your letter was that you preferred me not to come. The second was that you were very kind, just the same, to allow me the possibility of passing three days with you, and I was on the point of leaving. But then I was attacked by a sort of shame at pursuing you like this against your will; and finally, what decided me to stay, was the near-certainty that my presence would be disagreeable to your father and would spoil his pleasure in your company.

Now that it is too late, I am sorry I did not go. Wouldn't it have doubled the friendship we have for each other, perhaps, if we had passed three days together—and wouldn't it have given us strength not to forget each other in the two months and a half that separate us?

Are you a fatalist? Do you remember the day of Mi-Carême?* I had suddenly lost you in the crowd. It seems to me that our friendly relations will be suddenly interrupted in the same way without either of us desiring it. I am not a fatalist, but this will probably be a result of our characters. I shall never know how to act at the opportune moment.

For that matter it will be a good thing for you, for I do not know why I have got it into my head to keep you in France, to exile you from your country and family without having anything good to offer you in exchange for such a sacrifice.

Aren't you a little pretentious when you say you are perfectly free? We are all slaves at least of our affections, slaves of the prejudices of those we love; we must also earn our living, and thereby become a part of the machine, etc., etc.

The most painful thing is the concessions we are forced to make to the prejudices of the society that surrounds us; one makes them more or less often, according to one's strength or weakness. If we don't make enough we are crushed; and if we make too many we are vile and acquire a disgust for ourselves. I am now far away from the principles I held ten years ago. At that time I believed one ought to be excessive in everything and make no concession to environment. I thought I had to exaggerate defects as well as qualities; I wore only blue shirts like workmen, etc., etc.

So, you see, I have become very old and feel greatly weakened. I hope you will enjoy yourself very much.

Your devoted friend,

PIERRE CURIE.

* The mid-Lenten carnival.

Pierre Curie to Marie Sklodovska, September 7th, 1894:

. . . As you may imagine, your letter worries me. I strongly advise you to come back to Paris in October. It would be a great grief to me if you did not come back this year; but it is not out of a friend's selfishness that I tell you to come back. Only, I believe that you would work better here and can do a more solid and useful job.

What would you think of somebody who thought of butting his head against a stone wall in the hope of knocking it over? It might be an idea resulting from the finest feelings, but in fact that idea would be ridiculous and stupid. I believe that certain questions require a general solution, but are no longer capable of local solutions nowadays; and that when one engages in a course which has no issue one can do a great deal of harm. I further believe that justice is not of this world, and that the strongest system, or rather the most economic, is the one that must prevail. Man is worn out by work and has a miserable life just the same. that is a revolting thing, but it isn't for that reason that it will disappear. It will disappear, probably, because man is a kind of machine and there is an advantage, from the economic point of view, in making any sort of machine work in its normal way without forcing it.

You have an amazing way of understanding selfishness! When I was twenty I had a dreadful misfortune. I lost, in terrible circumstances, a childhood friend whom I loved. I haven't the courage to tell you all about it. I went through days and nights with a fixed idea, and experienced a sort of delight in torturing myself. Then I vowed, in all good faith, to lead a priest's existence; I promised myself to be interested only in *things* thereafter, and never again to think either of myself or of mankind. Since then I have often asked if this renunciation of life was not simply a trick which I used against myself to acquire the right to forget.

Is correspondence free in your country? I doubt it; and I think it would be better, in the future, to write no more dissertations which, even though purely philosophical, might be badly interpreted and could cause you trouble.

You can write to me, if you only will, at 13 Rue des Sablons.

Your devoted friend,

P. CURIE.

Pierre Curie to Marie Sklodovska, September 17th, 1894:

Your letter worried me a great deal; I felt that you were worried and undecided. Your letter from Warsaw reassures me a little; I feel you have regained your calm. Your picture pleases me enormously. How kind of you to send it to me! I thank you with all my heart.

And finally, you are coming back to Paris; that gives me great pleasure. I want very much for us to become at least inseparable friends. Don't you agree?

If you were French, you could easily manage to be a professor in the secondary schools or in a girls' normal school. Would that profession please you?

Your very devoted friend,

P. CURIE.

I showed your photograph to my brother. Was that wrong? He admired it. He added. "She has a very decided look, not to say *stubborn*."

Would it not in itself be a splendid title to fame, to have inspired such letters?

October came. Pierre's heart swelled with happiness: Marie, according to her promise, had returned to Paris. She was to be seen again at the lectures in the Sorbonne and at Lippmann's laboratory. But this year—her last in France, as she believed—she no longer lived in the Latin Quarter. Bronya had given her a room adjoining the surgery she had opened for consultation at 37 Rue de Châteaudun As the Dluskis still lived in La Villette and Bronya came to the Rue de Châteaudun only during the day, Marie could thus work in peace.

It was in this dark and rather dismal lodging that Pierre Curie resumed his tender entreaties. He bore within him the same faith as his future wife, a faith which was even more whole-hearted, purer by its lack of alloy. For Pierre, science was the only aim. Thus his was a strange and almost incredible adventure, for it mixed the essential aspiration of his mind into the movement of his heart. He felt himself drawn toward Marie by an impulse of love and at the same time by the highest necessity.

He was even ready to sacrifice what people call happiness to another happiness known to him alone. He made Marie a proposal which at first seems fantastic, which might pass for a ruse or an approach, but which was characteristic of his nature. If Marie had no love for him, he asked, could she resolve upon a purely friendly arrangement at least, and work with him "in an apartment in the Rue Mouffetard, with windows giving on a garden, an apartment which could be divided into two independent parts?"

Or else (since necessity names its own price) if he, Pierre Curie, went to Poland and obtained a position would she marry him? He could give French lessons; then, with whatever means at their disposal, he would engage in scientific research with her. . . .

Before the former governess who had once been disdained by a Polish squireen family, this man of genius became an humble supplicant.

Marie confided her perplexities and anxieties to Bronya, speaking of Pierre's offer to exile himself. She did not feel that she had the right to accept such sacrifice, but she was troubled and moved by the idea that Pierre loved her enough to have thought of it.

When he learned that the girl had spoken of him to the Dluskis, Pierre tried a new attack on that side. He went to see Bronya, whom he had already met several times; he won her over completely and asked her to come with Marie to his parents' house at Sceaux. Dr. Curie's wife took Bronya aside and in a gentle, touching voice asked her to speak to her younger sister.

"There isn't a soul on earth to equal my Pierre," Mme Curie insisted. "Don't let your sister hesitate. She will be happier with him than with anybody."

Ten more months had to pass before the obdurate Pole accepted the idea of marriage. Like a true Slavic "intellectual," Marie was encumbered with theories on life and duty. Some of her theories were generous and fine; others were only childish. Above all— and Pierre had understood this for a long time—it was not her theories that made Marie a superior being. The scientist made quick work of principles which Marie shared with several thousands of her cultivated compatriots. What held and fascinated him was her total devotion to work; it was her genius that he felt; it was also her courage and nobility. This graceful girl had the character and gifts of a great man.

Principles? He, too had lived on principles for a long time, and life had undertaken to demonstrate their absurdity. He, too, had sworn never to get married. He had no Poland to defend, but he had always believed marriage to be incompatible with an existence devoted to science. The tragic end of an ardent youthful love had turned him in upon himself and had kept him away from women. He no longer wanted to love: a salutary principle which had saved him from commonplace marriage and made him wait for this meeting with an exceptional woman, a woman "made for him"— for Marie. And now he would not be stupid enough to let the chance of great happiness and a wonderful collaboration escape him for the sake of a "principle." He would win the girl, the Pole and the physicist, three persons who had become indispensable to him . . .

Thus he gently reasoned with Mlle Sklodovska. By such words and by others more tender, by the protection he offered her and by the deep, irresistible charm of his daily presence, Pierre Curie gradually made a human being out of the young hermit.

On July 14th, 1895, Marie's brother Joseph sent her the affectionate absolution of the Sklodovski family:

. . . As you are now M. Curie's fiancée, I offer you first of all my sincerest good wishes, and may you find with him all the happiness and joy you deserve in my eyes and in the eyes of all who know your excellent heart and character.

. . . I think you are right to follow your heart, and no just person can reproach you for it. Knowing you, I am convinced that you will remain Polish with all your soul, and also that you will never cease to be part of our family in your heart. And we, too, will never cease to love you and to consider you ours.

I would infinitely rather see you in Paris, happy and contented, than back again in our country, broken by the sacrifice of a whole life and victim of a too subtle conception of your duty. What we must do now is try to see each other as often as possible, in spite of everything.

A thousand kisses, dear Manya; and again let me wish you happiness, joy and success. Give my affectionate regards to your fiancé. Tell him that I welcome him as a future member of our family and that I offer him my friendship and sympathy without reserve. I hope that he will also give me his friendship and esteem.

A few days later Marie wrote to Kazia, her girlhood friend, and announced the decision she had taken:

When you receive this letter your Manya will have changed her name. I am about to marry the man I told you about last year in Warsaw. It is a sorrow to me to have to stay for ever in Paris, but what am I to do? Fate has made us deeply attached to each other and we cannot endure the idea of separating.

I haven't written, because all this was decided only a short time ago, quite suddenly. I hesitated for a whole year and could not resolve upon an answer. Finally I became reconciled to the idea of settling here. When you receive this letter, write to me: Madame Curie, School of Physics and Chemistry, 42 Rue Lhomond.

That is my name from now on. My husband is a teacher in that school. Next year I shall bring him to Poland so that he will know my country, and I shall not fail to introduce him to my dear little chosen sister, and I shall ask her to love him. . . .

On July 26th Marie awoke for the last time in her lodging in the Rue de Châteaudun. It was a marvellous day. The girl's face was beautiful. Something her student comrades had never seen was alight in her face: to-day Mlle Sklodovska was to become Mme Pierre Curie.

She dressed her lovely hair and put on her wedding dress, a present from Casimir Dluski's aged mother, who now lived in the Rue d'Allemagne. "I have no dress except the one I wear every day," Marie had said. "If you are going to be kind enough to give me one, please let it be practical and dark, so that I can put it on afterwards to go to the laboratory."

Guided by Bronya, Mme Glet, a little dressmaker in the Rue Dancourt, had made the dress: a navy-blue woollen suit with a blue blouse with ligher blue stripes, in which Marie looked pretty, fresh and young.

Marie loved the idea of her wedding, which was to be, in every detail of the great day, different from all other weddings. There would be no white dress, no gold ring, no "wedding breakfast." There would be no religious ceremony: Pierre was a freethinker and Marie, for a long time past, had ceased the practices of religion. There were no lawyers necessary, as the marriage pair possessed nothing in the world—nothing but two glittering bicycles, bought the day before with money sent as a present from a cousin, with which they were going to roam the countryside in the coming summer.

It was to be a wonderful wedding indeed, for neither indifference, curiosity nor envy was to be present. At the city hall in Sceaux and in the little garden at Pierre's parents' house in the Rue des Sablons there would be Bronya and Casimir, a few very close friends—university people—and Professor Sklodovski, who had come from Warsaw with Hela. . . . The professor made it a point of honour to talk to old Dr. Curie in the most correct and careful French; but first of all he would say, in his lowest tone, very moved, these words straight from his good heart: "You will have a daughter worthy of affection in Marie. Since she came into the world she has never caused me pain."

Pierre came to get Marie. They had to go to the Luxembourg station for the train to Sceaux, where their parents were waiting. They went up the Boulevard Saint-Michel on the top of an omnibus in the bright sun, and from the height of their triumphal chariot looked down on the passing of familiar places.

In front of the Sorbonne, at the entrance to the Faculty of Science, Marie squeezed her companion's arm a little and sought his glance, luminous and at peace.

CHAPTER XI

A Young Couple

MARIE always succeeded in her undertakings. It was thus with her marriage. She had hesitated for more than a year before marrying Pierre Curie. Now that she was his wife, she organised their conjugal life with such far-sighted tenderness that she was to make a wonderful thing of it

The first days of their life together were picturesque: Pierre and Marie roamed the roads of the Ile-de-France on their famous bicycles. In the baggage straps they strung up a few clothes and two long rubberised cloaks which the rainy summer had forced them to buy. They lunched on bread and cheese, peaches and cherries, seated on the moss of some woodland glade. In the evening, they stopped by chance at some unknown inn. There they found thick, hot soup and a room with faded wallpaper on which the candle made shadows dance. They were alone in the mock-silence of the night fields, broken by far-off barking, the cooing of birds, the lewd complaints of cats and the dramatic crackling of boards in the floor

When they wanted to explore the woods or rocks they interrupted their journey by a walk. Pierre loved the country passionately, and no doubt his long, silent walks were necessary to his genius; their equal rhythm encouraged his scientist's meditation. He could not remain quiet when he was outside in a garden He did not know how to rest. Neither did he care for the classic excursions with itineraries provided in advance He had no notion of time: why ought one to walk by day more than by night, and why should the hours for meals be fixed once and for all?

Since his childhood he had had the habit of going off when he liked, sometimes at dawn, sometimes at dusk, without knowing whether he would come back in three days or in an hour. He retained a wonderful memory of these wanderings in the old days with his brother:

Oh! what a good time that was, in grateful solitude, far from the thousand irritating little things which tortured me in Paris. . . . No, I do not regret my nights in the woods or my days that slipped by alone. If I had time I would willingly ramble on about the day-dreams I had there. I should like to describe my delicious valley too—all embalmed in aromatic plants; the lovely jungle, so cool and wet, through which the Bièvre flowed, the fairy palace with colonnades of hop plants, the stony hills, red with briar, where we enjoyed ourselves so much. Yes: I shall always remember the woods of La Minière with gratitude. Of all the places I have known, it is the one I loved most, where I was happiest. I often went off in the evening, up the valley, and came back with dozens of ideas in my head. . . .

The summer's tramping in 1895, a "wedding tramp," was sweeter still; love exalted it and made it beautiful. At the cost of some thousands of pedal strokes and a few francs for village lodgings, the young couple attained the luxury of solitude shared between them for long enchanted days and nights.

One day, leaving their machines in a peasant's house, Pierre and Marie left the big road and went off on a chance trail taking nothing with them but a little compass and some fruit. Pierre strode on ahead and Marie followed him without fatigue. Sacrificing the proprieties, she had shortened her skirts a little so as to be able to walk freely. Her head was bare; she wore a white bodice, fresh and pretty, heavy shoes, and around her waist a leather belt, practical but not graceful, which harboured a knife, some money and a watch in its pockets.

Pierre went on thinking aloud about the work on crystals that preoccupied him, without even turning round to catch his wife's eyes. He knew that Marie understood, and that what she would reply would be intelligent, useful and original. She, too, had great plans for the next university year: she was going to prepare for the Fellowship competition and it was almost certain that the director of the School of Physics, Schutzenberger, would authorise her to make her researches in the same laboratory with Pierre. Thus they could live constantly together, never separate.

In the midst of the thicket they came upon a pond surrounded by reeds. Pierre discovered the flora and fauna of this sleeping pool with joy. He had a wonderful knowledge of air and water animals, of salamanders, dragon-flies and tritons. While his young wife stretched out on the bank, he stepped nimbly out on a fallen tree-trunk and, risking a fall and an unwanted bath, stretched his hands forward to gather yellow irises and pale floating water-lilies.

Marie, at peace and almost dozing, looked up at the sky where light clouds drifted. Suddenly she cried out sharply as she felt something cold and wet on her opened hand. It was a green frog, panting, which Pierre had delicately dropped into her palm. He had no intention of playing a joke; familiar acquaintance with frogs was an absolutely natural thing to him.

"Pierre. . . . Really, Pierre!" she protested, with a movement of childish terror.

The physicist was shocked.

"Don't you like frogs?"

"Yes, but not in my hands."

"You are quite wrong," he said, unmoved. "It is very amusing to watch a frog. Open your hand gently. Now see how nice it is!"

He took the animal back and Marie smiled in relief. He put the frog down on the edge of the pond and gave it its freedom; then, already tired of this halt, he made off down the trail, and his wife followed him, wearing her wild ornaments of iris and water-lily.

Caught up again by the haunting thought of work, Pierre Curie had suddenly forgotten woods and skies frog and pool. He mused upon the tenuous, immense difficulty of his research, the troubled mystery of the growth of crystals. He described the apparatus he was going to construct for a new experiment; and again he heard Marie's faithful voice, her lucid questions and reflective answers.

During these happy days was formed one of the finest bonds that ever united man and woman. Two hearts beat together, two bodies were united, and two minds of genius learned to think together. Marie could have married no other than this great physicist, than this wise and noble man. Pierre could have married no woman other than the fair, tender Polish girl, who could be childish or transcendent within the same few moments; for she was a friend and a wife, a lover and a scientist.

Toward the middle of August, delighted and tired by their wonderful summer, the young couple settled down near Chantilly on a farm called The Hind. This, too, was one of Bronya's discoveries; she had taken the peaceful dwelling for several months. There Marie and Pierre rejoined old Mme Dluska, Casimir, Bronya and their daughter Helen, nicknamed "Lou," Professor Sklodovski and Hela, who had prolonged their stay in France.

This holiday was to become a precious and dazzling memory to that group of people who were destined seldom to meet again. They felt the charm of a poetic old house standing alone in the woods full of pheasants and hares, its ground carpeted with lilies-of the-valley; the charm of a friendship embracing two races and three generations.

Pierre Curie made a permanent conquest of his new family. He talked about science with his father-in-law Sklodovski and had serious interviews with little Lou, who was pretty, funny and very gay at the age of three and was the delight of them all. Sometimes Dr. Curie and his wife came for a visit from Sceaux to Chantilly. Then there were two more places laid at the big table, and the conversation grew animated passing from chemistry to medicine and to the education of children, from social ideas to general views on France and Poland.

Pierre had not a trace of that instinctive distrust of foreigners which is so common among our compatriots. He was, on his side, captivated by the Dluskis and Sklodovskis. To give his wife a new proof of love he forced himself, in spite of Marie's delighted protests into a most touching effort: he tried to learn Polish, the most difficult of languages. and—since it was the speech of a country which had been abolished—the most useless.

Pierre took his "Polonisation" treatment at The Hind; and at Sceaux, where he brought his young wife in September, it was

Marie's turn to become Gallicised. She asked nothing better. She already loved her husband's parents, whose affection was to comfort her exile when M. Sklodovski and Hela had gone back to Warsaw.

Pierre's marriage to a poor foreign girl, found in a garret in the Latin Quarter, had neither shocked nor surprised the old people; theirs were gifted minds They admired Marie from the first moment. It was not only her "Slavic charm" that affected them and their elder son Jacques, who had a great friendship for his sister-in-law; they were dazzled by the masculine intelligence of Pierre's wife, and by her character.

One of the few surprises Marie was to experience in the circle at Sceaux, no doubt, was the ardour of her father-in-law's political passions and that of his friends Dr Curie, still in love with the ideas of 1848, was intimately associated with the radical Henri Brisson. He had a fighting spirit. Marie, who had been brought up in the struggle against foreign oppressors and the pacific devotion to a social ideal, learned to know party quarrels, so dear to Frenchmen. She listened to long arguments and the explanation of burning theories. When she was a little tired of them she took refuge with her husband, who kept to himself, dreamy and silent. If the Sunday guests in the little garden of the Rue des Sablons tried to get Pierre into one of their friendly disputes over events of the day, the physicist sometimes answered gently, as if to excuse himself: "I am not much good at getting angry."

Pierre Curie was little inclined to take an active part in politics [Marie was to write] By education and feeling he was attached to democratic and socialist ideas, but he was dominated by no party doctrine. . . . In public as in private life he did not believe in the use of violence.

The Dreyfus case was to be one of the few occasions on which Pierre Curie, coming out of his reserve, would grow impassioned in political struggle; but there again his conduct was not to be dictated by sectarian spirit: he quite naturally took the part of the innocent and persecuted. He was to fight against an iniquity that filled him with horror, because he was a just man.

The little flat at 24 Rue de la Glacière, where the young couple settled in October, had windows giving on a big garden. This lodging, which was singularly lacking in comfort, possessed no other charm.

Marie and Pierre had done nothing to decorate their three tiny rooms. They even refused the furniture offered them by Dr. Curie: every sofa and chair would be one more object to dust in the morning and to furbish up on days of full cleaning. Marie could not do it; she hadn't time. In any case, what was the good of a sofa or chair, as the Curies had agreed to do away with meetings and calls? The troublesome person who risked his neck on the four flights of stairs in order to disturb the young couple in their lair was rebuffed once for all when he got into the conjugal office with its bare walls, furnished with books and a white wooden table. At one end of the table was Marie's chair; at the other, Pierre's On the table were treatises on physics, a petroleum lamp, a bunch of flowers; and that was all Before these two chairs, neither of which was for him and before the politely astonished gaze of Pierre and Marie the most daring visitor could only flee.

Pierre's existence tended toward one ideal only: to engage in scientific research at the side of the beloved woman who also lived for scientific research. Marie's was a harder life, because to the obsession of work was added the humble and tiring tasks of womankind. She could no longer neglect material life, as she had done in the austere and careless days of her study at the Sorbonne; and her first purchase on their return from holiday was a black account book with the great word EXPENSES printed in letters of gold on its cover.

Pierre Curie now earned five hundred francs a month at the School of Physics. These five hundred francs were the couple's only resource until Marie's diploma as fellow of the university would permit her to teach in France.

This would do well enough: with such a sum a modest pair could live, and Marie knew how to be economical. The difficult thing was to get the crushing work of one day into twenty-four hours Marie passed the whole morning and afternoon at the laboratory of the school, where a place had been found for her. The laboratory was happiness; and yet there were a floor to sweep

and a bed to make at the Rue de la Glacière. Pierre's clothes had to
be kept in good condition and his meals had to be suitable. With
no maid. . . .

So Marie got up early to go to market; and in the evenings as
she was coming home from school on Pierre's arm she took him
into the grocer's shop or the dairy. She peeled the vegetables for
the noonday meal in the morning before she went to the laboratory.
Where were the days when the careless Mlle Sklodovska didn't
know the strange ingredients of soup? Mme Pierre Curie made it a
point of honour to learn them. As soon as her marriage had been
decided, the student had gone secretly to ask for cookery lessons
from old Mme Dluska and Bronya. She practised cooking a
chicken and fried potatoes, and dutifully prepared wholesome meals
for Pierre, who was indulgence itself, and so absent-minded that
he never even noticed the great effort she made.

Marie was stimulated by a puerile conceit; what a mortification
it would be for her if her French mother-in-law, face to face some
day with an unsuccessful omelette, wondered aloud what on earth
they taught the young girls in Warsaw! Marie read and re-read her
cookery book and annotated it conscientiously in the margins,
reporting her trials, failures and successes in brief phrases of
scientific accuracy.

She invented dishes which needed little preparation, and still
others which could be left to "cook themselves" during the hours
she passed at the school. But cooking was as difficult and mysterious as chemistry. What could she do to keep the macaroni
from sticking? Should she put boiled beef into cold or hot water?
How long should runner beans boil? In front of her oven Marie,
her cheeks afire, heaved many a sigh. It had been so simple
in the old days to live on buttered bread and tea, radishes and
cherries!

Little by little she improved in housekeeping wisdom. The gas
heater, which on several occasions had taken the liberty of burning
the roast, now knew its duty. Before going out, Marie would
regulate the flame with a physicist's precision; then, casting one
last worried glance at the stewpans she was entrusting to the fire,
she shut the door on the landing, flew down the stairs and caught
up with her husband, to walk with him toward the school.

In a quarter of an hour, bent over other containers, she would regulate the height of flame on a laboratory burner with the same careful gesture.

Eight hours of scientific research and two or three hours of housekeeping were not enough. In the evening, after writing down the details of daily expenses in the account-book columns so pompously headed "Monsieur's Expenditure" and "Madam's Expenditure," Marie Curie sat down at one end of the white-wood table and became absorbed in preparing for the Fellowship competition. On the other side of the lamp Pierre was drawing up the programme of his new course at the School of Physics. Often, when she felt her husband's fine eyes upon her, she lifted her own eyes to receive a message of love and admiration. And a little smile was silently exchanged between this man and woman who loved each other. There was a light at the window of their room until two or three in the morning, and the ardent pianissimo of the turning page, the running pen, could be heard in their office with its two chairs.

Marie to Joseph Sklodovski, November 23rd, 1895:
. . . Everything goes well with us; we are both healthy and life is kind to us. I am arranging my flat little by little, but I intend to keep it to a style which will give me no worries and will not require attention, as I have very little help: a woman who comes for an hour a day to wash the dishes and do the heavy work. I do the cooking and housekeeping myself.

Every few days we go to Sceaux to see my husband's parents. This does not interrupt our work; we have two rooms on the first floor there, with everything we need; we are therefore perfectly at home and can do all the part of our work that cannot be done in the laboratory.

When it is fine we go to Sceaux by bicycle; we only take the train when it is raining cats and dogs.

My "lucrative" employment is not yet settled. I hope to get some work this year that I can do in the laboratory. It is half-scientific, half-industrial occupation, which I prefer to giving lessons.

Marie to Joseph Sklodovski, March 18th, 1896:

. . . Our life is always the same, monotonous. We see nobody but the Dluskis and my husband's parents in Sceaux. We hardly ever go to the theatre and we give ourselves no diversions. At Easter we shall allow ourselves several days' holiday, perhaps, and shall go off on an excursion.

I am sorry not being able to go to Hela's wedding If none of us lived in Warsaw, perhaps, in spite of the difficulties, I might get together the money for the journey. But happily Hela is not altogether abandoned. I must therefore deprive myself of this great joy, because I cannot indulge it without scruple.

It has been very hot here for several weeks. Everything is green in the country. At Sceaux, simple violets were showing themselves already in February, and now there are quantities of them; the rockery in the garden is full of them. In the streets of Paris they sell masses of flowers at very reasonable prices, and we always have bunches of them at home. . . .

Marie to Joseph and to his wife, July 16th, 1896:

Dear ones, I should so much have liked to come home this year and take you both in my arms! I can't think of it, alas; I have neither the time nor the money. The competitive examination for a Fellowship, which I am passing now, may go on until the middle of August.

In the examination for a Fellowship in Secondary Education Mme Curie passed first. Pierre, without a word, flung his proud, protecting arm around Marie's neck. They went to the Rue de la Glacière arm in arm; and as soon as they got there they blew up the tyres of their bicycles and packed their bags. They were off to Auvergne on a journey of exploration.

How prodigal they were of their mental and physical powers! Their holidays, too, were an orgy of energy.

Marie was to write later:

A radiant memory remains from one sunny day when, after a long and difficult ascent, we traversed the fresh green fields of Aubrac in the pure air of the high plateau. Another living memory is that of an evening when, loitering at dusk in the gorges of the Truyère, we were particularly taken by a folk-song dying away in the distance, sung on a boat that was going down the current of the water. Having planned our stages badly, we could not get back to our lodging before dawn: a meeting with some carts whose horses were frightened at our bicycles made us cut across the tilled fields. We took the road afterward across the high plateau bathed in the unreal light of the moon, while the cows who were passing the night in enclosures came to contemplate us gravely with their great, tranquil eyes.

The second year of their marriage differed from the first only in Marie's state of health, which was upset by her pregnancy. Mme Curie had wanted a child, but she was vexed at being so ill and at being unable to stand before the apparatus and study the magnetisation of steel. She complained:

Marie to Kazia, March 2nd, 1897:
Dear Kazia, I am very late with my birthday letter, but I have been very unwell all these last weeks, and that deprived me of the energy and freedom of mind for writing.

I am going to have a child, and this hope has a cruel way of showing itself. For more than two months I have had continual dizziness, all day long from morning to night. I tire myself out and get steadily weaker, and although I do not look ill, I feel unable to work and am in a very bad state of spirits.

My condition irks me particularly because my mother-in-law is now seriously ill.

Marie to Joseph Sklodovski, March 31st, 1897:
Nothing new here. I am ill all the time, although I look well instead of showing it. My husband's mother is still ill, and as it is an incurable disease (cancer of the breast) we are very depressed. I am afraid, above all, that the disease will reach its end at the same time as my pregnancy. If this should happen my poor Pierre will have some very hard weeks to go through. . . .

In July 1897 Pierre and Marie, who had hardly been apart for an hour during the preceding two years, were separated for the first time. Professor Sklodovski came to pass the summer in France and settled with his daughter at the little Hotel of the Grey Rocks at Port Blanc; he watched over her until Pierre, who was detained in Paris, could come and join them.

Pierre to Marie, July 1897:
My little girl. so dear, so sweet, whom I love so much, I had your letter to-day and was very happy. . . . Nothing new here, except that I miss you very much: my soul flew away with you. . . .

These lines were traced with great industry, in Polish, the barbarian language in which the physicist had wanted to know all the tenderest words. Also in Polish, and in short little sentences that a novice could understand, Marie answered:

My dear husband, it is fine, the sun shines, it is hot. I am very sad without you, come quickly, I expect you from morning to night and I don't see you coming. . . . I am well, I work as much as I can, but Poincaré's book is more difficult than I had thought. I must speak to you about it and we can read over again together those parts which seemed to me important—and hard to understand.

Returning to French, Pierre, in letters beginning "My dear little child whom I love," hastily describes his life at Sceaux and the details of his work at the end of the year. He speaks with serious-ness and exactness about the swaddling clothes, jackets and little shirts of the infant that was about to be born:

I sent you a parcel to-day by post. You will find in it two knitted jackets coming from Mme P., I believe. They are of the smallest size and of the size next to it. The smallest size will do for jackets in elastic knit, but we must have a larger one in linen or cotton. You have to have jackets in both sizes. . . .

Suddenly he found grave and rare words to express his love:
I think of my dearest who fills my life, and I should like to have

new faculties. It seems to me that in concentrating my mind exclusively on you, as I have just been doing, I should be able to see you, to follow what you are doing, and also to make you feel that I am all yours in this moment—but I don't succeed in getting a clear picture.

At the beginning of August Pierre ran away to Port Blanc. It might be supposed that he would be so softened by Marie's condition, in her eighth month of pregnancy, as to pass a quiet summer with her; but this was not so. With the thoughtlessness of the insane—or rather of the scientist—the pair went off to Brest on their bicycles, covering stages as long as they usually did. Marie declared that she felt no fatigue, and Pierre was quite willing to believe her. He had a vague feeling that she was a supernatural being, who escaped from human laws.

This time, just the same, the young wife's body had to beg for mercy. Marie was forced, in great humiliation, to cut short the trip and go back to Paris, where she gave birth to a daughter on September 12th: Irène, a beautiful baby and a future Nobel prize-winner. Dr. Curie took charge of the delivery, which Mme Curie endured without a cry, her teeth clenched.

The confinement seems to have attracted little attention and cost very little money. On September 12th we find in the account book, under the heading of unusual expenses: "*Champagne 3 fr. Telegrams 1 fr. 10.*" Under the heading of "illnesses" the young mother has written: "*Chemist and nurse: 71 fr. 50.*" The total expenses of the Curie household for September—430 fr. 40—were thus so enlarged that Marie, to show her indignation, underlined the figure of 430 fr. with two great raging strokes.

The idea of choosing between family life and the scientific career did not even cross Marie's mind. She was resolved to face love, maternity and science all three, and to cheat none of them. By passion and will, she was to succeed.

Marie to M. Sklodovski, November 10th, 1897:
. . . I am still nursing my little Queen, but lately we have been seriously afraid that I could not continue. For three weeks

the child's weight had suddenly gone down, Irène looked ill, and was depressed and lifeless. For some days now things have been going better. If the child gains weight normally I shall continue to nurse her. If not, I shall take a nurse, in spite of the grief this would be to me, and in spite of the expense; I don't want to interfere with my child's development for anything on earth

It is still very fine here, hot and sunny. Irène goes out with me for a walk every day, or else with the servant. I bathe her in a little washing basin.

Marie was soon obliged to give up nursing her daughter by the doctor's orders; but morning, noon, evening and night she changed, bathed and dressed her. The nurse trundled the baby in the Parc Montsouris, while the young mother worked at the laboratory, finished and edited her work on magnetisation for the Bulletin of the Society for Encouragement of National Industry.

Thus, in the same year, within an interval of three months, Marie Curie brought into the world her first child and the results of her first research.

Sometimes her acrobatic system of life seemed impossible to continue. Her health had deteriorated since her pregnancy. Casimir Dluski and Dr. Vauthier, the Curie family doctor, spoke of a tubercular lesion in the left lung. Alarmed by Marie's heredity, as her mother had died of phthisis, they advised several months in a sanatorium. But the stubborn scientist listened to them absentmindedly and flatly refused to obey.

She had other things to worry about. She had the laboratory, her husband, her home and her daughter. Little Irène's tears as she was cutting teeth; a cold in the head; any minor accident troubled the calm of the household and made the two scientists pass nights of sleepless anxiety. Or else Marie, panic-stricken, would suddenly fly from the School of Physics toward the Parc Montsouris: had the nurse lost the child? No; she could see afar off, on their accustomed round, the woman and the little carriage in which something white could be discerned.

She found kindly and precious help in her father-in law. Dr. Curie, whose wife had died a few days after Irène's birth, had attached himself passionately to the baby. He watched over her first steps in the garden of the Rue des Sablons. When Pierre and Marie left the Rue de la Glacière for a little house in the Boulevard Kellermann, the old man was to come and live with them. He was to be Irène's first teacher and best friend.

The Polish girl had travelled far since the morning in November 1891 when she had arrived at the Gare du Nord, laden with parcels, in a third-class carriage. Manya Sklodovska had discovered physics, chemistry and the whole life of a woman. She had conquered humble and gigantic obstacles without for a moment suspecting that to do so she had called upon unequalled tenacity and exceptional courage.

These struggles and victories had transformed her physically; they had given her a new face. It is impossible to look unmoved at a photograph of Marie Curie taken a little after her thirtieth year. The solid and rather thick-set girl had become an ethereal creature. One would like to say: "What an attractive, odd and pretty woman!"—but one does not dare, in front of the immense brow, of that gaze into another world.

Mme Curie had a tryst with fame. She had made herself beautiful.

CHAPTER XII

The Discovery of Radium

WHILE a young wife kept house, washed her baby daughter and put pans on the fire, in a wretched laboratory at the School of Physics a woman physicist was making the most important discovery of modern science.

At the end of 1897 the balance-sheet of Marie's activity showed two university degrees, a fellowship and a monograph on the magnetisation of tempered steel. No sooner had she recovered from childbirth than she was back again at the laboratory.

The next stage in the logical development of her career was the doctor's degree. Several weeks of indecision came in here. She had to choose a subject of research which would furnish fertile and original material. Like a writer who hesitates and asks himself questions before settling the subject of his next novel, Marie, reviewing the most recent work in physics with Pierre, was in search of a subject for a thesis.

At this critical moment Pierre's advice had an importance which cannot be neglected. With respect to her husband, the young woman regarded herself as an apprentice: he was an older physicist, much more experienced than she. He was even, to put it exactly, her chief, her "boss."

But without a doubt Marie's character, her intimate nature, played a great part in this all-important choice. From childhood the Polish girl had carried the curiosity and daring of an explorer within her. This was the instinct that had driven her to leave Warsaw for Paris and the Sorbonne, and had made her prefer a solitary room in the Latin Quarter to the Dluskis' downy nest.

In her walks in the woods she always chose the wild trail or the unfrequented road.

At this moment she was like a traveller musing on a long voyage. Bent over the globe and pointing out, in some far country, a strange name that excites his imagination, the traveller suddenly decides to go there and nowhere else: so Marie, going through the reports of the latest experimental studies, was attracted by the publication of the French scientist Henri Becquerel of the preceding year. She and Pierre already knew this work; she read it over again and studied it with her usual care.

After Rontgen's discovery of X-rays, Henri Poincaré conceived the idea of determining whether rays like the X-ray were emitted by fluorescent bodies under the action of light. Attracted by the same problem, Henri Becquerel examined the salts of a rare metal, uranium. Instead of the phenomenon he had expected, he observed another, altogether different and incomprehensible: he discovered that uranium salts *spontaneously* emitted, without exposure to light, some rays of unknown nature. A compound of uranium, placed on a photographic plate surrounded by black paper, made an impression on the plate through the paper. And, like the X-ray, these astonishing uranic salts discharged an electroscope by rendering the surrounding air a conductor.

Henri Becquerel made sure that these surprising properties were not caused by a preliminary exposure to the sun and that they persisted when the uranium compound had been maintained in darkness for several months. For the first time, a physicist had observed the phenomenon to which Marie Curie was later to give the name of *radioactivity*. But the nature of the radiation and its origin remained an enigma.

Becquerel's discovery fascinated the Curies. They asked themselves whence came the energy—tiny, to be sure—which uranium compounds constantly disengaged in the form of radiation. And what was the nature of this radiation? Here was an engrossing subject of research, a doctor's thesis! The subject tempted Marie most because it was a virgin field: Becquerel's work was very recent and so far as she knew nobody in the laboratories of Europe had yet attempted to make a fundamental study of uranium rays. As a point of departure, and as the only bibliography. there existed some communications presented by Henri Becquerel at the Academy of Science during the year 1896. It was a leap into great adventure, into an unknown realm

There remained the question of where she was to make her experiments—and here the difficulties began. Pierre made several approaches to the director of the School of Physics with practically no results: Marie was given the free use of a little glassed-in studio on the ground floor of the school. It was a kind of store-room, sweating with damp, where unused machines and lumber were put away. Its technical equipment was rudimentary and its comfort *nil*.

Deprived of an adequate electrical installation and of everything that forms material for the beginning of scientific research, she kept her patience, sought and found a means of making her apparatus work in this hole.

It was not easy. Instruments of precision have sneaking enemies: humidity, changes of temperature. Incidentally the climate of this little workroom, fatal to the sensitive electrometer, was not much better for Marie's health. But this had no importance. When she was cold, the young·woman took her revenge by noting·the degrees of temperature in centigrade in her notebook. On February 6th, 1898, we find, among the formulas and figures: "Temperature here 6°25." Six degrees . . . !* Marie, to show her disapproval, added ten little exclamation points.

The candidate for the doctor's degree set her first task to be the measurement of the "power of ionisation" of uranium rays—that is to say, their power to render the air a conductor of electricity and so to discharge an electroscope. The excellent method she used, which was to be the key to the success of her experiments, had been invented for the study of other phenomena by two physicists well known to her: Pierre and Jacques Curie. Her technical installation consisted of an ionisation chamber, a Curie electrometer and a piezoelectric quartz.

At the end of several weeks the first result appeared: Marie acquired the certainty that the intensity of this surprising radiation was proportional to the quantity of uranium contained in the samples under examination, and that this radiation, which could be measured with precision, was not affected either by the chemical

* About 44° Fahrenheit.

state of combination of the uranium or by external factors such as lighting or temperature.

These observations were perhaps not very sensational to the uninitiated, but they were of profound interest to the scientist. It often happens in physics that an inexplicable phenomenon can be subjected, after some investigation, to laws already known, and by this very fact loses its interest for the research worker. Thus, in a badly constructed detective story, if we are told in the third chapter that the woman of sinister appearance who might have committed the crime is in reality only an honest little housewife who leads a life without secrets, we feel discouraged and cease to read.

Nothing of the kind happened here. The more Marie penetrated into intimacy with uranium rays, the more they seemed without precedent, essentially unknown. They were like nothing else. Nothing affected them In spite of their very feeble power, they had an extraordinary individuality.

Turning this mystery over and over in her head, and pointing toward the truth, Marie felt, and could soon affirm, that the incomprehensible radiation was an *atomic* property. She questioned: Even though the phenomenon had only been observed with uranium, nothing proved that uranium was the only chemical element capable of emitting such radiation. Why should not other bodies possess the same power? Perhaps it was only by chance that this radiation had been observed in uranium first, and had remained attached to uranium in the minds of physicists. Now it must be sought for elsewhere. . . .

No sooner said than done. Abandoning the study of uranium, Marie undertook to examine *all known chemical bodies*, either in the pure state or in compounds. The result was not long in appearing: compounds of another element, thorium, also emitted spontaneous rays like those of uranium and of similar intensity. The physicist had been right: the surprising phenomenon was by no means the property of uranium alone, and it became necessary to give it a distinct name. Mme Curie suggested the name of *radioactivity*. Chemical substances like uranium and thorium, endowed with this particular "radiance," were called *radio elements*.

Radioactivity so fascinated the young scientist that she never tired of examining the most diverse forms of matter, always by the same method. Curiosity, a marvellous feminine curiosity, the first virtue of a scientist, was developed in Marie to the highest degree. Instead of limiting her observation to simple compounds, salts and oxides, she wanted to assemble samples of minerals from the collection at the School of Physics and make them undergo, almost casually, for her own information, a kind of customs inspection, which is an electrometer test. Pierre approved, and chose, with her, the veined fragments, hard or crumbly, oddly shaped, which she wanted to examine.

Marie's idea was simple—sinple as the stroke of genius. At the cross-roads where Marie now stood hundreds of research workers might have remained, nonplussed for months or even years After examining all known chemical substances, and discovering—as Marie had done—the radiation of thorium, they would have continued to ask themselves in vain whence came this mysterious radioactivity. Marie, too, questioned and wondered But her surprise was translated into fruitful acts. She had used up all evident possibilities. Now she turned toward the unplumbed and the unknown.

She knew in advance what she would learn from an examination of the minerals, or rather she thought she knew. The specimens which contained neither uranium nor thorium would be revealed as totally "inactive." The others, containing uranium or thorium, would be radioactive.

Experiment confirmed this prevision. Rejecting the inactive minerals, Marie applied herself to the others and measured their radioactivity. Then came a dramatic revelation: the radioactivity was a *great deal stronger* than could have been normally foreseen by the quantity of uranium or thorium contained in the products examined!

"It must be an error in experiment," the young woman thought; for doubt is the scientist's first response to an unexpected phenomenon.

She started her measurements over again, unmoved, using the same products—repeated them ten times, twenty times; and she was forced to yield to the evidence: the quantities of uranium and thorium found in these minerals were by no means sufficient to justify the exceptional intensity of the radiation she observed.

Where did this excessive and abnormal radiation come from? Only one explanation was possible: the minerals must contain, in small quantity, a *much more powerfully radioactive substance* than uranium and thorium.

But what substance? In her preceding experiments, Marie had already examined *all known chemical elements.*

The scientist replied to the question with the sure logic and the magnificent audaciousness of a great mind: The minerals certainly contained a radioactive substance, which was at the same time a chemical element until then unknown: *a new element.*

A new element! It was a fascinating and alluring hypothesis—but still a hypothesis For the moment this powerfully radioactive substance existed only in the imagination of Marie and of Pierre. But it did exist there. It existed strongly enough to make the young woman go to see Bronya one day and tell her in a restrained, ardent voice:

"You know, Bronya, the radiation that I couldn't explain comes from a new chemical element. The element is there and I've got to find it We are sure! The physicists we have spoken to believe we have made an error in experiment and advise us to be careful. But I am convinced that I am not mistaken."

These were unique moments in her unique life. The layman forms a theatrical—and wholly false—idea of the research worker and of his discoveries. "The moment of discovery" does not always exist: the scientist's work is too tenuous, too divided, for the certainty of success to crackle out suddenly in the midst of his laborious toil like a flash of lightning, dazzling him by its fire. Marie, standing in front of her apparatus, perhaps never experienced the sudden intoxication of triumph. This intoxication was spread over several days of decisive labour, made feverish by a magnificent hope But it must have been an exultant moment when, convinced by the rigorous reasoning of her brain that she was on the trail of new matter, she confided the secret to her elder sister, her ally always. . . . Without exchanging one affectionate word, the two sisters must have lived again, in a dizzying breath of memory, their years of waiting, their mutual sacrifices, their bleak lives as students, full of hope and faith.

It was barely four years earlier that Marie had written:

Life is not easy for any of us. But what of that? We must have perseverance and, above all, confidence in ourselves. We must believe that we are gifted for something, and that this thing, at whatever cost, must be attained.

That "something" was to direct science towards a path hitherto unsuspected.

In a first communication to the Academy, presented by Professor Lippmann and published in the *Proceedings* on April 12th, 1898, "Marie Sklodovska Curie" announced the probable presence in pitch-blende ores of a new element endowed with powerful radio-activity. This was the first stage of the discovery of radium.

By the force of her own intuition the physicist had shown to herself that the wonderful substance must exist. She decreed its existence. But its incognito still had to be broken. Now she would have to verify hypothesis by experiment, isolate this material and see it. She must be able to announce with certainty: "It is there."

Pierre Curie had followed the rapid progress of his wife's experiments with passionate interest. Without directly taking part in Marie's work, he had frequently helped her by his remarks and advice. In view of the stupefying character of her results he did not hesitate to abandon his study of crystals for the time being in order to join his efforts to hers in the search for the new substance.

Thus, when the immensity of a pressing task suggested and exacted collaboration, a great physicist was at Marie's side—a physicist who was the companion of her life. Three years earlier, love had joined this exceptional man and woman together—love, and perhaps some mysterious foreknowledge, some sublime instinct for the work in common.

The available force was now doubled. Two brains, four hands, now sought the unknown element in the damp little workroom in the Rue Lhomond. From this moment onward it is impossible to distinguish each one's part in the work of the Curies. We know that Marie, having chosen to study the radiation of uranium as the subject of her thesis, discovered that other substances were also radioactive. We know that after the examination of minerals she was able to announce the existence of a new chemical element, powerfully radioactive, and that it was the capital importance of this result which decided Pierre Curie to interrupt his very different research in order to try to isolate this element with his wife. At that time—May or June 1898—a collaboration began which was to last for eight years, until it was destroyed by a fatal accident.

We cannot and must not attempt to find out what should be credited to Marie and what to Pierre during these eight years. It would be exactly what the husband and wife did not want. The personal genius of Pierre Curie is known to us by the original work he had accomplished before this collaboration. His wife's genius appears to us in the first intuition of discovery, the brilliant start; and it was to reappear to us again, solitarily, when Marie Curie the widow unflinchingly carried the weight of a new science and conducted it, through research, step by step, to its harmonious expansion. We therefore have formal proof that in the fusion of their two efforts, in this superior alliance of man and woman, the exchange was equal.

Let this certainty suffice for our curiosity and admiration. Let us not attempt to separate these creatures full of love, whose handwriting alternates and combines in the working notebooks covered with formulæ, these creatures who were to sign nearly all their scientific publications together. They were to write "We found" and "We observed"; and when they were constrained by fact to distinguish between their parts, they were to employ this moving locution:

Certain minerals containing uranium and thorium (pitchblende, chalcolite, uranite) are very active from the point of view of the emission of Becquerel rays. In a previous communication, *one of us* showed that their activity was even greater than that of uranium and thorium and stated the opinion that this effect was due to some other very active substance contained in small quantity in these minerals.

(Pierre and Marie Curie: *Proceedings of the Academy of Science*, July 18th, 1898.)

Marie and Pierre looked for this "very active" substance in an ore of uranium called pitch-blende, which in the crude state had shown itself to be four times more radioactive than the pure oxide of uranium that could be extracted from it. But the composition of this ore had been known for a long time with considerable precision. The new element must therefore be present in very small quantity or it would not have escaped the notice of scientists and their chemical analysis.

According to their calculations—"pessimistic" calculations, like those of true physicists, who always take the less attractive of two probabilities—the collaborators thought the ore should contain the new element to a maximum quantity of one per cent. They decided that this was very little. They would have been in consternation if they had known that the radioactive element they were hunting down did not count for more than a millionth part of pitch-blende ore.

They began their prospecting patiently, using a method of chemical research invented by themselves, based on radioactivity: they separated all the elements in pitch-blende by ordinary chemical analysis and then measured the radioactivity of each of the bodies thus obtained. By successive eliminations they saw the "abnormal" radioactivity take refuge in certain parts of the ore. As they went on, the field of investigation was narrowed It was exactly the technique used by the police when they search the houses of a neighbourhood, one by one, to isolate and arrest a malefactor.

But there was more than one malefactor here: the radioactivity was concentrated principally in two different chemical fractions of the pitch-blende. For M. and Mme Curie it indicated the existence of two new elements instead of one. By July 1898 they were able to announce the discovery of one of these substances with certainty.

"You will have to name it," Pierre said to his young wife, in the same tone as if it were a question of choosing a name for little Irène.

The one-time Mlle Sklodovska reflected in silence for a moment. Then, her heart turning toward her own country which had been erased from the map of the world, she wondered vaguely if the scientific event would be published in Russia, Germany and Austria—the oppressor countries—and answered timidly:

"Could we call it 'polonium'?"

In the *Proceedings of the Academy* for July 1898 we read:

We believe the substance we have extracted from pitch-blende contains a metal not yet observed, related to bismuth by its analytical properties. If the existence of this new metal is confirmed we propose to call it *polonium*, from the name of the original country of one of us.

The choice of this name proves that in becoming a Frenchwoman and a physicist Marie had not disowned her former enthusiasms. Another thing proves it for us: even before the note "On a New Radioactive Substance contained in Pitch-blende" had appeared in the *Proceedings of the Academy*, Marie had sent the manuscript to her native country, to that Joseph Loguski who directed the little laboratory at the Museum of Industry and Agriculture where she had made her first experiments. The communication was published in Warsaw in a monthly photographic review called *Swiatlo* almost as soon as it was in Paris.

Life was unchanged in the little flat in the Rue de la Glacière. Marie and Pierre worked even more than usual: that was all. When the heat of summer came, the young wife found time to buy some baskets of fruit in the markets and, as usual, she cooked and put away preserves for the winter, according to the recipes used in the Curie family. Then she locked the shutters on her windows, which gave on burnt leaves; she registered their two bicycles at the Orleans station, and, like thousands of other young women in Paris, went off on holiday with her husband and her child.

This year the couple had rented a peasant's house at Auroux, in Auvergne. Happy to breathe fresh air after the noxious atmosphere of the Rue Lhomond, the Curies made excursions to Mende, Puy, Clermont, Mont-Dore. They climbed hills, visited grottoes, bathed in rivers. Every day, alone in the country, they spoke of what they called their "new metals," polonium and "the other"— the one that remained to be found. In September they would go back to the damp workroom and the dull minerals; with freshened ardour they would take up their search again. . . .

One grief interfered with Marie's intoxication for work: the Dluskis were on the point of leaving Paris They had decided to settle in Austrian Poland and to build a sanatorium for tubercular sufferers at Zakopane in the Carpathian Mountains The day of separation arrived: Marie and Bronya exchanged broken-hearted farewells; Marie was losing her friend and protector, and for the first time she had the feeling of exile.

Marie to Bronya, December 2nd, 1898:
You can't imagine what a void you have made in my life. With you two, I have lost everything I clung to in Paris except my husband and child. It seems to me that Paris no longer exists, apart from our lodging and the school where we work

Ask Mme Dluska if the green plant you left behind should be watered, and how many times a day. Does it need a great deal of heat and sun?

We are well, in spite of the bad weather, the rain and the mud. Irène is getting to be a big girl. She is very difficult about her food, and except milk tapioca she will eat hardly anything regularly, not even eggs. Write me what would be a suitable menu for persons of her age. . . .

In spite of their prosaic character—or perhaps because of it—some notes written by Mme Curie in that memorable year 1898 seem to us worth quoting. Some are to be found in the margins of a book called *Family Cooking*, with respect to a recipe for gooseberry jelly:

I took eight pounds of fruit and the same weight in crystallised sugar. After boiling for ten minutes, I passed the mixture through a rather fine sieve. I obtained fourteen pots of very good jelly, not transparent, which "took" perfectly.

In a school notebook covered with grey linen, in which the young mother had written little Irène's weight day by day, her diet and the appearance of her first teeth, we read under the date of July 20th, 1898, some days after the publication of the discovery of polonium:

Irène says "thanks" with her hand. She can walk very well now on all fours. She says "Gogli, gogli, go" She stays in the garden all day at Sceaux on a carpet. She can roll, pick herself up, and sit down.

On August 15th, at Auroux.
Irène has cut her seventh tooth, on the lower left. She can stand for half a minute alone. For the past three days we have bathed her in the river. She cries, but to-day (fourth day) she stopped crying and played with her hands in the water.

She plays with the cat and chases him with war cries. She is not afraid of strangers any more She sings a great deal. She gets up on the table when she is in her chair.

Three months later, on October 17th, Marie noted with pride:

Irène can walk very well, and no longer goes on all fours.

On January 5th, 1899:
Irène has fifteen teeth!

Between these two notes—that of October 17th, 1898, in which Irène no longer goes on all fours, and that of January 5th, in which Irène has fifteen teeth—and a few months after the note on the gooseberry preserve, we find another note worthy of remark.

It was drawn up by Marie and Pierre Curie and a collaborator called G. Bémont Intended for the Academy of Science, and published in the *Proceedings* of the session of December 26th, 1898, it announced the existence of a second new chemical element in pitch-blende.

Some lines of this communication read as follows:

The various reasons we have just enumerated lead us to believe that the new radioactive substance contains a new element to which we propose to give the name of RADIUM.

The new radioactive substance certainly contains a very strong proportion of barium; in spite of that its radioactivity is considerable. The radioactivity of radium, therefore, must be enormous.

CHAPTER XIII

Four Years in a Shed

A MAN chosen at random from a crowd to read an account of the discovery of radium would not have doubted for one moment that radium existed: beings whose critical sense has not been sharpened and simultaneously deformed by specialised culture keep their imaginations fresh. They are ready to accept an unexpected fact, however extraordinary it may appear, and to wonder at it

The physicist colleagues of the Curies received the news in slightly different fashion. The special properties of polonium and radium upset fundamental theories in which scientists had believed for centuries. How was one to explain the spontaneous radiation of the radioactive bodies? The discovery upset a world of acquired knowledge and contradicted the most firmly established ideas on the composition of matter Thus the physicist kept on the reserve. He was violently interested in Pierre and Marie's work he could perceive its infinite developments, but before being convinced he awaited decisive results

The attitude of the chemist was even more downright. By definition, a chemist only believes in the existence of a new substance when he has seen the substance, touched it weighed and examined it, tested it with acids, bottled it, and when he has determined its "atomic weight."

Now, up to the present, nobody had *seen* radium, nobody knew its atomic weight. The chemists, faithful to their principles, therefore concluded: "No atomic weight, no radium. Show us some radium and we will believe you."

To show polonium and radium to the incredulous, to prove to

the world the existence of their "children," and to complete their own conviction, M. and Mme Curie were now to labour for four years.

The aim was to obtain pure radium and polonium. In the most strongly radioactive products which the scientists had prepared, these substances figured only in imperceptible traces. Pierre and Marie already knew the method by which they could hope to isolate the new metals, but the separation could not be made except by treating very large quantities of crude material.

Here arose three agonising questions:

How were they to get a sufficient quantity of ore? What premises could they use to effect their treatment? What money was there to meet the inevitable cost of the work?

Pitch-blende, in which polonium and radium were hidden, was a costly ore, treated at the St. Joachimsthal mines in Bohemia for the extraction of uranium salts used in the manufacture of glass. Tons of pitch-blende would cost a great deal: far too much for the Curie household.

Ingenuity was to make up for wealth. According to the expectation of the two scientists, the extraction of uranium should leave, intact in the ore, such traces of polonium and radium as the ore contains. There was no reason why these traces should not be found in the residue. And whereas crude pitch-blende was costly, its residue after treatment had very slight value. By asking an Austrian colleague for a recommendation to the directors of the mines of St Joachimsthal would it not be possible to obtain a considerable quantity of such residue for a reasonable price?

It was simple enough; but somebody had to think of it.

It was necessary, of course, to buy this crude material and pay for its transportation to Paris. Pierre and Marie appropriated the required sum from their meagre savings. They were not so foolish as to ask for official credits. . . . If two physicists on the scent of an immense discovery had asked the University of Paris or the French government for a grant to buy pitch-blende residue they would have been laughed at. In any case their letter would have been lost in the files of some office, and they would have had to wait months for a reply, probably unfavourable in the end. Out of the traditions and principles of the French Revolution, which had created the metric system, founded the Normal School, and encouraged science in many circumstances, the State seemed to have retained, after more than a century, only the deplorable words pronounced by Fouquier-Tinville at the trial in which Lavoisier was condemned to the guillotine: "The Republic has no need for scientists "

But at least could there not be found, in the numerous buildings attached to the Sorbonne, some kind of suitable workroom to lend to the Curie couple? Apparently not. After vain attempts, Pierre and Marie staggered back to their point of departure, which is to say to the School of Physics where Pierre taught, to the little room where Marie had done her first experiments. The room gave on a courtyard, on the other side of which was a wooden shack, an abandoned shed, with a skylight roof in such bad condition that it admitted the rain. The Faculty of Medicine had formerly used the place as a dissecting room, but for a long time now it had not even been considered fit for a mortuary. There was no floor and an uncertain layer of bitumen covered the earth It was furnished with some worn kitchen tables, a blackboard which had landed there for no known reason, and an old cast-iron stove with a rusty pipe.

A workman would not willingly have worked in such a place: Marie and Pierre, nevertheless, resigned themselves to it. The shed had one advantage: it was so untempting, so miserable, that nobody thought of refusing them the use of it. Schutzenberger, the director of the school, had always been very kind to Pierre Curie and no doubt regretted that he had nothing better to offer. However that may be, he offered nothing else; and the couple, very pleased at not being put out into the street with their material, thanked him, saying that "this would do" and that they would "make the best of it."

As they were taking possession of the shed, a reply arrived from Austria. Good news! By extraordinary luck, the residue of recent extractions of uranium had not been scattered The useless material had been piled up in a no-man's-land planted with pine-trees, near the mine of St. Joachimsthal. Thanks to the intercession of Professor Suess and the Academy of Science of Vienna, the Austrian government, which was the proprietor of the State factory there, decided to present a ton of residue to the two French "lunatics" who thought they needed it. If, later on, they wanted a greater quantity of the material, they could obtain it at the mine on the best terms. For the moment the Curies had to pay only the transportation charges on a ton of ore.

One morning a heavy wagon, like those which deliver coal, drew up in the Rue Lhomond before the School of Physics. Pierre and Marie were notified. They hurried bareheaded into the street in their laboratory gowns. Pierre, who was never excited, remained calm; but the more exuberant Marie could not restrain her joy at the sight of the sacks that were being unloaded. It was pitch-blende, *her* pitch-blende for which she had received a notice some days before from the freight station. Full of curiosity and impatience, she wanted to open one of the sacks and contemplate her treasure without further waiting. She cut the strings, undid the coarse sackcloth and plunged her two hands into the dull brown ore, still mixed with pine-needles from Bohemia.

That was where radium was hidden. It was from there that Marie must extract it, even if she had to treat a mountain of this inert stuff like dust on the road.

Marya Sklodovska had lived through the most intoxicating moments of her student life in a garret: Marie Curie was to know wonderful joys again in a dilapidated shed. It was a strange sort of beginning over again, in which a sharp subtle happiness (which probably no woman before Marie had ever experienced) twice elected the most miserable setting.

The shed in the Rue Lhomond surpassed the most pessimistic expectations of discomfort. In summer, because of its skylights, it was as stifling as a hothouse; in winter one did not know whether to wish for rain or frost; if it rained, the water fell, drop by drop, with a soft, nerve-racking noise, on the ground or on the work-tables, in places which the physicists had to mark in order to avoid putting apparatus there; if it froze, one froze. There was nothing to do about it. The stove, even when it was stoked high, was a complete disappointment. If one went near enough to touch it one received a little heat, but two steps away and one was back in the zone of ice.

It was almost better for Marie and Pierre to get used to the cruelty of the outside temperature, since their technical installation —hardly existent—possessed no chimneys to carry off noxious gases, and the greater part of their treatment had to be made in the open air, in the courtyard. When a shower of rain came the physicists hastily moved their apparatus inside: to keep on working without being suffocated they set up draughts between the opened door and windows.

Marie probably did not boast to Dr. Vauthier of this very peculiar cure for attacks of tuberculosis.

We had no money, no laboratory and no help in the conduct of this important and difficult task [she was to write later] It was like creating something out of nothing, and if Casimir Dluski once called my student years "the heroic years of my sister-in-law's life," I may say without exaggeration that this period was, for my husband and myself, the heroic period of our common existence.

. . . And yet it was in this miserable old shed that the best and happiest years of our life were spent, entirely consecrated to work. I sometimes passed the whole day stirring a boiling mass, with an iron rod nearly as big as myself. In the evening I was broken with fatigue.

In such conditions M. and Mme Curie worked for four years, from 1898 to 1902.

During the first year they busied themselves with the chemical separation of radium and polonium and they studied the radiation of the products (more and more active) thus obtained. Before long they considered it more practical to separate their efforts Pierre Curie tried to determine the properties of radium, and to know the new metal better; Marie continued those chemical treatments which would permit her to obtain salts of pure radium.

In this division of labour Marie had chosen the "man's job." She accomplished the toil of a day labourer. Inside the shed her husband was absorbed by delicate experiments. In the courtyard, dressed in her old dust-covered and acid-stained smock, her hair blown by the wind, surrounded by smoke which stung her eyes and throat, Marie was a sort of factory all by herself.

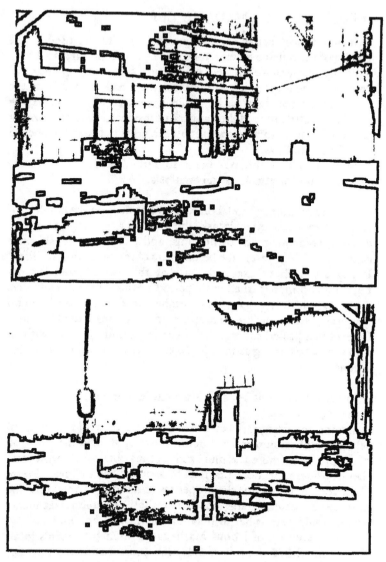

TWO VIEWS OF THE SHED AT THE SCHOOL OF PHYSICS
ON THE RUE LHOMOND WHERE RADIUM WAS
DISCOVERED

On the Blackboard in the Upper Picture Can Be Seen Pierre Curie's Writing

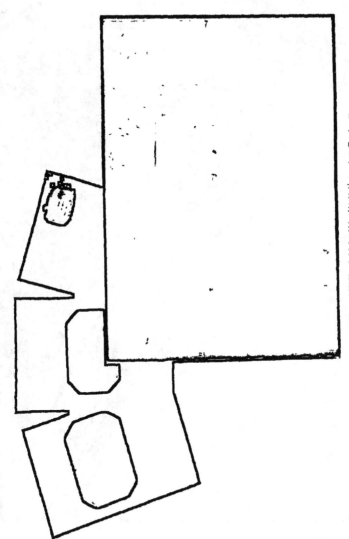

PLATE FRONT. MRH CURH'S WORK BOOKS, 1507–1516

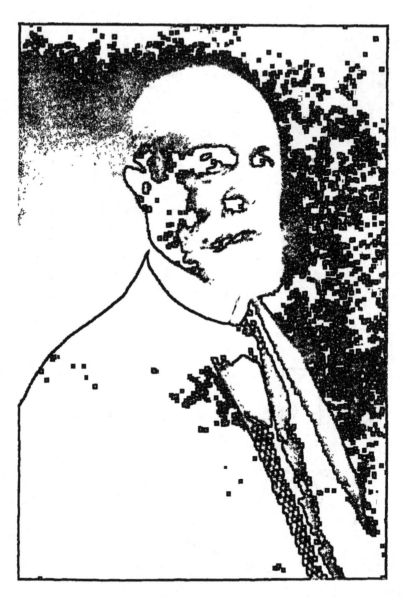

HENRI BECQUEREL
The First Scientist to Observe the Phenomenon of Radioactivity

PIERRE AND MARIE CURIE
With the Bicycles on Which, During Their Early Married Life
They Roamed the Roads of France Together

I came to treat as many as twenty kilogrammes of matter at a time [she writes], which had the effect of filling the shed with great jars of precipitates and liquids. It was killing work to carry the receivers, to pour off the liquids and to stir, for hours at a stretch, the boiling matter in a smelting basin.

Radium showed no intention of allowing itself to be known by human creatures. Where were the days when Marie naïvely expected the radium content of pitch-blende to be *one per cent?* The radiation of the new substance was so powerful that a tiny quantity of radium, disseminated through the ore, was the source of striking phenomena which could be easily observed and measured. The difficult, the impossible thing was to isolate this minute quantity, to separate it from the gangue in which it was so intimately mixed.

The days of work became months and years: Pierre and Marie were not discouraged. This material, which resisted them, which defended its secrets, fascinated them. United by their tenderness, united by their intellectual passions, they had, in a wooden shack, the "anti-natural" existence for which they had both been made, she as well as he.

At this period we were entirely absorbed by the new realm that was, thanks to an unhoped-for discovery, opening before us [Marie was to write]. In spite of the difficulties of our working conditions, we felt very happy. Our days were spent at the laboratory. In our humble shed there reigned a great tranquillity: sometimes, as we watched over some operation, we would walk up and down, talking about work in the present and in the future; when we were cold a cup of hot tea taken near the stove comforted us. We lived in our single preoccupation as if in a dream.

. . . We saw only very few persons at the laboratory; among the physicists and chemists there were a few who came from time to time, either to see our experiments or to ask for advice from Pierre Curie, whose competence in several branches of physics was well known. Then took place some conversations before the blackboard—the sort of conversation one remembers well because it acts as a stimulant for scientific interest and the ardour for work without interrupting the course of reflection and without troubling

that atmosphere of peace and meditation which is the true atmosphere of a laboratory.

Whenever Pierre and Marie, alone in this poor place, left their
apparatus for a moment and quietly let their tongues run on, their
talk about their beloved radium passed from the transcendent to
the childish

"I wonder what *It* will be like, what *It* will look like," Marie said
one day with the feverish curiosity of a child who has been promised a toy. "Pierre, what form do you imagine *It* will take?"

"I don't know," the physicist answered gently. "I should like
it to have a very beautiful colour . . ."

It is odd to observe that in Marie Curie's correspondence we
find, upon this prodigious effort, none of the sensitive comments,
decked out with imagery, which used to flash suddenly amid the
familiarity of her letters. Was it because the years of exile had
somewhat relaxed the young woman's intimacy with her people?
Was she too pressed by work to find time?

The essential reason for this reserve is perhaps to be sought
elsewhere. It was not by chance that Mme Curie's letters ceased to
be original at the exact moment when the story of her life became
exceptional. As student, teacher or young wife, Marie could tell
her story. . . . But now she was isolated by all that was secret and
inexpressible in her scientific vocation. Among those she loved
there was no longer anybody able to understand, to realise her
worries and her difficult design. She could share her obsessions
with only one person, Pierre Curie, her companion. To him alone
could she confide rare thoughts and dreams. Marie, from now on,
was to present to all others, however near they might be to her
heart, an almost commonplace picture of herself. She was to paint
for them only the bourgeois side of her life. She was to find sometimes accents full of contained emotion to express her happiness as
a woman. But of her work she was to speak only in laconic, inex-
pressive little phrases: news in three lines, without even attempting
to suggest the wonders that work meant to her. Through subtle
modesty, and also through horror of vain talk and everything
superfluous, Marie concealed herself, dug herself in; or rather, she

offered only one of her profiles. Shyness, boredom, or reason, whatever it may have been, the scientist of genius effaced and dissimulated herself behind "a woman like all others."

Marie to Bronya, 1899:

Our life is always the same. We work a lot but we sleep well, so our health does not suffer. The evenings are taken up by caring for the child In the morning I dress her and give her her food, then I can generally go out at about nine During the whole of this year we have not been either to the theatre or a concert, and we have not paid one visit. For that matter, we feel very well . . . I miss my family enormously, above all you, my dears, and Father. I often think of my isolation with grief. I cannot complain of anything else, for our health is not bad, the child is growing well, and I have the best husband one could dream of; I could never have imagined finding one like him. He is a true gift of heaven, and the more we live together the more we love each other.

Our work is progressing. I shall soon have a lecture to deliver on the subject. It should have been last Saturday, but I was prevented from giving it, so it will no doubt be this Saturday, or else in a fortnight.

This work, which is so dryly mentioned in passing, was in fact progressing magnificently. In the course of the years 1899 and 1900 Pierre and Marie Curie published a report on the discovery of "induced radioactivity" due to radium, another on the effects of radioactivity, and another on the electric charge carried by the rays And at last they drew up, for the Congress of Physics of 1900, a general report on the radioactive substances, which aroused immense interest among the scientists of Europe.

The development of the new science of radioactivity was rapid, overwhelming—the Curies needed fellow-workers. Up to now they had had only the intermittent help of a laboratory assistant named Petit, an honest man who came to work for them outside his hours of service—working out of personal enthusiasm, almost in secret. But they now required technicians of the first order. Their discovery had important extensions in the domain of chemistry, which demanded attentive study.

They wished to associate competent research workers with them.

Our work on radioactivity began in solitude [Marie was to write]. But before the breadth of the task it became more and more evident that collaboration would be useful. Already in 1898 one of the laboratory chiefs of the school, G. Bémont, had given us some temporary help. Toward 1900 Pierre Curie entered into relations with a young chemist, André Debierne, assistant in the laboratory of Professor Friedel, who esteemed him highly. André Debierne willingly accepted work on radioactivity. He undertook especially the research of a new radio element, the existence of which was suspected in the group of iron and rare clays. He discovered this element, named "actinium" Even though he worked in the physico-chemical laboratory at the Sorbonne directed by Jean Perrin, he frequently came to see us in our shed and soon became a very close friend to us, to Dr. Curie and later on to our children.

Thus, even before radium and polonium were isolated, a French scientist, André Debierne, had discovered a "brother," *actinium*.

At about the same period [Marie tells us], a young physicist, Georges Sagnac, engaged in studying X-rays, came frequently to talk to Pierre Curie about the analogies that might exist between these rays, their secondary rays, and the radiation of radioactive bodies. Together they performed a work on the electric charge carried by these secondary rays.

Marie continued to treat, kilogramme by kilogramme, the tons of pitch-blende residue which were sent her on several occasions from St. Joachimsthal. With her remarkable patience she was able to be, every day for four years, physicist, chemist, specialised worker, engineer and labouring man all at once Thanks to her brain and muscle, the old tables in the shed held more and more concentrated products—products richer and richer in radium. Mme Curie was approaching the end: she no longer stood in the courtyard, enveloped in bitter smoke, to watch the heavy basins of material in fusion. She was now at the stage of purification and of the "fractional crystallisation" of strongly radioactive solutions.

But the poverty of her haphazard equipment hindered her work more than ever. It was now that she needed a spotlessly clean workroom and apparatus perfectly protected against cold, heat and dirt. In this shed, open to every wind, iron- and coal-dust was afloat which, to Marie's despair, became mixed with the products purified with so much care. Her heart sometimes constricted before these little daily accidents, which absorbed so much of her time and her strength.

Pierre was so tired of the interminable struggle that he would have been quite ready to abandon it. Of course, he did not dream of dropping the study of radium and of radioactivity. But he would willingly have renounced, for the time being, the special operation of preparing pure radium. The obstacles seemed insurmountable. Could they not resume this work later on, under better conditions? More attached to the meaning of natural phenomena than to their material reality, Pierre Curie was exasperated to see the paltry results to which Marie's exhausting effort had led. He advised an armistice.

He counted without his wife's character. Marie wanted to isolate radium and she *would* isolate it. She scorned fatigue and difficulties, and even the gaps in her own knowledge which complicated her task. After all, she was only a very young scientist: she still had not the certainty and great culture Pierre had acquired by twenty years' work, and sometimes she stumbled across phenomena or methods of calculation of which she knew very little and for which she had to make hasty studies.

So much the worse! With stubborn eyes under her great brow, she clung to her apparatus and her test-tubes.

In 1902, forty-five months after the day on which the Curies announced the probable existence of radium, Marie finally carried off the victory in this war of attrition: she succeeded in preparing a decigramme of pure radium, and made a first determination of the atomic weight of the new substance, which was 225.

The incredulous chemists—of whom there were still a few—could only bow before the facts, before the superhuman obstinacy of a woman.

Radium officially existed.

It was nine o'clock at night. Pierre and Marie Curie were in their little house at 108 Boulevard Kellermann, where they had been living since 1900. The house suited them well. From the boulevard, where three rows of trees half hid the fortifications, could be seen only a dull wall and a tiny door. But behind the one-storey house, hidden from all eyes, there was a narrow provincial garden, rather pretty and very quiet. And from the "barrier" of Gentilly they could escape on their bicycles toward the suburbs and the woods. . . .

Old Dr. Curie, who lived with the couple, had retired to his room. Marie had bathed her child and put her to bed, and had stayed for a long time beside the cot. This was a rite. When Irène did not feel her mother near her at night she would call out for her incessantly, with that "Mé!" which was to be our substitute for "Mamma" always. And Marie, yielding to the implacability of the four-year-old child, climbed the stairs, seated herself beside her and stayed there in the darkness until the young voice gave way to light, regular breathing. Only then would she go down again to Pierre, who was growing impatient. In spite of his kindness, he was the most possessive and jealous of husbands. He was so used to the constant presence of his wife that her least eclipse kept him from thinking freely. If Marie delayed too long near her daughter, he received her on her return with a reproach so unjust as to be comic:

"You never think of anything but that child !"

Pierre walked slowly about the room. Marie sat down and made some stitches on the hem of Irène's new apron. One of her principles was never to buy ready-made clothes for the child: she thought them too fancy and impractical. In the days when Bronya was in Paris the two sisters cut out their children's dresses together, according to patterns of their own invention. These patterns still served for Marie.

But this evening she could not fix her attention. Nervous, she got up; then, suddenly:

"Suppose we go down there for a moment?"

There was a note of supplication in her voice—altogether superfluous, for Pierre, like herself, longed to go back to the shed they had left two hours before. Radium, fanciful as a living creature, endearing as a love, called them back to its dwelling, to the wretched laboratory.

The day's work had been hard, and it would have been more reasonable for the couple to rest. But Pierre and Marie were not always reasonable As soon as they had put on their coats and told Dr Curie of their flight, they were in the street. They went on foot, arm in arm, exchanging few words After the crowded streets of this queer district, with its factory buildings, wastelands and poor tenements, they arrived in the Rue Lhomond and crossed the little courtyard. Pierre put the key in the lock. The door squeaked, as it h'd squeaked thousands of times, and admitted them to their realm, to their dream.

"Don't light the lamps!" Marie said in the darkness. Then she added with a little laugh:

"Do you remember the day when you said to me: 'I should like radium to have a beautiful colour'?"

The reality was more entrancing than the simple wish of long ago. Radium had something better than "a beautiful colour"; it was spontaneously luminous. And in the sombre shed, where, in the absence of cupboards, the precious particles in their tiny glass receivers were placed on tables or on shelves nailed to the wall, their phosphorescent bluish outlines gleamed, suspended in the night.

"Look . . Look!" the young woman murmured.

She went forward cautiously, looked for and found a straw-bottomed chair. She sat down in the darkness and silence. Their two faces turned toward the pale glimmering, the mysterious sources of radiation, toward radium—their radium. Her body leaning forward, her head eager, Marie took up again the attitude which had been hers an hour earlier at the bedside of her sleeping child.

Her companion's hand lightly touched her hair.

She was to remember for ever this evening of glow-worms, this magic.

CHAPTER XIV

A Hard Life

THE existence of Pierre and Marie might have been altogether happy if they had been able to devote their strength to the impassioned struggle with nature in their poor laboratory.

Unfortunately, they had to engage in other struggles, from which they did not always emerge victorious.

For his salary of five hundred francs a month, Pierre gave a course of a hundred and twenty lessons a year at the School of Physics and directed the students' experiments. This tiring instruction, over which he took great pains, was in addition to his research work. So long as the Curies had no children and Marie could manage the domestic work herself, five hundred francs covered their expenses. But after Irène's birth the cost of a servant and a nurse made heavy inroads into the budget. First Pierre and then Marie went on the warpath: new resources had to be found.

There are few more distressing things than the awkward and unhappy attempts of these superior beings to assure themselves of the two or three thousand francs a year that they needed. The problem was not simply to find some subordinate work which would cover the deficit. Pierre Curie, as we know, considered scientific research as a vital necessity. It was more indispensable to him to work in the laboratory—or in the shed, rather, as there was no laboratory—than to eat or sleep. But his work in the school took up the greater part of his time. Rather than add other obligations to those he already possessed, the ideal would have been to lighten his task. But money was needed. What could he do?

The solution was simple—too simple. If Pierre were appointed professor at the Sorbonne, a post for which his work obviously fitted him, he would receive ten thousand francs a year, he would give fewer hours' lessons than at the school, and his scientific knowledge would enrich the students and increase the prestige of the university. And if the use of a laboratory were added to these duties, Pierre Curie would have nothing further to ask of fate. His humble ambition was contained in these words: a professor's chair for earning his living and teaching young physicists; a laboratory for work—a laboratory with all that was so cruelly missing from the shed: electrical and technical equipment, room for some assistants, a little heat in winter. . . .

Wild demands, over-ambitious dreams! Pierre was not to obtain the post of professor until 1904, after the whole world had acclaimed his worth. The laboratory was never to be accorded him. Death is quicker than public officials to claim great men.

The fact was that Pierre, so beautifully fitted for puzzling out mysterious phenomena and for the subtle struggle against hostile matter, was awkwardness itself when it came to canvassing for a place. His first disadvantage was that he had genius, which arouses secret, implacable bitterness in the competitions of personalities. He knew nothing about underhand methods or combinations. His most legitimate qualifications were of no use to him: he did not know how to make them valued.

Always ready to efface himself before his friends or even before his rivals, he was what they call a "wretchedly bad candidate" [Henri Poincaré was to write of him, adding]: But in our democracy, candidates are not what we most lack.

In 1898 a chair of physical chemistry fell vacant at the Sorbonne and Pierre Curie decided to ask for it. In equity his nomination should have been assured. But he had not gone through either the normal or the polytechnic school, and was deprived of the decisive support given by those institutions to their former students Moreover, the discoveries he had been publishing for the past fifteen years were not "exactly" in the realm of physical chemistry, certain captious professors asserted. . . . His candidature was rejected.

We are beaten [one of his partisans, Professor Friedel, wrote to him] and I should be left with nothing but regret for having encouraged you in such an unsuccessful candidature if the discussion had not been much more favourable than the vote. But in spite of the efforts of Lippmann, Bouty, Pellat and myself, in spite of the eulogies your work elicited even from your opponents, what can be done against a normal-school man and against the prejudices of mathematicians?

The fact that "the discussion had been favourable" to Pierre was a purely platonic compensation. No post of interest was vacant for months, and the Curies, absorbed by their great work on radium, preferred to muddle along rather than waste their time further in antechambers They made the best of a bad job and did not complain. Five hundred francs, after all, was not abject poverty. Life could be managed . . . badly

Marie to Joseph Sklodovski, March 19th, 1899:
We have to be very careful and my husband's salary is not quite enough for us to live on, but up to now we have had some unexpected extra resources every year, which keep us from having a deficit.

I hope, in any case, that my husband and I may soon find steady work. Then we could not only make both ends meet but also save something to ensure the future of our child I only want to pass my doctor's examination before looking for work At the moment we have so much work with our new metals that I cannot prepare for my doctorate. It is based on this work, it is true, but it requires extra study which I cannot take up at the moment.

Our health is good My husband no longer suffers as much from rheumatism since he has been on a diet consisting chiefly of milk, eggs and vegetables, doing without wine and red meat and drinking a great deal of water. I am very well; I don't cough at all, and I have nothing the matter with my lungs, as has been shown by medical examinations and several analyses of sputum

Irène is developing normally. I weaned her at eighteen months, but naturally I had been giving her milk soups for a long time. Now I feed her on such soups and on fresh eggs "straight from the hen"!

1900 . . . In the account book the expenses were rising, surpassing the income. Old Dr Curie lived with his son now, and to lodge the household—five persons, including a servant—Marie had rented the house in the Boulevard Kellermann: fourteen hundred francs rent. Driven by necessity, Pierre asked for and obtained a place as tutor in the Polytechnic School He was to receive two thousand five hundred francs a year for this drudgery.

Suddenly there came an unhoped-for offer—but not from France. The discovery of radium, without having reached the general public, was known by physicists. The University of Geneva was willing to make an exceptional effort to get a man and a woman whom it considered in the first rank of European scientists: the dean offered Pierre Curie a chair in physics, a salary of ten thousand francs, an allowance for residence, and the direction of a laboratory, "the appropriation for which will be increased by agreement with Professor Curie, and to which two assistants will be assigned. After an examination of the resources of the laboratory the collection of instruments of physics will be completed " An official position was to be accorded to Marie in the same laboratory.

Facetious on such occasions, fate allowed itself to bestow what had been desired above all things—but with one small variation that made it impossible. If the heading on the generous letter from the "Republic and Canton of Geneva" had read "University of Paris" the Curies would have been overwhelmed with happiness.

The position in Geneva was offered to Pierre with so much cordiality and deference that on first impulse he accepted it. In July he and Marie went to Switzerland and were given a warm welcome by their colleagues, but during the summer their scruples were aroused. Were they to take several months and consecrate them to the preparation of new and important teaching? To interrupt their research on radium, which was not easy to transport, and postpone their work on purification of the new substance? It was asking too much of these two scientists, two haunted ones.

Pierre Curie, sighing, sent off to Geneva a letter of excuses, thanks and resignation. He put the temptation of the easy way aside, and made up his mind to remain in Paris for the love of radium. Exchanging one task for another better paid, he left the

Polytechnic School in October for a post teaching at the P.C.N ,*
an annex of the Sorbonne in the Rue Cuvier. Marie, who wanted
to do her share of work, put in her application for a professorship
in the Higher Normal School for Girls, at Sèvres, near Versailles.
She received a letter of appointment from the vice-rector, reading:

MADAME,—

I have the honour to inform you that, on my recommendation,
you are charged with the lectures in physics for the first-and
second-year students of the Normal School at Sèvres for the school
year 1900–1901.

Will you put yourself at the disposal of the directors from
Monday next, 29th?

Here were two "successes." The budget was balanced for a long
time to come—and the Curies were burdened with an enormous
increase of work at the very moment when their experiments in
radioactivity called for all their energy. The only position worthy
of Pierre had been refused him: that of professor at the Sorbonne.
But the authorities were only too willing to entrust this master
with time-filling lessons of secondary importance.

M. and Mme Curie bent over their text-books, invented subjects
for problems, picked out experiments to make in class. Pierre now
had charge of two courses of instruction and the experimental work
of two series of students. Marie, impressed by her first steps in
French teaching, took the very greatest pains to prepare her
lectures and organise the experiments of the Sèvres girls. She
renovated the methods, and developed such original lessons that
Lucien Poincaré, rector of the university, was struck by them and
congratulated the young woman. Marie did not know how to do
things by halves.

But what energy was wasted, what hours stolen from their true
work! Carrying a portfolio crammed with corrected "home-
work," Marie made the journey to Sèvres several times a week, in a
maddeningly slow tram for which she sometimes waited half an
hour at a time, standing on the pavement. Pierre scurried from the
Rue Lhomond to the Rue Cuvier, where the P.C.N. was, and from

* Physics, Chemistry, Natural Science.

the Rue Cuvier to the shed in the Rue Lhomond. Hardly had he begun an experiment when he had to leave his apparatus to go and question the beardless physicists of the schools.

He had hoped that a laboratory would be attached to his new post. A laboratory would have consoled him for everything. But at the P.C.N. he was given only two tiny rooms. The disappointment was so great that he overcame his horror of asking for things and tried to get a larger place to work in. No success.

Those who have made similar demands [Marie was to write] know the financial and administrative difficulties one runs into, and may remember the considerable number of official letters, visits and requests which are indispensable if one is to obtain the slightest advantage. Pierre Curie was extremely tired and discouraged because of them.

The effort had an effect on the working power of the Curies and even upon their strength. Pierre, especially, felt such exhaustion that it became urgent to cut down the number of his "hours." A chair of mineralogy fell vacant at the Sorbonne just then—a chair for which the scientist who had evolved decisive theories on crystalline physics was particularly qualified. He presented himself. His competitor obtained the chair.

"With great merit and even greater modesty," Montaigne wrote, "one can remain unknown for a long time."

Pierre Curie's friends sought by all means to bring him a little nearer to that inaccessible place of professor. In 1902 Professor Mascart insisted on making Pierre present himself as a candidate for the Academy of Science. His election was certain and would be of great use afterward to his material position.

He hesitated, and then obeyed without pleasure. He found it hard to make the customary visits to the academicians, as required by a tradition which seemed to him stupid and humiliating. But the physics section of the Academy pronounced unanimously in his favour. He was touched by this and became a candidate. Duly coached by Mascart, he asked for an audience from each member of the illustrious company.

When fame had come, and journalists began to dig up striking anecdotes about the celebrated scientist, one of them was to write of Pierre Curie's round of visits in May 1902 in the following terms:

. . . To climb stairs, ring, have himself announced, say why he had come—all this filled the candidate with shame in spite of himself; but what was worse, he had to set forth his honours, state the good opinion he had of himself, boast of his science and his work—which seemed to him beyond human power. Consequently he eulogised his opponent sincerely and at length, saying that M. Amagat was much better qualified than he, Curie, to enter the Institute. . . .

On June 9th the results of the election were published. Between Pierre Curie and M. Amagat, the academicians had chosen the latter

Pierre announced the news thus to his intimate friend, Georges Gouy:

My dear friend, as you had foreseen, the election turned in favour of Amagat, who received 32 votes whereas I got 20 and Gernez 6.

I regret, when all is said, having lost time in paying visits for this brilliant result. The section had presented me at the head of the list unanimously, and I allowed them to go ahead.

. . . I tell you all this chatter because I know you rather like it, but do not believe that I am sensibly affected by these little happenings.

Your devoted
PIERRE CURIE.

The new dean, Paul Appell—whose lessons Marie had listened to with ecstasy in the old days—was soon to attempt another means of serving Pierre's interests. He knew Curie's uncompromising nature and prepared the way:

Paul Appell to Pierre Curie:
The Ministry has asked me to propose names for the Legion of Honour. You *must* be on my list. I ask you as a service to the

faculty to allow yourself to be named. I realise that the decoration has no interest for a man of your worth, but I intend to propose the men of most merit in the faculty, those who have most distinguished themselves by their discoveries and their work. It is one way of making them known to the Minister and showing how we work at the Sorbonne. If you are named, you may wear or not wear your decoration, as it may please you, naturally—but I ask of you to let me propose you.

Excuse me, dear colleague, for annoying you like this, and believe me your cordially devoted

PAUL APPELL.

Paul Appell to Marie Curie:

. . . I have spoken several times to Rector Liard of M. Curie's fine work, of the insufficiency of his equipment, and of the reasons which exist for giving him a bigger laboratory The rector spoke of M. Curie to the Minister, seizing the occasion offered by the presentations of July fourteenth for the Legion of Honour The Minister appeared to take great interest in M. Curie—perhaps he would like to show his interst, as a start, by decorating M. Curie. On this hypothesis I ask you to use all your influence to *keep M. Curie from refusing it*. The thing in itself is obviously without interest, but from the point of view of practical results (laboratories, credits, etc.) it has *considerable* worth.

I ask you to insist, in the name of science and in the highest interests of the faculty, that M. Curie allow us to name him.

This time Pierre Curie did not "submit to anything " His deep-seated aversion for honours would have been enough to justify his attitude, but he was animated by still another feeling. It seemed to him a bit too comic that a scientist should be refused the means of working and should at the same time, by way of "encouragement," of "good note," be offered a little enamelled cross hung on the end of a red silk ribbon.

His reply to the dean was as follows:

Please be so kind as to thank the Minister and to inform him that I do not feel the slightest need of being decorated, but that I am in the greatest need of a laboratory.

The hope of an easier life was abandoned. In the absence of the desired laboratory the Curies contented themselves with the shed for their experiments, and the ardent hours passed in this wooden shack consoled them for all their set-backs. They continued to teach. They did so with a good will and without bitterness. More than one boy was to remember Pierre's lessons, so clear and vivid, with gratitude; more than one Sèvres girl was to owe her love for science to Marie, the fair-haired professor whose Slavic accent made even the scientific demonstrations sing.

Torn between their own work and their jobs, they forgot to eat and sleep. The rule of "normal" life, as set up formerly by Marie, and her performances as cook and housekeeper, were forgotten. Unconscious of their folly, the pair used and abused their ebbing strength. On several occasions Pierre was obliged to take to his bed by attacks of pain, of intolerable violence, in the legs. Marie, upheld by her tense nerves, had not yet had a collapse: she considered herself invulnerable since she had cured—by scorn and daily imprudence—the attack of tuberculosis that had disquieted her family. But in the little notebook where she kept a regular record of her weight, the figure grew lower every week: in four years of work in the shed, Marie lost seven kilogrammes * The friends of the couple noticed her pallor and the emaciation of her face; one of them, a young physicist, even wrote to Pierre Curie to beg him to spare Marie's health and his own. The letter is an alarming picture of the life of the Curies, and of the way they sacrificed themselves:

Georges Sagnac to Pierre Curie:
. . . I have been struck, when I have seen Mme Curie at the Society of Physics, by the alteration in her appearance. I know very well that she is overworked because of her thesis. . . . But this is an occasion for me to observe that she has not sufficient sources of resistance to live such a purely intellectual life as that which both of you lead; and what I say of her, you can take also for yourself.

Only one example to dwell upon: you hardly eat at all, either of you. More than once I have seen Mme Curie nibble two slices of

* Fifteen pounds five ounces.

sausage and swallow a cup of tea with it. Do you think even a robust constitution would not suffer from such insufficient nourishment? What would become of you if Mme Curie lost her health?

Her own indifference or stubbornness will be no excuse for you. I foresee the following objection: "She is not hungry. She is old enough to know what she has to do!" Well, frankly, no: she is behaving at the present time like a child   I tell you this with all the conviction of my friendship.

You do not give enough time to your meals. You take them at any random hour, and in the evening you eat so late that your stomach, weakened by waiting, finally refuses to do its work. No doubt your researches may cause you to dine late one evening, but you have no right to make this into a habit. . . . It is necessary not to mix scientific preoccupations continually into every instant of your life, as you are doing. You must allow your body to breathe. You must sit down in peace before your meals and swallow them slowly, keeping away from talk about distressing things or simply things that tire the mind. You must not read or talk physics while you eat. . . .

To warnings and reproaches, Pierre and Marie answered ingenuously: "But we do rest; we take holidays in the summer."

And in fact they did so—or rather, thought they did. During the fine weather they wandered about, stage by stage, as in the old days. For them "rest" meant, in 1898, exploring the Cévennes on bicycles; two years later they followed the coast of the Channel from Havre to St. Valéry-sur-Somme, then they went off to the Ile de Noirmoutier. In 1901 we see them at Le Pouldu, in 1902 at Arromanches, in 1903 at Le Tréport and afterward at St. Trojean.

Did these journeys bring them the physical and spiritual relaxation they needed? It is permissible to doubt it. The one responsible was Pierre, who could not stay at peace: after two or three days passed in the same place he became preoccupied and absent-minded. Unable to stand it any longer, he would speak of going back to Paris and would say gently to his wife, as if to excuse himself:

"We have been doing nothing for a long time now."

In 1899 the Curies undertook a distant expedition which gave them great pleasure: for the first time since her marriage, Marie returned to her fatherland, not to Warsaw but to Zakopane in Austrian Poland, where the Dluskis were building their sanatorium. The Pension Eger, next door to the yard where the masons were at work, harboured an affectionate group. Professor Sklodovski was there, still very active, and rejuvenated by the happiness of seeing his four children and their four households united.

How the years had flown! Not long ago his son and his three daughters had been scouring Warsaw to find pupils. To-day, Joseph, a highly reputed doctor, had a wife and children. Bronya and Casimir were founding a sanatorium. Hela was making a career as a teacher, while her husband, Stanislav Szalay, directed a prosperous enterprise in photography. And little Manya was working in a laboratory and having her researches published—the dear "little rascal," as he had used to call the baby of the family.

Pierre Curie, "the foreigner," was the object of many attentions. His Poles were proud to show Poland to him At first without great enthusiasm for the severe countryside, where the dark points of pine-trees struck sharply at the sky, Pierre made an excursion to the summits of the "Rysy" and was moved by the poetry and grandeur of the high mountains. In the evening he said to his wife, in front of her family:

"This country is very beautiful. I understand now why you love it."

He purposely spoke in his brand-new Polish, which, in spite of the bad accent, dazzled his brothers-in-law and sisters-in-law; and he caught the smile of pride on Marie's glowing face.

Three years later, in May, 1902, Marie was to take the train for Poland again—but with what painful anxiety! Letters had informed her of her father's sudden illness and of an operation on his gall bladder which had resulted in the extraction of huge stones. She received reassuring news at first, and then suddenly a telegram. It was the end. Marie wanted to leave at once, but the passport formalities were complicated; hours went by before the red tape was all in order. After two and a half days' travel, she arrived in Warsaw, at Joseph's house where M. Sklodovski had been living. Too late!

Marie could not endure the thought that she was never to see that face again. She learned of her father's death during the journey, and begged her sisters by telegram to put off the funeral. She penetrated into the funereal chamber where there was nothing but the coffin and some flowers. With a strange obstinacy, she demanded that the coffin be broken open. This was done. And to the serene, lifeless face, streaked by a thin line of blood from one of the nostrils, Marie said farewell and asked for forgiveness. She had always secretly reproached herself for remaining in France, and for disappointing the old man who had counted on finishing his days with her. Before the open bier, in silence, she repented and accused herself, until her brother and sisters put an end to the painful scene.

Marie had the demon of scruple within her: she was torturing herself unjustly. The last years had been kind to her father—and kinder still because of her. The affection of his family, the satisfactions of a father and a grandfather had made M. Sklodovski forget the vicissitudes of a life without brilliance. His last and strongest joys had come to him through Marie. The discovery of polonium and radium, the startling communications signed with his daughter's name in the *Proceedings of the Academy of Science* of Paris, had been a source of intense emotion for the professor of physics, who had always been kept from making disinterested research by his daily tasks. He had followed his daughter's work stage by stage. He understood its importance and foresaw its later renown. Just recently, Marie had informed him that she had obtained, after four years of perseverance, some pure radium. And in his last letter, six days before his death, M. Sklodovski traced these words in a shaky hand which sadly deformed his fine and regular script:

And now you are in possession of salts of pure radium! If you consider the amount of work that has been spent to obtain it, it is certainly the most costly of chemical elements! What a pity it is that this work has only theoretical interest, as it seems!

Nothing new here. The weather is moderate, still rather cool. I must go back to bed now; I shall end, then, and embrace you tenderly. . . .

The happiness and pride of the good man would have been indescribable if he had been able to live another two years to learn that fame had seized upon his daughter's name, and that the Nobel Prize had been given to Henri Becquerel, to Pierre Curie and to Marie Curie, his little girl, his "Anciupecio."

Paler and thinner than ever, Marie left Warsaw. In September she was to go back to Poland. After this grief the Sklodovski "children" felt the need of gathering together, to prove that fraternal solidarity survived.

October . . . Pierre and Marie were back in the laboratory. They were tired. Marie, as she collaborated in research, was also drawing up the results of her work on the purification of radium. But she was without zest, and nothing aroused her. The terrible regimen she had inflicted on her nervous system for so long had strange repercussions: at night, slight attacks of somnambulism made her get up and walk unconsciously through the house.

The coming years were to bring unhappy events. The first was a pregnancy, accidentally interrupted. Marie took this disappointment tragically:

Marie to Bronya, August 25th, 1903:
I am in such consternation over this accident that I have not the courage to write to anybody. I had grown so accustomed to the idea of the child that I am absolutely desperate and cannot be consoled. Write to me, I beg of you, if you think I should blame this to general fatigue—for I must admit that I have not spared my strength. I had confidence in my organism, and at present I regret this bitterly, as I have paid dearly for it. The child—a little girl—was in good condition and was living. And I had wanted it so badly!

Later on, again from Poland, came bad news: Bronya's second child, a boy, had died within a few days of tubercular meningitis.

I am quite overwhelmed by the misfortune that has fallen upon the Dluskis [Marie writes to her brother]. That child was the picture of health. If, in spite of every care, one can lose a child like that, how can one hope to keep the others and bring them up? I can no longer look at my little girl without trembling with terror. And Bronya's grief tears me to pieces

These sorrows darkened Marie's life, which was undermined by another torment, the gravest of all: Pierre was not well. The violent attacks of pain to which he was subject, which the doctors —for lack of more precise signs—called rheumatism, came at frequent intervals and left him terribly weak. Shot through and through with pain, he moaned for entire nights, watched over by his frightened wife.

Just the same, Marie had to teach her classes at Sèvres; Pierre had to question his numerous students and supervise their laboratory work. And, far from the laboratory they had dreamed of in vain, the two physicists had to continue their minute experiments.

Once, and only once, Pierre allowed a complaint to escape him. He said, under his breath:

"It's pretty hard, this life that we have chosen."

Marie tried to protest. But she did not succeed in dissimulating her own anxiety. If Pierre was discouraged to this point, his strength must be leaving him. Perhaps he was affected by some terrible, implacable disease? And could she, Marie, ever conquer this dreadful fatigue? For months past, the idea of death had prowled about this woman and obsessed her.

"Pierre!"

The scientist, surprised, turned toward Marie, who had called him with distress, in a strangled voice.

"What's the matter? Darling, what is the matter with you?"

"Pierre . . . if one of us disappeared . . . the other should not survive. . . . We can't exist without each other, can we?"

Pierre shook his head slowly. Marie, in pronouncing those words of a woman in love, forgetting for an instant her mission, had made him remember that a scientist had no right to desert Science, the object of his life.

He contemplated Marie's twisted grief-stricken face for a moment. Then he said firmly:

"You are young. Whatever happens, even if one has to go on like a body without a soul, one must work just the same."

CHAPTER XV

A Doctor's Thesis

WHAT does it matter to Science if her passionate servants are rich or poor, happy or unhappy, healthy or ill? She knows that they have been created to seek and to discover, and that they will seek and find until their strength dries up at its source It is not in a scientist's power to struggle against his vocation even on his days of disgust or rebellion his steps lead him inevitably back to his laboratory apparatus.

We cannot, therefore, be surprised at the brilliance of the researches Pierre and Marie carried out successfully during these difficult years. Radioactivity grew and developed, exhausting little by little the pair of physicists who had given it life.

From 1899 to 1904 the Curies published, sometimes together and sometimes separately, or sometimes in collaboration with one of their colleagues, thirty-two scientific communications. The titles of these notes are grim, and their text bristles with diagrams and formulæ which frighten the layman Each of them, nevertheless, represents a victory. In reading the dry enumeration of the most important reports, let us think of how much curiosity, obstinacy and genius lie within them.

On the Chemical Effects of Radium Rays. Marie Curie and Pierre Curie, 1899.

On the Atomic Weight of Radiferous Barium. Marie Curie, 1900.

The New Radioactive Substances and the Rays They Emit. Marie Curie and Pierre Curie, 1900.

On Induced Radioactivity Provoked by Radium Salts. Pierre Curie and André Debierne, 1901.

The Physiological Action of Radium Rays. Pierre Curie and Henri Becquerel, 1901.

On Radioactive Bodies. Marie Curie and Pierre Curie, 1901.

On the Atomic Weight of Radium. Marie Curie, 1902.

On the Absolute Measure of Time. Pierre Curie, 1902

On Induced Radioactivity and on the Emanation of Radium. Pierre Curie, 1903.

On the Heat Spontaneously Disengaged by Radium Salts. Pierre Curie and A Laborde, 1903.

Researches on Radioactive Substances. Marie Curie, 1903.

On the Radioactivity of Gases Freed by the Water of Thermal Springs. Pierre Curie and A. Laborde, 1904.

The Physiological Action of the Emanation of Radium. Pierre Curie, Charles Bouchard and V. Balthazard, 1904

Radioactivity, born in France, rapidly conquered in foreign countries. From 1900 onwards, letters signed by the greatest names in science arrived in the Rue Lhomond from England, Germany, Austria, Denmark, all bubbling over with requests for information. The Curies thus had a continuous correspondence with Sir William Crookes, with Professors Suess and Boltzmann of Vienna, with the Danish explorer Paulsen The "parents" of radium were lavish of explanations and technical advice to their colleagues. In several countries, research workers rushed into the search for unknown radioactive elements. They hoped to achieve new discoveries. It was a fruitful pursuit, to which we owe mesothorium, radiothorium, ionium, protactinium and radio-lead.

In 1903 two English scientists, Ramsay and Soddy, demonstrated that radium continually disengaged a small quantity of a gas, helium. This was the first known example of a transformation of atoms. A little later, still in England, Rutherford and Soddy, taking up a hypothesis considered by Marie Curie as early as 1900, published a striking *Theory of Radioactive Transformation.* They affirmed that radio elements, even when they seemed to be unchangeable, were in a state of spontaneous evolution: the more rapid their rate of transformation, the more powerful their "activity."

Here we have a veritable theory of the transmutation of simple bodies, but not as the alchemists understood it [Pierre Curie was to write]. Inorganic matter must have evolved, necessarily, through the ages, and followed immutable laws.

Prodigious radium! Purified as a chloride, it appeared to be a dull-white powder, which might easily be mistaken for common kitchen salt. But its properties, better and better known, seemed stupefying. Its radiation, by which it had become known to the Curies, passed all expectation in intensity; it proved to be two million times stronger than that of uranium. Science had already analysed and dissected it, subdividing the rays into three different kinds, which traversed the hardest and most opaque matter— undergoing modification of course. Only a thick screen of lead proved to be able to stop the insidious rays in their invisible flight.

Radium had its shadow, its ghost: it spontaneously produced a singular gaseous substance, the *emanation* of radium, which was also active and destroyed itself clearly even when enclosed in a glass tube, according to rigorous law. Its presence was to be proved in the waters of numerous thermal springs.

Another defiance of the theories which seemed the immovable basis of physics was that radium spontaneously gave off heat. In one hour it produced a quantity of heat capable of melting its own weight of ice. If it was protected against external cold it grew warmer, and its temperature would go up as much as ten degrees centigrade or more above that of the surrounding atmosphere

What could it not do? It made an impression on photographic plates through black paper; it made the atmosphere a conductor of electricity and thus discharged electroscopes at a distance; it coloured the glass receivers which had the honour of containing it with mauve and violet; it corroded and, little by little, reduced to powder the paper or the cottonwool in which it was wrapped.

We have already seen that it was luminous.

This luminosity cannot be seen by daylight [Marie wrote] but it can be easily seen in half-darkness. The light emitted can be strong enough to read by, using a little of the product for light in darkness. . . .

Nor was this the end of the wonders of radium: it also gave phosphorescence to a large number of bodies incapable of emitting light by their own means.

Thus with the diamond:

The diamond is made phosphorescent by the action of radium and can so be distinguished from imitations in paste, which have very weak luminosity.

And, finally, the radiation of radium was "contagious"— contagious, like a persistent scent or a disease. It was impossible for an object, a plant, an animal or a person to be left near a tube of radium without immediately acquiring a notable "activity" which a sensitive apparatus could detect. This contagion, which interfered with the results of precise experiments, was a daily enemy to Pierre and Marie Curie.

When one studies strongly radioactive substances [Marie writes], special precautions must be taken if one wishes to be able to continue taking delicate measurements. The various objects used in a chemical laboratory, and those which serve for experiments in physics, all become radioactive in a short time and act upon photographic plates through black paper. Dust, the air of the room, and one's clothes all become radioactive. The air in the room is a conductor. In the laboratory where we work the evil has reached an acute stage, and we can no longer have any apparatus completely isolated.

Long after the death of the Curies, their working notebooks were to reveal this mysterious "activity," so that after thirty or forty years the "living activity" would still affect measuring apparatuses.

Radioactivity, generation of heat, production of helium gas and emanation, spontaneous self-destruction—how far we had travelled from the old theories on inert matter, on the immovable atom! Not more than five years before, scientists had believed our universe to be composed of defined substances, elements fixed for ever. Now it was seen that with every second of passing time radium particles were expelling atoms of helium gas from themselves and were hurling them forth with enormous force. The residue of this tiny, terrifying explosion, which Marie was to call the "cataclysm of atomic transformation," was a gaseous atom of emanation which, itself, was transformed into another radioactive body which was transformed in its turn. Thus the radio elements formed strange and cruel families in which each member was created by the spontaneous transformation of the mother substance: radium was a "descendant" of uranium, polonium a descendant of radium. These bodies, created at every instant, destroyed themselves according to eternal laws: each radio element lost half its substance in a time which was *always the same*, which was to be called its "period." To diminish itself by one half, uranium required several thousand million years, radium sixteen hundred years, the emanation of radium four days, and the "descendants" of emanation only a few seconds.

Motionless in appearance, matter contained births, collisions, murders and suicides. It contained dramas subjected to implacable fatality: it contained life and death.

Such were the facts which the discovery of radioactivity revealed. Philosophers had only to begin their philosophy all over again and physicists their physics.

The last and most moving miracle was that radium could do something for the happiness of human beings. It was to become their ally against an atrocious disease, cancer.

The German scientists Walkhoff and Giesel announced in 1900 that the new substance had certain physiological effects; Pierre Curie at once applied the technique which seemed to him most practical. Indifferent to danger, he exposed his arm to the action of radium. To his joy, a lesion appeared. He watched over it, followed its evolution and, in a report to the Academy, phlegmatically described the symptoms observed.

After the action of the rays, the skin became red over a surface of six square centimetres; the appearance was that of a burn, but the skin was not painful, or barely so. At the end of several days the redness, without growing larger, began to increase in intensity; on the twentieth day it formed scabs, and then a wound which was dressed with bandages; on the forty-second day the epidermis began to form again on the edges, working toward the centre, and fifty-two days after the action of the rays there was still a surface of one square centimetre in the condition of a wound, which assumed a greyish appearance indicating deeper mortification.

I may add that Mme Curie, in carrying a few centigrammes of very active matter in a little sealed tube, received analogous burns, even though the little tube was enclosed in a thin metallic box. One action lasting less than half an hour, in particular, produced a red spot at the end of fifteen days, which left a blister similar to that of a superficial burn and took fifteen more days to cure.

These facts show that the duration of the evolution of the changes varies with the intensity of the active rays and with the duration of the action which originally excites them.

Besides these lively effects, we have had various effects on our hands during researches made with very active products. The hands have a general tendency toward desquamation; the extremities of the fingers which have held tubes or capsules containing very active products become hard and sometimes very painful; with one of us, the inflammation of the extremities of the fingers lasted about a fortnight and ended by the scaling of the skin, but their painful sensitiveness had not yet completely disappeared at the end of two months.

Henri Becquerel, carrying a glass tube of radium in the pocket of his waistcoat, was also burned, but not because he had wished to be. Astonished and angry, he hurried to the Curies to tell them about his mishap and the exploits of their terrible "child." He declared, by way of conclusion:

"I love this radium, but I've got a grudge against it !"

Then he hastened to draw up the results of the involuntary experiment, which appeared in the *Proceedings* of June 3rd, 1901, alongside Pierre's observations.

Struck by this surprising power of the rays, Pierre studied the action of radium on animals. He collaborated with two medical men of high rank, Professors Bouchard and Balthazard. Their

conviction was soon formed: by destroying diseased cells, radium
cured growths, tumours and certain forms of cancer. This
therapeutic method was to be called Curietherapy. French
practitioners (Daulos, Wickam, Dominici, Legrais, etc) made the
first treatments of diseased persons with success, employing tubes
of emanation of radium lent by Marie and Pierre Curie.

The action of radium on the skin was studied by Dr. Daulos at
St. Louis' Hospital [Marie Curie was to write]. Radium gave
encouraging results from this point of view: the epidermis,
partially destroyed by its action, formed again in a healthy state.

Radium was *useful*—magnificently useful.
The immediate consequence of such revelations can be guessed.
The extraction of the new element no longer had merely experimental interest. It had become indispensable, salutary. A
radium *industry* was about to be born
Pierre and Marie watched over the beginning of this industry,
which could not have been created without their dv ce They
prepared with their own hands the first gramme oi radium that
saw the light—by the hands of Marie, chiefly—in treating eight
tons of pitch-blende residue at the shed behind the School of
Physics, according to a process of their invention Little by little
the magic properties of radium excited other imaginations, and the
couple found practical help in organising production on a vast
scale.
The wholesale treatment of ores was begun under the direction
of André Debierne at the Central Chemical Products Company,
which consented to effect the operation without making a profit.
In 1902 the Academy of Science awarded the Curies a credit of
20,000 francs "for the extraction of radioactive matter." They
began at once to purify five tons of ore.
In 1904, a French industrialist who was intelligent and bold,
Armet de Lisle, had the idea of founding a factory to make radium
and to furnish it to doctors for the treatment of malignant tumours.
He offered Pierre and Marie a laboratory attached to this factory,
where the scientists could successfully carry out work which the
narrow limits of their wooden shed made impracticable. The

Curies found collaborators such as F. Haudepin and Jacques Danne, to whom Armet de Lisle confided the extraction of the precious substance

Marie was never to be separated from her first gramme of radium which she bequeathed to her laboratory. It never had, and was never to have, a value other than that of her tenacious effort. When the shed had been knocked down by the wrecker's axe and Madame Curie was no more, this gramme of radium was to remain as the shining symbol of a great work and of the heroic period of two existences

The grammes which followed had a different value: a value in gold. Radium, regularly put on sale, became one of the dearest substances in the world: during these first years, it was estimated at 750,000 gold francs by gramme.

Such an aristocratic material was worth commenting upon: in January 1905 appeared the first number of a review, *Radium*, which was to treat exclusively of radioactive products.

Radium had acquired a commercial personality. It had its market value and its press. On the letter-paper of the Armet de Lisle factory was soon to be read, in big letters:

RADIUM SALTS—RADIOACTIVE SUBSTANCES
Telegraphic address: RADIUM, NOGENT-SUR-MARNE

If the fruitful work of scientists in several countries, the creation of an industry, and the first trials of a wonderful treatment for disease had been possible to accomplish, it was because a blonde young woman, carried away by her passionate curiosity, had chosen in 1897 to study Becquerel's rays as the subject of her thesis It was because she had been able to guess at the presence of a new substance and, joining her efforts to those of her husband, to prove the existence of this substance. It was, because she had succeeded in isolating pure radium.

We see this young woman on June 25th, 1903, before the blackboard in a little hall of the Sorbonne, the students' hall, reached by a twisting hidden staircase. Five years had gone by since Marie had attacked the subject of her thesis. Involved in the whirlwind of an immense discovery, she had put off her doctor's examination

again and again, as she could not find the necessary time to
assemble her material. To-day she was presenting herself before
her judges.

According to custom, she had sent the examiners, MM.
Lippmann, Bouty and Moissan, the text of the work she was
submitting for their approval: "Researches on Radioactive
Substances, by Madame Sklodovska Curie." And—incredible
event!—she had bought herself a new dress, all black, in "silk and
wool." To be exact, Bronya, who had come to Paris for the
presentation of the thesis, had made Marie ashamed of her shiny
clothes and had carried her off by force to a shop. It was Bronya
who had debated with the saleswoman, fingered the stuffs, and
decided on the alterations, without paying any attention to the
sulky, absent-minded face of her younger sister.

Did the two sisters remember that it was exactly twenty years
since, in the radiant month of June 1883, Bronya had dressed Marie
for another occasion? It was a solemn morning· little Manyusya,
dressed in black, was to receive from the hands of a Russian official
the gold medal of the Gymnasium in the Krakovsky Boulevard. . . .

Mme Curie was standing very straight. On her pale face and
rounded brow, completely bared by her fair hair brushed back in a
crest, a few lines marked the traces of the battle she had fought and
won. Physicists and chemists were crowded into the sun-filled
room where more chairs had had to be added: the exceptional
interest of the researches to be spoken of here had attracted men of
science.

Old Dr. Curie, Pierre Curie and Bronya had taken their places at
the back of the room, squeezed in between students. Near them
could be seen a group of young girls, fresh and chattering: they
were Sèvres girls, pupils of Marie, who had come to applaud their
professor.

The three examiners in evening dress sat behind a long oak table.
They took turns in asking questions of the candidate. To M.
Bouty, to Lippmann, her first master, with subtle inspired features,
and to M. Moissan, whose impressive beard seemed to go on for
ever, Marie answered in a gentle voice. Sometimes she traced the
design of an apparatus or the signs of a fundamental formula on

the blackboard with a piece of chalk. She explained the results of her research in sentences of technical dryness, with dull adjectives. But in the brains of the physicists around her, young and old, pontiffs and disciples, a transmutation of another order took place: Marie's cold words changed into a dazzling and exciting picture· that of one of the greatest discoveries of the century.

Scientists disapprove of eloquence and comments. In conferring on Marie Curie the rank of doctor, the judges gathered at the Faculty of Science were to use, in their turn, words without brilliance, to which their extreme simplicity, as one re-reads them thirty years later, gives deep emotional value

M. Lippmann, the president, pronounced the sacred formula:

"The University of Paris accords you the title of Doctor of Physical Science, with the mention '*très honorable.*'"

When the unobtrusive applause of the audience had been stilled, he simply added in friendship, with the timid voice of an old scholar:

"And in the name of the jury, Madame, I wish to express to you all our congratulations"

These austere examinations, these serious and modest ceremonies, taking place in exactly the same way for the genius of research and for the conscientious worker, are not fit subjects for irony. They have their style and their greatness.

Some time before the presentation of the thesis, and before the industrial treatment of radium had been developed in France and abroad, Pierre and Marie Curie took a decision to which they did not attach special importance, but which was to have a great influence over the rest of their lives.

By purifying pitch-blende and isolating radium Marie had invented a technique and created a process for its manufacture.

Since the therapeutic effects of radium had become known, radioactive ores were sought for everywhere. Plans for exploitation had been made in several countries, particularly in Belgium and in America. But these factories could only produce the "fabulous metal" if their engineers knew the secret of the delicate operations involved in preparing pure radium.

Pierre explained these things to his wife one Sunday morning in the little house in the Boulevard Kellermann. The postman had just brought a letter from the United States. The scientist had read it attentively, folded it up again and placed it on his desk.

"We must speak a little about our radium," he said thoughtfully. "The industry is going to be greatly extended; that is certain now. The recent cures of malignant tumours have been conclusive; in a few years the whole world will be wanting radium. Just now, in fact, this letter has come in from Buffalo—some technicians who want to exploit radium in America ask me to give them information."

"Well, then?" Marie said, taking no vivid interest in the conversation.

"Well, then, we have a choice between two solutions. We can describe the results of our research without reserve, including the processes of purification . . ."

Marie made a mechanical gesture of approval and murmured:

"Yes, naturally."

"Or else," Pierre went on, "we can consider ourselves to be the proprietors, the 'inventors' of radium. In this case it would be necessary, before publishing exactly how one worked to treat pitch-blende, to patent the technique and assure ourselves in that way of rights over the manufacture of radium throughout the world."

He made an effort to clarify the position in objective fashion. It was not his fault if, in pronouncing words with which he was only slightly familiar, such as "patent" and "assure ourselves of the rights," his voice had a hardly perceptible inflection of scorn.

Marie reflected a few seconds. Then she said:

"It is impossible. It would be contrary to the scientific spirit."

Pierre's serious face lightened. To settle his conscience, he dwelt upon it.

"I think so too. . . . But I do not want this decision to be taken lightly. Our life is hard—and it threatens to be hard for ever. We have a daughter; perhaps we may have other children. For them, and for us, this patent would represent a great deal of money, a fortune. It would be comfort made certain, and the suppression of drudgery . . ."

He mentioned, too, with a little laugh, the only thing which it was cruel for him to give up:

"We could have a fine laboratory too."

Marie's gaze grew fixed. She steadily considered this idea of gain, of material compensation. Almost at once she rejected it.

"Physicists always publish their researches completely. If our discovery has a commercial future, that is an accident by which we must not profit. And radium is going to be of use in treating disease. . . . It seems to me impossible to take advantage of that."

She made no attempt to convince her husband, she guessed that he had spoken of the patent only out of scruple. The words she pronounced with complete assurance expressed the feelings of both of them, their infallible conception of the scientist's role.

In the silence Pierre repeated, like an echo, Marie's phrase:

"No. It would be contrary to the scientific spirit."

He was appeased. He added, as if settling a question of no importance:

"I shall write to-night, then, to the American engineers, and give them the information they ask for."

In agreement with me [Marie was to write twenty years later] Pierre Curie decided to take no material profit from our discovery: in consequence we took out no patent and we have published the results of our research without reserve, as well as the processes of preparation of radium. Moreover, we gave interested persons all the information they requested. This was a great benefit to the radium industry, which was enabled to develop in full liberty, first in France and then abroad, furnishing to scientists, and doctors the products they needed. As a matter of fact, this industry is still using to-day, almost without modification, the processes which we pointed out.

The "Buffalo Society of Natural Science" has offered me, as a souvenir, a publication on the development of the radium industry in the United States, accompanied by photographic reproductions of the letters in which Pierre Curie replied most fully to the questions asked by the American engineers [1902 and 1903].

A quarter of an hour after this little Sunday-morning talk, Pierre and Marie passed the Gentilly gate on their beloved bicycles, and, pedalling at a good pace, headed for the woods of Clamart.

They had chosen for ever between poverty and fortune. In the evening they came back exhausted, their arms filled with leaves and bunches of field flowers.

CHAPTER XVI

The Enemy

THOUGH Switzerland was the first country to offer the Curies a position worthy of their merit—remember the University of Geneva's letter—their first honours came from England.

In France some scientific rewards had been given them: Pierre received the Planté Prize in 1895 and the Lacaze Prize in 1901. Marie had received the Gegner Prize three times. But no distinction of great brilliance had yet come their way when, in June 1903, the Royal Institution officially invited Pierre Curie to lecture on radium. The physicist accepted and went to London with his wife for this ceremonial.

A familiar face welcomed them, shining with friendliness and benevolence: Lord Kelvin. The illustrious old man made the success of the young couple his personal business, and was as proud of their researches as if they had been his own. He took them to see his laboratory; as they went along, he threw a paternal arm over Pierre's shoulder. With touching pleasure he showed his collaborators the present that had been brought him from Paris· it was a true physicist's present, a precious particle of radium enclosed in a glass tube.

On the evening of the lecture Lord Kelvin was seated beside Marie—the first woman who had ever been admitted to the sessions of the Royal Institution. In the crowded hall, the whole of English science gathered: Sir William Crookes, Lord Rayleigh, Lord Avebury, Sir Frederick Bramwell, Sir Oliver Lodge, Professors Dewar, Ray Lankester, Ayrton, S. P. Thompson, Armstrong. . . Speaking in French, with his slow voice, Pierre described the properties of radium. Then he asked for darkness and proceeded to make several striking experiments: by the witchcraft of radium he discharged a gold-leaf electroscope at a distance, rendered a screen of zinc sulphate phosphorescent, made impressions on photographic plates wrapped in black paper, and proved the spontaneous release of heat from the marvellous substance.

The enthusiasm aroused by that evening had its repercussion on the morrow: all London wanted to see the "parents" of radium. "Professor and Madame Curie" were invited to dinners and banquets.

At these brilliant receptions they listened to the toasts given in their honour and replied by brief words of gratitude. Pierre, dressed in the rather shiny suit of tails in which he always lectured at the P.C.N., gave, in spite of his great politeness, the impression of being elsewhere, of understanding with difficulty that these compliments were addressed to him. Marie uneasily felt thousands of glances fixed upon her—on this rarest of animals, this phenomenon: a woman physicist !

Her dress was dark, only slightly cut out at the neck; her hands, ruined by acids, were bare: there was not even a wedding ring to be seen on them Near her, over bare throats, there gleamed the finest diamonds in the empire. Marie looked upon these jewels with sincere pleasure and noticed with surprise that her husband, ordinarily so absent-minded, also had his eyes fixed on the necklaces and jewelled collars.

"I didn't even imagine that such jewels existed," she said to Pierre that evening as she was undressing. "How pretty they are!"

The physicist began to laugh.

"Do you know, during dinner, when I didn't know what to think about, I discovered a game: I calculated how many laboratories could be built with the stones that each woman present was wearing around her neck. When the time for the speeches arrived I had got up to an astronomical number of buildings."

After a few days the Curies went back to their shed They had formed solid friendships in London and planned various collaborations: Pierre was to publish soon, with his English colleague, Professor Dewar, a study on the gases released by radium bromide.

Anglo-Saxons are faithful to those whom they admire. In November 1903 a letter announced to Pierre and Marie that the Royal Society of London wished to mark its esteem of them by one of its highest awards: the Davy Medal.

Marie, who was ill, let her husband go to the ceremony without her. Pierre brought back from England a heavy gold medal on which their names were engraved. He looked for a place for the medal in their house in the Boulevard Kellermann. He handled it awkwardly; he lost and found it again. Finally, seized with a sudden inspiration, he confided it to his daughter Irène, who had never had such a gala day in her six years

When his friends came to see him, the scientist showed them the child amusing herself with the new toy.

"Irène adores her big new penny!" he said by way of conclusion.

The brilliance of two brief journeys, and a little girl playing with a golden disc: such was the prelude of the symphony which was now approaching its all-powerful crescendo.

It was from Sweden, this time, that the conductor gave the signal.

In its "solemn general meeting" of December 10th, 1903, the Academy of Science of Stockholm publicly announced that the Nobel Prize in Physics for the current year was awarded half to Henri Becquerel and half to M. and Mme Curie for their discoveries in radioactivity.

Neither of the Curies was present at the session. The French Minister received the diplomas and gold medals in their names from the King's hands. Unwell and overworked, Pierre and Marie had shrunk from the long journey in mid-winter.

Professor Aurivillius to M. and Mme Curie, November 14th, 1903:
M. AND MME CURIE,

As I have had the honour of informing you telegraphically, the Swedish Academy of Science, in its session of November 12th, decided to bestow on you half of the Nobel Prize in Physics for this year, as evidence of its appreciation of your extraordinary work in common on the Becquerel rays.

On December 10th, at the ceremonial general meeting, the decisions of the various bodies charged with the distribution of prizes—which must be kept *strictly secret* until then—will be published, and on the same occasion the diplomas and gold medals will also be distributed.

In the name of the Academy of Science, I therefore invite you to be present at this meeting to receive your prize in person.

According to Article 9 of the statute of the Nobel Foundation, you are required to make a public lecture in Stockholm during the six months following the meeting, on the subject of the work for which the prize is awarded. If you come to Stockholm at the said time, it would no doubt be best to discharge this obligation during the days immediately following the meeting, if that arrangement suits you.

Hoping that the Academy will have the great pleasure of seeing you in Stockholm, I beg of you, monsieur and madame, to accept the assurance of my distinguished regard.

Pierre Curie to Professor Aurivillius, November 19th, 1903:
Mr. SECRETARY,*

We are very grateful to the Academy of Science of Stockholm for the great honour it does us in awarding us half of the Nobel Prize for Physics. We beg you to be kind enough to transmit the expression of our gratitude and of our sincerest thanks.

It is very difficult for us to go to Sweden for the ceremonial meeting on December 10th.

We cannot go away at that time of year without greatly upsetting the teaching which is confided to each of us. If we went to the meeting we could only stay a very short time, and we should barely have time to make the acquaintance of the Swedish scientists.

Finally, Mme Curie has been ill this summer and is not yet completely recovered.

I wish to ask you to postpone the time of our journey and the lecture to a later date. We could go to Stockholm at Easter, for

* Professor Aurivillius was the *secrétaire perpétuel* of the Swedish Academy of Science, a position of great eminence and authority, which the English word "secretary" hardly conveys.

example, or, which would suit us better still, toward the middle of June.

Please accept, Mr. Secretary, the assurance of our respect.

After these phrases of official courtesy we must quote another letter—unexpected and astonishing. Written by Marie in Polish, it was addressed to her brother. The date is worthy of remark: December 11th, 1903, the day after the public meeting in Stockholm. The first day of fame!—when Marie should have been intoxicated by her triumph. Her adventure was indeed extraordinary: no woman had heretofore achieved renown in the difficult realm of science. She was the first, and for the moment the only, celebrated woman scientist in the world.

Marie Curie to Joseph Sklodovski, December 11th, 1903:
DEAR JOSEPH,

I thank both of you most tenderly for your letters. Don't forget to thank Manyusya [Joseph's daughter] for her nice letter, so well written, which gave me great pleasure. I shall answer her as soon as I have a free moment.

At the beginning of November I had a sort of influenza which left me with a slight cough. I went to see Dr. Landrieux, who examined my lungs and found nothing wrong But on the other hand, he says I am anæmic. I feel strong, just the same, and I succeed in working more now than I did in the autumn, without too much fatigue.

My husband has been to London to receive the **Davy Medal** which has been given us. I did not go with him for fear of fatigue.

We have been given half of the Nobel Prize. I do not know eaxctly what that represents; I believe it is about seventy thousand francs. For us, it is a huge sum I don't know when we shall get the money, perhaps only when we go to Stockholm. We are obliged to lecture there during the six months following December 10th.

We did not go to the ceremonial meeting because it was too complicated to arrange. I did not feel strong enough to undertake such a long journey (forty-eight hours without stopping, and more if one stops along the way) in such an inclement season, in a cold country, and without being able to stay there more than three or four days: we could not, without great difficulty, interrupt our courses for a long period

We are inundated with letters and with visits from photographers and journalists. One would like to dig into the ground somewhere to find a little peace. We have received a proposal from America to go there and give a series of lectures on our work. They ask us how much we want. Whatever the terms may be, we intend to refuse. With much effort we have avoided the banquets people wanted to organise in our honour We refuse with the energy of despair, and people understand that there is nothing to be done.

My Irène is well. She is going to a little school rather far from the house. It is very difficult in Paris to find a good school for small children.

I kiss you all tenderly, and implore you not to forget me.

"We have been given half of the Nobel Prize . . . I don't know when we shall get the money."

These words, written by a creature who had just willingly renounced wealth, assume a special value. The thunderous notoriety, the homage of Press and public, official invitations and the bridge of gold offered from America, Marie only mentions with bitter complaints. This Nobel Prize, which suddenly made of Pierre Curie and herself a famous couple, represented in her eyes one thing only: seventy thousand gold francs. It was a recompense accorded by Swedish scientists to the work of two of their colleagues, and it was not "contrary to the scientific spirit" to accept it—a unique chance of releasing Pierre from his hours of teaching, of saving his health!

On January 2nd, 1904, the blessed cheque was paid in to the branch bank in the Avenue des Gobelins, which harboured the couple's slender savings. Pierre at last could leave off teaching at the School of Physics, where an eminent physicist, Paul Langevin, his former pupil, was to replace him. The Curies engaged, at their own expense, a laboratory assistant: it was simpler and quicker than waiting for the phantom collaborators promised by the university. Marie sent twenty thousand Austrian crowns as a loan to the Dluskis, to help in the beginnings of their sanatorium, and the rest of the little fortune, which was soon to be swollen by the fifty thousand francs of the Osiris Prize, awarded half to Marie Curie and half to Edouard Branly, was evenly divided between French *rentes* and bonds of the City of Warsaw.

In the black account book can be found traces of a few other sumptuary expenses. There were presents in money and loans to Pierre's brother, to Marie's sisters—liberalities which the extreme discretion of their beneficiaries was to reduce to modest proportions. There were also subscriptions to scientific societies.

Gifts: to Polish students, to a childhood friend of Marie's, to laboratory assistants, to a Sèvres girl in need. . . . Finding in her memory the name of a very poor woman who had once lovingly taught her French—a Mlle de St. Aubin, now Mme Kozlovska, born in Dieppe, but settled and married in Poland—whose great dream was to see the land of her birth again, Marie wrote to her, invited her to France, received her in her house and paid for her journey from Warsaw to Paris and from Paris to Dieppe; the good lady was to speak of this immense unexpected joy with tears.

Marie bestowed such ingenious and subtle kindnesses judiciously, without fuss. She had no unmeasured generosities and no whims and decided to help those who needed her for as long as she lived. She wished to do so according to her means, so as to be able to continue to do so always.

She also thought of herself. She installed a modern bathroom in the house in the Boulevard Kellermann and repapered a little room which needed it. But it never entered her head to mark the occasion of the Nobel Prize by buying a new hat, and though she insisted on Pierre's leaving the School of Physics, for her part she kept on with her teaching at Sèvres. She loved her pupils and felt strong enough to continue with the lessons which assured her of a salary.

It may be thought strange to enumerate so minutely the expenses of two scientists at the moment when Fame opened her arms to them. I ought perhaps to describe the mob of the curious and of the journalists of all countries who besieged the Curie house and the shed in the Rue Lhomond; I ought to count the telegrams which piled up on the huge work-table, the newspaper articles in their thousands, and depict the physicists posing for photographers.

I have no desire to do so. I know that the commotion which was now beginning brought my parents nothing but displeasure. We must seek for their satisfactions not in such evidence but elsewhere: Pierre and Marie were happy to see their discovery appreciated at its worth by the members of the Swedish Academy, happy also to find, among the heaps of .congratulations, enthusiastic messages from a few persons whom they admired. The joy of their relations moved them, and the seventy thousand francs which lightened the burden of daily drudgery were welcome. The rest— that "rest" for which men are capable of such effort, and often of such baseness—was nothing but misery and torment to them.

A permanent misunderstanding separated them from the public which turned its sympathy towards them. The Curies reached in this year of 1903 a moment which was perhaps the most pathetic of their lives. They were at an age where genius, served by experience, could give its maximum. They had successfully accomplished, in a barrack sodden with rain, the discovery of radium which astonished the world But the mission was not finished; their brains contained the possibility of other unknown riches. They wanted to work; they had to work.

But fame took little account of the future towards which Pierre and Marie were straining. Fame leaps upon the great, hangs its full weight upon them, attempts to arrest their development. The publicity given by the Nobel Prize fixed upon the couple of research workers the attention of millions of beings, men and women, philosophers, workers, professors, business men and people in society. These millions of beings offered their praises to the Curies. But what pledges they claimed in exchange! The advantages which the scientists had presented them with in advance—the intellectual capital of the discovery, its power of help against a terrible evil—did not suffice for them. They consigned radioactivity, although it was still in an embryonic stage, to the class of acquired victories and busied themselves less with helping in its development than in savouring the picturesque details of its birth. They wished to break in upon the intimacy of the surprising

couple about whom a double genius, a transparent life and a total
disinterestedness were already creating a legend. Their eager
homage rummaged through the existence of their idols—of their
victims—and dispossessed them of the only treasures they wished
to preserve: meditation and silence.

In the newspapers of the period, along with photographs of
Pierre, or Marie ("a fair young woman, distinguished, slender in
figure"—or "a charming mother whose exquisite sensibility is
accompanied by a spirit curious about the unfathomable") of their
"adorable little girl" and of Didi, the alley cat rolled up into a
ball before the stove in the dining-room, there also appeared
eloquent descriptions of the little house and of the laboratory,
those retreats whose charm and chaste poverty the two physicists
had wished to keep for themselves. The house in the Boulevard
Kellermann became "the sages' dwelling," described as "a pretty
house, far off in the unknown and solitary Paris, in the shadow of
the fortifications, a house which harbours the intimate happiness
of two great scientists."

And the Shed rose to honour:

Behind the Panthéon, in a narrow, dark and deserted street such
as those shown in the etchings to illustrate melodramatic old
novels, the Rue Lhomond, between black and fissured houses,
beside a trembling pavement, a miserable barrack raises its wooden
wall: it is the Municipal School of Physics and Chemistry.

I went through a courtyard, a lamentable enclosure which had
endured the worst insults of time, and then through a solitary
archway where my steps re-echoed, and found myself in a soggy
blind alley where a twisted tree was dying in a corner between
wooden planks. There extended several cabins of a sort, long,
low, grassed-in, where I perceived small steady flames and glass
instruments of various forms. No noise: a deep, melancholy
silence; the echo of the town did not even enter here.

I knocked at a door chosen at random and entered a laboratory
of astonishing simplicity: the floor was of rugged beaten earth,
the walls of ruined plaster, the ceiling of rather shaky laths, and
the light came in weakly through dusty windows. A young man,
bent over a complicated piece of apparatus, lifted his head.

"M. Curie," he said, "is in there." At once he resumed his work. Minutes went by. It was cold. Drops of water were falling from a tap. Two or three gas burners were alight.

Finally there entered a tall, thin man with a bony face and a rough grey beard, wearing a battered little cap. It was M Curie.

(Echo de Paris, Paul Acker.)

Fame is an astonishing mirror, sometimes faithful, sometimes distorting like the convex glasses of an amusement park, it projects into space a thousand pictures of its chosen ones and takes possession of their least gestures to exalt them by caricature. The life of the Curies furnished fashionable cabarets with subjects for sketches; when the newspapers announced that M. and Mme Curie had accidentally lost part of their stock of radium, a skit played in a Montmartre theatre promptly showed them locked up in their shed, allowing nobody to enter, sweeping the floor themselves and comically exploring every corner of the stage to find the lost substance.

And here is how the event was told by Marie:

Marie to Joseph Sklodovski:
A great misfortune has overtaken us recently: in the course of a delicate operation with radium, we lost an important quantity of our stock, and we still cannot understand the cause of the disaster. On this account I find myself forced to put off the work on the atomic weight of radium, which I should have begun by Easter. We are both of us in consternation.

In another letter, speaking of the radium which was her only care, she writes:

Marie to Joseph Sklodovski, December 23rd, 1903:
It is possible that we may succeed in preparing a greater quantity of this luckless substance. For this we need ore and money. We have the money now, but up to the present it has been impossible for us to get the ore. We are given some hope at the moment, and we shall probably be able to buy the necessary stock which was refused us before. The manufacture will therefore

develop. But if you only knew how much time, patience and money must be spent to extract this tiny amount of radium from several tons of matter!

Such were Marie's preoccupations thirteen days after the awarding of the Nobel Prize. In the course of these thirteen days the whole world had, in its turn, made a discovery: the Curies. A "great couple"! But Pierre and Marie did not get inside the skin of these new characters.

Pierre Curie to Georges Gouy, January 22nd, 1904:

MY DEAR FRIEND,

I wanted to write to you a long time ago; excuse me if I didn't; it is because of the stupid life I am leading just now.

You have seen this sudden fad for radium This has brought us all the advantages of a moment of popularity; we have been pursued by the journalists and photographers of every country on earth; they have even gone so far as to reproduce my daughter's conversation with her nurse and to describe the black-and-white cat we have at home. Then we have received letters and visits from all the eccentrics, from all the unappreciated inventors. . . . We have had a large number of requests for money. Last of all, collectors of autographs, snobs, society people and sometimes even scientists come to see us in the magnificent establishment in the Rue Lhomond which you know With all this, there is not a moment of tranquillity in the laboratory, and a voluminous correspondence to be sent off every night. On this regime I can feel myself being overwhelmed by brute stupidity. . . .

The Curies, who had supported poverty, overwork and even the injustice of mankind without a complaint, now for the first time betrayed a strange nervousness. As their renown increased, this nervousness grew in proportion.

Pierre Curie to Charles Edouard Guillaume:

. . . We are asked for articles and lectures, and when several years have passed, the very people who are asking us for them would be astonished to see that we have done no work. . . .

Pierre Curie to Charles Edouard Guillaume, January 15th, 1904.
MY DEAR FRIEND,

My lecture will take place on February 18th; the newspapers were misinformed. To this piece of false news, I owe 200 requests for tickets, to which I have given up replying.

Absolute and *invincible* inertia regarding Flammarion's lecture. I long for calmer days passed in a quiet place, where lectures will be forbidden and newspapermen persecuted.

Marie Curie to Joseph Sklodovski, February 14th, 1904:

. . . Always a hubbub. People are keeping us from work as much as they can. Now I have decided to be brave and I receive no visitors—but they disturb me just the same. Our life has been altogether spoiled by honours and fame.

Marie Curie to Joseph Sklodovski, March 19th, 1904:
DEAR JOSEPH,

I send you my most affectionate greetings for your birthday. I wish you good health and success for all your family—and also that you may never be submerged by such a correspondence as inundates us at this moment, or by the assaults to which we are subjected.

I regret a little that I threw away the letters we received; they were instructive enough. There were sonnets and poems on radium, letters from various inventors, letters from spirits, philosophical letters. Yesterday an American wrote to ask if I would allow him to name a racehorse after me. And then, naturally, hundreds of requests for autographs and photographs. I hardly reply to these letters, but I lose time by reading them.

Pierre Curie to Georges Gouy, March 20th, 1904:

. . . As you have been able to observe, fortune favours us at the moment; but the favours of fortune do not come without numerous worries. Never have we been less at peace. There are days when we have hardly the time to breathe. And to think that we had dreamed of living like wild people, far from human beings!

Marie Curie to her cousin Henrietta, spring of 1904:
Our peaceful and laborious existence is completely disorganised:
I do not know if it will ever regain its equilibrium.

The irritation, the pessimism, and I might almost say the
bitterness of these letters are not misleading: the scientists had
lost their inner peace

The fatigue resulting from an effort which surpassed our
strength, and which had been imposed upon us by the unsatisfactory physical conditions of our work, was increased by the
invasion of publicity [Marie was to write later]. The shattering
of our voluntary isolation was a cause of real suffering to us and
had all the effects of a disaster.

By way of compensation, fame should have brought the Curies
certain advantages: the chair, the laboratory, the collaborators and
the credits so long desired. But when would these benefactions
come? Their anxious waiting was prolonged. . .

Here we touch upon one of the essential causes of Pierre's and
Marie's bitterness. France was the country where their worth had
been recognised last, and nothing less than the Davy Medal and
the Nobel Prize were required before the University of Paris
bothered to create a chair in physics for Pierre Curie. The two
scientists were saddened by this. The compensations which came
from abroad underlined the desolate conditions under which they
had successfully pursued the great discovery—conditions which
did not seem likely to change soon.

Pierre thought of the positions which had been refused him for
the past four years, and made it a point of honour to pay public
homage to the only institution which had encouraged and supported his efforts within the poor means at its disposal: the School
of Physics and Chemistry. In a lecture delivered at the Sorbonne
before a large audience he was to say, as he recalled the bareness
and magic of the old shed:

I wish to point out here that we made all our researches at the
School of Physics and Chemistry of the City of Paris.
In all scientific production the influence of the surroundings in

which work is done has a very great importance, and part of the results obtained is due to this influence. For more than twenty years I have been working at the School of Physics. Schutzenberger, the first director of this school, was an eminent man of science. I remember with gratitude that he procured the means of work for me when I was only an assistant; later on, he permitted Mme Curie to come and work with me, an authorisation which at that time, was an innovation far out of the ordinary. The present directors, MM. Lauth and Gariel, have maintained the same kindliness toward me.

The professors of the school and the pupils who have finished their studies constitute a benevolent and productive circle which was very useful to me. It is among the former pupils of the school that we found our collaborators and friends, and I am happy to be able to thank them all here.

The aversion which celebrity inspired in the Curies had still other sources besides their passion for work or their fright at the loss of time.

With Pierre, who was naturally detached, the attack of popularity encountered the resistance of principles he had always held He hated hierarchies and classifications. He found it absurd that there should be "firsts" in a class, and the decorations which grown persons coveted seemed to him as superfluous as the medals awarded children in school. This attitude, which had made him refuse the Legion of Honour, was equally his in the realm of science. He was devoid of all spirit of competition, and in the "race for discoveries" he was able to endure being beaten by his colleagues without annoyance. "What difference does it make if I didn't publish such and such a work," he had the habit of saying, "since somebody else has published it?"

This almost inhuman indifference had had a deep influence on Marie. But when she fled before the evidences of admiration it was not in order to imitate her husband and not to obey him. The war against fame was not a principle with her: it was an instinct—an irresistible timidity, a painful shrinking congealed her as soon as curious glances were fastened upon her, and even provoked disturbances which brought on dizziness and physical discomfort.

Also, her existence was too crowded with obligations for her to squander a single atom of energy uselessly. Carrying the full weight of her work, of her household, of motherhood and teaching all at once, Mme Curie advanced on her difficult road like an acrobat. Only one more "part" to play, and the equilibrium was gone: she fell from the tight rope. Wife, mother, scientist, teacher, Marie had not one second of time available for playing the part of the celebrated woman.

By differing routes, Pierre and Marie thus arrived at the same position. One might imagine that creatures who had accomplished a great work together might react to fame in different ways. Pierre might have been distant, Marie vain. . . . Nothing of the sort occurred. The two souls, like the two brains, were of equal quality. After all their trials the couple traversed this one too victoriously, and in their withdrawal from honours they remained united.

I must confess that I have sought with passion for some disobedience to a law which I found cruel. I should have liked to feel that such prodigious success, a scientific reputation without precedent for a woman, had brought my mother some moments of happiness. That this unique adventure should have made its heroine suffer constantly seemed to me too unjust, and I should have given a great deal to find at the end of a letter, in the midst of a confidence, some movement of selfish pride, a cry or a sigh of victory.

It was a childish hope. Marie, promoted to the rank of "the celebrated Mme Curie," was still to be happy at times, but only in the silence of her laboratory or the intimacy of her home. Day after day, she made herself dimmer, more effaced, more anonymous, in order to escape from those who would have dragged her on to the stage, to avoid being the "star" in whom she could never have recognised herself. For many long years, to unknown persons who came up to her, asking with insistence: "Aren't you Mme Curie?" she was to reply in a neutral voice, dominating a little spasm of fear and condemning herself to impassibility: "No, you are mistaken."

In the presence of her admirers, or of the potentates of the day, who now treated her like a sovereign, she—like her husband—

showed only astonishment, lassitude, an impatience more or less
covered over and, above all, boredom: the crushing mortal
boredom which dragged her down when people rambled on about
her discovery and her genius.

One anecdote out of a thousand sums up beautifully the response
of the Curies to what Pierre called "the favours of fortune." The
couple were dining at the Elysée Palace with President Loubet. In
the course of the evening a lady came up to Marie and asked:

"Would you like me to present you to the King of Greece?"

Marie, innocently and politely, replied in her gentle voice, all
too sincere:

"I don't see the utility of it."

She recognised the lady's stupefaction—and also, with horror,
perceived that the lady, whom she had not recognised, was, in fact,
Mme Loubet. She blushed, caught herself up, and said precipi-
tately:

"But—but—naturally, I shall do whatever you please. Just as
you please."

The Curies, who had always liked to "live like wild people,"
now had another reason for seeking solitude: they were fleeing
from the curious. More than ever they haunted isolated villages,
and if they had to pass the night in a country inn they registered
there under a false name.

But their best disguise was still their natural appearance. To
look at this tall, ungainly man, carelessly dressed, leading his
bicycle along some hollow road in Brittany, and the young woman
who accompanied him, accoutred like a peasant girl, who could
imagine them to be the laureates of the Nobel Prize?

Even the most knowing had difficulty in recognising them. An
American journalist, having cleverly followed the trail of the
physicists and found them at Le Pouldu, stopped, perplexed, in
front of their fisherman's cottage. His newspaper had sent him to
interview Mme Curie, the illustrious scientist. Where could she
be? He would have to find out from somebody. . . . From this
woman, for instance, who was sitting barefoot on the stone steps
at the door, shaking the sand out of her bathing shoes.

The woman lifted her head, fixed her ash-grey eyes on the

intruder . . . and all at once she resembled a hundred or a thousand photographs that had appeared in the Press. It was she! The reporter was stunned for a moment, and then dropped down beside Marie and drew out his notebook.

Seeing that flight was impossible, she resigned herself, and answered her interlocutor's questions by short phrases. Yes, Pierre Curie and she had discovered radium. Yes, they were continuing their work.

Meanwhile she brandished her sandals, beat them against the stone to empty them thoroughly, and then put them back on her fine bare feet scratched by rocks and brambles Magnificent occasion for a journalist! A scene of "intimacy" sketched from life, by the luckiest of chances. . . . Quickly the good reporter took advantage of it and put some questions of a less general nature. If he could get some confidences about Marie's youth, her methods of work, or the psychology of a woman devoted to research. . . .

But at that moment the surprising face was turned from him In one single sentence which she was to repeat often as a sort of motto, which depicted character, existence and vocation—a sentence which tells more than a whole book—Marie put an end to the conversation:

"In science we must be interested in things, not in persons."

CHAPTER XVI

Every Day

THE name of Curie was now a "great name." The couple were richer in money, less rich in happy moments.

Marie, especially, had lost her movements of ardour, and joy. She was not as entirely absorbed by scientific thought as Pierre. Her sensibility, her nerves were affected by the events of each day—and they responded badly

The hubbub which celebrated radium and the Nobel Prize irritated her without distracting her for an instant from the care which was poisoning her life: Pierre's illness.

Pierre Curie to Georges Gouy, January 31st, 1905:
My rheumatism is leaving me alone at the moment, but I had a violent attack this summer and had to give up going to Sweden. As you can see, we are thus completely out of favour with the Swedish Academy. The truth is that I can only keep myself in condition by avoiding all physical fatigue. My wife is in the same state as myself, and we can't dream of the long working days we used to have.

Pierre Curie to Georges Gouy, July 24th, 1905:
.   We still lead the same life, people very busy doing nothing of interest. A whole year has passed since I was able to do any work, and I have not one moment to myself. Evidently I have not yet found the way of defending us against all this frittering away of our time, and yet it is very necessary that I should do so. It is a question of life or death from the intellectual point of view.

My pains appear to come from some kind of neurasthenia rather than from true rheumatism, and I am getting better since I have been eating more suitably and taking strychnine.

Pierre Curie to Georges Gouy, September 19th, 1905:
. . . I was wrong when I told you I was in better health. I have had several new attacks and the slightest fatigue brings them on. I wonder if I shall ever be able to work seriously in the laboratory, in the state I am now in.

There was no question now of the holidays of yore, charming, imprudent and foolish, in which the couple took to the road like schoolboys. Marie had rented a little country house near Paris in the valley of Chevreuse There she cared for her husband and daughter.

Marie to Mme Jean Perrin (from St. Rémy-lès-Chevreuse):
. . . I am not very pleased with Irène, who has had a lot of trouble getting over her whooping-cough; from time to time she begins to cough again, though she has been in the country for three months. My husband is very tired; he can't go for walks, and we pass our time studying memoranda on physics and mathematics.
Irène now has a little bicycle and knows how to use it very well. She rides it in a boy's costume and is very amusing to watch.

Worn in body, and feeling, as he did, some grave menace hanging over him, Pierre was obsessed by the flight of time. Did this man, so young, fear that he was soon to die? He seemed to be competing in fleetness with an invisible enemy. He was all determination and haste; he nagged his wife affectionately and transmitted his disquiet to her. The work went on too slowly for his liking. They would have to accelerate the rhythm of the research, utilise every instant, pass more hours at the laboratory. . . .
Marie forced herself into a more intense effort, which passed the limit of her nervous resistance.
Hers was a severe fate. For twenty years—ever since the day when, as a little Polish girl of sixteen, her head filled with the memory of dances, she had come back from the country to Warsaw

to earn her bread—she had never ceased to labour. She had lived her youth in solitude, bent over manuals of physics in an icy garret; and when love came at last, it came in the guise of work.

Fusing into one single fervour her love of science and her love for a man, Marie had condemned herself to an implacable existence. Pierre's tenderness and her own were of equal power and their ideal was the same. But Pierre had had long periods of laziness in the old days, an ardent adolescence and lively passions. Marie, since she had become a woman, had never for an instant stepped aside from her task, and she would have liked sometimes to know the simple charm of living. She was a wife and mother, most tender. She dreamed of sweet respites, days of rest and carelessness.

In this she astonished and shocked Pierre. Dazzled at having discovered a companion in genius, he intended her to sacrifice herself entirely, as he sacrificed himself, to what he called "their dominating thoughts."

She obeyed him—she always obeyed—but she felt tired in body and mind. She grew discouraged and accused herself of intellectual impotence, of "stupidity." The truth was simpler: in this woman of thirty-six the sheer animal life, worn down for too long, was claiming its rights. Marie needed to cease being "Mme Curie" for some time, to forget radium—to eat, sleep and think of nothing.

This could not be. Every day brought new obligations. The year 1904 was to be exhausting—especially exhausting for Marie, who was pregnant. The only favour she asked was a brief holiday from the school at Sèvres. And in the evening, tired and heavy, coming back from the laboratory on Pierre's arm, she sometimes bought, in memory of Warsaw, a tiny portion of pressed caviar, for which she felt an irresistible, morbid longing.

When the end of her second pregnancy arrived her prostration was extreme. Apart from her husband, whose health was her torment, it seemed that she no longer loved anything; neither science nor life, not even the child which was about to be born. Bronya, who had come from Poland for the delivery, was in consternation before this new Marie, this defeated woman.

"Why am I bringing this creature into the world?" she never ceased asking. "Existence is too hard, too barren. We ought not to inflict it on innocent ones . . ."

The lying-in was painful, interminable. Finally, on December 6th, 1904, a plump baby was born, crowned with shaggy black hair. Another daughter: Eve.

Bronya's apparent calm, her sensible mind, somewhat dissipated Marie's melancholy. When she went away again she left more serenity behind her.

The smiles and antics of the new-born child, who was cared for by a nurse, enlivened the young woman. Very small children softened her to tenderness. In a grey notebook she listed, as she had done for Irène, the story of Eve's first movements and her first teeth; and as the child developed the nervous condition of the mother grew better. Relaxed by the forced rest which accompanied childbirth, Marie insensibly regained her taste for life She approached her laboratory apparatus with a pleasure she had forgotten; soon she was seen again at Sevres.

Vacillating for a moment, she had found her steady step again: she had returned to her hard road.

Everything interested her again: the house, the laboratory. She followed the events which shook her native country with passionate interest: in Russia, the Revolution of 1905 had broken out and the Poles, carried away by the mad hope of deliverance, supported the anti-Tsarist agitation.

Marie to Joseph Sklodovski, March 23rd, 1905:
I see that you have the hope that this painful trial will bring some benefit to our country. This is also Bronya's opinion and Casimir's. May that hope not be disappointed! I ardently wish for this, and think of it without ceasing. In any case I believe it is necessary to support the Revolution. I shall shortly be sending some money to Casimir for this purpose, since I cannot—alas!—be of any direct use. . . .

. . . Nothing new at home. The children are growing well. Little Eve sleeps very little, and protests energetically if I leave her lying awake in her cradle. As I am not a stoic, I carry her in my arms until she grows quiet. She does not resemble Irène. She has dark hair and blue eyes, whereas up to now Irène has rather light hair and green-brown eyes.

We are still living in the same house, and now that spring is here we are beginning to enjoy the garden. The weather is magnificent to-day, which delights us all the more as the winter was wet and disagreeable.

I resumed teaching at Sèvres on the first of February. In the afternoons I am at the laboratory, and in the mornings at home, except for two mornings a week spent at Sèvres. . . . I have a great deal of work, what with the housekeeping, the children, the teaching and the laboratory, and I don't know how I shall manage it all.

The weather was fine, Pierre felt stronger, and Marie was in better spirits. The moment had come to fulfil a duty which had been too often postponed. the visit to Stockholm and the Nobel lecture. The couple undertook the splendid journey—that journey which, in our family, was to become a tradition. . . .

On June 6th, 1905, in the name of his wife and himself, Pierre Curie spoke on radium before the Academy of Science of Stockholm. He evoked the consequences of the discovery of radium. In physics it profoundly modified the fundamental principles of mechanics. In chemistry it stirred up bold hypotheses on the source of energy which supplied the radioactive phenomena. In geology, in meteorology, it was the key to phenomena which had never been explained before. In biology, last of all, the action of radium on cancerous cells had proved efficacious.

Radium had enriched Knowledge and served the Good. But could it also serve Evil?

One may also imagine [Pierre said in concluding] that in criminal hands radium might become very dangerous, and here we may ask ourselves if humanity has anything to gain by learning the secrets of nature, if it is ripe enough to profit by them, or if this knowledge is not harmful. The example of Nobel's discoveries is characteristic: powerful explosives have permitted men to perform admirable work. They are also a terrible means of destruction in the hands of the great criminals who lead the peoples towards war

I am among those who think, with Nobel, that humanity will obtain more good than evil from the new discoveries.

The welcome given them by the Swedish scientists gave the

Curies pleasure They had been afraid of the pomp of this distant expedition. But, organised with wisdom, it proved to have unexpected attractiveness. No crowds, very few official personages. Pierre and Marie visited at will in a country which charmed them, and talked with men of science; they went home delighted.

Pierre Curie to Georges Gouy, July 24th, 1905:

. . . My wife and I have just made a very agreeable journey to Sweden. We were free of all care, and it was a rest for us. Anyhow there was hardly anybody in Stockholm in June and the official side of things was a great deal simplified by this fact.

Sweden is composed of lakes and arms of the sea, with a little land round about, pines, moraines, houses of red wood; it is a rather uniform landscape, but very pretty and restful. There was no night at all during the time of our journey, and an autumn sun shone nearly always.

Our children and my father are very well, and my wife and I are much better, although we get tired easily.

In the house in the Boulevard Kellermann, protected like a fortress against intruders, Pierre and Marie led the same simple, hidden life. The cares of housekeeping were reduced to the essentials. A charwoman did the heavy work, a maid of all work prepared the meals and brought the dishes to the table. She beheld the absorbed faces of her strange employers with amazement and waited in vain for some flattering remark on the roast or the mashed potatoes.

One day, unable to stand it any longer, the honest creature stopped before Pierre and demanded in a firm voice his opinion on the beefsteak he had just eaten with appetite. But the answer left her perplexed.

"Did I eat a beefsteak?" the scientist murmured. Then he added conciliatorily: "It's quite possible."

Even at periods of great overwork Marie reserved time for the care of her children. Her work obliged her to entrust her daughters to servants, but until she had verified on her own account that Irène and Eve had slept and eaten well, that they were washed and combed, had no colds or ills of any sort, she was never at ease.

For that matter, even if she had been less attentive Irène would have known how to remind her. Irène was a despotic child. She took jealous possession of her mother and barely allowed her to care for "the little one." In the winter Marie made long journeys across Paris to discover the pippins and bananas which her elder child consented to eat, and without which she did not dare go home.

The couple spent most of their evenings in dressing gowns and slippers, going through scientific publications or scribbling complicated calculations in their notebooks Even so, they were to be seen at exhibitions of painting, and seven or eight times a year they permitted themselves two hours at a concert or the theatre.

There were wonderful actors in Paris at the beginning of the century. Pierre and Marie watched for the occasional appearances of Eleanora Duse. The eloquence of Mounet-Sully and the art of Sarah Bernhardt touched them less than the natural playing of Julia Bartet and Jeanne Granier or the power of Lucien Guitry

They followed the "advanced" productions, which have always had the favour of university people. At the Théatre de l'Œuvre, Suzanne Desprès was playing the dramas of Ibsen and Lugné Poë was producing *The Powers of Darkness*. From these performances Pierre and Marie would come home content—and depressed for several days. The mocking smiles of Dr. Curie welcomed them. The old Voltairian, who had small liking for the morbid, fixed his azure gaze upon their long faces and never failed to say ironically:

"Don't forget that you went there for pleasure!"

A certain taste for the mysterious, combined with the eternal scientific curiosity of the Curies, led them at this period into a strange path: they were present at séances of spiritism, given with the help of the celebrated medium Eusapia Paladino. They went not as adepts but as observers They attempted lucidly to explore this dangerous region of consciousness. Pierre especially took passionate interest in such exhibitions, and in the darkness he would measure the "levitation" of objects imaginary or real. . . .

For his impartial spirit these tests were disconcerting; they had neither the rigorousness nor the honesty of laboratory experiments. Sometimes the medium obtained stupefying results, and the two scientists were quite near being convinced. But suddenly they discovered gross frauds, and scepticism was born again. Their final opinion was to remain uncertain. After a few years Marie was to abandon completely the study of such phenomena.

Pierre and Marie avoided receptions: they were never to be seen in society. But they could not always get out of official dinners or banquets in honour of foreign scientists. It therefore sometimes happened that Pierre would put off the thick woollen suit he wore every day and don his evening clothes, as Marie would put on her one evening dress

This dress, which she kept for years and years, to be transformed from time to time by a little dressmaker, was made of black grenadine bordered with ruches on a foundation of faille, or else—supreme boldness!—of white Chantilly lace mixed with black velvet. A smart woman would have looked upon it with disdain: Marie knew nothing of fashions and had no taste. But the discretion and reserve which were the very mark of her character saved her from being conspicuous and created a sort of style in her dress. When she changed her laboratory clothes, which were far from æsthetic, for an evening dress, when she wound her ash-blonde hair into a crest and timidly hung a light necklace of gold filigree about her neck, she was exquisite. Her slender body and inspired face suddenly unveiled their charm. Beside Marie, with her immense pale forehead and her powerful gaze, other women did not cease to be pretty: but many among them appeared both stupid and vulgar.

One evening, when they were going out, Pierre contemplated Marie's outlines with unusual attention—her free neck, her bare arms, so feminine and noble. A shadow of regret passed over the face of this man made stoop-shouldered by science.

"It's a pity," he murmured. "Evening dress becomes you!"

With a sigh, he added:

"But there it is, we haven't got time."

If Marie invited a few persons to their home, by any chance, she made an effort to see that the food was suitable and the house pleasing. She wandered, preoccupied, among the little carts of first fruits and vegetables in the Rue Mouffetard or the Rue d'Alésia, chose the best fruits, and gravely questioned the creamery man on the comparative quality of his cheeses. She picked out of a flower vendor's basket some bunches of roses, tulips or lilacs. . . . Back at home again, she would "make bouquets" while the maid of all work emotionally prepared to cook dishes a little more complicated than usual, and the pastry-shop man in the neighbourhood would deliver some ice-cream with great pomp. In this home of work, the most modest gathering was preceded by such a general stir. At the last moment Marie would inspect the table and rearrange the furniture.

For the Curies at last had some furniture. The family chairs, which they had refused to admit into their lodgings in the Rue de la Glacière, were welcomed in the Boulevard Kellermann. Sofas of curved mahogany, covered with shiny old velvet of watery green, one of which served as a bed for little Irène, and Restoration arm-chairs gave some human graciousness to the sitting-room covered in pale paper. But in the placid, commonplace interior, on the shelves of two high bookcases, thick volumes stood guard with the titles: *Treatise on Physics* and *Differential and Integral Calculus*.

There were some guests of note: foreign colleagues who were passing through Paris; or else Poles bringing news to Marie. Mme Curie also organised children's parties to amuse her shy Irène: a Christmas tree, decked out by her in garlands, coloured candles and gilded nuts, was to leave great memories in the younger generation.

On some occasions the house served as a setting for an even more magic spectacle than that of the illuminated tree. Mechanics placed theatre projectors and a row of electric lights in the dining-room; and after dinner, before the Curies and two or three of their friends, these lights were to caress the floating veils of a dancer who could make herself in turn a flame or a flower, a goddess or a witch.

The dancer was Loïe Fuller, the "light fairy" whose fantastic inventions enchanted Paris; a picturesque friendship united her to the two physicists. Having read in the newspapers that radium was luminous, the star of the Folies-Bergère had imagined a sensational costume, the phosphorescence of which was to puzzle the spectators. She asked the Curies for information. Her naïve letter made the scientists smile, and they revealed to Loïe how fanciful was her plan for "butterfly wings of radium."

The American dancer, applauded every night in the theatre,

astonished her kindly correspondents; she made no boast of her letter from the Curies and did not ask the physicists to come and applaud her. She wrote to Marie: "I have only one means of thanking you for having answered me. Let me dance one evening at your house, for the two of you."

Pierre and Marie accepted. An odd, badly dressed girl, with a Kalmuck face innocent of make-up, her eyes as blue as a baby's, came to their door, followed by a troop of electricians laden with material. A little worried, the couple left the room to the invaders and went off to the laboratory. And Loie laboured for hours, tried different combinations of light, and arranged the curtains and rugs she had ordered to reconstruct her enchanting spectacle in the narrow dining-room of the two professors.

The severe little house with the well-guarded gate thus welcomed a goddess from the music-halls. Loie happened to have a delicate soul. She always showed Marie Curie the rarest sort of admiration: that which asks for nothing in return, which makes itself ingenious in rendering service and giving pleasure. She came back to dance at the house in the Boulevard Kellermann in the same privacy. When they knew her better, Pierre and Marie returned her visits. At her house they met Auguste Rodin, with whom they established friendly relations. In the course of these years Pierre, Marie, Loie Fuller and Rodin could have been seen sometimes talking peaceably in the sculptor's studio among the clay and the marbles.

Seven or eight intimate friends were always welcome in the Boulevard Kellermann: André Debierne, Jean Perrin and his wife, who was Marie's best woman friend, Georges Urbain, Paul Langevin, Aimé Cotton, Georges Sagnac, Charles Edouard Guillaume, a few students from the School at Sèvres. . . . Scientists, all scientists!

On Sunday afternoons in fine weather the group would meet in the garden. Marie installed herself in the shade with her work, near Eve's baby carriage. But the mending or sewing did not keep her from following the general conversation, which, for another woman, would have been more mysterious than a discussion in Chinese.

It was the time of day when the latest gossip went the rounds: thrilling revelations about "alpha," "beta" and "gamma" rays of radium. . . Perrin, Urbain and Debierne were making research, on and off, on the origin of the energy emitted by radium. In order to explain it, it was necessary to abandon either Carnot's principle or that of the conservation of energy or the conservation of elements. Pierre suggested the hypothesis of radioactive transmutations, but Urbain exclaimed in horror. He would not hear of it, and defended his own point of view with passion And what of Sagnac's work, by the way? And what news of Marie's experiments on the atomic weight of radium? . . .

Radium, radium, radium! The magic word came up ten or twenty times, passed from tongue to tongue, and sometimes provoked a regret in Marie: chance had arranged things badly in making radium such a prodigious substance and polonium—the first element the Curies had discovered—an unstable body of secondary interest. The patriotic Marie could have wished that polonium, with its symbolic name, had drawn fame upon itself.

More human sounds at times traversed these transcendent exchanges of ideas: Dr. Curie talked politics with Debierne and Langevin, Urbain amiably chaffed Marie, criticised the severity of her dress, and reproached her with her disdain for coquetry—and the young woman, surprised at the unexpected sermon, listened speechless. Jean Perrin, abandoning atoms, the "infinitely small," lifted his enthusiastic face to the sky and, like a fervent Wagnerian, hurled forth themes from the *Rheingold* or the *Meistersinger*. At the end of the garden, a little to one side, Mme Perrin was telling a fairy story to her children, Aline and Francis, and to Irène, their playmate.

The Perrins and Curies saw each other every day: they lived in neighbouring houses and their two gardens were separated only by a trellis covered with rose vines. When Irène had something urgent to confide to her friends, she called them "to the trellis." Through these rusty bars the accomplices exchanged bits of chocolate, toys and confidences—until such time as they, too, like the grown-ups, could talk physics.

The "grown-ups," especially Pierre and Marie, were vibrating with plans. A new era opened before the Curies: France had taken notice of their existence and was thinking of supporting their efforts.

The first and indispensable stage was the nomination of Pierre to the Academy of Science. The scientist submitted himself for the second time to the ordeal of a round of visits. His adherents, fearing that he would not behave like "a good candidate," showered him with worried advice:

E. Mascart to Pierre Curie, May 22nd, 1905:
MY DEAR CURIE,—

. . . Naturally you are placed at the top of the list, without serious competitors, and the nomination is no longer in doubt.

Just the same, it is *necessary* for you to take your courage in your two hands and make a round of calls on the members of the Academy, except that you can leave a visiting card *turned down at one corner* when you don't find anybody at home Start doing this next week, and in about a fortnight the job will be finished.

E. Mascart to Pierre Curie, May 25th, 1905:

My dear Curie, arrange it *any way you like,* but before the twentieth of June you must make the sacrifice of a final round of calls on the members of the Academy, even if you have to rent a motor car by the day.

The reasons you give me are excellent in principle, but one must make some concessions to the exigencies of practice. You must also think of the fact that the title of Member of the Institute will enable you more easily to be of service to others.

On July 3rd, 1905, Pierre Curie entered the Academy—but only just ! Twenty-two scientists, fearing no doubt the injustice of making him their equal, had voted for his opponent, M. Gernez.

Pierre Curie to Georges Gouy, July 24th, 1905:

. . . I find myself in the Academy without having desired to be there and without the Academy's desire to have me. I only made one round of visits, leaving cards on the absent ones, and everybody told me it was agreed that I would have fifty votes. That's probably why I nearly didn't get in!

. . . What's the use? In that house they can do nothing simply, without intrigues. Apart from a little campaign, cleverly conducted, I had against me also the lack of sympathy of the clericals, and of those who thought I had not paid enough calls. S. asked me which academicians were going to vote for me, and I told him I did not know; that I had not asked them. "That's it," he said, "you didn't *deign* to ask!" And the rumour is put about that I am proud.

Pierre Curie to Georges Gouy, October 6th, 1905:

. . I went to the institute on Monday, but I must really say I don't know what I was doing there. I have nothing to do with any of the members, and the interest of the meetings is null. I feel very clearly that these circles are not mine.

Pierre Curie to Georges Gouy, October, 1905:
I have not yet discovered what is the use of the Academy.

Pierre, though a lukewarm admirer of the illustrious company, took the liveliest interest in the decisions taken in his favour by the university: his work depended upon them. At the beginning of 1904 the rector, Liard, had obtained for him the creation of a chair in physics. Here at last was the post, so long desired, of titular professor. Before accepting the promotion Pierre asked where would be the laboratory attached to his work.

A laboratory? What laboratory? There had been no question of a laboratory.

In a second the laureates of the Nobel Prize, parents of radium, discovered that if Pierre left his position in the P.C.N. to teach at the Sorbonne he would run the risk of being able to do no work at all. No space was offered the new professor, and the two rooms he had been using at the P.C.N would be, as was only natural, assigned to his successor. He was left with the prospect of conducting his experiments in the street.

With his accomplished pen, Pierre wrote his chiefs a polite but firm letter: since the position created for him did not bring with it either a room to work in or an appropriation for research, he had decided to give it up. He could keep on at the P.C.N.—with its

MARIE AND PIERRE CURIE,
with Their Daughter Irene, in the Garden of the House on Boulevard Kellermann, 1904

MARIE CURIE AND PIERRE CURIE
and Their Daughter Irène in the Garden of the House on Boulevard Kellermann 1908

MARIE CURIE
and her two daughters Eve and Irene in 1908

MARIE CURIE IN HER LABORATORY, 1912,
the Year Following the Award of Her Second Nobel Prize

excessive hours of teaching—the little place where he and Marie, somehow or other, could do useful work.

More palavers. Then, with a great gesture, the university at last asked the Chamber of Deputies to create a laboratory with a hundred and fifty thousand francs appropriation. The project was adopted—or almost! There was decidedly no room for Pierre at the Sorbonne, but a place with two rooms would be built in the Rue Cuvier. A credit of twelve thousand francs a year would be allotted to M. Curie, who would receive thirty-four thousand francs in addition for the cost of installation.

The naïve Pierre imagined "cost of installation" to mean that he could buy apparatus and complete his equipment. Yes, he could do so—but only when the price of the new building was subtracted from this small sum. In the mind of the public authorities, building and "cost of installation" were the same thing!

Thus the official plans shrivelled.

Pierre Curie to Georges Gouy, January 31st, 1905:
I have kept two rooms at the P.C.N., where we work, and then they are building two other rooms for me in a courtyard. They will cost twenty thousand francs, which are taken out of my appropriation for the purchase of instruments.

Pierre Curie to Georges Gouy, November 7th, 1905:
I begin my courses to-morrow, but I find myself in very bad conditions for preparing experiments: the lecture hall is at the Sorbonne and my laboratory in the Rue Cuvier. Moreover, a great many other lectures are given in the lecture hall, and I have only one morning to prepare the course there.

I am neither very well nor very ill. But I get tired easily, and I no longer have more than a very feeble capacity for work. My wife, on the contrary, leads a most active life, between her children, the school at Sèvres and the laboratory. She does not lose a minute, and attends much more regularly than I do to the progress of the laboratory, in which she passes the greater part of her day.

Slowly, the stingy State made a place for Pierre Curie within the framework of its officialdom. Workrooms for him were reluctantly yielded square foot by square foot; on an inconvenient bit of land were built two rooms which were known in advance to be insufficient.

A rich woman, moved by this paradoxical situation, offered her help to the Curies, and spoke to them of building an institute in some quiet suburb. Regaining hope, Pierre Curie confided his plans and desires to her.

Pierre Curie to Madame de X . . . February 6th, 1906:
MADAME,

Enclosed you will find the indications you asked for about the desired laboratory. These indications are not absolute, and can be modified in taking account of the situation, of the space and the resources at our disposal.

. . . We have insisted strongly on this question of a laboratory in the country because it is of capital importance for us to live with our children where we work. Children and a laboratory exact the constant presence of those who take care of them. And, for my wife especially, life is very difficult when the house and the laboratory are far from each other. At times the double task is beyond her strength.

A calm life outside of Paris would be very favourable to scientific research and the laboratories could only gain by being transferred there. On the other hand, life in the middle of the city is destructive for children, and my wife cannot decide to bring them up under such conditions.

We are extremely touched by your solicitude with respect to us.

I beg of you, madame, to accept our respectful greetings with my thanks.

This generous plan came to nothing. Eight years more of patience were required before Marie was to install radioactivity in a home worthy of it—a home which Pierre was never to see. The harrowing idea that her companion had waited in vain for his beautiful laboratory—the single ambition of his life—until the very end, was to live within her always.

Speaking of the two rooms in the Rue Cuvier, awarded *in extremis* to Pierre, she was to write:

One cannot keep one's self from feeling some bitterness at the thought that this concession was the last, and that when all is said and done, one of the best French scientists never had a suitable laboratory at his disposal although his genius had been revealed from the age of twenty. No doubt if he had lived longer he would have benefited, sooner or later, by satisfactory conditions of work —but at forty-seven years of age he was still without them. Can one imagine the regret of the enthusiastic and disinterested artisan of a great work, delayed in the realisation of his dream by the constant lack of means? And can we think without pain of the waste, above all things irreparable, of the nation's greatest good: the genius, strength and courage of its best sons?

. . . It is true that the discovery of radium was made in precarious conditions: the shed which sheltered it seems clouded in the charms of legend. But this romantic element was not an advantage: it wore out our strength and delayed our accomplishment. With better means, the first five years of our work might have been reduced to two, and their tension lessened.

Of all the Minister's decisions, one alone gave the Curies real pleasure: Pierre was to have three co-workers henceforth, a chief of laboratory work, a laboratory assistant, and a laboratory aid. The chief of laboratory work was to be Marie.

Up to now the presence of the young woman in the laboratory had only been tolerated. Marie had accomplished her researches in radium without any rank or salary. In November 1904, a steady, paid position—paid at the rate of two thousand four hundred francs a year!—gave her, for the first time, official rights in her husband's laboratory.

University of France.

Madame Curie, Doctor of Science, is named chief-of work in Physics (Chair of M. Curie) in the Faculty of Science of the University of Paris, dating from the first of November, 1904.

Madame Curie will receive in that capacity an annual salary of two thousand four hundred francs, dating from November 1st, 1904.

Farewell to the shed! Pierre and Marie moved such apparatus as remained in the old barracks to the new place in the Rue Cuvier. The old shed was dear to them; it represented such days of effort and happiness that on several occasions they were to come back, arm in arm, to see its wet walls and rotten planks again.

They adapted themselves to the new life. Pierre prepared his new course. Marie, as in the past, gave her courses at Sèvres. The couple met in the badly arranged rooms of their new realm, where André Debierne, Albert Laborde, an American, Professor Duane, and several assistants or students pursued research. They bent over the fragile structure of their experiments of the moment:

Madame Curie and I are working to dose radium with precision by the amount of emanation it gives off [Pierre Curie wrote on April 14th, 1906]. That might seem to be nothing, and yet here we have been at it for several months and are only now beginning to obtain regular results.

Madame Curie and I are working . . .
These words, written by Pierre five days before his death, express the essence and the beauty of a union which was never to be weakened. Each progress of the work, each of their disappointments and victories, was to link this husband and wife more closely together.

Have I sufficiently pointed out the charm, confidence and familiar good humour of their collaboration of genius? Ideas big and little, questions, remarks and advice were thrown back and forth at every hour of the day between Pierre and Marie. Gay compliments, too, and friendly reproaches. Between these two equals, who admired each other passionately but could never envy, there was a worker's comradeship, light and exquisite, which was perhaps the most delicate expression of their profound love.

In the laboratory in the Rue Cuvier [their assistant, Albert Laborde, recently wrote to me] I was working with a mercury apparatus. Pierre Curie was there. Mme Curie came, grew interested in a detail of the mechanism, and at first did not understand. The detail was, for that matter, very simple. Nevertheless, when the explanation was given she insisted upon refuting it.

Then Pierre Curie launched out with a happy, tender, indignant "Well, really, Marie—!" which remained in my ears, and of which I wish I could convey the nuance.

Some days later, some comrades entangled in a mathematical formula asked for help of the Master. He advised them to wait for the arrival of Mme Curie whose knowledge of integral calculus would, he said, soon get them out of the difficulty. And in fact Mme Curie found the difficult solution in a few minutes.

When Pierre and Marie were alone, an affectionate abandon softened their faces and manners. These very strong personalities, these differing characters—he calmer and dreamier, she more ardent and more human—did not oppress each other. During eleven years they had very rarely needed to rely upon those "reciprocal concessions" without which, it is said, no marriage can last. Naturally, they thought the same way, and even in the tiniest circumstances of life they acted only together.

If a friend—Mme Perrin—came to ask Pierre if she could take Irène to play with her children, he would answer with a timid and almost submissive smile: "I don't know . . . Marie is not in yet; I can't tell you without asking Marie." If Marie, ordinarily not talkative, allowed herself to discuss a scientific point fierily in a meeting of scientists, she could be seen to blush to interrupt, herself in confusion, and to turn towards her husband to give him the floor; so lively was her conviction that Pierre's opinion was a thousand times more precious than her own.

He was all I could have dreamed at the moment of our union, and more [she wrote later] My admiration for his exceptional qualities, on a level so rare and high, constantly increased, so that he sometimes seemed to me like an almost unique being, by his detachment from all vanity and from those pettinesses which one finds in one's self and in others, and which one judges with indulgence, though not without aspiring to a more perfect ideal.

Radiant weather illumined the Easter holidays in 1906. Pierre and Marie gave themselves several days of country air in their quiet house at St-Rémy-lès-Chevreuse. They resumed their country habits, went to get the milk at the near-by farm with their daughters, and Pierre laughed to see the tottering Eve, who was just fourteen months old, stubbornly attempt to follow the dried cart tracks with her awkward trot.

On Sunday, with the bells ringing afar off, the couple rode their bicycles into the woods of Port-Royal. They brought back branches of flowering mahonia and a bunch of big water ranunculi. Too tired, the next day, for another jaunt, Pierre stretched out lazily on the grass in a meadow. A light and heavenly sun slowly dissipated the morning mist which hung over the valley. Eve was squalling, while Irène, brandishing a tiny green net, pursued butterflies and greeted her rare captures with gleeful cries. She was hot; she had taken off her jumper; and Pierre and Marie, stretched out beside each other, admired the grace of their child, oddly dressed in a girl's blouse and a boy's knickers.

Either on that morning or during the evening before, calmed by the charm and silence of an intoxicating spring day, Pierre looked at his daughters capering on the grass, and at Marie, motionless beside him; he touched his wife's cheeks and fair hair and murmured: "Life has been sweet with you, Marie."

In the afternoon, taking turns at carrying Eve on their shoulders, the couple wandered slowly through the woods. They looked for the pond covered with lilies, which they had admired in the days of their great wandering, when they were first married. The pond was dry, the lilies had disappeared. Around the muddy hollow was a resplendent stiff crown of flowering gorse, brilliantly yellow. Near there, beside a road, the couple plucked violets and some periwinkles.

After a hasty dinner, Pierre took the return train in the cooler air. He left his family at St. Rémy, his only companion being the bouquet of ranunculi, which he would arrange in a glass and put on his desk in the Boulevard Kellermann.

After another day of sun and country Marie, on Wednesday night, brought Irène and Eve back to Paris, left them at home and joined Pierre in the laboratory. When she came in she saw him, standing as usual before the window of the big room, examining apparatuses. He was waiting for her. He put on his overcoat and hat, and took his wife's arm to go to Foyot's Restaurant, for the traditional dinner of the Physics Society. With colleagues whom he admired, such as Henri Poincaré, his neighbour at table, he spoke of the problems which preoccupied him just then: the measurement of the emanation of radium, the experiments in spiritism at which he had recently been present, the education of girls, upon which he had original theories, wishing to turn it resolutely in the direction of natural science

The weather had changed. One could never have believed that summer had seemed so near on the evening before. It was cold, a sharp wind was blowing, the rain beat on the glass. The pavement was soaked, slippery and shining.

CHAPTER XVIII

April 19, 1906

THURSDAY began sullenly: it was still raining, it was dark, and the Curies could not even forget the April showers by absorbing themselves in work. Pierre had to go to a luncheon of the Association of Professors in the Faculty of Science, and afterwards to his publishers', Gauthier-Villars, to correct proofs, and finally to call at the Institute. Marie had several errands to do.

In the morning's rush, the couple hardly saw each other. Pierre hailed Marie from the ground floor and asked if she was going to the laboratory. Marie, who was dressing Irène and Eve on the first floor, said she would probably not have time—but her words were lost in the noise. The front door slammed. Pierre had gone in a hurry.

While Marie was lunching with her daughters and Dr Curie, Pierre was chatting amicably with his colleagues at the Hotel des Sociétés Savantes in the Rue Danton. He enjoyed these quiet meetings where people talked shop, the Sorbonne and research work. The general conversation turned toward the accidents that occur in laboratories, and Pierre at once offered his support to a plan for limiting the dangers run by research workers.

Towards half-past two, smiling, he got up, said good-bye to his comrades, and shook hands with Jean Perrin, whom he was supposed to meet again that evening. On the threshold he looked up into the air mechanically and made a face at the clouded sky. Opening his big umbrella, he went out into the downpour and walked toward the Seine.

At Gauthier-Villars' he found closed doors: there was a strike going on. He left Gauthier-Villars', followed the Rue Dauphine, sonorous with the cries of coachmen and the screeching of tram-cars which passed along the neighbouring tracks. This overladen street in Old Paris was hopelessly encumbered. The pavement barely allowed two lines of traffic to pass, and for the numerous pedestrians at this hour of the afternoon the sidewalk was very narrow. Pierre, by instinct, sought for a free road. He walked sometimes on the stone curb, sometimes in the street itself, with the uneven step of a man who pursues his thoughts. What was he thinking of then, with his eyes concentrated and his face so grave? Of an experiment he was making? Of his friend Urbain's work, explained in the note to the Academy which he now carried in his pocket? Of Marie? . . .

He had been treading the asphalt for several minutes behind a closed cab which slowly rolled along toward the Pont Neuf. At the corner of the street and the Quai, the noise was intense: a tramcar going toward the Place de la Concorde had just passed along the river. Cutting across its route, a heavy wagon drawn by two horses emerged from the bridge and entered the Rue Dauphine at a trot.

Pierre wanted to cross the pavement and reach the other side-walk. With the sudden movement of an absent-minded man, he abandoned the shelter of the cab, the square box which had been obscuring his view, and made a few steps toward the left. But he ran into one of the horses of the wagon, which was passing the cab at that same second. The space between the two vehicles narrowed dizzily. Surprised, Pierre, in an awkward movement, attempted to hang on to the chest of the animal, which suddenly reared. The scientist's heels slipped on the wet pavement. A cry arose, made of a dozen shouts of horror: Pierre had fallen beneath the feet of the powerful horses. Pedestrians cried "Stop! Stop!" The driver pulled on the reins, but in vain: the team of horses kept on.

Pierre was down, but alive and unhurt. He did not cry out and hardly moved. His body passed between the feet of the horses without even being touched, and then between the two front wheels of the wagon. A miracle was possible. But the enormous mass, dragged on by its weight of six tons, continued for several yards more. The left back wheel encountered a feeble obstacle which it crushed in passing: a forehead, a human head. The cranium was shattered and a red, viscous matter trickled in all directions in the mud: the brain of Pierre Curie!

Policemen picked up the warm body, from which life had been taken away in a flash. They hailed several cabs in succession, but no coachman wanted to take into his carriage a dead body covered with mud and dripping with blood. Minutes passed; the curious assembled and crowded round. A thicker and thicker crowd besieged the motionless lorry, and cries of fury broke out against the driver, Louis Manin, the involuntary author of the drama. Finally, two men brought a stretcher. The dead man was laid on it, and, after an unnecessary stop in a pharmacy, was carried to the near-by police station, where his wallet was opened and his papers examined. When the rumour spread that the victim was Pierre Curie, a professor, a celebrated scientist, the tumult doubled and the police had to intervene to protect the driver Manin, threatened by many fists.

A doctor, M. Drouet, sponged the bruised face, scrutinised the open wound of the head, and counted the sixteen bony fragments of what had been, twenty minutes before, a cranium. The Faculty of Science was notified by telephone. Soon, in the obscure police station in the Rue des Grands-Augustins, a politely sympathetic commissary and secretary looked upon the bent figures of the physicist's laboratory assistant, M. Clerc, who was sobbing, and of the driver, Manin, whose red face was swollen with tears.

Between them Pierre was extended, his forehead bandaged, his face intact and open, indifferent to everything.

The wagon, twenty feet long, loaded to the brim with military uniforms, was drawn up at the door. Little by little the rain effaced the stains of blood on one of its wheels. The heavy young horses, vaguely disturbed by the absence of their master, snorted with fear and struck the pavement with their hoofs.

Misfortune charged down upon the Curie household. Motor-cars and cabs wandered, undecided, along the fortifications and stopped in the deserted boulevard. A representative of the President of the Republic rang at the door, and then, learning that "Mme Curie was not back yet," went away without delivering his message. Another ring: the dean of the faculty, Paul Appell, and Professor Jean Perrin entered the house.

Dr. Curie, who was alone in the silent house with a servant, was astonished at such important callers. He advanced toward the two men and perceived the stricken look on their faces. Paul Appell, whose mission it was to notify Marie first, kept an embarrassed silence before her father-in-law. But the tragic doubt did not long endure. The tall old man looked at these faces for another instant. Then, without asking a question, he said:

"My son is dead!"

On hearing the account of the accident his dry, wrinkled face was furrowed with the bitter tracks of a very old man's tears. His tears expressed revolt as much as grief. With vehement tenderness and despair, Dr. Curie accused his son of the absentmindedness that had cost him his life, and obstinately repeated the same heartbroken reproach: "What was he dreaming of this time?"

Six o'clock: the noise of a key turning in a lock. Marie, gay and vivid, appeared in the doorway of the room. She vaguely perceived, in the too deferential attitude of her friends, the disquieting signs of compassion. Paul Appell gave an account of the facts again. Marie remained so motionless, so fixed, that one might have supposed her to understand nothing of what they said. She did not fall into their affectionate arms; she neither moaned nor wept. She seemed as inanimate and insensible as a woman of straw. After a long, haggard silence, her lips moved at last and she asked in a low voice, hoping madly for some sort of denial:

"Pierre is dead? Dead? Absolutely dead?"

It is commonplace to say that a sudden catastrophe may transform a human being for ever. Nevertheless, the decisive influence of these minutes upon the character of my mother, upon her destiny and that of her children, cannot be passed over in silence. Marie Curie did not change from a happy young wife to an inconsolable widow. The metamorphosis was less simple and more serious. The interior tumult that lacerated Marie, the nameless horror of her wandering ideas, were too virulent to be expressed in complaints or in confidences. From the moment when those three words, "Pierre is dead", reached her consciousness, a cope of solitude and secrecy fell upon her shoulders for ever. Mme Curie, on that day in April, became not only a widow but at the same time a pitiful and incurably lonely woman.

The witnesses of the drama felt the invisible wall between her and them. Their melancholy words of comfort passed her by. With dry eyes and a face grey with pallor, she scarcely seemed to hear them and answered the most urgent questions only with difficulty. In a few laconic words she refused the autopsy which would have completed the judicial inquiry, and asked that Pierre's body be brought back to the Boulevard Kellermann. She begged her friend Mme Perrin to take in Irène for a time, she sent a brief telegram to Warsaw, saying, "Pierre dead result accident." Then she went out into the wet garden and sat down, her elbows on her knees and her head in her hands, her gaze empty. Deaf, inert, mute, she waited for her companion

First they brought her relics found in the pockets of Pierre's clothes: a fountain pen, some keys, a wallet, a watch which was still going with even its glass intact. Finally, at eight o'clock, an ambulance stopped before the house Marie climbed into it, and, in the half darkness, saw the kindly, peaceful face.

Slowly, painfully, the stretcher was edged through the narrow door André Debierne, who had gone to the police station to fetch his master, his friend, supported the lugubrious burden The dead man was lying in a room on the ground floor, and Marie remained alone with her husband. She kissed his face, his supple body, still almost warm, his hand which could still be moved She was taken by force into another room so as not to be present at the dressing of the body. She obeyed, as if unconscious, and then, seized by the idea that she had allowed herself to be robbed of these minutes, that she should not have permitted anybody else to handle these sacred remains, she came back and clung to the body.

On the following day the arrival of Jacques Curie released Marie's contracted throat and opened the floodgates of her tears. Alone with the two brothers, one living and the other annihilated, she abandoned herself at last to sobs. Then, stiffening again, she wandered through the house and asked if Eve had been washed and combed as usual. Going across the garden, she called for Irène, who was playing blocks at the Perrins', and talked to her across the railing. She said "Pe" had hurt himself badly in the head and that he needed rest. Careless, the child returned to her game.

After some weeks had passed, Marie, incapable of speaking of her woe before human beings, lost in a silence, a desert which sometimes made her cry out with horror, was to open a grey note-book and hurl on to the paper, with writing which trembled, the thoughts that were stifling her. Through these scratchy, tear-splotched pages, of which only fragments can be published, she addressed Pierre, called upon him and asked him questions. She tried to fix every detail of the drama which had separated them in order to torture herself with it for ever afterward. The brief, intimate diary—the first and the only one Marie ever kept—reflected the most tragic hours of this woman's life.

. . . Pierre, my Pierre, you are there, calm as a poor wounded man resting in sleep, with his head bandaged. Your face is sweet and serene, it is still you, lost in a dream from which you cannot escape Your lips, which I used to call greedy, are livid and colourless. Your little beard is grey. Your hair can hardly be seen, because the wound begins there, and above the forehead, on the right, the bone that has been broken can be seen. Oh! how you have suffered, how you have bled, your clothes are soaked in blood What a terrible shock your poor head has felt, your poor head that I have so often caressed in my two hands. I kissed your eyelids which you used to close so that I could kiss them, offering me your head with a familiar movement. . . .

. . . We put you into the coffin Saturday morning, and I held your head up for this move. We kissed your cold face for the last time. Then a few periwinkles from the garden on the coffin and the little picture of me that you called "the good little student" and that you loved. It is the picture that must go with you into the grave, the picture of her who had the happiness of so pleasing you that you did not hesitate to offer to share your life with her, even when you had seen her only a few times. You often told me that this was the only occasion in your life when you acted without hesitation, with the absolute conviction that you were doing well. My Pierre, I think you were not wrong. We were made to live together, and our union had to be.

Your coffin was closed and I could see you no more. I didn't allow them to cover it with the horrible black cloth. I covered it with flowers and I sat beside it.

. . . They came to get you, a sad company; I looked at them, and did not speak to them. We took you back to Sceaux, and we saw you go down into the big deep hole. Then the dreadful procession of people. They wanted to take us away. Jacques and I resisted. We wanted to see everything to the end. They filled the grave and put sheaves of flowers on it. Everything is over, Pierre is sleeping his last sleep beneath the earth, it is the end of everything, everything, everything.

Marie had lost her companion, and the world had lost a great man. This atrocious departure, in the rain and mud, had struck the popular imagination. The newspapers of all countries described in pathetic stories, over several columns, the accident in the Rue Dauphine. Messages of sympathy accumulated in the house in the Boulevard Kellermann, with the names of kings, ministers, poets and scientists mixed with obscure names. Among these bundles of letters, articles, telegrams, are to be found some cries of true emotion:

Lord Kelvin:
Grievously distressed by terrible news of Curie death. When will funeral be? We arrive Hotel Mirabeau to-morrow morning.

Marcelin Berthelot:
. . . We have been struck by this terrible news as if by lightning. So many services already rendered to science and humanity, so many services that we expected from this discoverer of genius——! All that vanished in an instant, or already passed into the state of memory!

G. Lippmann:
It seems to me that I have lost a brother: I did not know by what bonds I was attached to your husband, but I know it to-day.
I suffer also for you, madame.

Charles Cheveneau, Pierre Curie's laboratory assistant:

Some of us had developed a true cult for him. For me he was, after my own family, one of the men I loved most; such had been the great and delicate affection with which he knew how to surround his modest collaborator. And his immense kindness extended even to his humblest servants, who adored him: I have never seen sincerer or more harrowing tears than those shed by his laboratory attendants at the news of his sudden decease.

On this occasion, as on all others, the woman who was to be known hereafter as an "illustrious widow" fled from the attacks of fame. To avoid an official ceremony, Marie advanced the date of the funeral to Saturday, April 21st. She refused processions, delegations and speeches, and asked that Pierre be buried as simply as possible in the grave where his mother rested at Sceaux. Aristide Briand, then Minister of Public Instruction, nevertheless defied orders: in a gesture of generosity he joined the relations and intimates of the Curies and accompanied Pierre's body in silence to the far-off little suburban cemetery.

Journalists, concealed behind the tombstones, watched the figure of Marie hidden under thick mourning veils:

. . . Mme Curie, on her father-in-law's arm, followed her husband's coffin to the grave hollowed out at the foot of the wall of the enclosure in the shadow of the chestnut trees. There she remained motionless for a moment, always with the same fixed, hard gaze; but when a sheaf of flowers was brought near the grave, she seized it with a sudden movement and began to detach the flowers one by one to scatter them on the coffin.

She did this slowly, composedly, and seemed to have totally forgotten the watchers, who, profoundly moved made no noise, no murmur.

The master of ceremonies, nevertheless, thought he must ask Mme Curie to receive the condolences of the persons present. Then, allowing the bouquet she held to fall to the earth, she left the cemetery without saying a word and rejoined her father-in-law.

(*Le Journal*, April 22nd, 1906.)

During the following days, eulogies of the vanished scientist were pronounced at the Sorbonne and in the French and foreign scientific societies which counted Pierre Curie among their members. Henri Poincaré exalted the memory of his friend at the Academy of Science:

All those who knew Pierre Curie know the pleasantness and steadiness of his friendship, the delicate charm which exhaled, so to speak, from his gentle modesty, his candid uprightness, and the fineness of his mind.

Who could have believed that so much gentleness concealed an uncompromising soul? He did not compromise with the generous principles upon which he had been nourished, or with the special moral ideal he had been taught to love, that ideal of absolute sincerity, too high, perhaps, for the world in which we live. He did not know the thousand little accommodations with which our weakness contents itself. He did not separate the cult of this ideal from that which he rendered to science, and he has shown us by a brilliant example what a high conception of duty can come out of the simple and pure love of truth. It matters little what god one believes in; it is the faith, and not the god, that makes miracles.

Marie's diary:
    . . . The day after the burial I told Irène everything; she was at the Perrins'. . . . She did not understand, at first, and let me go away without saying anything; but afterward, it seems, she wept and asked to see us. She cried a great deal at home, and then she went off to her little friends to forget. She did not ask for any detail and at first was afraid to speak of her father. She made great worried eyes over the black clothes that were brought to me. . . . Now she no longer seems to think of it at all.
    Arrival of Joseph and Bronya. They are good, Irène plays with her uncles; Eve, who toddled about the house with unconscious gaiety all through these events, plays and laughs; everybody talks. And I see Pierre, Pierre on his deathbed.
    . . . On the Sunday morning after your death, Pierre, I went to the laboratory with Jacques for the first time. I tried to make a measurement, for a graph on which we had each

made several points. But I felt the impossibility of going on.

In the street I walk as if hypnotised, without attending to anything. I shall not kill myself. I have not even the desire for suicide But among all these vehicles is there not one to make me share the fate of my beloved?

Dr. Curie, his son Jacques, Joseph Sklodovski and Bronya observed with terror the movements of this icy, calm, black-robed woman, the automaton Marie had become. Even the sight of her children did not awaken feeling in her. Stiff, absent-minded, the wife who had not joined the dead seemed already to have abandoned the living.

But the living busied themselves about her and worried over that future in which she believed so little. The decease of Pierre Curie had brought up some important problems. What was to be the fate of the research work Pierre had left in suspense, and of his teaching at the Sorbonne? What was to become of Marie?

Her relatives discussed these questions in low voices, and listened to the suggestions of the representatives of the Ministry and the university, who succeeded each other at the house in the Boulevard Kellermann. On the morrow of the obsequies the government officially proposed to award the widow and children of Pierre Curie a national pension. Jacques submitted this plan to Marie, who refused flatly. "I don't want a pension," she said. "I am young enough to earn my living and that of my children."

In her suddenly strengthened voice could be heard the first faint echo of her habitual bravery.

Between the authorities and the Curie family the exchanges of views wavered somewhat. The university was disposed to keep Marie in its faculty. But with what title, and in what laboratory? Could this woman of genius be put under the orders of a chief? And where was there a professor capable of directing Pierre Curie's laboratory?

Consulted as to her own wishes, Mme Curie answered vaguely that she was not able to reflect, that she did not know . . .

Jacques Curie and Bronya and the most faithful of Pierre's friends, Georges Gouy, felt that they must make the decisions and take the initiative in Marie's place. Jacques Curie and Georges

Gouy informed the dean of the faculty of their conviction: that Marie was the only French physicist capable of pursuing the work she and Pierre had undertaken. Marie was the only teacher worthy of succeeding Pierre. Marie was the only chief of laboratory who could replace him. Traditions and customs must be swept away so as to name Mme Curie professor at the Sorbonne.

On the strong insistence of Marcelin Berthelot, of Paul Appell and Vice-Rector Liard, the public authorities made a frank and generous gesture on this occasion. On May 13th, 1906, the council of the Faculty of Science unanimously decided to maintain the chair created for Pierre Curie and to confide it to Marie, who would take the title of *chargée de cours*.

University of France

Mme Pierre Curie, Doctor of Science, chief of research work in the Faculty of Science of the University of Paris, is charged with a course in physics in the said faculty.

Mme Curie will receive in this capacity an annual salary of ten thousand francs, dating from the first of May, 1906.

This was the first time that a position in French higher education had been given to a woman.

Marie listened distractedly, almost with indifference, to her father-in-law giving the details of the heavy mission she owed it to herself to accept. She answered in a few syllables: "I will try."

A phrase pronounced in other days by Pierre, a phrase which was a moral testament, an order, came up in her memory and formally indicated her course:

"Whatever happens, even if one has to go on like a body without a soul, one must work just the same . . ."

Marie's diary:

I am offered the post of successor to you, my Pierre: your course and the direction of your laboratory. I have accepted. I don't know whether this is good or bad. You often told me you would have liked me to give a course at the Sorbonne. And I would like at least to make an effort to continue your work.

Sometimes it seems to me that this is how it will be most easy for me to live, and at other times it seems to me that I am mad to attempt it.

May 7th, 1906:

My Pierre, I think of you without end, my head is bursting with it and my reason is troubled. I do not understand that I am to live henceforth without seeing you, without smiling at the sweet companion of my life.

For two days the trees have been in leaf and the garden is beautiful. This morning I looked at the children there. I thought you would have found them beautiful and that you would have called me to show me the periwinkles and the narcissus in bloom. Yesterday, at the cemetery, I did not succeed in understanding the words "Pierre Curie" engraved on the stone. The beauty of the countryside hurt me, and I put my veil down so as to see everything through my crêpe

May 11th:

My Pierre, I got up after having slept rather well, relatively calm. That was only a quarter of an hour ago, and now I want to howl again—like a wild beast.

May 14th:

My little Pierre, I want to tell you that the laburnum is in flower, the wistaria, the hawthorn and the iris are beginning—you would have loved all that.

I want to tell you, too, that I have been named to your chair, and that there have been some imbeciles to congratulate me on it.

I want to tell you that I no longer love the sun or the flowers. The sight of them makes me suffer. I feel better on dark days, like the day of your death, and if I have not learned to hate fine weather it is because my children have need of it.

May 22nd:

I am working in the laboratory all day long, it is all I can do: I am better off there than anywhere else, I conceive of nothing any more that could give me personal joy, except perhaps scientific work—and even there—— no, because if I succeeded with it, 1 could not endure you not to know it.

June 10th:
Everything is gloomy. The preoccupations of life do not even allow me time to think of my Pierre in peace

Jacques Curie and Joseph Sklodovski had left Paris. Soon Bronya was to rejoin her husband at their sanatorium in Zakopane.

One evening, one of the last the two sisters passed together, Marie made a sign to her elder sister to follow her. She led Bronya into her own bedroom, where, in spite of the summer heat, a great wood fire was flaming, and locked the door behind her. Bronya, surprised, questioned the widow's face It was even paler and more bloodless than usual. Without a word, Marie took a stiff, bulky packet, wrapped in waterproof paper, out of the cupboard. Then she sat down before the fire and signed to her sister to sit down beside her. She had a pair of strong scissors ready on the mantelpiece.

"Bronya," she murmured, "you must help me."

Slowly she undid the string and opened the paper. The flames lit up her trembling hands. A bundle appeared, carefully knotted into a cloth Marie hesitated an instant—then she unfolded the white cloth and Bronya restrained a cry of horror: the wrapping enclosed a hideous mass of clothing, of linen, of dried mud and blackened blood. Marie had been keeping near her, for days past, the clothes Pierre had worn when the wagon struck him in the Rue Dauphine.

The silent widow took the scissors and began to cut up the dark coat. She threw the pieces one by one into the fire and watched them shrivel up, smoke, be consumed and disappear. But suddenly she stopped, struggling in vain against the tears that darkened her tired eyes. In the half-congealed folds of the cloth appeared some viscous fragments of matter: the last scraps of the brain in which, a few weeks before, noble thoughts and the discoveries of genius had been born.

Marie contemplated these corrupt remnants fixedly; she touched them and kissed them desperately until Bronya dragged the clothing and the scissors away from her and began in her turn to cut and throw the pieces of cloth into the fire.

The task was finished at last, without a single word pronounced between the two women. The wrapping paper, the cloth, the towel with which they dried their hands, all in their turn were the prey of the flames.

"I could not have endured having this touched by indifferent hands," Marie said at last, in a strangling voice. Then, coming near Bronya:

"And now, tell me how I am going to manage to live. I know that I must, but how shall I do it? How can I do it?"

Breaking down into a horrible outburst of sobs, coughs, tears and cries, she hung upon her sister, who supported her, tried to calm her and finally undressed and put to bed this poor human creature who was at the end of her strength.

On the morrow Marie again became the icy automaton that had moved in her place since April 19th. It was this automaton that Bronya was to clasp in her arms as she got into the train for Warsaw. Bronya was to remain long obsessed by the picture of Marie motionless on the platform, in her mourning veils.

A sort of "normal life" was taken up again in that house, so impregnated with the memory of Pierre that on certain evenings, when the outside door slammed, Marie had, for the quarter of a second, the mad idea that the catastrophe was a bad dream and that Pierre Curie was about to appear. On the faces around her, young and old, could be read an expression of waiting. Projects, a plan for the future, were expected of her. This woman of thirty-eight, worn out by grief, was now the head of a family.

She made her decisions: she would stay in Paris all summer to work in the laboratory and to prepare the teaching which she was to begin in November. Her course at the Sorbonne must be worthy of Pierre Curie's. Marie got together her notes and books, and ran through the notes left by her husband. Once again she was buried in study.

During these sombre holidays her daughters skipped about in the country: Eve at St-Rémy-lès-Chevreuse with her grandfather, Irène at the seaside at Vaucottes, under the guardianship of Hela Szalay, Marie's second sister, who, to offer her affectionate help, had come to pass the summer in France.

In the autumn, Marie, who could not bear to stay in the Boulevard Kellermann, went in search of a new dewelling-place. She chose to live at Sceaux, where Pierre had lived when she met him—and where he now rested.

When this move was proposed, Dr. Curie, intimidated perhaps for the first time in his life, approached his daughter-in-law.

"Now that Pierre is no longer here, Marie, you have no reason to go on living with an old man. I can quite easily leave you, go to live alone, or with my elder son. Decide!"

"No, you decide," Marie murmured. "If you went away it would hurt me. But you should choose what you prefer."

Her voice was troubled by anxiety. Was she also going to lose this friend and faithful companion? It would be natural for Dr Curie to go and live with Jacques, rather than to stay with her—with a foreign woman, a Pole. . . . But the desired answer came at once:

"What I prefer, Marie, is to stay with you always."

He added the phrase, "Since you are willing," into which penetrated the emotion he did not wish to confess. And, very quickly, he turned away and went to the garden, where Irène's happy cries called him.

A widow, an old man of seventy-nine, a little girl and a baby—this was the Curie family now.

Mme Curie, widow of the illustrious scientist who died so tragically, who has been appointed to the chair occupied by her husband at the Sorbonne, will deliver her first lecture on Monday, November 5th, 1906, at half-past one in the afternoon.

Mme Curie, in this inaugural lecture, will explain the theory of ions in gases, and will treat of radioactivity.

Mme Curie will speak in a lecture hall. These halls contain about a hundred and twenty seats, most of which will be occupied by the students.' The public and the Press, which also have some rights, will be obliged to share at most twenty seats between them! On this occasion, an occasion unique in the history of the Sorbonne, why could the regulations not be abandoned so as to put the great amphitheatre at Mme Curie's disposition for her first lecture only?

Such extracts from the newspapers of the time reflect the interest and impatience with which Paris watched for the first public appearance of the "celebrated widow." The reporters, society people, pretty women, artists who besieged the secretariat of the Faculty of Science and grew indignant when they were not given "invitation cards" were moved neither by compassion nor by the desire to receive instruction. They cared little indeed about the "theory of ions in gases," and Marie's suffering on this cruel day was only an added sauce for their curiosity. Even sorrow has its snobs.

For the first time a woman was about to speak at the Sorbonne—a woman who was at the same time a genius and a despairing wife. Here was enough to draw the public of theatrical *premières*—the audience for great occasions.

At noon, at the hour when Marie, standing before the grave in the cemetery at Sceaux, was speaking in an undertone to him whose succession she assumed to-day, the crowd had already filled the little graded amphitheatre, stopped up the corridors of the Faculty of Science, and overflowed even into the square outside. In the hall, great and ignorant minds were mixed, and Marie's intimate friends were scattered among the indifferent. The worst off were the real students, who had come to listen and to take notes, but who had to cling to their seats to keep from being dislodged.

At one-twenty five the noise of conversation grew heavy. There were whisperings and questions; necks were craned so as not to miss any part of Mme Curie's entrance. All those present had the same thought: what would be the new professor's first words—the first words of the only woman the Sorbonne had ever admitted among its masters? Would she thank the Minister, thank the university? Would she speak of Pierre Curie? Yes, undoubtedly: the custom was to begin by pronouncing a eulogy of one's predecessor. But in this case the predecessor was a husband, a working companion. What a strong situation! The moment was thrilling, unique. . . .

Half-past one. . . . The door at the back opened, and Marie Curie walked to the chair amidst a storm of applause. She inclined her head. It was a dry little movement intended as a salute. Standing, with her hands firmly holding on to the long table laden with apparatus, Marie waited for the ovation to cease. It ceased suddenly: before this pale woman, who was trying to compose her face, an unknown emotion silenced the crowd that had come for a show.

Marie stared straight ahead of her and said:

"When one considers the progress that has been made in physics in the past ten years, one is surprised at the advance that has taken place in our ideas concerning electricity and matter . . ."

Mme Curie had resumed the course at the precise sentence where Pierre Curie had left it.

What was there so poignant in these icy words: "When one considers the progress that has been made in physics . . ."? Tears rose to the eyes and fell upon the faces there.

In the same firm, almost monotonous voice, the scientist gave her lesson that day straight to the end. She spoke of the new theories on the structure of electricity, on atomic disintegration, on radioactive substances. Having reached the end of the arid exposition without flinching, she retired by the little door as rapidly as she had come in.

PART THREE

CHAPTER XIX

Alone

WE admired Marie when, supported by a man of genius, she was able both to manage her home and to take her part in a great scientific task It did not seem possible to us that she could lead a harder life or put forth a more powerful effort.

Compared to the life that awaited her, this condition was mild. The responsibilities of "the widowed Mme Curie" would have frightened a robust, happy and courageous man.

She had to bring up two young children, earn their livelihood and her own, and to fill her place as professor with success. Deprived of the masterly collaboration of Pierre Curie, she had to pursue and carry out the researches undertaken with her companion. Her assistants and students had to receive orders and advice from her. One essential mission also remained: to build a laboratory worthy of Pierre's disappointed dreams, where young research workers could develop the new science of radioactivity.

Marie's first care was to give her daughters and father-in-law a comfortable existence. At 6 Rue du Chemin de Fer, at Sceaux, she rented a house without charm, embellished by an agreeable garden. Irène, to her joy, entered into possession of a square of earth which she acquired the right to cultivate in her own way. Under the eyes of her governess, Eve hunted through the tufts of grass on the lawn for her favourite turtle and chased the black cat or the tabby cat down the narrow walks.

Mme Curie paid for this arrangement by additional fatigue: a half-hour by train separated her from the laboratory. Every morning she was to be seen going to the station, with her fine, hurried step that called to mind some tardiness to be made up, some tireless errand. This woman in deep mourning, who always got into the same second-class compartment of the same smelly train, soon became a familiar figure to the travellers on the line

She rarely had time to lunch at Sceaux. She renewed her acquaintance with the creameries of the Latin Quarter, where she had gone in the old days, alone as she was to-day—only then she had been young, filled with unconscious hope. Or else, walking the length and breadth of her cramped laboratory, she nibbled at a piece of bread or some fruit.

In the evening, often very late, she would take the return train home. In winter her first thought was to inspect the big stove in the vestibule, to replenish it with coal and regulate its draught. The idea was firmly fixed in her head that nobody in the world except herself was capable of keeping up a good fire—and it was true that she knew how to place the paper and kindling, and the hard coal or logs above, like an artist or a chemist. When the stove purred to her satisfaction Marie would stretch out on a sofa and get her breath again after the exhausting day

Too reserved to let her grief be seen, she never wept before anybody, and she refused to be pitied or consoled. To nobody did she confide her cries of despair or the dreadful nightmares that persecuted her sleep. But her near ones watched uneasily when her dull gaze was vaguely fixed on nothing, her hands agitated by the beginning of a tic: the nervous fingers, irritated by numerous radium burns, rubbed against each other in an irrepressible and obsessing movement.

It sometimes happened that her physical resistance abandoned her so suddenly that she did not have time to send her daughters away, to isolate herself. One of my earliest childhood memories is that of my mother collapsing to the floor in a faint, in the dining-room at Sceaux—and of her pallor, her mortal inertia.

Marie to her friend Kazia, 1907:
Dear Kazia, I was not able to see your protégé, Monsieur K. The day when he came, I was very unwell, which is often the case, and also I had a lecture to give the next day. My father-in-law, who is a

doctor, had forbidden me to see anybody at all, knowing that conversations tire me a great deal.

As for the rest, what can I tell you? My life is upset in such a way that it will never be put right again I think it will always be like this and I shall not try to live otherwise. I want to bring up my children as well as possible, but even they cannot awaken life in me They are both good, sweet and rather pretty. I am making great efforts to give them a solid and healthy development. When I think of the younger one's age, I see it will take twenty years to make grown persons of them. I doubt if I shall last so long, as my life is very fatiguing, and grief does not have a salutary effect upon strength and health.

Financially I am in no difficulty, I earn enough to bring up my children, even though, naturally, my circumstances are a great deal more modest than they were when my husband was alive.

In the darkest moments of a solitary life two persons brought help to Marie. One was Marya Kamienska, Joseph Sklodovski's sister-in-law, a sweet and delicate woman who, at Bronya's request, had accepted the post of governess and housekeeper in the Curie family. Her presence gave Marie a little of that Polish intimacy of which her exile had often seemed to deprive her too much When Mlle Kamienska was forced by bad health to go back to Warsaw, other Polish governesses, less reliable and less charming, were to take her place with Irène and Eve.

Marie's other ally, and her most precious, was Dr. Curie. Pierre's disappearance had been for him a terrible trial. But the old man drew a certain kind of courage, of which Marie was not capable, from his rigid rationalism He scorned sterile regrets and the cult of tombs. After the funeral he was never again to return to the cemetery. Since nothing remained of Pierre, he refused to be tortured by a ghost.

His stoical serenity had a beneficial effect on Marie. Before her father-in-law, who compelled himself to lead a normal life, to talk and laugh, she was ashamed of the stupor into which her grief had plunged her, and tried in her turn to show a quiet countenance.

The presence of Dr. Curie, so sweet to Marie, was sheer joy to the children. Without the blue-eyed old man their childhood would have been stifled in mourning. He was their playmate and master far more than their mother, who was ever away from home —always kept at that laboratory of which the name was endlessly rumbling in their ears. Eve was still too young for a true intimacy to be created between them, but he was the incomparable friend of the elder girl, of that slow, untamed child, so profoundly like the son he had lost.

He was not content with introducing Irène to natural history and botany, with communicating to her his enthusiasm for Victor Hugo, and with writing her letters during the summer, reasonable, instructive and very droll letters, in which his mocking spirit and exquisite style were reflected: he polarised her intellectual life in a decisive way. The spiritual equilibrium of the present Irène Joliot-Curie, her horror of suffering, her implacable attachment to the real, her anticlericalism and even her political sympathies come to her in the direct line from her grandfather.

Mme Curie was to pay her debt of gratitude to this excellent man by an affectionate and constant devotion. In 1909 the consequences of a lung congestion kept the doctor in bed for a whole year. She passed all her free moments at the bedside of the sick man, who was both difficult and impatient, trying to distract him.

On February 25th, 1910, the old man died. At the cemetery of Sceaux, frozen and swept bare by winter, Marie demanded an unexpected labour from the grave-diggers. She asked that Pierre's coffin be removed from the grave: Dr. Curie's was then placed at the bottom, and Pierre's was lowered upon it. Above the husband from whom she did not want to be separated in death there was an empty place for Marie, which she contemplated, unafraid, for a long time.

Marie Curie was now left to herself to bring up Irène and Eve. She had definite ideas on the care and early education of children which successive governesses interpreted with more or less success.

Every day began with an hour's work, intellectual or manual, which Marie tried to make attractive. She watched passionately for the awakening of her daughter's gifts, and noted in her grey notebook Irène's successes in arithmetic, Eve's musical precocity.

As soon as their daily task was finished, the little girls were sent into the open air. In all weathers they took long walks and

physical exercises. Marie had a cross-bar installed in the garden at
Sceaux, with a trapeze, flying rings and a slippery cord. After
these exercises at home, the two girls became enthusiastic pupils
at a gymnasium from which they brought home some flattering
first prizes for their prowess on the rigging.

Their hands and limbs were constantly in service. They did
gardening, modelling, cooking and sewing. Marie, however tired
she might be, compelled herself to accompany them on their jaunts
on bicycles. In the summer she went into the water with them
and supervised their progress as swimmers.

She could not leave Paris for long, and it was under the
guardianship of their aunt Hela Szalay that Irène and Eve passed
the greater part of their holidays. They were to be seen, in the
company of one or several of their cousins, disporting themselves
upon the less frequented beaches of the Channel or the ocean.
In 1911 they made their first journey to Poland with their mother;
Bronya welcomed them at her sanatorium at Zakopane. The little
girls learned to ride horseback, made excursions of several days'
duration into the mountains, and slept at mountaineer cabins.
Sack on back and shod with hobnailed boots, Marie preceded them
on the trails.

She did not encourage her children to acrobatic imprudence,
but she wanted them to be hardy. There was never to be any
question of being "afraid of the dark" with Irène and Eve—or
of hiding their heads under a pillow when a storm broke, or
being afraid of burglars or epidemics. Marie had known all these
terrors of old: she saved her children from them. Even the
memory of Pierre's fatal accident did not make a nervous watcher
out of her. The little girls were to go out alone very early, at
eleven or twelve years of age; soon they were to travel without
an escort.

Their spiritual health was no less dear to her. She tried to
preserve them from nostalgic reverie, from regret, from the
excesses of sensibility. She took a singular decision: that of never
speaking of their father to the orphans. This choice was, above
all, 'due to a physical impossibility in her. Until the end of her
days it was with the greatest difficulty that Marie could pronounce
"Pierre" or "Pierre Curie" or "your father" or "my husband,"

and her conversation, in order to get round the little islets of memory, was to employ incredible stratagems. She did not judge this silence to be blameworthy with regard to her daughters. Rather than plunge them into an atmosphere of tragedy, she deprived them, and deprived herself, of noble emotions.

And as she had not established the cult of the vanished scientist in her house, neither did she establish the cult of martyred Poland. She wished Irène and Eve to learn Polish, and for them to know and love her native land But she deliberately made true Frenchwomen of them. Ah, let them never feel torn between two countries, or suffer in vain for a persecuted race! . . .

She did not have her daughters baptized and gave them no sort of pious education. She felt herself incapable of teaching them dogmas in which she no longer believed: above all, she feared for them the distress she had known when she lost her faith. There was no anticlerical sectarianism in this. Absolutely tolerant, Marie was to affirm on many occasions to her children that if they wanted to give themselves a religion later on, she would leave them perfectly free.

Mme Curie was content that her daughters should know nothing of the uneasy childhood, drudging adolescence and poverty-stricken youth that had been hers. At the same time she did not wish for them to live in luxury. On several occasions Marie had had the opportunity of assuring a great fortune to Irène and Eve. She did not do so. When she became a widow she had to decide what to do with the gramme of radium that she and Pierre had prepared with their own hands, which was her private property. Against the advice of Dr. Curie and of several members of the family council, she decided, sharing the views of him who was no more, to make to her laboratory a gift of this precious particle, which was worth more than a million gold francs.

In her mind, if it was inconvenient to be poor, it was superfluous and shocking to be very rich. The necessity for her daughters to earn their living later on seemed healthy and natural to her.

The programme of education so carefully drawn up by Marie had but one thing lacking: education itself—good manners. In the house of mourning only intimate friends were received: the Perrins, the Chavannes. On Sundays, André Debierne brought books and toys to the girls and for hours he patiently amused a taciturn Irène, drawing for her on white sheets of paper processions of animals, elephants of all sizes. . . . Irène and Eve did not see anybody other than indulgent and affectionate friends. When Irène met strangers, she was panic-stricken, became completely mute, and obstinately refused to "say how do you do to the lady." She would never completely get over this habit of hers.

To smile, to be amiable, to pay visits, to receive people, to say words of politeness, to accomplish the ritual gestures imposed by ceremony: Irène and Eve were ignorant of all this. In ten years', twenty years' time they would perceive that life has its exactions, its laws, and that to "say how do you do to the lady" is, unfortunately, a necessity.

When Irène had won her study certificate and reached the age for going to school, Marie anxiously sought for a means of instructing her daughter above and beyond routine.

This whole-souled worker was haunted by the idea of the over-work to which children were condemned. It seemed to her barbarous to install young beings in ill-ventilated schoolrooms and to steal innumerable sterile "hours of attendance" from them at the age when they should be running free. She wanted Irène to study very little but very well. How was she to set about it?

She reflected, she consulted her friends—professors at the Sorbonne like herself, and, like herself, heads of families. Under her impetus was born the original idea of collective teaching, in which great minds would share the task of instructing all their children according to new methods.

An era of excitement and intense amusement opened for some ten little monkeys, boys and girls, who, dispensing with school, went every day to hear one single lesson given by a chosen master. One morning they invaded the laboratory at the Sorbonne where Jean Perrin taught them chemistry; the next day the little battalion moved to Fontenay-aux-Roses: mathematics taught by Paul Langevin. Mmes Perrin and Chavannes, the sculptor Magrou, and Professor Mouton taught literature, history, living languages, natural science, modelling and drawing. Last of all, in an unused room in the School of Physics, Marie Curie devoted Thursday afternoons to the most elementary course in physics that these walls had ever heard.

Her disciples—some of whom were future scientists—were to retain a dazzling memory of these fascinating lessons, of her familiarity and kindness. Thanks to her, the abstract and boring phenomena of the manuals were most picturesquely illustrated: bicycle ball-bearings, dipped in ink, were left on an inclined plane where, describing a parabola, they verified the law of falling bodies. A clock inscribed its regular oscillations on smoked paper A thermometer, constructed and graduated by the pupils, consented to operate in agreement with the official thermometers, and the children were immensely proud of it. . . .

Marie transmitted her love of science and her taste for work to them. She also taught them the methods which a long career had developed in her. A virtuoso in mental arithmetic, she insisted or having her protégés practise it: "You must get so that you *never* make a mistake," she insisted. "The secret is in not going too fast." If one of the apprentices created disorder or dirt in constructing an electric pile. Marie grew red with anger. "Don't tell me you will clean it *aft rwards!* One must *never* dirty a table during an experiment "

The laureate of the Nobel Prize sometimes gave these ambitious infants simple lessons in good sense.

"What would you do to keep the liquid contained in this jug hot?" she asked one day.

At once Francis Perrin, Jean Langevin, Isabelle Chavannes, and Irène Curie—the scientific stars of the class—proposed ingenious solutions· to wrap the jug in wool, to isolate it by refined—and impracticable—processes.

Marie smiled and said:

"Well, if I were doing it, I should start by putting the lid on."

On these homely words ended the lesson for that Thursday. The door was already opening, a servant was bringing in the enormous stock of rolls, chocolate bars and oranges for their collective tea, still chewing and arguing, the children tumbled out into the courtyard of the school.

On the watch for Mme Curie's slightest gesture, the newspapers of the day seized upon these lessons to make merry fun of the intrusion—very discreet and carefully supervised—of the scientists' sons and daughters into official laboratories:

This little company which hardly knows how to read or write [said a gossip writer], has permission to make manipulations, to engage in experiments to construct apparatus and to try reactions. . . . The Sorbonne and the building in the Rue Cuvier have not exploded yet, but all hope is not yet lost.

The collective teaching, fragile as other human enterprises, came to an end after two years. The parents were overworked by their personal tasks, the children, for whom the trials of the baccalaureate examination were in store, had to work according to the official programmes. Marie chose for Irène a private establishment, the Collège Sévigné, where the number of classroom hours was somewhat restricted. It was in this excellent school that the elder girl was to finish her secondary education and it was there that Eve was to make her studies later on.

Were Marie's touching efforts to protect her daughters' personalities from their earliest childhood successful? Yes and no. "Collective teaching" gave the elder girl, in default of a complete literary equipment, a first-class scientific education which she could not have obtained in any secondary school. Spiritual education? It would be too much to expect it to modify the intimate nature of young people, and I do not think we became a great deal better under our mother's wing. Several things, nevertheless, were permanently imprinted upon us: the taste for work—a thousand times more victorious in my sister than in me!—a certain indifference toward money, and an instinct of independence which convinced us both that in any combination of circumstances we should know how to get along without help.

The struggle against sorrow, active in Irène, had little success in my case: in spite of the help my mother tried to give me, my young years were not happy ones. In one single sector Marie's victory was complete: her daughters owe to her their good health and physical address, their love of sports. Such is, in this matter, the most complete success achieved by that supremely intelligent and generous woman.

It is not without apprehension that I have striven to grasp the principles that inspired Marie Curie in her first contacts with us. I fear that they suggest only a dry and methodical being, stiffened by prejudice. The reality is different. The creature who wanted us to be invulnerable was herself too tender, too delicate, too much gifted for suffering. She, who had voluntarily accustomed us to be undemonstrative, would no doubt have wished, without confessing it, to have us embrace and cajole her more. She, who wanted us to be insensitive, shrivelled with grief at the least sign of indifference. Never did she put our "insensibility" to the test by chastising u for our pranks. The traditional punishments, from a harmless box on the ear to "standing in the corner" or being deprived of pudding, were unknown at home. Unknown, too, were cries and scenes: my mother would not allow anybody to raise his voice, whether in anger or in joy. One day when Irène had been impertinent, she wanted to "make an example" and decided not to speak to her for two days. These hours were a painful trial for her and for Irene—but, of the two of them, the more punished was Marie: unsettled, wandering miserably about the mournful house, she suffered more than her daughter.

Like a great many children, we were probably selfish and inattentive to shades of feeling. Just the same we perceived the charm, the restrained tenderness and the hidden grace of her whom we called—in the first line of our letters spotted with ink, stupid little letters which, tied up with confectioners' ribbons, Marie kept until her death—"Darling Mé," "My sweet darling," "My sweet," or else, most often, "Sweet Mé."

Sweet, too sweet "Mé," who could hardly be heard, who spoke to us almost timidly, who wanted to be neither feared nor respected nor admired. . . . Sweet Mé who, along the years, neglected completely to apprise us that she was not a mother like every other mother, not a professor crushed under daily tasks, but an excep tional human being, an illustrious woman.

CHAPTER XX

Successes and Ordeals

EVERY morning a woman who was very thin, very pale, whose face was getting a little worn and whose fair hair was suddenly turning grey, entered the narrow rooms of the school in the Rue Cuvier, took a coarse linen smock down from its peg to cover her black dress, and set to work.

Although Marie was not aware of it, it was during this dull period of her life that her physical aspect was to attain its perfection It has been said that as they grow older human beings acquire the faces they deserve. How true this was of my mother! If the adolescent Manya Sklodovska had been simply "nice," if the student and the happy wife had had much charm, the matured and grief-stricken scientist she had now become showed striking beauty. Her Slavic features, illuminated by the life of the mind, had no need of such superfluous ornaments as freshness and gaiety. An air of melancholy courage, a more and more evident fragility, were her noble adornments soon after her fortieth year. It was this ideal appearance that Marie Curie was to retain in the eyes of Irène and Eve for many long years—up to the day when they were to perceive with terror that their mother had become a very old woman.

Professor, research worker and laboratory director, Mme Curie worked with the same incomparable intensity. She continued to teach at Sèvres. At the Sorbonne—where she had been promoted to the titular professorship in 1908—she was giving the first, and for the moment the only, course on radioactivity in the world. Great efforts! Although secondary education in France seemed to her defective, she regarded French higher education with lively admiration. She wanted to make herself the equal of the masters who once had dazzled a young Pole.

After two years of professorship, Marie undertook to write down her lessons. She published in 1910 a masterly *Treatise on Radioactivity*. Nine hundred and seventy-one pages of text barely sufficed to sum up the knowledge acquired in this realm since the day, not so long ago, when the Curies had announced the discovery of radium.

The portrait of the author did not figure as frontispiece for this work. Opposite the title-page Marie had placed a photograph of Pierre. Two years earlier, in 1908, this same photograph decorated the title of another volume of six hundred pages: the *Works of Pierre Curie*, collected, put in order and corrected by Marie.

The widow composed, for this latter book, a preface which retraced Pierre's career. She lamented his unjust death with restraint:

The last years of Pierre Curie's life were very productive. His intellectual faculties were in full development, as well as his experimental skill.

A new period of his life was about to open :it would have been, with more powerful means of action, the natural prolongation of an admirable scientific career. Fate did not wish it thus, and we are obliged to bow before its incomprehensible decision.

The number of Mme Curie's students grew larger every day. The American philanthropist Andrew Carnegie had bestowed on her in 1907 a series of annual scholarships which permitted her to welcome some novices in the Rue Cuvier. They joined the assistants paid by the university and some benevolent volunteer workers. A tall boy, remarkably gifted, Maurice Curie, son of Jacques Curie, was among them. Marie was proud of his successes. She was always to give her nephew a maternal love. Over this squad of eight or ten persons an old collaborator, a sure friend and a first-class scientist, watched with Marie: André Debierne.

Mme Curie had a programme of new researches. She performed them in spite of the steady deterioration to her health.

She purified a few decigrammes of chloride of radium and made a second determination of the atomic weight of the substance. She then undertook the isolation of radium metal. Up to now, every time she had prepared "pure radium," it had been *salts* of radium (chlorides or bromides) which constituted its only stable form. Marie collaborated with André Debierne in bringing the metal itself to light, undamaged by alterations due to atmospheric agents. The operation—one of the most difficult known to science—was never to be repeated.

André Debierne also helped Mme Curie to study polonium and the rays it emitted. Finally, Marie, in independent work, discovered a method of measuring radium by the measurement of the emanation it disengaged.

The universal development of Curietherapy made it necessary to separate tiny particles of the precious matter with rigorous precision. When the thousandth part of a milligramme is in question, balances are not of much use. Marie had the idea of "weighing" radioactive substances by the rays that they emitted. She brought this difficult technique to the point of practicability and created a "service of measures" in her laboratory where scientists, doctors and even ordinary citizens might have active ores or products examined and receive a certificate indicating their radium content.

At the time when she was publishing a *Classification of the Radioelements* and a *Table of Radioactive Constants*, she was performing another work of general importance: the preparation of the first international standard of radium. This light glass tube which Marie, with emotion, had closed with her own hands, contained twenty one milligrammes of chloride of pure radium. It was to serve as a model for the standards afterward dispersed through the five continents, and was solemnly deposited at the office of Weights and Measures at Sèvres, near Paris.

After the fame of the Curie couple, the personal fame of Mme Curie mounted and spread like a rocket. Diplomas of doctor *honoris causa* or of corresponding member of foreign academies arrived by the dozen to encumber the desks at the house in Sceaux, though the laureate never dreamed of making a show of them or even of drawing up a list of them.

France has only two ways of honouring her great men during their lifetime: the Legion of Honour and the Academy. The cross of chevalier was offered to Marie in 1910, but, inspired by the attitude of Pierre Curie, she refused it.

Why did she not oppose the same resistance to the over-zealous adherents who persuaded her, a few months later, to present herself for the Academy of Sciences? Had she forgotten the humiliating ballots to which her husband had been subjected in defeat, and even in victory? And was she unaware of the network of envy all about her?

Yes, she was unaware of it. And above all, like a naïve Polish woman, she was afraid of seeming pretentious or ungrateful by refusing the distinction which—she imagined—her adopted country was offering her.

Edouard Branly, a scientist of high rank and a well known Catholic, was her competitor. Between "Curistes" and "Branlystes," between freethinkers and clericals, between partisans and adversaries of that sensational novelty, the admission of a women to the Academy, a struggle broke out on all fronts. Marie, powerless and dismayed, beheld these controversies, which she had not foreseen.

The greatest scientists, Henri Poincaré, Dr. Roux, Emile Picard, Professors Lippmann, Bouty and Darboux at their head, conducted a campaign in her favour; but the other camp prepared a vigorous defence.

"Women cannot be part of the Institute of France," said M. Amagat with virtuous indignation—that same M. Amagat who had been, eight years earlier, the successful competitor of Pierre Curie. Kindly informers declared to the Catholics that Marie was a Jewess, and recalled to the freethinkers that she was a Catholic. On January 23rd, 1911, the day of the election, the president, when he opened the meeting, said very loudly to the ushers:

"Let everybody come in, women excepted."

And an almost blind academician, a lively partisan of Mme Curie, complained that he had very nearly voted against her, with a false ballot which had been slipped into his hand.

At four o'clock the excited journalists rushed off to write

"stories" of disappointment or of victory: Marie Curie had missed being elected by one vote.

In the Rue Cuvier her assistants, even her laboratory servant, awaited the verdict with more impatience than the candidate. Certain of success, they had bought a big bunch of flowers in the morning and had hidden it under the table which held the precision balances. Defeat left them stupefied. Louis Ragot, the mechanician, his heart heavy, caused the useless bouquet to disappear. The young workers silently prepared words of comfort, but they had no need to pronounce them. Marie appeared from the little room which served as her working office. She was not to comment by so much as a word upon this set-back which in no wise afflicted her.

In the story of the Curies, it seems that foreign countries were constantly correcting the attitudes of France. In December the Swedish Academy of Sciences, wishing to recognise the brilliant work accomplished by the woman scientist since her husband's death, awarded her the Nobel Prize in Chemistry for the year 1911. No other laureate, man or woman, had been, or was to be, judged worthy of receiving such a recompense twice.

Weakened and ill, Marie asked Bronya to make the journey to Sweden with her. She also took her elder daughter, Irène, with her. The child was present at the solemn meeting. Twenty-four years later, in the same hall, she was to receive the same prize.

Apart from the customary receptions and the King's dinner, special rejoicings had been organised in Marie's honour. She was to retain a delightful memory of one peasant festival, in which hundreds of women, dressed in vivid colours, wore crowns of lighted candles on their heads like trembling diadems.

In her public address, Marie offered the homage which had been lavished upon her to the shade of Pierre Curie.

Before approaching the subject of the lecture, I wish to recall that the discovery of radium and that of polonium were made by Pierre Curie in common with me. We also owe to Pierre Curie, in the domain of radioactivity, some fundamental studies which he carried out either alone or in common with me or in collaboration with his pupils.

' The chemical work which had as its aim the isolation of radium in the state of pure salt and its characterisation as a new element was carried out especially by me, but is intimately linked with the work in common. I therefore believe I shall interpret exactly the Academy's thought in admitting that the high distinction bestowed upon me is motivated by this work in common and thus constitutes a homage to the memory of Pierre Curie.

A great discovery, universal celebrity, and two Nobel prizes had fixed the admiration of a great many contemporaries upon Marie—and therefore the animosity of a great many others

Malice burst upon her in a sudden squall and attempted to annihilate her. A perfidious campaign was set going in Paris against this woman of forty-four, fragile, worn out by crushing toil, alone and without defence.

Marie, who exercised a man's profession, had chosen her friends and confidants among men And this exceptional creature exercised upon her intimates, upon one of them particularly, a profound influence. No more was needed. A scientist, devoted to her work, whose life was dignified, reserved, and in recent years especially pitiable, was accused of breaking up homes and of dishonouring the name she bore with too much brilliance.

It is not for me to judge those who gave the signal for the attack, or to say with what despair and often with what tragic clumsiness Marie floundered. Let us leave in peace those journalists who had the courage to insult a hunted woman, pestered by anonymous letters, publicly threatened with violence, with her life itself in danger. Some among these men came to ask her pardon later on, with words of repentance and with tears. . . . But the crime was committed Marie had been led to the brink of suicide and of madness, and, her physical strength forsaking her, she had been brought down by a very grave illness.

Let us retain only the least murderous but the basest of these knife thrusts, the one which was to be levelled at her all along the way. Every time an occasion offered to humiliate this unique woman, as during the painful days of 1911, or to refuse her a title, a recompense or an honour—the Academy, for instance—her origins were basely brought up against her: called in turn a Russian, a German, a Jewess and a Pole, she was "the foreign

woman" who had come to Paris like a usurper to conquer a high
position improperly. But whenever, by Marie Curie's gifts, science
was honoured, every time she was acclaimed in another country
and unprecedented praise heaped upon her, she at once became, in
the same newspapers and over the signatures of the same writers,
"the ambassadress of France," the "purest representative of our
race's genius," and a "national glory." With equal injustice, the
Polish birth of which she was proud was then passed over in
silence.

Great men have always been subjected to the attacks of those
who long to discover imperfect human creatures beneath the
armour of genius. Without the terrible magnet of renown which
had drawn sympathies and hatreds upon her, Marie Curie would
never have been criticised or calumniated. She now had another
reason for hating fame

Friends can be counted in adversity. Hundreds of letters, signed
by names known and unknown, came to tell Marie how her trials
were arousing pity and indignation. André Debierne, M. and Mme
Jean Perrin, M. and Mme Chavannes, a charming English friend,
Mrs. Ayrton, and many others as well, among them her assistants
and pupils, fought for Marie. In the university world, persons who
hardly knew her drew near in this cruel moment—such as the
mathematician Émile Borel and his wife. Along with her brother
Joseph, with Bronya and Hela, who had hurried to France to help
her, her firmest defender was Pierre's brother, Jacques Curie.

These evidences of affection restored some of Marie's courage.
But her physical depression grew more marked every day. She no
longer felt strong enough to make the journey to Sceaux, and she
had taken an apartment in Paris, at 36 Quai de Béthune, where she
intended to live from January 1912. She was not able to stay so
long as she had intended, and on December 29 she was taken—
dying, condemned to death—to a nursing home. She conquered
the illness, however, but the profound lesions, by which her kid-
neys were attacked demanded an operation Marie, who had been
carried on stretchers from her house to the clinic several times in
two months and was only a bloodless creature now, asked that the
operation should be performed in March and not before: she

wanted to be present at a congress of physicists at the end of February.

She was operated upon and marvellously cared for by the great surgeon Charles Walther, but her health was compromised for a long time. Marie was pitifully thin and could hardly stand up. The crises of fever and kidney pains which she was enduring without complaint would have obliged any other woman to lead an invalid's life.

Tracked down by physical ills and human baseness, she hid herself like a beast at bay. Her sister had taken a little house for her at Brunoy, near Paris, under the name of "Dluska"; the patient passed some time there, and then installed herself incognito at Thonon for some melancholy weeks of cure. In the summer her friend, Mrs. Ayrton, received her and her daughters in a peaceful house on the English coast. There she found care and protection.

At the moment when Marie was considering the future with the utmost discouragement, an unexpected proposal came to fill her with emotion and uncertainty.

Since the Revolution of 1905 Tsarism, slowly crumbling, had made some concessions to liberty of thought in Russia, and even in Warsaw the conditions of existence had lost some of their rigour. A society of sciences, very active and relatively independent, had named Marie "honorary member" in 1911. A few months later a grandiose plan was formed among the intellectuals: to create a laboratory of radioactivity at Warsaw, to offer its directorship to Mme Curie, and to bring the greatest woman scientist in the world back to her fatherland.

In May 1912 a delegation of Polish professors presented itself at Marie's house, and the writer Henryk Sienkiewicz, the most celebrated and the most popular man in Poland, addressed to her, without knowing her personally, an appeal in which a pathetic familiarity was mixed with the formulas of respect:

Deign, most honoured madame, to transport your splendid scientific activity to our country and our capital. You know the reasons why, in these later times, our culture and science have declined. We are losing confidence in our intellectual faculties, we are being lowered in the opinion of our enemies, and we are abandoning hope for the future.

. . . Our people admire you, but would like to see you working here, in your native town. It is the ardent desire of the whole nation Possessing you in Warsaw, we should feel stronger, we should lift our heads now bent under so many misfortunes. May our prayers be granted. Do not repulse our hands which are stretched out to you.*

For a less scrupulous person, what an opportunity to leave France with effect, to turn one's back on calumny and cruelty! ·

But Marie never adopted the counsels of rancour. She anxiously and honestly tried to find where her duty lay. The idea of returning to her own country attracted and frightened her at the same time. In the state of physiological misery in which this woman found herself, any decision became terrifying. There was something else: the construction of the laboratory the Curies had so long wanted had at last been decided upon, in 1909. To renounce Paris and flee from France was to reduce this plan to nothing, to kill a great dream.

At a moment in her life when she felt hardly strong enough for anything, Marie was torn between two duties which excluded each other After how many homesick hesitations, with what suffering, she addressed her letter of refusal to Warsaw! Still, she accepted the task of directing the new laboratory from afar and placed it under the practical control of two of her best assistants: the Poles Danysz and Wertenstein.

Marie, still very ill, went to Warsaw in 1913 for the inauguration of the radioactivity building The Russian authorities deliberately ignored her presence: no official took part in the fêtes organised in her honour. The welcome given by her native land was therefore all the more tumultuous. For the first time in her life, Marie pronounced, in a hall packed to its limits, a scientific lecture in Polish.

I am doing my best to render the most possible service here before I go away again [she wrote to one of her colleagues]. On

* The first paragraph here quoted is in the formal style of address in Polish and the second paragraph in the familiar, with "thee" and "thou."

Tuesday I made a public lecture. I have also been present, and shall be present again, at various meetings. I find a good will which must be put to use. This poor country, massacred by an absurd and barbarous domination, really does a great deal to defend its moral and intellectual life. A day may come perhaps when oppression will have to retreat, and it is necessary to last out until then. But what an existence! What conditions!

I have seen again the places to which my memories of childhood and youth are attached. I have seen the Vistula again, and the tomb in the cemetery. These pilgrimages are at the same time sweet and sad, but one can't help making them.

One of the ceremonies took place in the Museum of Industry and Agriculture, in the very building where, twenty two years earlier, Marie had made her first experiments in physics On the next day a banquet was offered to "Mme Sklodovska Curie" by the Polish women. In one of the rows of guests was seated a very old lady with white hair who contemplated the scientist in ecstasy: it was Mlle Sikorska, the directress of the boarding school where, in the old days, the tiny fair-haired Manya had begun her education. Leaving her place, Marie made her way between the beflowered tables, joined the old lady, and with a timid impulsiveness, as on the far-off days of prize-giving, she kissed her on both cheeks. Poor Mlle Sikorska dissolved into tears while the audience applauded frantically.

Marie's health grew sufficiently better for her to resume her normal life. During the summer of 1913 she tried her strength by a walking tour in the Engadine, rucksack on back. Her daughters accompanied her with their governess, and the group of excursionists also included the scientist Albert Einstein and his son. A charming comradeship of genius had existed for several years between Mme Curie and Einstein. They admired each other; their friendship was frank and loyal, and sometimes in French, sometimes in German, they loved to pursue interminable palavers in theoretical physics.

In the vanguard gambolled the young ones, who were enormously amused by this journey. A little behind, the voluble

Einstein, inspired, would expound to his confrère the theories which obsessed him, and which Marie, with her exceptional mathematical culture, was one of the rare persons in Europe to understand.

Irène and Eve sometimes caught words on the fly which seemed to them rather singular. Einstein, preoccupied, passed alongside the crevasses and toiled up the steep rocks without noticing them. Stopping suddenly, and seizing Marie's arm, he would exclaim· "You understand, what I need to know is exactly what happens to the passengers in a lift when it falls into emptiness."

Such a touching preoccupation made the younger generation roar with laughter, far from suspecting that the imaginary fall in a lift posed problems of transcendent "relativity."

After this brief holiday Marie went to England, where she was called for scientific ceremonies. Again she received a degree of doctor *honoris causa*, at Birmingham. For once in a way she endured the ceremony with good humour and described it to Irène in picturesque style:

They dressed me in a fine red robe with green facings, the same as my companions in misery, which is to say the other scientists who were to receive the doctor's degree. We each heard a little speech celebrating our merits, and then the vice-chancellor of the university declared to each of us that the university awarded us the degree. Then we took our places on the platform. Afterward we went off again, taking part in a sort of procession composed of all the professors and doctors of the university, in costumes rather similar to our own. All this was rather amusing. I had to take the solemn engagement to observe the laws and customs of the University of Birmingham.

Irène was carried away with enthusiasm. She wrote to her mother:

DARLING,

I can see you in your fine red robe with green facings; how beautiful you must be in it! Did you keep this fine robe, or was it only lent you for the ceremony?

In France, all storms forgotten, the scientist was at the zenith of her fame. For the past two years the architect Nénot had been building the Institute of Radium for her on the ground allotted in the Rue Pierre Curie.

Things did not arrange themselves easily; just after the death of Pierre, the public authorities had proposed to Marie the opening of a national subscription for the building of a Curie institute. The widow, not wishing to turn the fatal accident of the Rue Dauphine into money, had refused. The authorities fell back into their lethargy. But in 1909 Dr. Roux, director of the Pasteur Institute, had the generous and bold idea of building a laboratory for Marie Curie. If this had happened, she would have left the Sorbonne and become a star of the Pasteur Institute.

The heads of the university suddenly pricked up their ears. . . . Let Mme Curie go? Impossible? Cost what it may, she must be retained on the official staff!

An understanding between Dr. Roux and Vice-Rector Liard put an end to the discussions. At their common expense—400,000 gold francs each—the university and the Pasteur Institute founded the Institute of Radium, which was to comprise two parts: a laboratory of radioactivity, placed under the direction of Marie Curie; and a laboratory for biological research and Curietherapy, in which studies on the treatment of cancer and the care of the sick would be organised by an eminent physician, Professor Claude Regaud. These twin institutions, materially independent, were to work in co-operation for the development of the science of radium.

Now Marie was to be seen scurrying from the Rue Cuvier to the builders' scaffoldings, where she drew plans and argued with the architect. The greying woman was brimful of new and modern ideas. She was thinking of her own work; but above all she wanted to create a laboratory which could still be used in thirty years, in fifty years, long after she was dead. She demanded vast rooms, big windows which would inundate the research halls with sunlight. And even though the costly innovation might make the government's engineers indignant, she had to have a lift.

As for the garden—the pet worry of that eternal peasant—she was to compose it with love. Deaf to the arguments of those who wanted to "save space," she eagerly defended every square foot of the ground that separated the buildings. She picked out young trees one by one, like a connoisseur, and had them transplanted under her own eyes, long before the foundations had been laid. She confided to her collaborators:

"By buying my plane-trees and my lime-trees right away I am gaining two years. When we open the laboratory the trees will have grown and whole clumps will be in bloom. But don't say a word! I haven't spoken about it to M. Nénot!"

And a little flame of youth and gaiety reappeared in her grey eyes.

She planted the rambler roses herself, wielding the spade and tamping down the earth with her hands at the foot of the unfinished walls. Every day she watered them. When she straightened up it seemed that there, standing in the wind, she watched alike the growth of the dead stones and of the living plants.

One day when Marie was absorbed in an experiment in the Rue Cuvier her former laboratory servant, Petit, came to her, much moved. Work-halls were being built also at the School of Physics, and the shed, Pierre's and Marie's poor damp barrack, was about to fall beneath the wrecker's axe.

With that humble friend of the past, Marie arrived in the Rue Lhomond for her last farewell. The shed was there, still intact. The blackboard, by pious care, had been preserved untouched, and bore some lines in Pierre's handwriting. It seemed as though the door was about to open, to give entrance to a tall, familiar figure.

Rue Lhomond, Rue Cuvier, Rue Pierre Curie. . . . Three addresses, three stages. On this day Marie had retraced, without even noticing it, the road of her beautiful yet painful life as a scientist. Before her the future was clearly outlined. In the biological laboratory, which had just been finished, Professor Regaud's assistants were already at work, and lighted windows were to be seen at night shining from the new building. In a few months Marie, in her turn, would leave the P.C.N. and transfer her apparatus to the Rue Pierre Curie.

This victory came upon its heroine when she was no longer either young or strong, and when she had lost her happiness. What did it matter, since she was surrounded by fresh forces, since enthusiastic scientists were at hand to aid her in the struggle? No, it was not too late.

The glaziers were singing and whistling on every floor of the little white building. Above the entrance could already be read these words, cut into the stone: INSTITUT DU RADIUM, PAVILLON CURIE

Before these sturdy walls and this exalting inscription Marie evoked the words of Pasteur:

If conquests useful to humanity touch your heart; if you stand amazed before the surprising effects of electric telegraphy, the daguerreotype, anæsthesia and so many other admirable discoveries; if you are jealous of the part your country can claim in the further flowering of these wonders—take an interest, I urge upon you, in those holy dwellings to which the expressive name of laboratories is given. Ask that they be multiplied and adorned. They are the temples of the future, of wealth and well-being It is there that humanity grows bigger, strengthens and betters itself. It learns there to read in the works of nature, works of progress and universal harmony, whereas its own works are too often those of barbarity, fanaticism and destruction.

In that wonderful month of July the "temple of the future" in the Rue Pierre Curie was at last finished. It was ready now for its radium, its workers and its director.

Only, this July was the July of 1914.

CHAPTER XXI

War

MARIE had rented a little villa in Brittany for the summer Irène and Eve were already there, with a governess and a cook, and their mother had promised to join them there on the third of August. The end of the university year had kept her in Paris. She was used to staying alone like this, during the dog-days, in the empty apartment in the Quai de Bethune without even a house-maid to take care of her. She passed her days at the laboratory and returned home, where the concierge had presumably done some sketchy cleaning, only late at night.

Marie to her daughters, August 1st, 1914:
Dear Irène, dear Eve,—Things seem to be getting worse: we expect mobilisation from one minute to the next. I don't know if I shall be able to leave. Don't be afraid, be calm and courageous. If war does not break out, I shall come and join you on Monday. If it does, I shall stay here and send for you as soon as possible. You and I, Irène, will try to make ourselves useful.

August 2nd.
My dear daughters,—Mobilisation has begun, and the Germans have entered France without a declaration of war. We shall not be able to communicate with each other easily for some time.

Paris is calm and gives a good impression, in spite of the grief of the farewells.

August 6th:

My dear Irène,—I, too, want to bring you back here, but it is impossible for the moment. Be patient.

The Germans are crossing Belgium and fighting their way Brave little Belgium did not allow them to pass without defending itself. . . . All the French are hopeful, and think that the struggle, although it may be hard, will take a good turn.

Poland is partly occupied by the Germans. What will be left of it after their passage? I know nothing about my family.

An extraordinary emptiness had been created all around Marie Her colleagues and all her laboratory workers had joined their regiments. Only her mechanician, Louis Ragot, who had not been mobilised on account of a weak heart, and a little charwoman about as high as the table, remained with her.

The Polish woman forgot that France was only her adoptive country; the mother did not dream of going to join her children; the frail, suffering creature disdained her own ills, and the scientist put off her personal work until better times. Marie had only one thought: to serve her second fatherland. In the terrible contingency her intuition and initiative revealed themselves once more.

She ruled out the easy solution, which would have been to close the laboratory and become, like a great many courageous Frenchwomen, a nurse in a white veil. . . . Having registered herself at once on the organisation of the medical service, she discovered in it a blank which did not seem to bother the authorities but which, to her, seemed tragic: the hospitals, both at the front and behind the front, were almost unprovided with X-ray equipment.

The discovery of X-rays by Röntgen in 1895 had made it possible to explore, without surgical aid, the interior of the human body, to "see" and to photograph the bones and the organs; in 1914 only a limited number of Röntgen machines existed in France and were used by radiographic doctors. The wartime Military Health Service had provided equipment in certain big centres considered worthy of the luxury: that was all.

A luxury, the magic arrangement whereby, a rifle bullet or a fragment of shell could at once be discovered and localised in the wound?

Marie's work had never dealt with X-rays, but she had devoted several lectures to them every year at the Sorbonne. She knew the subject admirably well. By a spontaneous transposition of her scientific knowledge, she foresaw what the horrible carnage would require: a large number of radiological stations must be created at once. And in order to follow the movements of the armies easily, light equipment would be necessary.

Marie had recognised her field and acquired her impetus. In a few hours she drew up the inventory of the apparatus existing in the university laboratories, her own included, and made a round of visits to the manufacturers: all the X-ray material that could be used was collected together and distributed to the hospitals in the region of Paris. Volunteer operators were recruited from among professors, engineers and scientists.

But how could they help the wounded who were brought in crowds, with terrifying frequency, to the still unprovided ambulances? Some of these were even without electric equipment to which the apparatus could be attached.

Mme Curie found the solution. She created, with funds from the Union of Women of France, the first "radiological car"; it was an ordinary motor-car in which she put a Rontgen apparatus and a dynamo which, driven by the motor of the car, furnished the necessary current. This complete mobile station circulated from hospital to hospital from August 1914 onward; it was the only one to take care of the examination of the wounded evacuated toward Paris during the Battle of the Marne.

The rapid advance of the Germans gave Marie a difficult problem to decide. Should she stay in Paris or go to join her daughters in Brittany? And if the enemy threatened to occupy the capital, should she follow the retreat of the medical organisations?

She calmly considered these alternatives and took her decision: she would remain in Paris, whatever happened. It was not only the benevolent task she had undertaken that kept her; she was thinking of her laboratory, of her delicate instruments in the Rue Cuvier and of the new halls of the Rue Pierre Curie. "If I am there," she thought, "perhaps the Germans will not dare plunder them: but if I go away, everything will disappear."

Thus she reasoned, not without some hypocrisy, and discovered logical excuses for the instinct by which she was guided. This obstinate, tenacious, proud Marie did not like the act of flight. To be afraid was to serve the adversary. Nothing in the world would induce her to give a triumphant enemy the satisfaction of occupying a deserted Curie laboratory.

She confided her daughters to her brother-in-law Jacques, preparing them for a possible separation:

Marie to Irène, August 28th, 1914:

. . . They are beginning to face the possibility of a siege of Paris, in which case we might be cut off. If that should happen, endure it with courage, for our personal desires are nothing in comparison with the great struggle that is now under way. You must feel responsible for your sister and take care of her if we should be separated for a longer time than I expected.

August 29th:

' Dear Irène,—You know there is nothing to prove that we shall be cut off, but I wanted to tell you that we must be ready for all sorts of alternatives . . . Paris is so near the frontier that the Germans might very well approach it. That must not keep us from hoping that the final victory will be for France. So, courage and confidence! Think of your rôle as elder sister, which it is time you took seriously. .

August 31st, 1914:

I have just received your sweet letter of Saturday, and I wanted so much to kiss you that I almost cried.

Things are not going very well, and we are all heavy-hearted and disturbed in soul. We need great courage, and I hope that we shall not lack it. We must keep our certainty that after the bad days the good times will come again. It is in this hope that I press you to my heart, my beloved daughters.

Although she could look serenely forward to a life in Paris besieged, bombarded or even conquered, there was one treasure which she wished to protect against the aggressor: the gramme of

radium her laboratory possessed. She would not have dared to
confide the precious particle to any messenger, and decided to take
it to Bordeaux herself.

So Marie appeared in one of those groaning trains which were
carrying away the government officials and important personages
—Marie in a black alpaca dust-coat laden with a small overnight
bag and a gramme of radium, that is to say, with a heavy case
wherein were the tiny tubes in the shelter of their leaden covers.
Mme Curie miraculously found an end of a bench to sit on and was
able to arrange the heavy packet in front of her. Resolutely deaf
to the pessimistic talk that filled the carriage, she contemplated the
sunny countryside through the window: but there, too, everything
spoke of defeat: on the national road alongside the railway there
ran an uninterrupted procession of motor cars fleeing to the west.

Bordeaux was invaded by the French. Porters, taxis and hotel
rooms were equally difficult to find. When night fell Marie was
still standing in the station square, near her burden which she was
not strong enough to carry. The crowd shoved and pushed about
her without impairing her good nature: she was amused by her
situation. Was she going to have to mount guard all night over
this case which was worth a million francs? No: an employee of
one of the ministries, her travelling companion, saw her and came
to her rescue. This saviour obtained a room for her in a private
apartment. The gramme of radium, weighing twenty kilogrammes
in its case, was given shelter. On the following morning Marie
deposited her troublesome treasure in the safety vault of a bank
and, freed from this anxiety, took the road to Paris again.

She had passed unnoticed on her journey down, but her
departure toward the capital excited lively comment. A crowd
collected around the phenomenon: "the woman who is going back
there." The "woman" took care not to reveal her identity, but,
more talkative than usual, she tried to calm the alarming rumours
and asserted gently that Paris would hold out, that its inhabitants
were incurring no danger.

The troop train into which she, the only civilian, had mounted
made its way with incredible slowness. It was stopped in the open
fields several times for hours at a stretch. Marie, famished,
accepted a big piece of bread that a soldier pulled out of his

knapsack for her. Since the day before, when she left the laboratory, she had not had time to eat anything.					$\blacklozenge$

Paris, silent and threatened, seemed to her, in this exquisite light of early September, to have a beauty and a value never before attained. Must such a jewel be lost? But already news was spreading in the streets with the violence of a tidal wave. Mme Curie, covered with the dust of her journey, hurried to enquire: the German advance was broken, the Battle of the Marne had begun.

Marie joined her friends Appell and Borel at the Superior Normal School: she wanted to offer her services without delay to the medical organisation they had founded, the National Aid. Paul Appell, president of the charity, was filled with pity for this poor exhausted woman. He made Marie lie down on a sofa and urged her to take some rest during the coming days. She was not listening to him. She wanted to act, to do something. . . . "On that sofa, with her face so pale and her eyes so big, she was all flame," Appell was to say of her later.

Marie to Irène, September 6th, 1914:

. . . The theatre of war is changing at the moment: the enemy seems to be going farther away from Paris. We are all hopeful, and we have faith in final success.

. . . Make young Fernand Chavannes do his problems in physics. If you cannot work for France just now, work for its future. Many people will be gone, alas, after this war, and their places must be taken. Do your mathematics and physics as well as you can.

Paris was saved. Marie sent for her daughters, who were protesting energetically against their exile. Eve went back to school, while Irène took her course for the nurse's diploma.

Mme Curie had foreseen everything—that the war would be long and murderous, that the wounded would have to be operated upon more and more in the places where they were found, and that the surgeons and radiologists would have to be at hand in the front ambulances; that it was urgently necessary to organise the intensive manufacture of Röntgen apparatus—and, finally, that the radiological cars would be called upon to render invaluable service.

These cars, nicknamed "little Curies" in the army zones, were equipped by Marie at the laboratory, one by one, regardless of the indifference or the latent hostility of the bureaucrats. Our timid woman had suddenly become an exacting and authoritative personage. She nagged at the lazy officials, demanded passes from them, visas and requisitions. They made difficulties, brandished the regulations at her. . . . "Civilians mustn't bother us!"—such was the spirit that animated many among them. But Marie hung on, argued and won.

She held up individual citizens mercilessly. At her request such generous women as the Marquise de Ganay and the Princess Murat gave or lent her their limousines, which she immediately transformed into radiological stations. "I shall give you back your motor car after the war," she would promise with slightly mocking assurance. "Truthfully, if it's not useless by then, I shall give it back to you!"

Of the twenty cars which she thus put into service, Marie kept one for her personal use: a flat-nosed Renault with a body like that of a lorry. Aboard this chariot of regulation grey, ornamented by a red cross and a French flag painted on its plates, she led the life of an adventurer, of a great captain.

A telegram or a telephone call would notify Mme Curie that an ambulance laden with wounded demanded a radiological post in a hurry. Marie would immediately verify the equipment of her car and attach her apparatus and dynamo. While the military chauffeur took on petrol, she would go home and get her dark cloak, her little travelling hat, soft and round, which had lost both form and colour, and her baggage: a yellow leather bag, cracked and peeling. She climbed in beside the driver, on the seat exposed to the wind, and soon the stout car was rolling at full speed—namely, the "twenty-miles-an-hour average," which was its best—toward Amiens, Ypres, Verdun.

After various stops and palavers with untrustful sentries, the hospital appeared. To work! Mme Curie rapidly chose one room as a radiological hall and had her cases brought in there. She unpacked the instruments and assembled them from their separate pieces. The cable which connected the apparatus with the dynamo in the motor car was rolled out: the chauffeur, at a given signal, started the dynamo, and Marie tested the intensity of the current. Before beginning the examination of the wounded she prepared the radioscopic screen and ranged her protecting gloves and glasses near at hand, along with special marking pencils and the leaden indicator which found the projectiles. She darkened the room by stopping up the window with the black curtains she had brought, or even with ordinary hospital blankets. At one side, in an improvised photographic dark-room, were placed the baths of chemicals where the plates would be developed. Half an hour after Marie's arrival, everything was ready.

The melancholy procession began. The surgeon shut himself and Mme Curie into the dark-room, where the apparatus in action was surrounded by a mysterious halo. One after the other the stretchers laden with suffering bodies were brought in. The wounded man would be extended on the radiological table. Marie regulated the apparatus focused on the torn flesh so as to obtain a clear view. The bones and organs showed their precise outlines, and in the midst of them appeared a thick dark fragment: the shot or piece of shell.

An assistant wrote down the doctor's observations while Marie made a quick copy of the picture or took a photograph which would guide the surgeon in extracting the projectile. Sometimes the operation was made immediately "under the rays," and on the radioscopic screen the surgeon could follow the picture of his pincers probing the wound and going round the obstacles of the skeleton to seize upon the bit of shell.

Ten wounded men, fifty, a hundred. . . . Hours passed, and sometimes days. So long as there were any patients Marie remained almost constantly shut into the dark-room. Before leaving the hospital she studied means of installing a fixed radiological post there. Then, having packed up her material, she would climb into the front seat of her magic chariot and start back to Paris.

This ambulance station would see her again very soon: she had moved heaven and earth to find an available apparatus and came out to install it. A manipulator would accompany her, a man whom she had found somehow or other and had instructed somehow or other in his work. From now on the hospital, furnished with an X-ray room, would have no need of her.

Apart from the twenty motor cars she equipped, Marie installed *two hundred* radiological rooms. The total number of wounded men examined by these 220 posts, fixed or mobile—posts created and started going by Mme Curie personally—rose to above a million.

Her science and her courage were not her only support. Marie possessed in the highest degree that humble, precious gift of "getting on with it," and she made masterly use of the super-method which the French in war time called "System D"—the defeat of red tape by ingenuity. She imposed systematic training on herself· at a time when she was perfecting her technique with Röntgen apparatus and reading anatomical treatises to acquire the culture of a perfect medical radiologist she was also learning how to drive a car, passing for her licence, and initiating herself into mechanics. She wanted to avoid what she hated most: calling for help, or having herself waited upon.

If her chauffeur was not available she would take the wheel of the Renault herself and drive it, somehow or other, over the bad roads. She could be seen in the coldest weather energetically turning the crank of the recalcitrant motor. She was to be seen putting her weight on the jack to change a tyre, or cleaning a dirty carburettor with scientific thoroughness, her brows frowning with attention. If she had apparatus to carry by train, she would put it into the van herself, and on arrival it was she who unloaded and unpacked it, watching to see that nothing went astray. . . .

Indifferent to the lack of comfort, she asked for no particular consideration and no favourable treatment. Never was a famous woman less troublesome. She would eat no matter how and sleep anywhere—in a nurse's room or else, as in the Hoogstade hospital, under a tent in the open air. She, the student who once had chattered with cold in a garret, now became a soldier of the Great War without an effort.

Marie to Paul Langevin, January 1st, 1915:
The day I leave is not fixed yet, but it can't be far off. I have had a letter saying that the radiological car working in the Saint-Pol region has been damaged. This means that the whole northern

area is without any radiological service! I am taking the necessary
steps to hasten my departure and am resolved to put all my
strength at the service of my adopted country since I cannot do
anything for my unfortunate native country just now, bathed as it
is in blood after more than a century of suffering.

In Paris, Irène and Eve were living more or less like the
daughters of combatants. Their mother gave herself "leave" only
when a kidney attack forced her to stay in bed for several days. If
she was at home, it meant that she was ill. If she was not ill, she was
at Suippes, at Reims, Calais, Poperinghe—in one of the three or
four hundred French and Belgian hospitals that she was to visit
while hostilities lasted Eve's letters to her mother announcing her
successes in history or French composition were sent to strange
and changing addresses:

"Mme Curie, Hôtel de la Noble Rose, Furnes."

"Mme Curie, Auxiliary Hospital II, Morvillars, Haut-Rhin."

"Mme Curie, Hospital 112."

Post cards hastily scribbled by the wanderer at various stops
brought laconic news to Paris:

January 20th, 1915:

Dear children,—Here we are at Amiens, where we slept. We
have only burst two tyres. Greet everybody.—Mé.

The same day:

Arrived at Abbeville. Jean Perrin, with his car, ran into a tree.
Luckily no great harm done. Continuing to Boulogne.—Mé.

January 24th, 1915:

Dear Irène,—After various incidents we have arrived at
Poperinghe, but we can't work until we have had some changes
made at the hospital. They are building a shelter for the car and a
partition to enclose the radiological room inside a big ward of
wounded. All this delays me, but it is difficult to do otherwise.

Some German aeroplanes dropped some bombs at Dunkirk; a
few people were killed, but the population showed no great fright.
At Poperinghe, too, such accidents happen, but less often. We can

hear the cannon rumbling almost constantly. It is not raining: it
has frozen a little. I was received with extreme cordiality at the
hospital: I have a nice room and they give me a fire in a stove. I
am better off than at Furnes. I take my meals at the hospital. I
embrace you tenderly.—Mé.

May 1915:
Darling,—I had to wait at Châlons for eight hours and only
reached Verdun this morning at five. The car also arrived. We
are organising!—Mé.

One evening in April, 1915 Marie came home a little paler and a
little less agile than usual. Without answering the worried
questions that arose, she shut herself in her room to sulk.

She was sulking because, on her way back from the hospital at
Forges, a sudden twist of the wheel by the chauffeur had thrown
her car into a ditch The car overturned, and Marie, who was
travelling inside, seated among her apparatus, was buried underneath the crashing cases. She was very vexed, not because she was
so badly bruised, but to think—as she did at once—that her
radiological plates must be shattered: But, underneath the cases
which were gradually crushing her, she could not help laughing
just the same, when she heard her little chauffeur, who had lost all
his presence of mind and all his logic, running around the wrecked
car inquiring in a whisper: "Madame! Madame! Are you dead?"

Without telling the story of her adventure, she hid herself to
treat her wounds, which were slight. An account of the accident
appeared in a newspaper, and some bits of blood-stained linen
found in her dressing-room gave her away to the family; but she
was already off again with her yellow bag and her round hat, with
the wallet in her pocket—the big black leather wallet, man's size—
which she had bought "to go to war."

In 1918 she was to leave this wallet forgotten in a drawer, and it
was not touched again until 1934, after her death. It then yielded
up an identity card made out to "Mme Curie, director of the
Service of Radiology," a paper from the under-secretariat of state
for artillery and munitions "authorising Mme Curie to make use of
military cars," and about ten "special-mission" orders from the

Union of the Women of France. Four photographs: one of Marie, one of her father, and two of her mother, Mme Sklodovska; and two little empty bags which had contained seeds—seeds which she had no doubt planted, between trips, in the flower-beds at the laboratory. On these little bags were inscribed the following words: "Officinal rosemary, to be sown from April to June, in the nursery."

Mme Curie adopted no special costume for this surprising life of hers. All her old clothes, in turn, were ornamented by an arm-band of the Red Cross. She never wore a nurse's veil, but worked with bare head in the hospitals, dressed in an ordinary white laboratory blouse.

Irène tells me you are in the neighbourhood of Verdun [her nephew Maurice Curie, an artilleryman at Vauquois, wrote her] I stick my nose into every medical car that passes along the road, but I never see anything but much-striped caps, and I don't imagine that the military authorities have taken steps to regularise your coiffure, which is hardly according to regulations. . . .

This nomad could not take care of her own house. A certain disorder reigned there. Irène and Eve continued their studies, well or badly, knitted sweaters for their adopted soldiers, and followed the march of operations by sticking little flags into strategic points on the big map on the wall of the dining-room. Marie made her children take holidays without her—but her care stopped at that. She allowed Irène and Eve to stay in bed during bombardments instead of going down to shiver in the cellar, and she let them enlist in the gang of harvest workers in Brittany in 1916 to replace men who had gone to the front. For a fortnight they cut and bound sheaves and worked as threshers. In 1918 they remained in Paris in spite of the bombardment of Big Bertha. I think Marie would not have liked her daughters to be too prudent or too exacting.

Eve could not make herself useful yet, but Irène, at seventeen, had been initiated in radiology without giving up her work for a school certificate and her courses at the Sorbonne. She had been her mother's "manipulator" at first, and then been given some

missions. Marie sent her to the hospitals and found it only natural
that Irène, charged with responsibilities for which she was very
young, should stay in the army zones at Furnes, Hoogstade and
Amiens. An intimate and charming comradeship linked Mme Curie
and this young girl. The Polish woman was solitary no longer.
She was able to talk of her work or of her personal worries now
with a collaborator and friend.

During the first months of the war she had had an important
consultatation with Irène.

"The government has asked citizens to bring in their gold, and
soon there will be some loans floated," she said to her daughter.
"I am going to give up the little gold I possess. I shall add to this
the scientific medals, which are quite useless to me. There is
something else: by sheer laziness I had allowed the money for my
second Nobel Prize to remain in Stockholm in Swedish crowns.
This is the chief part of what we possess. I should like to bring it
back here and invest it in war loans. The State needs it. Only, I
have no illusions: this money will probably be lost. I don't want to
commit such 'nonsense,' therefore, unless you approve."

Changed into francs, the Swedish crowns became bonds,
"national subscriptions" or "voluntary contributions," and were
frittered away as Marie had foreseen. She took her gold to the
Bank of France: the official who received her accepted the money
but indignantly refused to send the glorious medals to be melted
down. Marie was not flattered: she judged such fetishism absurd,
and took her collection back to the laboratory with a shrug of the
shoulders.

When an hour's respite was accorded her, Mme Curie sometimes sat down on a bench in the garden in Rue Pierre Curie
where her lime-trees were growing. She looked at the Radium
Institute, new and deserted. She thought of her collaborators, all
at the front, of her favourite assistant, the Pole Jan Danysz, who
had died like a hero. She sighed. When would this bloody horror
come to an end? And when would she be able to get back to
physics again?

She did not waste time with empty dreams, and without ceasing
to "make war," she slowly and quietly prepared for peace. She
found time to strip the laboratory in the Rue Cuvier and install it

in the Rue Pierre Curie. Packing, loading and unloading, driving
her old radiological car from one building to another, she accomplished this patient work, of which the result soon appeared: the
new laboratory was ready! Marie completed the installation by an
impressive fortification of sandbags around the annex which
contained radioactive substances. As early as 1915 she had
brought the gramme of radium back from Bordeaux and had put it
at the country's disposal.

Like X-rays, radium had various therapeutic effects upon the
human body. In 1914 no effort had yet been made by the State to
organise medical treatment, so that Marie once more had to create
and improvise. She consecrated her gramme of radium to an
"emanation service": every week she "milked" radium for the gas
it gave off, and enclosed this emanation in tubes which were
afterward sent to the Hospital of the Grand-Palais and to other
sanitary centres. It was to serve in curing "vicious" sores and
many skin lesions.

Radiological cars, radiological stations, emanation service. . . .
There was still more to come. The lack of trained manipulators
worried Marie. She proposed to found and conduct a course of
instruction in radiology. Before long about twenty nurses
gathered at the Radium Institute for the first course. The programme included theoretical lessons on electricity and X-rays,
practical exercises, and anatomy. The professors were Mme Curie,
Irène Curie, and a charming and learned woman, Mlle Klein.

The hundred and fifty technicians trained in this way by Marie
from 1916 to 1918 were recruited from all classes: some among
them were very poorly educated. The prestige of Mme Curie
intimidated them at first, but they were quickly won over by the
cordial and familiar welcome the scientist gave them. Marie had a
prodigious gift for making science accessible to simple minds. The
taste for work properly done was so strong in her that when one of
the apprentices—a former chambermaid—succeeded for the first
time in developing a radiographic plate like an artist, Mme Curie
was as delighted as if it had been her own triumph.

France's allies called upon her in their turn. Since 1914 she had
been making frequent visits to the Belgian hospitals. In 1918, at
the request of the Italian government, she went on a mission to

MARIE CURIE, left, WITH HER TWO SISTERS, ANH ZALA AND
ANH BRONYA, AND HER BROTHER M. SKLODOWSKI

Photographed in Warsaw in 1912

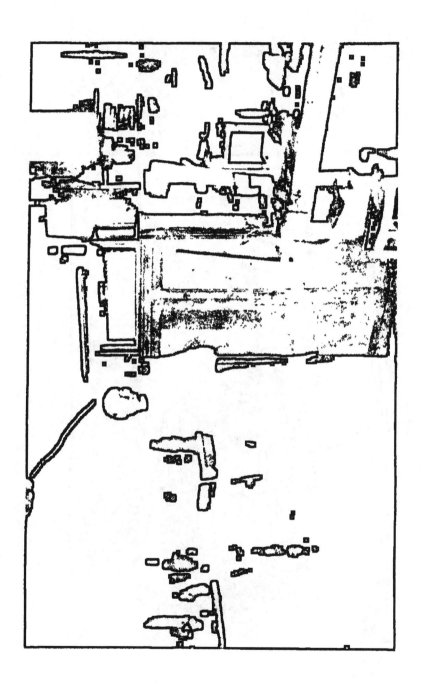

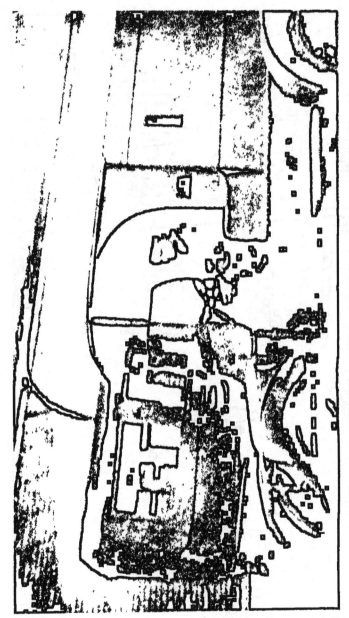

MARIE CURIE AT THE WHEEL OF THE LANGEVIN, WITH AR CONVERTED INTO A RADIOLOGICAL UNIT IN WHICH FROM AUGUST 1914 ON, SHE CARRIED AID FROM HOSPITAL TO HOSPITAL

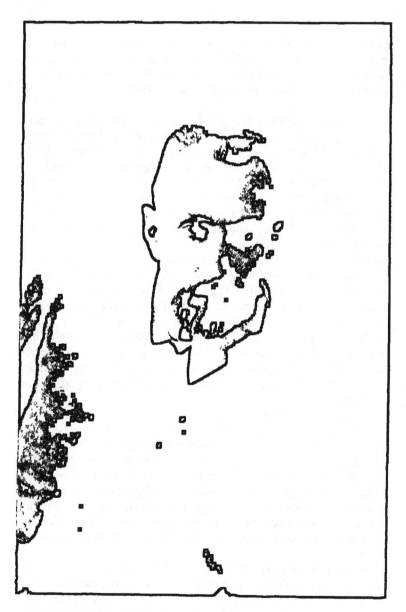

MARIE CURIE'S FAVORITE PORTRAIT OF HER HUSBAND

northern Italy, where she studied the country's resources in radioactive substances. A little later she was to welcome into her laboratory some twenty soldiers from the American Expeditionary Forces, whom she was to initiate to radioactivity.

Her new profession brought her into contact with the most varied types of human being. Certain surgeons, understanding the usefulness of the X-ray, treated her as a great colleague and a precious fellow-worker. Others, more ignorant, regarded her apparatus with deep distrust. After a few conclusive radioscopic experiments, they were astonished that "it worked" and could hardly believe their eyes when, at the spot indicated by the rays and pointed out by Marie, their scalpel encountered the bit of shell which had been vainly sought for in suffering flesh. Suddenly converted, they commented upon the event as upon a miracle. . . .

Fashionable women, the guardian angels of the hospitals, needed only one glance to classify this grey-haired woman, so indifferently dressed, who neglected to mention her name; and sometimes they treated her like a subordinate. Marie was amused by their misunderstandings. When such trivial manifestations of vanity had annoyed her a little, she purified her soul by remembering a nurse and a soldier, silent and tenacious, who were her working comrades at the hospital in Hoogstade: Queen Elizabeth and King Albert of Belgium.

Marie, often cold and distant, was charming to the wounded. Peasants and workmen sometimes grew frightened of the Rontgen apparatus and asked if the examination would hurt them. Marie reassured them: "You'll see, it's just the same as a photograph." She had what could be sweetest to them: a pleasing tone of voice, light hands, a great deal of patience, and an immense religious respect for human life. To save a man's life or to spare him suffering, an amputation or an infirmity, she was ready for the most exhausting efforts. She gave up only when every chance had been tried in vain.

She was never to speak of the hardships and dangers to which she exposed herself during these four years. She spoke neither of her tremendous fatigues, of the risk of death, nor of the cruel effect of X-rays and radium upon her damaged organism. She showed her working companions a careless and even a gay face—gayer than it had ever been. The war was to teach her that good humour which is the finest mask of courage.

She had very little joy in her soul, just the same. To the intimate anguish that distressed her when she thought of her interrupted work, or of her Polish family from whom she heard nothing, there was added her horror at the absurd frenzy that had taken possession of the world. The memory of the thousands of hacked-up bodies she had seen, of the groans and shrieks she had heard, was to darken her life for a long time.

The guns of the armistice surprised her in her laboratory. She wanted to dress flags on the institute, and took her collaborator Marthe Klein with her to search the shops of the neighbourhood for French flags. There were none left anywhere, and she ended by buying some bits of stuff in three colours which her charwoman, Mme Bardinet, hastily sewed together and displayed at the windows. Marie, trembling with nervousness and joy, could not keep still. She and Mlle Klein got into the old radiological car, battered and scarred by four years of adventure. An attendant from the P.C.N. acted as chauffeur and drove them up and down the streets, to and fro, through the eddying mass of a people both happy and grave. In the Place de la Concorde the crowd stopped the car. People clambered on the fenders of the Renault and hoisted themselves on to the roof. When Marie's car took up its route again, it carried off a dozen such extra passengers who continued to occupy this position for the rest of the morning.

For Marie there were two victories instead of one: Poland was born again from the ashes, and after a century and a half of slavery became a free country once more.

She who had been Mlle Sklodovska saw her oppressed childhood again and all the struggles of her youth. It was not in vain that she had attacked the Tsar's officialdom by dissimulation and ruse as a small child; that she had secretly joined her comrades of the Floating University in their meeting places in poor rooms in Warsaw; that she had taught little peasants of Szczuki to read. . . . The "patriotic dream" in the name of which she had once almost sacrificed her vocation, and even the love of Pierre Curie, was becoming a reality under her eyes.

Marie to Joseph Sklodovski, December, 1920:

So now we, "born in servitude and chained since birth,"* we have seen that resurrection of our country which has been our dream. We did not hope to live until this moment ourselves; we thought it might not even be given to our children to see it— and it is here! It is true that our country has paid dearly for this happiness, and that it will have to pay again. But can the clouds of the present situation be compared with the bitterness and discouragement that would have crushed us if, after the war, Poland had remained in chains and divided into pieces? Like you, I have faith in the future.

This faith and these dreams consoled Marie Curie for her personal troubles. The war had disorganised her scientific work, the war had used up her health, the war had ruined her. The money she had entrusted to the country had melted like snow, and when she examined her material situation she was anxious indeed: at the age of fifty and more, she was almost poor. For her living and that of her daughters she had only her salary as professor— twelve thousand francs a year. Would her strength allow her to pursue her teaching, to take care of her work as laboratory director for the years that separated her from the age of retirement?

Without abandoning her war work (for two years more, apprentices in radiology continued to come to the Institute of Radium for instruction) Marie threw herself again into the passion of her life: Physics. She was asked to write a book on *Radiology in War:* in it she exalted the good work of scientific discovery, eternal research and its human value. She had drawn from her tragic experience new reasons for adoring science.

The story of radiology in war offers a striking example of the unsuspected amplitude that the application of purely scientific discoveries can take under certain conditions.

X-rays had had only a limited usefulness up to the time of the

* Adam Mickievicz: *Messer Thaddeus.*

war. The great catastrophe which was let loose upon humanity, accumulating its victims in terrifying numbers, brought up by reaction the ardent desire to save everything that could be saved and to exploit every means of sparing and protecting human life.

At once there appeared an effort to make the X-ray yield its maximum of service. What had seemed difficult became easy and received an immediate solution. The material and the personnel were multiplied as if by enchantment. All those who did not understand gave in or accepted; those who did not know learned; those who had been indifferent became devoted. Thus the scientific discovery achieved the conquest of its natural field of action. A similar evolution took place in radium therapy, or the medical application of radiations emitted by the radioactive elements.

What are we to conclude from these unhoped-for developments revealed to us by science at the end of the nineteenth century? It seems that they must make our confidence in disinterested research more alive and increase our reverence and admiration for it.

It is very nearly impossible to discern in this drily technical little book how important were Marie Curie's own initiatives. What fiendish ingenuity she used to find impersonal formulas, what a rage for effacing herself, for remaining in the shadows! The "I" was not detestable to Marie: it did not exist   Her work seems to have been accomplished by mysterious entities which she names by turn "the medical organisations," or else "they," or, in cases of extreme necessity, "we." The discovery of radium itself is dissimulated among "the new radiations revealed to us by science at the end of the nineteenth century." And when she is compelled to speak of herself, Mme Curie attempts to merge into the nameless crowd:

Having wished, like so many others, to put myself at the service of the national defence during the years we have just traversed, I was at once directed toward radiology.

One detail, just the same, proves to us that Marie was conscious of having helped France as best she could. She had formerly refused—and later was to refuse again—the cross of the Legion of Honour. But her intimate friends know that if she had been proposed for the rank of chevalier in 1918 *as a soldier** she would have accepted this and no other ribbon.

This slight departure from her principles was spared her. A great many "ladies" received decorations and rosettes. She was given nothing. After some weeks, the part she had played in the great drama was effaced from all memories. And in spite of services which had been somewhat exceptional, nobody dreamed of pinning the little cross of a soldier on Mme Curie's dress.

---

* *A titre militaire*—the Legion of Honour gained on the field of battle is unlike the civil order.

CHAPTER XXII

Peace—Holidays at Larcouëst

THE world found its calm again. Marie, with a confidence and hope which were to grow weaker and weaker, followed from afar the labours of those who were organising the peace.

Very naturally, this idealist was bound to be attracted by the Wilsonian doctrines, and to have faith in the League of Nations. She obstinately sought remedies for the barbarity of the peoples and dreamed of a treaty which would truly efface rancour and hatred. "Either the Germans must be exterminated to the last man, which I could scarcely advocate," she sometimes said, "or else they must be given a peace which they can endure."

Relations between the scientists of the conquered and the conquering countries were resumed. Mme Curie showed a sincere will to forget the recent struggle. At the same time she refrained from the premature manifestations of fraternity and enthusiasm in which some of her colleagues engaged. She was inclined to ask before she would see a German physicist: "Did he sign the Manifesto of the Ninety-Three?" If he did, she would be polite and no more. If not, she was more friendly, and talked freely of science with her confrère as if the war had not taken place.

This fact, of only temporary consequence, illustrates Marie's very high idea of the role and duties of intellectuals in times of trouble. She did not think that great minds could remain "above the battle"; for four years she had served France loyally, she had saved human lives. But there were certain acts in which she could not acknowledge the intellectuals' right to complicity. Mme Curie blamed the writers and scientists of beyond the Rhine for signing

300

the Manifesto, just as, later on, she was to blame the Russian scientists who publicly approved the procedure of the Soviet police: an intellectual betrayed his mission if he was not the most constant defender of civilisation and freedom of thought.

Marie had become neither a war-monger nor a partisan by taking her part in the great struggle. It is a pure scientist that we find, in 1919, at the head of her laboratory.

She had looked forward with fervour to the moment when the buildings in the Rue Pierre Curie would hum with activity. Her first care was not to spoil the exceptional work accomplished during the war: the service of emanations, the distribution of "active" little tubes to the hospitals, continued under the direction of Dr. Regaud, who had taken possession of the biological building again on demobilisation. In the physical section, Mme Curie and her fellow-workers applied themselves to the experiments interrupted in 1914 and began some new ones.

A more normal life allowed the ageing woman to give more time to the future of Irène and Eve—two sturdy girls, bigger than she was. The elder, a student of twenty-one, calm and marvellously balanced, had never hesitated for an instant over her vocation: she would be a physicist, and she wanted, very definitely, to study radium. The fame and the achievement of her parents neither discouraged nor intimidated her. With a simplicity and naturalness worthy of admiration, Irène Curie set out on the road that had been followed by Pierre and Marie. She did not ask whether her career would be as brilliant as her mother's or not; she did not feel oppressed by a name too great. Her sincere love of science, her gifts, inspired in her only one ambition: to work for ever in that laboratory which she had seen go up, and in which, as early as 1918, she had been named assistant.*

Marie's personal experience and the happy example of Irène made it too easy for her to believe that young creatures can find their direction in the labyrinth of life without trouble. She was disconcerted by Eve's anguish, her veering and tacking about. A noble and excessive respect for the freewill of the young, an overestimate of their wisdom, kept her from exercising her authority

* *Préparateur délégué*—another laboratory position without an exact equivalent in English or American practice.

upon this adolescent. She would have liked Eve, well gifted in science, to become a doctor and to study the medical applications of radium. Nevertheless, she did not impose that course upon the child. With tireless sympathy she supported each of her daughter's capricious plans in turn, rejoiced to see her studying music, and left the choice of her teachers and her methods of work to herself.
. . . She was bestowing too much freedom upon a being undermined by doubt, who would have done better to obey firm indications. How could she perceive her error, she who had been led to her destiny, in spite of immense obstacles, by the infallible instinct of genius?

Her tenderness was to watch to the very end over these very different daughters whom she had brought into the world, without ever showing a preference between them. Irène and Eve were to find in her, in all circumstances of their lives, a protector and an ardent ally. Later on, when Irène was married and had children in her turn, Marie was to surround the two generations with her loving care:

Marie to Irène and Frédéric Joliot-Curie, December 29th, 1928:
My dear children,—I send you my best wishes for a happy New Year—that is to say, a year of good health, good humour and good work, a year in which you will have pleasure in living every day, without waiting for the days to be gone before finding charm in them, and without putting all hope of pleasure in the days to come. The older one gets the more one feels that the present must be enjoyed: it is a precious gift, comparable to a state of grace.

I am thinking of your little Hélène, and forming wishes for her happiness. It is so moving to see the evolution of this little creature who expects everything from you with unlimited confidence, and who certainly believes that you can interpose between her and all suffering. One day she will know that your power does not extend so far—nevertheless one could wish to be able to do that for one's children. At the very least one owes them every effort to give them good health, a peaceful and serene childhood in surroundings of affection, in which their fine confidence will last as long as possible.

Marie to her daughters, September 3rd, 1919:

. . . I often think of the year of work that is opening before us. I think also of each of you, and of the sweetness, joys and cares you give me. You are in all truth a great fortune to me, and I hope life still holds for me a few good years of existence in common with you.

Whether it was that her health had grown better after the exhausting years of the war, or that the appeasement of age was beginning, Marie became more serene after her fiftieth year. The grip of sorrow and illness was relaxed and the torments of old were deadened by time: Marie did not find her happiness again, but she learned to love the little joys of daily life. Irène and Eve, who had grown up in the shadow of a woman for ever struggling against illness, discovered a new companion now, with an older face but a younger heart and body. Irène, an indefatigable sportswoman, encouraged her mother to imitate her exploits, took long excursions on foot with her, and carried her off to skate, to ride horseback, and even to ski a little.

In the summer Marie joined her daughters in Brittany. In the village of Larcouëst, in a part of the country undisturbed by the vulgar crowd, the three friends passed enchanted holidays.

The population of this hamlet on the Channel coast near Paimpol was composed entirely of sailors, peasants and of professors at the Sorbonne. The discovery of Larcouëst by the historian Charles Seignobos and the biologist Louis Lapique in 1895 assumed the importance of Christopher Columbus's first journey, to the group of university people. Mme Curie, a latecomer in this colony of learned men which a witty journalist was to nickname "Port Science," lived at first in the house of one of the villagers, then rented a villa and finally bought one. She had chosen the most isolated and windswept place on the moor, dominating a tranquil sea dotted with innumerable large or tiny islands which kept the waves of the open sea from approaching the coast She had a love for lighthouses; the summer dwellings she rented and those which she was later to build all looked alike: a narrow house on a big field, rooms badly arranged, almost poorly furnished—and a sublime view.

The rare passers-by whom Marie met every morning—stoop-shouldered Breton women, slow-moving peasants, children whose smiles showed spoiled teeth—pronounced a sonorous "Bonjour, Madame Cû-û-ûrie," in which the Breton accent made the syllables drag. And—oh, miracle!—Marie, without attempting to run away, smiled and answered in the same tone: "Bonjour, Madame Le Goff. . . . Bonjour, Monsieur Quintin," or simply "bonjour" if, to her shame, she did not recognise her interlocutor. It is only after due consideration that the natives of a village accord these tranquil greetings, from equal to equal, in which there is neither indiscretion nor curiosity, but friendship alone. The mark of esteem had not come to Marie because of radium or because "her name was in the papers." She had been judged worthy of it after two or three seasons, when the women with their hair tight drawn under pointed white caps had recognised in her one of their own, a peasant.

Mme Curie's house was only a dwelling like all others. The house in Larcouëst that really counted, the centre of the colony, the palace of fashion, was a low, thatched cottage dressed to the roof in Virginia creeper, passion flowers and giant fuchsia. The cottage was called, in Breton, Taschen-Vihan: "the little orchard." Taschen possessed a sloping garden in which the flowers, planted without apparent design, formed long rows of bursting colour. Except when the east wind blew, the door of the house was always wide open. There dwelt a young sorcerer of seventy, Charles Seignobos, professor of history at the Sorbonne. He was a very small, very active old man, a trifle humpbacked, perpetually dressed in a suit of white flannel with thin black lines, patched and discoloured. The people of the country called him "Monsieur Seigno" and his friends called him "Captain." Words cannot indicate the charming devotion of which he was the object, nor, above all, by what characteristics of his nature he had deserved the veneration, tenderness and comradeship that surrounded him. This elderly bachelor had always had all men's friendship, and more wives than any pasha: thirty, forty companions, of ages from two to eighty. . . .

Marie went down to Taschen by a steep trail dominating the bay of Launay. Some fifteen initiates were already collected in front of the house, dawdling as they waited for the daily embarkation for the islands. The appearance of Mme Curie aroused no emotion in this assembly, which was a sort of cross between a convoy of emigrants and a troupe of gipsies. Charles Seignobos, whose charming eyes were concealed behind the glasses of the near-sighted, saluted her with crusty friendliness: "Ah! Here's Madame Curie! Bonjour, bonjour!" A few other "bonjours" echoed, and Marie, sitting down on the ground, took her place in the circle.

She wore a hat of washed-out linen, an old skirt and the indestructible swanskin pea-jacket which the woman "tailor" of the village, Elisa Leff, made according to a model which was the same for men and women, scientists and fishermen. Her feet were bare, in sandals. She placed in front of her a bag like fifteen other bags scattered about the grass, swollen with her bath-robe and bathing suit.

A reporter suddenly finding himself in the midst of the peaceful group would have been overjoyed. He would have had to take great care not to step on some member of the Institute of France, lazily stretched out on the ground, or not to kick a Nobel Prize winner. Intellect was abundantly represented. . . . If you wanted to talk physics there were Jean Perrin, Marie Curie, André Debierne, Victor Auger. Mathematics, integral calculus? Apply to Émile Borel, draped in his bath-robe like a Roman emperor in his toga. Biology, astrophysics? Louis Lapique or Charles Maurain could answer you. And as for the enchanter, Charles Seignobos, the numerous children of the colony whispered to each other in terror that he "knew all his history." . . .

But the miraculous thing about this assembly of scholars was that nobody ever talked physics, history, biology, or mathematics. Respect, hierarchies and even the conventions of politeness were forgotten here. Here, humanity was no longer divided into pontiffs and disciples, old and young: it was composed of exactly four categories of individuals. These were: the "philistines," the uninitiate strangers who strayed into the clan and had to be expelled as soon as possible; the "elephants," who were friends without great gifts for a nautical life, tolerated but made the victims of endless jokes; and then the Larcouëstians who were worthy of that name, the "sailors." Last of all came the super-sailors, technical experts on the currents in the bay, virtuosi of the crawl and of the rudder, denominated "crocodiles." Mme Curie, who had never been a "philistine," could hardly hope to attain the title of "crocodile." She had become a "sailor" after a short term as "elephant."

Charles Seignobos counted his flock and gave the signal for departure. From the flotilla anchored near the sho.e—two sail-boats and five or six rowboats—Eve Curie and Jean Maurain, the cabin boys on duty, had detached this morning's choice, the "big boat" and the "English boat," and had sculled them alongside, where the capriciously cut rocks served as a natural landing place. The troop of navigators was already on the bank Seignobos, in his abrupt, gay and sarcastic voice, cried out: "All aboard! All aboard!" And, as the boats filled with passengers: "Which is the first crew? I'll row stroke! Madame Curie will row bow, Perrin and Borel go to the oars, and Francis will steer."

These orders, which would have left many intellectuals per-plexed, were immediately followed. Four oarsmen—all four professors at the Sorbonne and celebrities—settled themselves on the banks and waited submissively for the orders of young Francis Perrin, the omnipotent master on board, since he was at the tiller. Charles Seignobos gave the first stroke and indi-cated the rhythm to his crew. Behind him, Jean Perrin pulled on his oar with such force that he made the boat swirl around. Emile Borel was behind Perrin, and behind Borel, in the bow, was Marie Curie.

The white-and-green boat advanced regularly across the sunny sea. Severe but just criticisms by the young coxswain broke the silence: "Number two is slacking!" (Émile Borel tried to deny his fault, but soon resigned himself, and, forgetting his laziness, pulled harder at the oar.) "Bow is not following stroke!" (Marie Curie, confused, corrected her error and applied herself to the rhythm.)

Mme Charles Maurain's beautiful, warm voice started the first notes of a "rowing song," soon taken up in chorus by the pas-sengers packed in behind:

*"My father had a house built
(Pull, pull on your oars!)
By eighty young masons . . ."**

A light north-west wind—the wind for fine weather—carried the slow, cadenced melody toward the second boat, which had made headway and could be seen on the other side of the bay. The oarsmen in the English boat in their turn set up a chant, one of those three or four hundred old songs which formed the colony's repertory, and which Charles Seignobos taught to each new generation of Larcouëstians.

Two or three songs brought the big boat to the point of La Trinité. The helmsman consulted his watch and cried: "The relief!" He did not care whether the oarsmen were tired or not, but the regulation ten minutes had passed since the start, and Marie Curie, Perrin, Borel and Seignobos gave up their places to four other members of the higher educational system. A new crew was needed to cut across the violent current in the channel and reach Roch Vras, the big violet-coloured rock, the deserted island where, nearly every morning, the Larcouëstians came to bathe.

The men undressed near the empty boats, on the beach covered with brown seaweed, the women in a corner carpeted with slick, rubbery weeds, which had been called "the ladies' cabin" since the beginning. Marie reappeared among the first, in her black bathing suit, and made for the sea. The bank was steep, and no sooner had one plunged into the water than one was out of one's depth.

The picture of Marie Curie swimming at Roch Vras in that cool deep water of ideal purity and transparence is one of the most delightful memories I have of my mother. She did not practise the "crawl" her daughters and their comrades loved. Methodically trained by Irène and Eve, she had learned an overarm stroke in good style. Her innate elegance and grace had done the rest. You forgot her grey hair, hidden under the bathing cap, and her wrinkled face, in admiring the slim, supple body, the pretty white arms and the lively, charming gestures of a young girl.

* "Mon père a fait bâtir maison
(Tirons donc sur nos avirons!)
Par quatre-vingt jeunes maçons . . ."

Mme Curie was extremely proud of her agility and of her aquatic talents; between her colleagues at the Sorbonne and herself there existed a concealed rivalry in sport. Marie observed scientists and their wives, in the little cove of Roch Vras, who swam with a respectable overhand stroke, or who floated in one place, flopping desperately, powerless to advance. She implacably counted the distances covered by her adversaries, and, without ever openly proposing a race, she put herself in training to break the records of speed and distance held by the university teaching body. Her daughters were at the same time her teachers and her confidants:

"I think I can swim better than Monsieur Borel," Marie sometimes remarked.

"Oh, a lot better, Mé. There isn't any comparison!"

"Jean Perrin gave a fine performance to-day. But I'd been farther than that yesterday, do you remember?"

"I saw you. It was very good. You've made great progress since last year."

She adored these compliments, which she knew to be sincere. At more than fifty years of age, she was one of the best swimmers of her generation.

After her swim she would warm herself in the sun, eating a bit of dry bread as she waited for the moment to go back. She made little happy exclamations: "How good it is!" Or else, before the thrilling picture of rocks, sky and water: "How beautiful!" Such brief judgments were the only comments upon Larcouést that its colonists would tolerate. It was so well understood that this was the most delightful place in the world, that the sea was bluer here— yes, blue, as blue as in the Mediterranean—and more hospitable, more varied than anywhere else, that nobody ever spoke of it, any more than one could have spoken of the scientific genius of the notable Larcouëstians. Only "philistines" would wax lyrical over these subjects, and that not for long in the face of the general irony.

Noon: The tide ebbed and the boats navigated prudently by the "Anterren channel" between blocks of weeds that looked like wet pastures. For the thousandth time the passengers noted the exact spot where the same boat, coming back from the same trip, had been caught by the ebb tide and marooned for four hours while its famished crew explored the deserted weeds in the hope of finding smelts or shellfish. Song succeeded song, relief followed relief. Here at last, below the house of Taschen, was the shore, the landing place—or rather the bank of seaweed which served as landing place at low tide. Feet and legs bare, sandals and bath-robe brandished aloft, Marie lifted her skirt and made her way bravely toward dry land through a black, smelly ooze in which she sank above the ankles. Any Larcouëstian who, through deference for her age, should have offered her help or asked to carry her bag, would have provoked her astonishment and disapproval. Nobody helped anybody here, and Article 1 of the law of the clan enjoined: "Take care of yourself!"

The sailors separated and went to lunch. At two o'clock they would meet again at Taschen for the daily trip on the *Eglantine*, the white-sailed yacht without which Larcouëst would not be Larcouëst. Mme Curie, this time, failed to answer the call. The idleness of a sailing boat wearied her. Alone in her lighthouse, deserted by her daughters, she would correct some scientific publication or else, getting out her tools, her spade and her pruning scissors, she would work in the garden. From these combats with gorse and briars, these mysterious plantation labours, she emerged scratched until the blood came, her legs striped with cuts, her hands earthy and full of thorns. It was a lucky day when the damage was no worse. Irène and Eve sometimes found their enterprising mother with a sprained ankle or a finger half crushed by a misdirected blow of the hammer.

Toward six o'clock Marie went down the landing for a second bathe and then, dressed again, she would go into Taschen by the ever-open door. In an arm-chair, behind the wide window which gave on the bay, was seated a very old, very witty and very pretty woman, Mme Marillier. She lived in the house and, from this place, watched every evening for the navigators' return. Marie waited with her until the sails of the *Eglantine* appeared on the paling sea gilded by the setting sun. After the work of disembarkation the troop of passengers climbed up the rail. There were Irène and Eve, with bronzed arms, in their cheap little dresses, their hair ornamented by red pinks from the garden which Charles Seignobos, according to an unalterable tradition, had given them before the trip started. Their shining glances spoke of the intoxication of an excursion to the mouth of the Trieux or to the isle of Modez, where the short grass incited to exhausting games of prisoner's base. Everybody, even the seventy-year-old captain, took part in this game, in which diplomas and Nobel prizes counted for nothing. Scientists who were swift kept all their prestige, but the less agile ones had to endure the condescension of the "leaders" on each side and, in the exchange of prisoners, were treated like a rabble of slaves

These customs of children or savages, living half-naked in the water and the wind, were later to become the fashion and to intoxicate all classes from the richest to the poorest. But in those years just after the war they aroused the shocked criticisms of the uninitiate. In advance of the fashion by some fifteen years, we discovered beach life, swimming races, sun-bathing, camping out on deserted islands, the tranquil immodesty of sport. Little thought was given to appearance: a bathing suit a hundred times mended, a pea-jacket, two pairs of sandals, and two or three cotton dresses made at home, formed the summer wardrobe of Irène and Eve. Later on, in a decadent Larcouëst invaded by "philistines" and—oh, horror!—robbed of its poetry by belching motor-boats, coquetry was to make its first appearance.

After dinner Mme Curie, wrapped in a shaggy monk's cloak that she had owned for fifteen or twenty years, strode up and down, arm-in-arm with her daughters. By dark trails the three figures reached Taschen—always Taschen! In the common room, for the third time in the day, the Larcouèstians were assembled. They were playing "letters" around the big table. Marie, one of the cleverest at forming complicated words with paper letters drawn from a sack, was rated as a champion: the others quarrelled over which side should claim her. Other colonists, grouped around the paraffin lamps, read or played draughts.

On gala days, amateur actor-authors played charades, songs with action, and revues in which the heroic events of the season were celebrated: an exciting race between two rival crews; the dangerous transportation of an enormous rock which had obstructed the landing place—an operation on a big scale, carried out by a body of highly excited technical experts; the misdeeds of the east wind, reviled by all; a tragic-comic shipwreck; the crimes of a ghostly badger, periodically accused of devastating the kitchen garden at Taschen. . . .

How is one to suggest the unique charm made of light, of songs childish laughter, fine silences, of a free and unconstrained comradeship between young people and their elders? This existence in which hardly anything ever happened, which cost almost nothing, and in which every day was like the day before, was to leave the richest of memories to Marie Curie and her daughters. In spite of the simplicity of the setting, it was always to represent to them the last word in luxury. No millionaire, on any beach, has been able to make the ocean yield up pleasures more vivid, rarer or more delicate than the clear-eyed sportsmen of the Sorbonne did in this corner of Brittany. And since the setting for the adventure was only a charming village—charming like a great many others, no doubt—the merit of the striking success must be attributed to the scientists who met there every year.

Several times, in writing this biography, I have asked myself if the reader, thinking of other things he has read, will not stop to murmur, with a smile of irony: "Lord, what 'nice people' they all are! What candid hearts, what sympathy and confidence!"

Well, yes. "Sympathetic characters" abound in this story. It is not my fault: they existed, and just as I have tried to depict them. Marie's companions, from those who witnessed her birth to the friends of her last days, would furnish very poor subjects for analysis to our novelists with their liking for dark colours. Strange, abnormal families, these Sklodovskis and Curies, in which parents and children did not hate each other, in which human beings were guided by tenderness, in which nobody listened at doors or dreamed of treacheries and inheritances, in which nobody murdered anybody—in which everybody was, in fact, perfectly honest! Strange circles, these groups of French and Polish university people, imperfect like all human groups, but devoted to one ideal which was never to be altered by bitterness or perfidy. . . .

I have spread the trump card of our Breton happiness upon the table. Perhaps shoulders may be shrugged at the thought that neither snobbishness nor quarrels ever secretly animated these enchanted summers. At Larcouëst the most penetrating observer would have been quite incapable of distinguishing the great scientist from the modest research worker, the rich man from the poor. Never once, in the sun and waves of Brittany, did I hear anybody speak of money. Our elder, Charles Seignobos, set us the finest example: without proclaiming himself the champion of theories or of doctrines, this liberal old man had made his property the property of us all. The house with the open door, the yacht *Eglantine*, the rowing boats, all belonged to him and still belong to him, but nobody is less their proprietor than himself. And when there was a dance in his dwelling, lighted by fluted paper lamps with candles inside, and the accordion played polkas, lancers and Breton peasant dances, the whirling couples were mixed without distinction of servants and employers, members of the Institute of France and the daughters of farmers, Breton sailors and Parisiennes.

Our mother was a silent witness of these festivals. Her friends, who knew the vulnerable point of her timid character, so reserved and almost severe to approach, never failed to tell her that Irène danced well or that Eve had on a pretty dress. And then suddenly, on the worn face of Marie Curie, there would appear an ingenuous and exquisite smile of pride.

CHAPTER XXIII

America

ONE morning in May, 1920, a lady was ushered into the tiny waiting-room of the Institute of Radium. She was called Mrs. William Brown Meloney, and she edited a great magazine in New York. It was impossible to see her as a business woman: she was small, very frail, almost an invalid; a childhood accident had made her slightly lame. She had grey hair and immense, poetic black eyes set in a lovely pale face. Trembling, she asked the servant who opened the door if Mme Curie had not forgotten the appointment with her.

She had been waiting for this appointment for years. Mrs. Meloney was one of those beings, more and more numerous, whose imaginations were exalted by the life and work of Marie Curie. The scientist represented the highest vision of womanhood to her. And, as this American idealist was at the same time a great reporter, she made determined efforts to draw near to her idol.

After several unanswered requests for an interview, Mrs. Meloney had sent Marie, through a scientist they both knew, a final letter of appeal containing the following words:

"My father, who was a medical man, used to say that it was impossible to exaggerate the unimportance of people. But you have been important to me for twenty years, and I want to see you for a few minutes."

The next morning Marie received her at the laboratory. Mrs. Meloney afterwards wrote:.*

* In her preface to the American edition of Mme Curie's brief biography, *Pierre Curie.*

315

The door opened and I saw a pale, timid little woman in a black cotton dress, with the saddest face I had ever looked upon. Her kind, patient, beautiful face had the detached expression of a scholar. Suddenly I felt like an intruder.

My timidity exceeded her own. I had been a trained interrogator for twenty years, but I could not ask a single question of this gentle woman in a black cotton dress. I tried to explain that American women were interested in her great work, and found myself apologising for intruding upon her precious time. To put me at my ease Mme Curie began to talk about America

"America," she said, "has about fifty grammes of radium. Four of them are in Baltimore, six in Denver, seven in New York." She went on, naming the location of every grain.

"And in France?" I asked.

"My laboratory has hardly more than a gramme."

"*You* have only a gramme?"

"I? Oh, I have none. It belongs to my laboratory."

. . . I suggested royalties on her patents. The revenue from such patents should have made her a very rich woman. Quietly, she said:

"Radium was not to enrich anyone Radium is an element. It belongs to all people."

"If you had the whole world to choose from," I asked impulsively, "what would you take?"

It was a silly question perhaps, but, as it happened, a fateful one.

. . . That week I learned that the market price of a gramme of radium was one hundred thousand dollars. I also learned that Mme Curie's laboratory, although practically a new building, was without sufficient equipment; that the radium held there was used only for cancer treatment.

The surprise, the amazement of this cultivated American woman must have been .extreme. Mrs. Meloney knew the powerful laboratories of the United States from having visited them—above all that of Edison, like a palace. After such grandiose establishments the Radium Institute, new and decent, but built on the modest scale of French university buildings, seemed very poor. Mrs. Meloney also knew the Pittsburgh factories where the radium ores were treated in mass. She remembered their plumes of black smoke and their long lines of cars laden with the carnotite which contained the precious matter. . . .

Here, in Paris, in a badly furnished office, face to face with the woman who had discovered radium, she asked: "What would you like to possess most?" And Mme Curie replied gently: "I need a gramme of radium to continue my researches, but I cannot buy it: radium is too dear for me."

Mrs. Meloney conceived of a magnificent plan: she wanted her compatriots to offer a gramme of radium to Marie Curie. On her return to New York she tried to persuade ten very rich women to give ten thousand dollars each to buy this present, but without success: she found only three Lady Bountifuls disposed to make such a gift. "But why look for ten rich women?" she then said to herself. "Why, not organise a subscription among all the women of America, rich and poor?"

Nothing is impossible in the United States. Mrs. Meloney formed a committee whose active members were Mrs. William Vaughan Moody, Mrs. Robert G. Mead, Mrs. Nicholas F. Brady, and Drs. Robert Abbe and Francis Carter Wood. They launched a national campaign for the Marie Curie Radium Fund in all the cities of the New World, and less than a year after her visit to the "woman in the black cotton dress," Mrs. Meloney wrote to Mme Curie: "The money has been found, the radium is yours."

The generous American women offered Marie Curie inestimable help; but in exchange they asked her gently, amicably: "Why should you not come to see us? We want to know you."

Marie hesitated. She had always fled from the crowd. The trials and display of a visit to America, to the one country in the world which most thirsted after publicity, terrified her.

Mrs. Meloney insisted and swept her objections away one by one.

"You say you don't want to leave your daughters? We invite your daughters too. Ceremonies tire you? We shall draw up the most reasonable and limited programme of receptions. Come! We shall make it a fine journey for you, and the gramme of radium will be solemnly presented to you at the White House by the President of the United States in person."

Mme Curie was touched. To collect her gramme of radium and to thank America for it she conquered her fears and accepted for the first time in her life, at the age of fifty-four, the obligations of a great official journey.

Her daughters, delighted with the adventure, made their preparations for departure. Eve made her mother buy a dress or two and persuaded her to leave her favourite costumes in Paris—the most worn and faded ones. Everybody around Mme Curie was excited. The newspapers described the ceremonies which awaited Marie on the other side of the Atlantic, and the public authorities wondered what distinctions they could bestow upon the scientist so that she might arrive in the United States with official titles worthy of her great reputation. It was hardly comprehensible to Americans that Mme Curie should not be part of the Academy of Sciences of Paris. It was surprising that she did not have the cross of the Legion of Honour. . . . The cross of the Legion was quickly offered to her, but for the second time she refused it. She was later on to ask that the rank of chevalier be accorded to Mrs. Meloney.

On the initiative of the periodical *Je Sais Tout* a farewell celebration was given in Marie's honour at the Paris Grand Opéra on April 27th, 1921, for the benefit of the Radium Institute.

Léon Bérard, Professor Jean Perrin and Dr. Claude Regaud made speeches, and afterward a programme was performed by the illustrious actors and musicians whom Sacha Guitry, the organiser of the fête, had got together: Sarah Bernhardt, then aged and infirm, and Lucien Guitry associated themselves in this tribute.

Some days later Mme Curie was on board the *Olympic*. Her two daughters were travelling with her. For the three women, for all their clothing, one trunk sufficed; but they occupied the most sumptuous apartment on the ship. Marie appreciated its comfort; nevertheless she made the instinctive grimace of a distrustful peasant before over-luxurious furniture and over-complicated food. Locked in her stateroom to escape those who would not leave her alone, she tried to forget her official mission by calling up the humble, peaceful memory of her ordinary life:

Mme Curie to Mme Jean Perrin, May 10th, 1921:
DEAR HENRIETTE,—

I found your sweet letter on board, and it did me good, for it is not without apprehension that I have left France to go on this distant frolic, so little suited to my taste and habits.

I didn't like the crossing; the sea was gloomy, dark and turbulent. Without being sick, I was dizzy, and I stayed in my cabin most of the time. My daughters seem to be very contented. Mrs. Meloney, who is travelling with us, does everything she can to get friendly with them. She is as amiable and as kind as it is possible to be.

. . . I think of Larcouëst, of the good time we shall soon be having there with our friends, of the garden where you will come to spend a few peaceful hours, and of the sweet blue sea that we both love, which is more hospitable than this cold, taciturn ocean. I am thinking, too, of the child your daughter expects, who will be the youngest member of our group of friends, the first of the new generation. After this one, I hope, there will be born a great many more children of our children. . . .

New York, delicate, bold and ravishing, appeared through a haze of fine weather. Mrs. Meloney, who had crossed with the Curie family, came to warn Marie that the journalists, photographers and cinema operators were waiting for her. An enormous mob, massed upon the landing pier, was on the watch for the scientist's arrival. These countless curious ones were to paw the ground for five hours before they saw her whom the newspapers, in giant headlines, were calling the *"benefactress of the human race."* Battalions of Girl Scouts and schoolgirls could be distinguished and a delegation of three hundred women waving red and white roses: they represented the Polish organisations of the United States. The blazing colours of the American, French and Polish flags floated above thousands of crowded shoulders and eager faces.

On the boat deck of the *Olympic* Marie was installed in a big armchair. Her hat and handbag were taken away from her. Imperious shouts from the photographers—"Look this way, Mme Curie! Turn your head to the right! Lift your head! Look this way! This way!"—rose above the incessant clicking of the forty photographic and cinematographic machines focused in a threatening semi-circle upon that astonished and tired face.

Irène and Eve served as bodyguard throughout these exhausting and fascinating weeks. The two girls were not able to form a very clear idea of the United States from their journeys in a private car, dinners for five hundred people, the ovations of mobs and the assaults of reporters. More freedom and more calm are needed before the charm of such a great country can be penetrated. This tour in the Barnum manner could teach them little about America: but in compensation it gave them certain revelations on their own mother. . . .

The determined efforts of Mme Curie to stay in the shadows had been partially crowned with success in France: the patient enemy to fame had succeeded in convincing her compatriots, and even those who came nearest her, that a great scientist was not an important personage. From the time of their arrival in New York the veil fell and the reality appeared: Irène and Eve discovered all at once what the retiring woman with whom they had always lived meant to the world.

Every speech, every movement of the mob, every article in the newspapers brought the same message; even before knowing her, the Americans had surrounded Mme Curie with an almost religious devotion and had placed her in the first rank of living men and women. Now that she was here among them, thousands of beings were subjected to the "SIMPLE CHARM OF TIRED VISITOR," and felt the pangs of love at first sight for the "JUST TIMID LITTLE WOMAN," the "PLAINLY DRESSED SCIENTIST."

I cannot dream of pretending to define the soul of a people, and —it goes without saying—I do not judge America by its newspaper headlines. Just the same, the irrepressible rush of enthusiasm with which the men and women of the United States welcomed Marie Curie was not without its profound meaning. The Latin peoples grant the Americans practical genius, but at the same time, by singular vanity, reserve to themselves a monopoly regarding idealism, sensibility and the dream world. Nevertheless it was a wave of idealism that broke at the feet of Marie Curie. A Mme

Curie sure of herself, haughty, enriched by her scientific dis‐
coveries might perhaps have provoked curiosity in the United
States; but she would not have aroused this collective tenderness.
Above and beyond the frightened scientist, the Americans were
acclaiming an attitude to life which moved them deeply: the scorn
for gain, devotion to an intellectual passion, and the desire to
serve.

In Mrs. Meloney's apartment, overflowing with flowers—a
horticulturist who had been cured of cancer by radium had been
lovingly at work for two months growing the magnificent roses he
now sent Marie—a council of war drew up the programme for the
journey. All the cities, all the colleges and all the universities of
America had invited Mme Curie to visit them. Medals, honorary
titles, and doctorates *honoris causa* were awaiting her by the
dozen. . . .

"Naturally you've brought your cap and gown?" Mrs. Meloney
asked. "They are indispensable for these ceremonies."

Marie's innocent smile provoked general consternation. She
had not brought a university gown, for the excellent reason that
she had never owned one. The masters of the Sorbonne are
obliged to have a gown, but Mme Curie, the only professor of her
sex, had left the pleasures of ordering such dress to the gentlemen.

A tailor, called in without delay, hastily ran up the majestic
vestment of black silk with velvet facings on which were to be
placed the brilliant hoods which accompany the doctor's degree.
When she tried it on Marie grew agitated, snorted impatiently,
asserted that the sleeves embarrassed her, that the stuff was too hot
—and above all that the silk irritated her poor fingers, ruined by
radium.

On May 13th, at last everything was ready. After a luncheon at
Mrs. Andrew Carnegie's and a rapid tour of New York, Mme
Curie, Mrs. Meloney, Irène and Eve departed on their meteoric
journey.

White-robed girls in line along the sunny roads; girls running by
the thousand across grassy slopes to meet Mme Curie's carriage;
girls waving flags and flowers, girls on parade, cheering, singing in
chorus. . . . such was the dazzling vision of the first days,

devoted to the women's colleges, Smith, Vassar, Bryn Mawr, Mount Holyoke. It had been a good, a very good idea to domesticate Marie Curie by introducing her first of all to an enthusiastic youth, to the girl students, her equals.

Delegates from these same colleges appeared some days later at Carnegie Hall in New York at the huge gathering of the Association of University Women. They bowed before Marie and each offered her a flower, one an "American Beauty" rose, and the next a lily. In the presence of American professors, the French and Polish ambassadors, and Ignace Paderewski, who had come to applaud his comrade of the old days, Mme Curie received titles, prizes, medals and what was then an exceptional distinction, the freedom of the city of New York.

At the ceremonies on the next two days, when five hundred and seventy-three representatives of the American scientific societies were gathered at the Waldorf Astoria to greet her, Marie was already staggering with fatigue. Between the robust, noisy, ardently demonstrative crowd and a frail woman who had left the life of a convent the struggle was unequal. Marie was stunned by the noise and the acclamations. The staring of innumerable people frightened her, as did the violence with which the public jostled to get a look when she passed through. She was vaguely afraid of being crushed in one of these terrible eddies. A fanatic was soon to injure her hand badly by an over-fervent shake, and the scientist was to complete her journey with one wrist bandaged and the arm in a sling—a casualty of fame.

The great day arrived. "PAY TRIBUTE TO HER WORK . . . HOMAGE TO GENIUS . . . BRILLIANT COMPANY AT WHITE HOUSE HONOURS NOTED WOMAN" . . . On May 20th, in Washington, President Harding presented Mme Curie with her gramme of radium—or rather with its symbol. A lead-lined casket had been specially built to contain the tubes; but these tubes were so precious —and also so dangerous, by their radiation—that they had been left safe in the factory. It was a coffer containing "imitation radium" that was exposed on a table in the middle of the East Room, where the diplomats and high officials of the magistracy, army and navy gathered with representatives of the universities.

Four o'clock. A double door opened for the entrance of the procession: Mrs. Harding on the arm of M. Jusserand, the French ambassador; Mme Curie on President Harding's arm; then Mrs. Meloney, Irène and Eve Curie, and the ladies of the "Marie Curie Committee."

The speeches began. The last was that of the President of the United States. He addressed himself cordially to the "noble creature, the devoted wife and loving mother who, aside from her crushing toil, had fulfilled all the duties of womanhood." He presented Marie with a roll of parchment tied with a tri-colour ribbon, and passed over her head a slight silken cord on which was hanging a tiny gold key: the key to the coffer.

Marie's brief words of gratitude were listened to religiously; then, in a happy rustle of commotion, the guests passed into the Blue room to file in front of the scientist. Mme Curie, seated in a chair, smiled silently at those who, one by one, advanced toward her. Her daughters shook hands in her place, and pronounced the formulas of politeness in English, Polish or French, according to the nationalities of the persons Mrs. Harding presented to them. Afterwards the procession formed again and went out on to the steps, where an army of photographers waited.

The privileged ones who were present at this celebration and the journalists who proclaimed that the "*Discoverer of Radium Is Given Priceless Treasure by American Friends*," would have been surprised to learn that Marie Curie had got rid of her gramme of radium before President Harding presented it to her. On the eve of the ceremony, when Mrs. Meloney submitted the deed of gift for her approval, she read the document carefully. Then she said with composure:

"This paper must be modified. The radium offered me by America must belong to science. So long as I am alive, it goes without saying that I shall use it only for scientific work. But if we leave things in this state, the radium would become the property of private persons after my death—of my daughters. This is impossible. I want to make it a gift to my laboratory. Can we call in a lawyer?"

"Well, yes, of course," said Mrs. Meloney, a little taken aback. "If you like, we can see to these formalities next week."

"Not next week. Not to-morrow. To-night. The act of gift will soon be valid, and I may die in a few hours."

A man of law, discovered with some difficulty at this late hour, drew up the additional legal paper with Marie. She signed it at once.

Before leaving the capital Mme Curie had to inaugurate the new low-temperature Laboratory of Mines in Washington. At the last moment the engineers were warned that she would be too tired to go down into the engine rooms, and, by quick improvisation, they created an ingenious arrangement for her use: she was to press an ordinary electric switch and all the motors would start at the same time. The ceremony took place as scheduled. The speaker, in front of a microphone said what he had to say, and then added in a loud voice: "Now Mme Curie will start the machines in this laboratory."

There were a few seconds of waiting. The assistants made despairing signs at the scientist without attracting her attention.

Marie was absorbed in the contemplation of a magnificent specimen of carnotite which had been offered her five minutes earlier, which she was turning over and over in her hands in order to admire it from all sides. In thought she must have been already choosing the exact spot, the shelf in the Radium Institute of Paris where this very rare specimen would be placed.

A renewed announcement from the speaker and some respectful digs of the elbow were necessary to bring her back from Paris to Washington. Embarrassed, she hastily pressed the magic button and thus reassured the thousands of invisible listeners who had been surprised by the unexpected hitch.

Philadelphia. Honorary titles. Doctorates. Presents were exchanged between Mme Curie and the scientific and industrial notables of the city: the owner of a factory gave the scientist fifty milligrammes of mesothorium. The members of the American Philosophical Society bestowed the John Scott Medal on her. As a mark of gratitude, Marie presented this society with a "historic" piezoelectric quartz, made and used by her during her first years of research.

She visited the radium factory in Pittsburgh, where her famous gramme had been isolated. Another doctor's degree at the university. . . . Marie wore her university gown, which was becoming and comfortable, but she refused to cover her grey hair with the traditional mortar-board, which she thought hideous and accused of "not staying on." She remained bareheaded, hat in hand, in the midst of the crowd of students and professors crowned with their stiff black mortar-boards. The most experienced coquette could not have calculated her effect better. Marie had no idea of the immaterial beauty of her face among all these black-framed faces.

She stiffened in order not to fall during the ceremony; she received bouquets, listened to speeches, hymns and choruses. . . . But on the next morning the news that had been feared was made public: Mme Curie was too weak to continue her journey. On the advice of her doctors, she gave up her tour in the cities of the West, where the receptions arranged in her honour were cancelled.

The American journalists, in an effervescent *mea culpa*, immediately accused their country of having inflicted trials beyond her strength upon an aged and delicate woman. Their articles were charming in spontaneity and picturesqueness.

"Too Much Hospitality," one newspaper proclaimed in enormous letters. "The American women showed fine intelligence when they came to the aid of the scientist, but bitter critics might well say that we had made Mme Curie pay with her own flesh for our gift, for the mere satisfaction of our pride." In another paper it was boldly asserted that "any circus or variety manager would have offered Mme Curie much more money for half as much work." Pessimists took the event tragically. "We have already almost killed Marshal Joffre by our excess of enthusiasm. Are we going to kill Mme Curie too?"

Marie had been frank and unreserved with her American admirers—and these latter had won the first round. From now on the organisers of the journey were to use every ruse to conserve her strength. Mme Curie acquired the habit of getting out of trains by the back way and crossing the rails in order to avoid the excited crowd that awaited her on the platform. When her arrival was announced at Buffalo she stopped at the station before—Niagara Falls—to visit the celebrated cascade in peace. It was a short respite. The reception committee in Buffalo had not given up hope of seeing Marie Curie. Motor cars streamed toward Niagara Falls and caught the fugitive there. . . .

Irène and Eve, who were at first simple members of the escort, became what in theatrical slang is called "doubles." Irène, dressed in the university gown, received degrees *honoris causa* in place of Mme Curie. Grave orators addressed to Eve—a girl of sixteen—the speeches they had prepared for the scientist, speaking to her of her "magnificent work," of her "long life of toil," and expected a pertinent reply from her. In cities where several ladies of the committee were disputing the honour of sheltering Marie, the Curie family was split asunder, and Irène and Eve were given as hostages to the most insistent hostesses.

When they were not representing their over-famous mother, the girls were sometimes offered amusements suited to their age: a party of tennis or boating, an elegant week-end on Long Island, an hour's swimming in Lake Michigan, a few evenings at the theatre, and a night of wild delight at the colossal amusement park at Coney Island.

But the most thrilling days were those on the journey to the West. Mrs. Meloney, who had given up the idea of having Mme Curie visit the whole of America, nevertheless wanted to show her the most astonishing marvel of the continent: the Grand Canyon of the Colorado. Marie was too tired to show her pleasure very strongly, but her daughters were carried away by enthusiasm. Everything amused them: the three days on the train by the Santa Fé line, across the sands of Texas: the exquisite meals in solitary little stations under a Spanish sun; the hotel at the Grand Canyon, an islet of comfort on the edge of that extraordinary gash in the earth's crust—a precipice sixty-five miles long and ten miles wide, of which the first sight, grandiose and almost terrifying, leaves the spectator voiceless.

Irène and Eve, mounted on hard Indian ponies, wandered along the crest of the chasm, and, from on high, watched the motionless chaos of mountains, rocks and sand pass from violet to red, from orange to pale ochre, enriched by rough shadows. Unable to resist, they soon adopted the classic itinerary and went down on mule-back to the bottom of the canyon, where, over mud and stones, the young Colorado rolled impetuously.

Only the most important ceremonies, the indispensable ones, had been carried out—and yet they would have sufficed to exhaust the most robust athlete. On May 28th, in New York, Mme Curie became a doctor *honoris causa* of Columbia University. In Chicago she was made an honorary member of the University of Chicago, received several degrees and was present at three receptions. At the first of these a large ribbon, stretched like a barrier, separated Mme Curie and her daughters from the crowd which filed past before them. At the second, in which the "Marseillaise," the Polish national hymn, and the "Star-Spangled Banner" were sung in turn, Marie almost disappeared under the heaps of flowers her admirers had brought. ·The last reception surpassed all others in fervour: it was given in the Polish quarter of Chicago for a public entirely composed of Poles. These *émigrés* were acclaiming one who was no longer a scientist, but the symbol of their far-away fatherland. Men and women in tears tried to kiss Marie's hands or to touch her dress.

On June 17th Mme Curie had to own herself beaten for the second time and interrupt her course. Her blood-pressure, which was terribly low, disturbed the doctors. Marie obtained some rest and recuperated enough to go to Boston and New Haven, to the universities of Harvard, Yale, Wellesley, Simmons and Radcliffe. On June 28th she embarked on the *Olympic*, where her cabin was piled high with telegrams and masses of flowers.

The name of another great "star" from France was soon to replace hers in the headlines of the newspapers: the boxer Georges Carpentier, preceded by his immense reputation, had just arrived in New York, and the reporters were in despair at their inability to extract from Mme Curie the slightest opinion upon the probable result of his match with Dempsey. . . .

Marie was very tired—and, to tell the truth, very content. In her letters she rejoiced at having "made a very small contribution to the friendship of America for France and Poland," and quoted the phrases of sympathy for her two fatherlands which had been pronounced by President Harding and Vice-President Coolidge. But the most stubborn modesty could not conceal from her the fact that her personal success in the United States had been enormous, that she had conquered the heart of millions of Americans and the sincere affection of all those who had come near her. Mrs. Meloney was to remain for her, up to the last day, the tenderest, most devoted of friends.

Marie Curie retained confused impressions of her exceptional expedition, lighted up brilliantly here and there by certain memories of special vividness. She was struck by the activity of American university life, by the brilliance and gaiety of the traditional ceremonies, and above all by the excellent conditions under which the students of the colleges practised sport and physical development.

She was impressed by the colossal power of the associations of women which had fêted her throughout her journey.

Finally, the perfect equipment of the scientific laboratories, and that of the numerous hospitals in which Curietherapy was utilised for the cure of cancer, left a little bitterness in her. She thought with discouragement that in this very year 1921 France still did not possess a single hospital given over to radium treatment.

The stock of radium which she had come to seek left America on the same ship with her, well sheltered behind the complicated locks of the purser's safe. This symbolic gramme inspires certain reflections upon the career of Marie Curie. In order to buy the tiny particle, it had been necessary to organise a campaign of magnificent begging across a whole continent. Marie had to appear in person in the philanthropic cities and offer her thanks. . . .

How can one not be obsessed by the idea that a simple signature given on a patent years ago would have been altogether more effective? How can one avoid thinking that a rich Marie Curie could have given laboratories and hospitals to her country? Had twenty years of struggle and difficulties given Marie any regret? Had they convinced her that by disdaining wealth she had sacrificed the development of her work to a chimera?

In some short autobiographical notes drawn up after her return from America Mme Curie asked herself these questions. She answered them:

A large number of my friends affirm, not without valid reasons,

THE RADIUM INSTITUTE AT WARSAW

RADIUM INSTITUTE AT PARIS

MISS GERTRUDE CURIE AND PUPILS FROM THE AMERICAN EMBROIDERY ART SCHOOL
AT THE INSTITUTE OF RADIUM IN PARIS

MARIE CURIE WITH DEAN PEGRAM DEAN OF THE
SCHOOL OF ENGINEERING AT COLUMBIA
UNIVERSITY 1921

MARTL CURB DISCUSSING A SCIENTIFIC PROBLEM AT BEHNER RGH
DURING THE AMERICAN TOUR

that if Pierre Curie and I had guaranteed our rights, we should have acquired the financial means necessary to the creation of a satisfactory radium institute, without encountering the obstacles which were a handicap to both of us, and which are still a handicap for me. Nevertheless, I am still convinced that we were right.

Humanity certainly needs practical men, who get the most out of their work, and, without forgetting the general good, safeguard their own interests. But humanity also needs dreamers, for whom the disinterested development of an enterprise is so captivating that it becomes impossible for them to devote their care to their own material profit.

Without the slightest doubt, these dreamers do not deserve wealth, because they do not desire it. Even so, a well-organised society should assure to such workers the efficient means of accomplishing their task, in a life freed from material care and freely consecrated to research.

CHAPTER XXIV

Full Bloom

I BELIEVE the journey to America had taught my mother something.

It had shown her that the voluntary isolation in which she confined herself was paradoxical. As a student she might shut herself in a garret with her books, and as an isolated research worker might cut herself off from the century and concentrate entirely on her personal work—and indeed she had to do so. But Mme Curie at fifty-five was something other than a student or a research worker; Marie was responsible for a new science and a new system of therapeutics. The prestige of her name was such that by a simple gesture, by the mere act of being present, she could assure the success of some project of general interest that was dear to her. From now on she was to reserve a place in her life for these exchanges and these missions.

I shall not describe all Marie's journeys: they were much alike. Scientific congresses, lectures, university ceremonies and visits to laboratories called Mme Curie to a large number of capitals. She was fêted and acclaimed in them all. She tried to make herself useful. Too often she was obliged to struggle against the weaknesses of her uncertain health.

When she had fulfilled her official duties, her best reward was to discover new landscapes and to satisfy her curiosity for nature. Thirty years of dry work had only vivified her pagan adoration for the beauty of the world. The trip across the South Atlantic on a quiet little Italian steamer gave her childlike pleasure:

We have seen some flying fish [she wrote to Eve]. **We have**

seen that our shadow can be reduced to almost nothing, and we
have had the sun on our heads. And then we have seen the known
constellations disappear into the sea: the Polar star, the Big Bear.
In the south has emerged the Southern Cross, a very beautiful
constellation. I know hardly anything about the stars one sees in
the heavens here. . . .

Four weeks at Rio de Janeiro, where she had gone with Irène to
deliver some lectures, were an agreeable interlude. Every morning
—incognita—she swam in the bay. In the afternoons she made
excursions on foot, by motor and even in a hydroplane. . . . .
Italy, Holland and England welcomed her on several occasions.
In 1932 she and Ève made a dazzling, never-to-be-forgotten
journey across Spain President Masaryk, a peasant like herself,
invited her to his country house in Czechoslovakia. In Brussels,
where she regularly attended the Solvay congresses, she was not
treated as a distinguished stranger but as a friend and neighbour.
She loved these meetings, in which those whom she called (in one
of her letters) "the lovers of Physics" discussed discoveries and
new theories. Usually such sojourns ended with a dinner or a visit
with the sovereigns: King Albert and Queen Elizabeth, whom
Marie had known on the Belgian front, honoured her with their
charming friendship.
There was not a corner of the world where her name was not
known. In an old provincial capital of China in the temple of
Confucius at Taiyuan-fu, there was a portrait of Mme Curie, placed
there among the "benefactors of humanity" by the wise men of the
country, along with Descartes, Newton, the Buddhas and the great
emperors of China. . . .

On May 15th, 1922, by unanimous vote, the Council of the
League of Nations named "Mme Curie-Sklodovska" a member of
the International Committee on Intellectual Co-operation. "Mme
Curie-Sklodovska" accepted.
This was an important date in Marie's life. Since she had become
celebrated, hundreds of charities, leagues and associations had
asked her for the support of her name. She had never once
accorded it. Marie did not want to become a member of com-

mittees in which she did not have time to do actual work. And, above all, she desired to maintain an absolute political neutrality in all circumstances She refused to abdicate her high title as "pure scientist" to throw herself into the welter of political controversy and even the most inoffensive manifesto could never obtain her signature.

The adherence of Mme Curie to the League of Nations effort therefore assumed special significance. It was to be her only infidelity to scientific research.

The International Committee on Intellectual Co-operation included brilliant personalities: Bergson, Gilbert Murray, Jules Destrée, Albert Einstein, Professor Lorentz, Paul Painlevé, and many others. Marie was to become its vice-president. She was to be a member of several committees of experts, as well as of the directors' committee of the Institute of Intellectual Co-operation in Paris.

It would show small knowledge of this practical idealist to imagine her in ecstasy before the vain jugglery of general ideas. Marie Curie worked at Geneva—and once again she succeeded in serving science.

She was struggling against what she called the "anarchy of scientific work" in the world, and tried to obtain an agreement among her confrères on a certain number of precise questions, humble in appearance, but on which the progress of knowledge depended: the international co-ordination of bibliography, to permit the worker to familiarise himself with other workers' results in his own domain; the unification of scientific symbols and terminology, of the format of scientific publications, and of the accounts of research work published in reviews; and the creation of the Tables of Constants.

Instruction in universities and laboratories claimed her attention for a long time. She would have liked to perfect its methods. She advocated "directed work" which should co-ordinate the efforts of research workers, and suggested a system of relationship between the chiefs, a true general staff which would guide scientific operations on the European continent.

All her life she had been obsessed by a certain thought: that of the intellectual gifts ignored and wasted in the classes unfavoured by fortune. In this peasant or that workman was hidden—perhaps—a writer, a scientist, a painter, a musician. . . . Marie was obliged to limit her activity. She devoted it altogether to the development of international scientific scholarships.

What is society's interest? [she asks in one of her reports]. Should it not favour the development of scientic vocations? Is it, then, rich enough to sacrifice those which are offered? I believe, rather, that the collection of aptitudes required for a genuine scientific vocation is an infinitely precious and delicate thing, a rare treasure which it is criminal and absurd to lose, and over which we must watch with solicitude, so as to give it every cnance of fruition.

And finally—paradox of paradoxes!—the physicist who had always avoided material profit for herself became the champion of "scientific property" for her confrères: she wanted to establish a copyright for scientists, so as to reward the disinterested work which serves as a basis for industrial applications. Her dream was thus to find a remedy for the poverty of the laboratories by obtaining subsidies for pure research from the profits of commerce.

Once only, in 1933, she abandoned these practical questions and went to Madrid to preside over a debate on "The Future of Culture," in which writers and artists of all countries took part: "Don Quixotes of the spirit, who are fighting their windmills," Paul Valéry, the initiator of the meeting, called them. She astonished her colleagues by her courteous authority and by the originality of her interpositions. The members of the congress were filled with alarm, denouncing the perils of specialisation and standardisation, and they made science in part responsible for the "crisis of culture" in the world. Here again we see Marie Curie—the most quixotic, perhaps, of all the Don Quixotes present—defending, with the same faith as of old, the love of research and the spirit of adventure and enterprise, in short, the passions which had guided her life always:

I am among those who think that science has great beauty [she told her interlocutors]. A scientist in his laboratory is not only a technician: he is also a child placed before natural phenomena

which impress him like a fairy tale. We should not allow it to be
believed that all scientific progress can be reduced to mechanisms,
machines, gearings, even though such machinery also has its own
beauty.

Neither do I believe that the spirit of adventure runs any risk of
disappearing in our world. If I see anything vital around me, it is
precisely that spirit of adventure which seems indestructible and
is akin to curiosity. . . .

The struggle for an international culture, respecting the different
national cultures; the defence of personality and talent wherever
they are to be found; the struggle to "strengthen the great spiritual
strength of science in the world", the struggle for "moral disarm-
ment" and for peace—such were the combats in which Mme Curie
engaged, without having the vanity to hope for an early victory.

Marie Curie to Eve Curie, July, 1919:
I believe international work is a heavy task, but that it is nevertheless indispensable to go through an apprenticeship in it, at the
cost of many efforts and also of a real spirit of sacrifice: however
imperfect it may be, the work of Geneva has a grandeur which
deserves support.

Two, three, four journeys to Poland. . . .
Mme Curie did not return to her own people in search of rest or
to forget care. Since Poland had become free again, Marie had been
haunted by a great project: she wanted Warsaw to possess a
radium institute, a centre for scientific research and the treatment
of cancer.

Her stubbornness alone was not enough to conquer the difficulties. Poland, convalescing from a long enslavement, was poor:
poor in money and poor in technicians. And Marie had not time
to make all the arrangements herself or to collect the funds.

The ally who was at her side at the first call hardly need be
named. Bronya, weighed down by age, but as enthusiastic and
valiant as thirty years ago, flung herself into the work. She was at
the same time architect, agent and treasurer. . . . The countryside
was soon flooded with posters and with stamps bearing Marie's

^face. Money was asked for—or rather, bricks: "Buy a brick for the Marie Sklodovska-Curie Institute!" was the injunction on thousands of postcards reproducing, in facsimile, the written declaration of the scientist: "My most ardent desire is the creation of an institute of radium in Warsaw." This campaign had the generous support of the State, of the city of Warsaw and of the most important Polish institutions.

The stock of bricks grew larger . . . and in 1925 Marie went to Warsaw to lay the corner stone of the institute. It was a triumphal visit: memories of the past, promises for the future. . . . The fervour of a whole people accompanied the woman who was called, by one of the orators, "the first lady-in-waiting of our gracious sovereign, the Polish Republic." The universities, the academies and the cities bestowed their finest honorary titles on her, and Marshal Pilsudski became her cordial friend in a few days. On a sunny morning the president of the republic laid the first stone of the institute, Mme Curie the second, and the mayor of Warsaw the third. . . .

There was no official stiffness in these ceremonies It was not out of simple politeness that the head of the state, Stanislav Wojciechowski, expressed his amazement at the perfection with which Marie spoke her native language after such a long exile. He had been Mlle Sklodovska's comrade in Paris; anecdotes tumbled out, one after the other.

"Do you remember the little travelling cushion you lent me thirty-three years ago when I went back to Poland on a secret political mission?" the president asked Marie. "It was very useful!"

"I even remember," Marie answered, laughing, "that you forgot to return it to me."

And M. Kotarbinski, that very old, very celebrated actor, who addressed a compliment to Mme Curie from the stage of the crowded Popular Theatre, was in fact the same M. Kotarbinski for whom the happy adolescent Manya had woven chaplets of field flowers long ago at Zwola. . . .

The years passed; the bricks became walls. Marie and Bronya were not at the end of their efforts: although each had given to the institute a good part of her savings, money was lacking for the stock of radium with which cancer treatment could be begun.

Marie did not lose courage: she explored the horizon and turned again toward the West—toward the United States where she had once been so magnificently helped, and toward Mrs. Meloney. The generous American woman knew that the institute in Warsaw was as dear to Marie's heart as her own laboratory. She accomplished a new miracle, and collected the money necessary for the purchase of a gramme of radium—the second gramme given by America to Mme Curie. The events of 1921 repeated themselves: in October 1929 Marie took ship again for New York, to thank America in the name of Poland. As in 1921, she was overwhelmed with honours. In the course of this visit she was the guest of President Hoover and stayed at the White House for several days.

I have been given a little ivory elephant, very sweet, and another tiny one [she wrote to Eve] It seems that this animal is the symbol of the Republican party, and the White House is full of elephants of all dimensions, isolated or in groups. . . .

America, devastated by the economic crisis, was in graver mood than in 1921, but its welcome was none the less warm. On her birthday the scientist received hundreds of presents sent her by unknown friends: flowers, books, objects, cheques intended for the laboratory and even— as presents from physicists—a galvanometer, some ampoules of "radon," and some specimens of rare earths. Before taking the ship again, Marie, piloted fraternally by Mr. Owen D Young, visited St. Lawrence University, where a magnificent figure of Mme Curie stands in sculptured low relief upon the entrance door. She was present at Edison's jubilee: all the speeches, and even the message sent from the South Pole by Commander Byrd, contained tributes to her.

On May 29th, 1932, the work performed in common by Marie Curie, Bronya Dluska and the Polish State was brought to its crowning point: in the presence of M. Moscicki, president of the republic—a chemical colleague and friend of Marie's—of Mme Curie and of Professor Regaud, the imposing Radium Institute of Warsaw was inaugurated. Bronya's practical sense and good taste had made it spacious, with harmonious lines. For several months it had already been admitting patients for treatment by Curietherapy.

This was the last time Marie was to see Poland, the old streets of her native town, and the Vistula, which she went to gaze at nostalgically on every visit, almost with remorse. In her letters to Eve she describes again and again this water, this land, these stones, to which she was attached by the most violent, primitive instinct.

I went for a walk alone toward the Vistula yesterday morning. . . . The river winds lazily along its wide bed, bluish green near at hand but made bluer far off by the reflection of the sky. The most adorable san banks, sparkling in the sun, are stretched out here and there, determining the capricious course of the water. On the edges of these banks, a piping of brilliant light marks the limit of the deeper water. I feel an irresistible desire to go and loiter on one of these luminous and magnificent beaches. I admit that this aspect of my river is not that of a self-respecting navigable body of water. One day it is going to be necessary to restrain its fancies a little, to the detriment of its beauty. . . .

There is a Cracow song in which they sing of the Vistula: "This Polish water has within itself such a charm that those who are taken by it will love it even unto the grave." This seems to be true, so far as I am concerned. The river has a profound attraction for me, the origins of which I do not know.

Good-bye, darling. Kiss your sister Irène for me. I embrace you both, with all my heart which belongs to you,

YOUR MOTHER.

In France . . .

On the generous initiative of Baron Henri de Rothschild, the Curie Foundation was created in 1920 as an independent institution to collect gifts and subsidies and to support the scientific and medical work of the Radium Institute.

In 1922 thirty-five members of the Academy of Medicine of Paris submitted the following petition to their colleagues:

The undersigned members think that the Academy would honour itself by electing Mme Curie as a free associate member, in recognition of the part she took in the discovery of radium and of a new treatment in medicine, Curietherapy.

This was a revolutionary document. Not only was it proposed to elect a woman academician but, breaking with custom altogether, it was proposed to elect her spontaneously, without the regular presentation of a candidacy. Sixty-four members of the illustrious company signed this manifesto with enthusiasm—thus giving a lesson to their brethren in the Academy of Sciences. All candidates to the vacant chair retired in favour of Mme Curie.

On February 7th, 1922, the election took place. M. Chauchard, president of the Academy, said to Marie from the tribune:

"We salute in you a great scientist, a great-hearted woman who has lived only through devotion to work and scientific abnegation, a patriot who, in war as in peace, has always done more than her duty. Your presence here brings us the moral benefit of your example and the glory of your name. We thank you. We are proud of your presence among us. You are the first woman of France to enter an Academy, but what other woman could have been so worthy?"

In 1923 the Curie Foundation decided to celebrate the twenty-fifth anniversary of the discovery of radium. The government associated itself with this intention and passed through Parliament, by unanimous vote, a law granting Mme Curie an annual pension of forty thousand francs as a "national recompense," with the right of inheritance to Irène and Eve.

On December 26th, twenty-five years after the meeting of the Academy of Science in 1898 at which the historic report of Pierre Curie, Mme Curie and G. Bémont *On a New and Strongly Radioactive Substance Contained in Pitch-blende* had been read, an enormous crowd invaded the great amphitheatre of the Sorbonne. The French and foreign universities, the scientific societies, the civil and military authorities, Parliament, the great schools, the students' associations and the Press were represented by delegations. On the platform were Alexandre Millerand, president of the republic, Léon Bérard, minister of public instruction, Paul Appell, rector of the Academy and president of the Curie Foundation, Professor Lorentz, who was to speak in the name of the foreign scientists, Professor Jean Perrin for the

Faculty of Science and Dr. Antoine Béclère for the Academy of Medicine.

In this group of eminent personages, could be seen a white-haired, serious-faced man and two elderly women who were wiping tears from their eyes: Hela, Bronya and Joseph had come from Warsaw to be present at Manya's triumph. The fame that had fallen upon the youngest of the Sklodovskis had neither altered nor spoiled their fraternal affection. Never were three faces more magnificently alight with emotion and pride.

André Debierne, the collaborator and friend of the Curies, read the scientific communications by which they had announced their discoveries concerning radioactive bodies. The chief of the staff at the Radium Institute, Fernand Holweck, assisted by Irène Curie, made several experiments on radium. The president of the republic offered Marie Curie the national pension "as a feeble but sincere witness of the universal sentiment of enthusiasm, respect and gratitude which follow upon her," and Mr Léon Bérard pointed out that "in order to propose and pass this law, which carries the signature of all the representatives of France, the Government and the two Houses had to resolve to act as if Mme Curie's modesty and disinterestedness had no legal existence."

Last of all, Mme Curie rose, saluted by interminable ovations. In a low voice she thanked those who had given her these tributes, taking care not to forget one of them. She spoke of the man who was no more, of Pierre Curie. Then she spoke of the future: not her own future, so very short, but that of the Radium Institute, for which she demanded help and support with insistent passion.

We have seen Marie Curie in the evening of her life at the mercy of the admiration of crowds, received by presidents, ambassadors and kings in all latitudes.

One picture, always the same, dominates the memory of these fêtes and processions for me: the bloodless, expressionless, almost indifferent face of my mother.

"In science," she had said long ago, "we must be interested in things, not in persons." The years had taught her that the public, and even the governments, did not know how to be interested in things except through persons. Whether she wished to do so or not, she had to use her prestige to honour and enrich science—to "dignify" it, as the Americans said—and she allowed her own legend to be the agent of propaganda for a cause which was dear to her.

But nothing in her had changed—neither the physical fear of crowds nor the timidity which froze her hands and dried her throat, nor, above all, her incurable inaptitude for vanity. In spite of a loyal effort, Marie did not succeed in making her pact with fame. She could never approve of the evidences of what she called "fetishism."

I find myself a long way from both of you [she wrote to me from one of these journeys] and very much exposed to manifestations which I neither like nor appreciate, because they wear me out—so I feel a little sad this morning.

In Berlin a crowd on the station platform was bustling and shouting to acclaim the boxer Dempsey, who got out of the same train with me. He looked quite content. After all, is there much difference between acclaiming Dempsey and acclaiming me? It seems to me that the mere fact of acclaiming in this way has in itself something not to be commended, whatever may be the object of the manifestation. I don't see, nevertheless, just how one ought to proceed, nor to what degree it is permissible to confound the person with the idea that person represents. . . .

How could exuberant tributes to a discovery made a quarter of a century ago satisfy the passionate student who survived inside this ageing woman? Discouraged words expressed her revolt against the premature burial which is called celebrity. "When *they* talk to me about my 'splendid work' it seems to me that I'm already dead—that I'm looking at myself dead," she murmured sometimes and added: "It seems to me that the services I might still render don't mean much to *them*—and my disappearance would put them more at their ease in paying me compliments."

Her dissatisfaction and her refusal contained, I believe, the secret of the exceptional power Mme Curie exercised over crowds. Unlike the great "stars" of popularity, politicians, monarchs, actors of the stage or cinema, who, the moment they step forward on a platform, become the accomplices of their admirers, Marie mysteriously escaped from the ceremonials at which she was present. And the profound impression produced by this motionless woman dressed in black was created, precisely, by the total absence of communication between the public and herself.

Persons even more amiable, attractive, and celebrated than Mme Curie have often been honoured by the world; but none of them, perhaps, has shown a face so locked and shuttered, an air of absence so complete. In the storm of acclamations, none of them can have seemed quite so solitary.

CHAPTER XXV

On the Ile Saint-Louis

WHEN Marie came home from some brilliant journey, one of her daughters would go to meet her on the station platform, watching for the appearance—at a window of the *wagon de luxe*—of that busy, poverty-stricken figure that Mme Curie was to remain until the end. The wanderer had a firm, cautious grip on her big handbag of brown leather, always the same one, given her years ago by an association of Polish women. It was swollen with papers, portfolios, and eyeglass cases. In the crook of her arm Marie carried a bunch of fading flowers, stiff and commonplace, which somebody had given her along the way; however troublesome they might be, she never dared to throw them out.

Relieved of her burdens, the scientist climbed up the three high storeys—without a lift—in her house of the Ile Saint-Louis. And while she examined her mail, Eve, kneeling on the floor in front of her, opened bags and unpacked for her.

She discovered, mixed in with the familiar clothing, pointed copes of velvet and silk, the emblems of new doctorates *honoris causa;* leather boxes containing medals; rolls of parchment and—more precious than all the rest—the menus of banquets, which Marie always cherished jealously. They were so convenient and so suitable, being made of thick, hard cardboard, for scribbling calculations in mathematics!

At last, with a crackle of unfolding tissue paper, appeared the "souvenirs" and presents for Irène and Eve, purchased by Marie. She had picked them out for their strangeness, their humbleness.

Bits of "petrified wood" from Texas became paper-weights,

blades of damascene from Toledo served to cut scientific books, and carpets of rough wool, woven by Polish mountaineers, were used to cover little tables. At the neck of Marie's black blouses were hung tiny jewels brought back from the Grand Canyon: these bits of crude silver, on which the Indians had cut lines of zigzag lightning, were, with a clasp of Bohemian garnet, a chain of gold filigree and a very pretty old fashioned amethyst brooch the only jewels my mother ever possessed. I doubt if all of them put together could have been sold for more than three hundred francs.

That apartment on the Quai de Béthune, very large and not very comfortable, all made of corridors and inside staircases, was a strange sort of family dwelling: twenty-two years of Mme Curie's life were passed there. The imposing rooms of a house dating from the time of Louis XIV called in vain for the majestic arm-chairs and sofas that would have suited their proportions and their style. The mahogany furniture inherited from Dr. Curie was grouped at random in the huge drawing-room—which was big enough for fifty but rarely held more than four—upon the skating rink of a fine waxed parquet which creaked and complained under one's footsteps. Neither carpets nor curtains: the high windows, on which the shutters were never closed, were barely veiled by thin net. Marie hated hangings, carpets and draperies. She liked a shining floor and naked glass windows that could not steal one ray of the sun from her. She wanted the Seine, the quais and the Ile-de-la-Cité—an admirable view—complete and unimpaired.

For years she had been too poor to make a beautiful dwelling place for herself. Now she had lost the desire to do so, and for that matter had no time to spend in altering the hasty simplicity of her life's background. However, successive alluvial deposits of gifts came to decorate the light, empty rooms. There were to be seen there some water colours of flowers, sent to Mme Curie by an anonymous admirer, a Copenhagen vase with bluish lights in it—the biggest and finest from the factory—a green and brown carpet given by a Rumanian manufacturer, a silver vase with a pompous inscription. . . . The only acquisition Marie had made was the grand piano she had bought for Eve, upon which the young girl practised for hours at a time, without ever causing Mme Curie to complain of the terrible deluge of arpeggios.

Irène had inherited the maternal indifference and, up to the time of her marriage, made herself perfectly comfortable in this icy apartment. In a big room which was her own lair, Eve made attempts at decoration—often disastrous—and renewed them as frequently as the state of her finances would permit.

The only room in the house that produced the emotion of life was Marie's workroom. A portrait of Pierre Curie, glassed-in shelves of scientific books, and a few pieces of old furniture created an atmosphere of nobility there.

This dwelling, chosen from all other possible dwellings for its calm, was one of the noisiest in the world. The pianist's scales, the strident call of the telephone, the marauding of the black cat whose speciality was cavalry charges through the corridors, and the robust clangour of the doorbell echoed and were magnified between these high walls. The insistent roaring of tugboats on the Seine used to draw Eve, young and lonely, to the window where she pressed her forehead against the glass and counted the steamers by groups. Family group of the Musketeers: Athos, Porthos. . . . Family of birds: Martin, Linnet, Swallow. . . .

In the morning, before eight o'clock, the noisy activity of an untrained servant and the light, hurried step of Mme Curie awoke the household. At a quarter to nine Mme Curie's little closed car stopped on the quay in front of the house and three honks of the klaxon resounded. Marie flung on her hat and coat and hastened downstairs. The laboratory was waiting for her.

The government's national pension and an annuity provided by American generosity had dissipated material cares. Mme Curie's income, which might have been considered absurdly small by many people, sufficed to assure her comfort, although she profited little by it. She never learned how to be waited upon by a maid. She could never make her chauffeur wait more than a few minutes without feeling vaguely guilty. And if she went into a shop with Eve, she never looked at the prices, but with infallible instinct she would point out, with her nervous hands, the simplest dress and the cheapest hat: these were the ones that pleased her.

She enjoyed spending money only for plants and stones and country houses. She built two such houses. one at Larcouëst and the other in the south. As age came on she went to the Mediterranean for a more ardent sun and warmer sea than in Brittany. To sleep in the open on the terrace of her villa at Cavalaire, to contemplate the view of the bay and of the isles of Hyères, to plant eucalyptus, mimosa and cypress on hillside gardens, were new joys to her. Two friends, two charming neighbours, Mme Sallenave and Mlle Clément, admired her aquatic feats with a certain fear. Marie bathed among jagged rocks, swimming from one to the other, and minutely described her adventures for her daughters.

The bathing is good, but one has to go a long way for it [she writes]. To-day I bathed between the rocks that overlook La Vigie —but what a climb!!! The sea has been calm for three days and I observe that I can swim for a long time, covering good distances. A distance of three hundred metres does not in the least frighten me in a calm sea, and no doubt I could do more.

Her dream would have been to abandon Paris and pass the winter at Sceaux, as in the old days. She bought land there and talked of building a house on it. The years passed without a decision being made; and every day, at lunch-time, she could be seen coming home on foot from the laboratory, crossing the bridge of La Tournelle with a step almost as lively as of yore, and, a little breathless, climbing the stairs of the old house in the Ile Saint-Louis.

When Eve was a child and Irène, Mme Curie's young assistant, lived and worked constantly with her mother, meals around the thick round table were often reduced to scientific dialogues between the scientist and her elder daughter. Technical formulæ struck Eve's ears, and she interpreted these transcendant propositions in her own way. The little girl derived great satisfaction, for example, from certain algebraic terms employed by her mother and sister: BB "prime" (BB) and Bb "square" (Bb²).* These unknown "babies" of whom Marie and Irène Curie were for ever talking must be charming, Eve thought. . . . But why

* BB, pronounced *bébé*.

square babies? And *prime* babies? What were their privileges?

One morning in 1926 Irène calmly announced to her family her engagement to Frédéric Joliot, the most brilliant and the most high-spirited of the workers at the Institute of Radium. The existence of the household was turned upside down. A man, a young man suddenly appeared in this female household where, except for a few familiars (such as André Debierne, Maurice Curie, the Perrins, the Borels and the Maurains), nobody ever penetrated. The young couple at first lived in the Quai de Béthune and then migrated to an independent flat Marie, content at the visible happiness of her daughter but disconcerted at not being able to live every hour with her working companion, tried in vain to conceal her inner dismay.

And then, when daily intimacy had made her better acquainted with Frédéric Joliot, the student who had become her son-in-law, and she was able to appreciate the exceptional qualities of the handsome, talkative boy brimming with vitality, she perceived that all was for the best. Two assistants instead of one could share her worries, discuss the research under way, receive her advice— and soon even make suggestions to her, bring her new ideas. The Joliots, very naturally, got into the habit of coming to lunch with Mme Curie four times a week.

And again, over the round table, they talked about "babies square" and "babies prime."

"Aren't you going to the laboratory, Mé?"

The ash-grey eyes, which for some years now had been sheltered behind shell-rimmed spectacles, turned their gentle, defenceless gaze upon Eve.

"Yes, I'm going there after a bit. But first I've got the Academy of Medicine. And since the meeting is not until three o'clock I think I shall have time to. . . . Yes, I can stop by the flower market, and perhaps a minute or two in the Luxembourg Gardens."

The klaxon of the Ford had already sounded three times in front of the house. In a few minutes Marie, wandering among the pots of flowers and baskets of slips, would be picking out the plants she wanted for the laboratory garden and depositing them with caution, well protected by newspapers, on the seat in her car.

The gardeners and flower-growers knew her well—but she practically never went inside a florist's shop. Some undefined instinct and the habits of poverty kept her away from precious flowers. Jean Perrin, the gayest and most attentive of her friends, made his irruptions into Mme Curie's house with his arms laden with bouquets. And as if she were admiring jewels, Marie would contemplate the big carnations and fine roses with surprise and with a little timidity.

Half-past two. The Ford dropped Marie at the gate of the Luxembourg Gardens, and the scientist hastened toward her appointment "near the lion on the left." Among the hundreds of children who were playing in the garden on this early afternoon there was one little girl who, when she saw her, would race toward her with all the speed of tiny legs: Hélène Joliot, Irène's child. In appearance Mme Curie was a reserved and undemonstrative grandmother, but she wasted a great deal of time and made long detours in order to spend a few minutes with this baby, dressed in bright red, who questioned her tyrannically: "Where are you going, Mé? Why don't you stay here with me, Mé?"

The clock on the Senate building marked ten minutes to three. Marie must leave Hélène and her sand pies. At the austere meeting hall in the Rue Bonaparte Marie took her usual place next to her old friend, Dr. Roux. And, the only woman among sixty venerable colleagues, she participated in the work of the Academy of Medicine.

"Ah! How tired I am!"

Nearly every evening Marie Curie, her face quite pale, worn and aged by fatigue, would murmur this phrase. She left the laboratory very late—at half-past seven or sometimes at eight o'clock. Her car brought her home, and the three storeys seemed harder to climb than ever before. She put on her slippers, threw a jacket of black wool over her shoulders and wandered aimlessly through the house, made more silent by the end of the day, as she waited for the maid to announce the meal.

It would have been no use for her daughter to say: "You work too hard. A woman of sixty-five cannot and ought not to work as you do, twelve or fourteen hours a day." Eve knew perfectly well that Mme Curie was incapable of working any less, and that working less, becoming reasonable would mean the dreadful indication of decrepitude. And the only wish that the young girl could formulate was that her mother might find the strength to work fourteen hours a day for a long time to come.

Since Irène no longer lived in the Quai de Béthune, Eve and her mother dined alone. The thousand incidents of a long day preoccupied Marie, and she could not refrain from commenting aloud on them Evening after evening these scattered remarks traced a mysterious and moving picture of the intense activity in that laboratory to which Mme Curie belonged, body and soul. Apparatus which Eve was never to see became familiar to her—familiar like those collaborators of whom Marie spoke warmly, almost tenderly, with the aid of many possessive adjectives:

"I am really very well pleased with 'my' young Grégoire. I knew he was very gifted! . . ." (Then, having finished her soup:) "Just think, to-day I went to see 'my' Chinese, in the Salle de Physique. We talk in English, and our conversations last for ever: in China it is impolite to contradict anybody, and when I state a hypothesis which this young man has just proved wrong by experiment, he continues to agree courteously. I have to guess when he has an objection to make! In front of these students from the Far East I am always ashamed of my bad manners. They are so much more civilised than we are!" (Taking some compôte:) "Ah, Evette, one of these evenings we must invite 'my' Pole, this year's Pole. I am afraid he must be very lost in Paris . . ."

Workers of many nationalities succeeded each other in the Tower of Babel that was the Radium Institute. There was always a Pole among them. When Mme Curie could not bestow a university scholarship on one of her compatriots without injustice to some better qualified candidate, she paid the expenses of the young man from Warsaw out of her own money—a generosity of which the young man never knew.

Suddenly Marie interrupted herself, threw off the obsession of the laboratory, leaned toward her daughter and said in another voice:

"Now, darling . . . tell me something. Give me some news of the world!"

One could tell her anything, even—and above all—childish

things. Eve's satisfied remarks upon the "forty-five-miles-an-hour average" that she got out of her car found the most understanding listener in Marie. Mme Curie, a prudent but ardent motorist, observed the sporting performances of her own Ford with emotion. Stories about her granddaughter Hélène, a quotation from the child's talk, would make her suddenly laugh to the point of tears, with an unexpected laugh of youth.

She also knew how to talk politics without bitterness. Ah! her comforting liberalism! . . . If Frenchmen praised dictatorships in front of her, she answered gently: "I have lived under a régime of oppression. You have not You don't understand your own good fortune in living in a free country . . ." The partisans of revolutionary violence met with the same opposition: "You can never convince me that it was useful to guillotine Lavoisier."

But she retained the audacity and vehemence of a young Polish "progressive." That France should be lacking in hospitals and schools, that thousands of families lived in unhealthy lodgings, that the rights of women should be precarious—all these were thoughts that tortured her.

Marie had never had time to be a perfect educator to her daughters. But Irène and Eve received one gift from her that they will never be able to appreciate enough: the incomparable benefit of living near an exceptional being—exceptional not only in her genius but by her humanity, by her innate refusal of all vulgarity and littleness Mme Curie avoided even that element of vanity that might most easily have been forgiven her: to let herself be cited as an example to other women. "It isn't necessary to lead such an anti-natural existence as mine," she sometimes said to calm her over-militant admirers. "I have given a great deal of time to science because I wanted to, because I loved research. . . . What I want for women and young girls is a simple family life and some work that will interest them."

During these calm evening meals it sometimes happened that Mme Curie and Eve talked of love. This woman, tragically and unjustly maltreated, had no great esteem for the passion of love. She would willingly have adopted the formula of one eminent French writer: "Love is not an honourable sentiment."

I think [she once wrote to Eve] that we must seek for spiritual strength in an idealism which, without making us vain, would oblige us to place our aspirations and our dreams very high—and I also think it is a source of disappointment to make all the interest of one's life depend upon sentiments as stormy as love. . . .

She knew how to receive all sorts of confidences and to keep their secret so delicately and faithfully that it seemed as if she had never heard them. She also knew how to hurry to the rescue of her own when they were threatened by danger or unhappiness But, with her, conversations on love were never real exchanges. Her judgments and her philosophy remained obstinately impersonal, and never, under any circumstances, did Marie open the gates of her sorrowful past to take lessons or memories from its store. That was an intimate realm into which nobody, however near to her heart, had the right to venture.

She allowed her daughter to divine only one thing, her home-sickness at growing old far from the two sisters and the brother to whom she had remained tenderly attached. First by exile and then by widowhood, she had been doubly deprived of the family warmth which was sweet to her. She wrote sad letters to the friends she regretted seeing so rarely—to Jacques Curie, living at Montpellier, to Joseph and to Hela, and to Bronya, whose life had been devastated like her own: Bronya had lost her two children and, in 1930, her husband, Casimir Dluski

Marie to Bronya, April 12th, 1932:
DEAR BRONYA,

I, too, am sad that we are separated. But even though you do feel lonely, you have one consolation just the same: there are three of you in Warsaw, and thus you can have some company and some protection. Believe me, family solidarity is, after all, the only good thing. I have been deprived of it, so I know Try to get some comfort out of it, and don't forget your Parisian sister: let us see each other as often as possible. . . .

If Eve was going out after dinner Mme Curie would come into her room, lie down on the divan and watch her dress.

Their opinions upon dress and feminine æsthetics were fundamentally different. But Marie had long since given up hope of imposing her principles. Of the two, it was rather Eve who oppressed her mother by an imperious insistence on renewing her black dresses before they were worn to rags. The discussions of the two women therefore remained academic, and it was with resignation, or even with gaiety and humour, that the mother made her comments to the daughter.

"Oh, my poor darling! What *dreadful* heels! No, you'll never make me believe that women were made to walk on stilts. . . . And what sort of new style is this, to have the *back* of the dress cut out? Décolletage in front was bearable, just; but these miles and miles of naked back! First of all, it's indecent; secondly, it makes you run the risk of pleurisy; thirdly, it is ugly; the third argument ought to touch you if the others don't. . . . However, apart from all this, your dress is pretty. But you wear black too much. Black isn't suited to your age . . ."

The most painful moments were those of the make-up box. After a prolonged effort toward what she judged to be a perfect result, Eve would answer her mother's ironic appeal: "Turn round a little so that I can admire you!" Mme Curie would examine her fairly, scientifically, and in the end with consternation.

"Well, of course, I have no objection in principle to all this daubing and smearing. I know it has always been done. In ancient Egypt the women invented far worse things. . . . I can only tell you one thing: I think it's dreadful. You torture your eyebrows, you daub at your lips without the slightest useful purpose . . ."

"But, Mé, I assure you it's better like this!"

"Better! Listen here; to console myself I'm coming to-morrow morning to kiss you in your bed, before you've had time to put those horrors on your face. I like you when you're not so tricked out. . . . And now you must run, my dear child. Good night. . . . Ah! by the way, you haven't anything you can give me to read?"

"Of course. What would you like?"

"I don't know . . . something that won't depress me. One has to be young like you to endure all these painful and distressing novels."

She never re-read the Russians, even Dostoievsky, whom she had once adored. Eve and she, in spite of differing literary tastes, had certain favourites in common: Kipling, Colette . . . Marie Curie was never tired of looking through the *Jungle Book*, the *Naissance du Jour,** Sido** or *Kim* for the magnificent living reflections of that nature which was always her comfort, her element And she knew by heart thousands of verses—in French, German, Russian, English or Polish. . . .

Holding the volume Eve had chosen for her, she would take refuge in her study, stretch out on the chaise-longue covered with red velvet, place a swansdown cushion under her head, and turn a few pages.

But at the end of half an hour, perhaps an hour, she put the book down. She rose, seized a pencil, notebooks, scientific manuals: she would work now, as was her habit, until two or three o'clock in the morning.

When Eve came in she would see the light in her mother's study through the round window on a narrow corridor; she crossed the corridor and pushed at the door. . . .

The spectacle was the same every night. Mme Curie, surrounded by papers, calculating rulers, and monographs, was seated on the floor. She had never been able to get used to working in front of a desk, installed in an arm-chair according to the tradition of "thinkers." She had to have limitless space to spread out her documents and her sheets of graphs.

She was absorbed in a difficult theoretical calculation, and although she had noticed her daughter's return, she did not lift her head. Her brows frowned and her face was preoccupied.

A notebook was on her knees. She scribbled signs and formulæ on it. From her lips escaped a murmur.

Mme Curie was pronouncing figures and numbers in an undertone. And like the little girl of sixty years ago in the arithmetic class at Mlle Sikorska's school, this professor at the Sorbonne was counting in Polish. . . .

' By Colette.

CHAPTER XXVI

The Laboratory

"Is Mme Curie there?"

"I am looking for Mme Curie. Has she come?"

"Have you seen Mme Curie?"

Young men, young women, persons in white under laboratory blouses, questioned each other in the vestibule by which the scientist had to pass when she arrived at the Radium Institute.

Five, ten or a dozen workers would gather in this way every morning to wait for her. Each one wanted—"without disturbing her"—to ask advice, to reap a little encouragement or a suggestion in passing. Thus was constituted what Marie laughingly called "the Soviet"

The Soviet had not long to wait. At nine o'clock the old car passed the gate in the Rue Pierre Curie and turned into the alley. The iron door clanged; Mme Curie appeared by the garden entrance. The group of soliciting students collected happily about her. Respectful, timid voices announced that such-and-such a measurement had just been completed, or gave news of the polonium solution, or insinuated that "if Mme Curie could come and look at the Wilson apparatus for a moment she would see interesting results."

Even though she sometimes complained of it, Marie adored the commotion of energy and curiosity that welcomed her from the beginning of the day. Far from attempting to slip away toward her own work, she would stay there, in coat and hat, standing in the middle of her collaborators. Each of the eager faces that met her glance recalled to her an experiment upon which she had reflected in solitude.

"M. Fournier, I have thought about what you told me. Your idea is good, but the procedure you suggest isn't practicable. I have found another that ought to succeed I shall come and talk to you about it. Mme Cotelle, what number did you get? Are you quite sure that the calculation was exact? Last night I did it over and I obtained a slightly different answer. However, we shall see . . ."

There was no disorder and no approximation in these remarks. During the minutes she devoted to a research worker, Marie Curie was entirely concentrated upon the problem he was studying, a problem which she knew in its slightest details. An instant later she was speaking of other work with another pupil. Her brain was marvellously gifted for this singular form of mental gymnastics· In the laboratory, where so many young intelligences laboured with determ nation, she resembled those chess champions who can follow thirty or forty games at a time without even looking at the pieces

Men passed, saluted and stopped. The Soviet grew larger. Marie would end by seating herself on one of the steps of the staircase without interrupting this somewhat unorthodox consultation. Thus seated looking up at the workers who stood round her or leaned against the wall, she did not have the classic attitude of a chief And yet——!

It was she who had chosen the students of the laboratory after a minute examination of their capacities. It was she, almost always, who designated their work It was to her that pupils in distress would come, with the certainty that Mme Curie would find the experimental error that had put them on the wrong road.

During forty years of scientific labour this white-haired scientist had amassed an immense amount of knowledge. She was the living library of radium; she had read, in the five languages of which she was a master, all the publications connected with the experiments undertaken at the institute. She discovered new developments of known phenomena, invented new techniques. And, finally—of inestimable value in disentangling the mixed skeins of knowledge and hypothesis—Marie possessed common sense. Fine-spun theories, attractive but fantastic suppositions, as exposed by certain of her disciples, encountered a rejection from her clear glance and her metallic reason. To work with this daring but prudent master was security.

Little by little the group assembled on the staircase was scattered. Those to whom Marie had given her day's suggestions made off with their loot. Mme Curie would accompany one of them as far as the "physics hall" or the "chemistry hall" and continue the conversation in front of an apparatus. . . . At last, set free, she would go into her own laboratory, put on her big black working blouse, and become absorbed in her personal work.

Her solitude was short. Somebody knocked at the door. One of the research workers reappeared, with sheets of manuscript in his hand. Behind him another was waiting. . . . On this Monday, the day of the weekly meeting at the Academy of Sciences, the authors of the communications that were to be presented that afternoon came to submit their reports to Mme Curie.

To read these papers Marie went into a very light, narrow, ordinary room, in which a stranger would have had difficulty recognising the study of an illustrious scientist. An office desk of oak, a file, bookshelves, an old typewriter, and a leather arm-chair like a hundred other leather arm-chairs, conferred upon it a decent anonymity. On the table there were a marble ink-stand, piles of brochures, a goblet stuck full of fountain pens and sharpened pencils, an "art object" offered by a students' association, and—surprise!—a little urn from the excavations at Ischia, dull brown, ravishing.

The hands which held out the reports to the Academy to Mme Curie often trembled with emotion. Their authors knew that the examination would be severe. The writing was never clear or chaste enough, to Marie's way of thinking. She tracked down not only the technical errors; she re-wrote whole sentences and corrected faults in syntax. "I think it might do now," she would say to the young scientist more dead than alive, as she handed him back his work.

But if the pupil's work had satisfied Marie, her smile and her pleased remarks—"Very good! That's perfect!"—compensated the physicist for his trouble and gave him wings for his journey to the laboratory of Professor Perrin. Professor Perrin customarily presented the communications of the Radium Institute to the illustrious company.

This same Jean Perrin repeated to all and sundry: "Mme Curie is not only a famous physicist: she is the greatest laboratory director I have ever known"

What was the secret of this master? First of all and above everything, the extraordinary chauvinism for the Radium Institute which animated Marie. She was the perfervid servant and the natural defender of the prestige and interests of the beloved place.

She made the most determined efforts to obtain the stock of radioactive substances necessary to research on a large scale Exchanges of courtesies and compliments between Mme Curie and the directors of the Belgian radium factory, the Union Minière du Haut-Katanga, invariably ended in the same way: the Union Minière would kindly send Mme Curie some tons of residue for nothing, and Marie, delighted, would immediately undertake the extraction of the coveted elements! . . .

From year to year she enriched her laboratory. She could be seen haunting the ministries with Jean Perrin, demanding subsidies, scholarships. Since she was "Mme Curie" the powers of the day listened to her. Thus she obtained, in 1930, an exceptional research credit of five hundred thousand francs

Sometimes, tired and a little humiliated by all the begging she forced herself to do, she described to Eve these waits in antechambers, these terrors, and concluded with a smile:

"I think they'll finish by throwing us out like beggars."

Workers in the Curie laboratory, guided by this sure pilot, explored the unexplored compartments of radioactivity one by one. From 1919 to 1934 *four hundred and eighty-three* scientific communications, of which thirty-four were theses, were published by the physicists and chemists of the Institute of Radium. Among these four hundred and eighty-three studies, Mme Curie had thirty-one publications to her credit.

Even though this number may seem high, it requires comment. During the last part of her life, Mme Curie was preparing the future with too much spirit of sacrifice, perhaps, and gave the greater part of her time to her role as director and teacher. What might have been her creative activity if she had been able to dedicate every one of her minutes to research, like the young men around her? And who can ever tell the part

Marie took in the work she inspired and guided step by step?

She asked herself no such questions. She rejoiced over the victories won by her side and with her aid, by that collective person which she did not even call "my laboratory, but, with an in-" expressible accent of secret pride, "The Laboratory." When she pronounced these two words no other laboratory existed on earth.

Psychological gifts—human ones—helped the solitary scientist to become an inspiration to and a director of the work of others. Mme Curie, so devoid of familiarity, knew how to gain the devotion of working companions whom she was still calling "Mademoiselle" or "Monsieur" after years of daily collaboration.

If Marie, absorbed in some scientific discussion, sometimes stayed out on a bench in the garden for half an hour at a time, the imploring voice of an assistant would recall her to reality.

"Madame, you'll catch cold! Madame, come in, please!" Discreet hands put bread and fruit beside her when she had forgotten to go to lunch. . . .

The laboratory journeymen and the workmen, like the others, felt her hidden attraction, an attraction unique in the world. On the day when Marie engaged a chauffeur of her own, the factotum of the institute—Georges Boiteux, who was day labourer, mechanic, chauffeur and gardener all in one—could be seen weeping bitterly at the idea that from now on another man would drive Mme Curie from the Rue Pierre Curie to the Quai de Béthune every day.

Marie was attached, by an affection, which she seldom showed to all those who worked with her; and it enabled her to distinguish the highest and most enthusiastic spirits in this big family. I hardly ever saw my mother so overwhelmed as she was in August, 1932, when she learned of the sudden death of one of her favourite pupils:

I had a great grief when I reached Paris [she wrote]. The young chemist Reymond, whom I liked so much, has been drowned in a river in Ardèche. I am quite overcome. His mother wrote to me to say that he had passed the best years of his life in the laboratory. What was the good of it if it had to end like this?

Such a fine youth, so much grace, nobility and charm, such remarkable intellectual gifts—all that wiped out because of a wretched cold bath. . . .

Her lucid glance discerned faults as well as qualities, and was inexorably arrested on the defects that would keep such-and-such a research worker from becoming a great scientist. Even more than vanity, she distrusted awkwardness. The material catastrophes that awkward hands brought upon the setting up of an experiment exasperated her. Of an experimenter without gifts she said one day to her intimates: "If everybody was like him there wouldn't be many daring flights in physics!"

When one of her collaborators passed his thesis, received his diploma, or had been judged worthy of a prize, a "laboratory tea" was given in his honour. In the summer the reunion took place out-of-doors, under the lindens in the garden. In winter the noise of crockery would suddenly disturb the peace of the biggest room in the building, the library. It was an odd sort of crockery: laboratory glasses served for teacups and champagne glasses, stirring rods took the place of spoons. The girl students handed things round, offering cakes to their comrades and chiefs and to the members of the small staff. Among the groups could be seen André Debierne, who was director of lectures at the Institute of Radium, Fernand Holweck, the chief assistant, and Marie in her most animated and talkative mood, protecting her glass of tea from the movements of the crowd.

But suddenly there was a silence—Mme Curie was about to congratulate the laureate. In a few warm phrases she would praise the originality of his work and throw light upon the difficulties he had overcome. There was vigorous applause for the friendly remarks that accompanied that sort of compliment: either an amiable word for the parents of the hero of the day, or else—if he was a foreigner—for his far-off fatherland. "When you go back to your beautiful country, which I know, where your compatriots received me so kindly, I hope you will retain a pleasant memory of the Institute of Radium. You have been able to observe that we work hard here, and that we do our best. . . ."

Some of the "teas" had special emotional value for Marie: one of them celebrated her daughter Irène's doctor's thesis, another that of her son-in-law, Frédéric Joliot. Mme Curie saw the gifts of these two research workers bloom under her direction. In 1934 the young couple won a magnificent victory: after working on the phenomena of transmutation of atoms, Irène and Frédéric Joliot discovered artificial *radioactivity*: by bombarding certain substances (aluminium for example) with the rays spontaneously emitted by the radio-elements, they succeeded in transforming these substances into new radioactive elements unknown in nature, which henceforth would be the source of rays. The consequences of this surprising creation of atoms upon chemistry, biology and medicine can easily be seen: the time is near, perhaps, when bodies possessing the properties of radium can be manufactured industrially for the requirements of Curietherapy.

At a meeting of the Physical Society when the couple explained their work, Marie, attentive and proud, was among the public. Encountering Albert Laborde, who was formerly her assistant and Pierre Curie's, she welcomed him with unusual exuberance: "Bonjour! They talked well, didn't they? We're back again in the fine days of the old laboratory."

She was too excited and tremulous not to prolong the evening. She came home on foot, along the quays, accompanied by several colleagues. And she commented endlessly upon the success of "her young people."

On the other side of the garden in the Rue Pierre Curie the collaborators of Professor Regaud, whom Marie familiarly called "the people across the way," waged their war on cancer by research and therapeutics. From 1919 to 1935, 8,319 patients were taken care of at the Radium Institute.

Claude Regaud was also a laboratory patriot. He had patiently collected the arms his fight demanded: radium, apparatus, space, a hospital. In front of the enormous number of cures obtained, and the urgency of the need, he was obliged to borrow radium—the Union Minière entrusted up to ten grammes to him!—and appeal to the government's subsidies and the gifts of citizens: Baron Henri de Rothschild and Lazard Frères were his chief benefactors, as well as a magnificent but modest anonymous donor who, employing complicated precautions to preserve his incognito, presented the Curie Foundation with 3,400,000 francs.

Thus was created, little by little, the most scientific centre of radiotherapy in France. Its prestige was immense: more than two hundred doctors came there from the five continents to learn the technique of cancer treatment.

Mme Curie, a physicist and chemist, took no part in the work of biology and medicine, but she followed their progress with passion. She got along admirably with Professor Regaud, a perfect colleague, high-minded and fiercely disinterested. Like Marie, he hated the noise of fame. Like her, he had always rejected material profits. By building up a practice he could have made a fortune: the notion did not even occur to him.

These two co-directors, who marvelled at the excellence of treatment when it was practised by technicians, were alike disturbed over one thing: exasperated and helpless, they beheld the unscrupulous exploitation of radium throughout the world. In one place ignorant doctors would treat patients with radioactive substances in hit-or-miss fashion, without even understanding the danger of such "cures." In another, patent medicines and even beauty products "on the basis of radium" were offered to the public —sometimes even under names similar to that of the Curies.

We need not judge such enterprises. We can simply say that my mother, the Curie family, Professor Regaud and the Institute of Radium had nothing whatever to do with them.

"See if there's anything important."

Marie, harassed and hurried, pointed out last night's mail to a gentle, intelligent secretary, Mme Razet.

The envelopes frequently bore simplified addresses: "Mme Curie, Paris," or "Mme Curie, scientist, France." A good half of them contained requests for autographs and letters from maniacs.

A printed card answered the autograph-hunters: "Mme Curie does not wish to give autographs or sign photographs and asks you to excuse her." To the hysterical writers of many of the other letters, in which inks of different colours alternated over eight or ten pages—misunderstood inventors, persecuted madmen, madmen in love, and threatening madmen—there was only one answer possible: silence.

MARIE CURIE AND PRESIDENT HARDING
During Her Tour of the United States in 1921

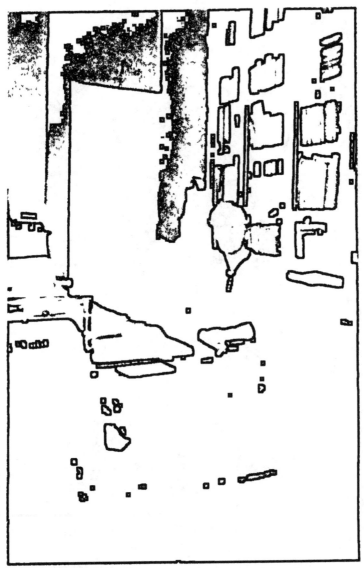

MME CURIE IN HER OFFICE AT THE RADIUM
INSTITUTE IN PARIS 1925

A GROUP PHOTOGRAPH MADE AT THE INSTITUTE
OF RADIUM IN PARIS
In the Front Row Are Irene Curie, Marie Curie, and Their
co-worker, Andre Debierne

MME CURIE AND HER DAUGHTER IRENE, 1925

There remained the other letters. Marie conscientiously dictated to her secretary messages for her colleagues abroad and answers to the desperate appeals of those who imagined that Mme Curie could cure any disease or alleviate any suffering. There were also the letters to the manufacturers of apparatus; estimates; bills; answers to the circulars sent by her hierarchical superiors to "Mme Veuve Curie, Professor in the Faculty of Science": an overwhelming administrative flood of paper which Marie filed methodically into forty-seven folders.

She conformed strictly to university customs. Her fame and her quality as a woman did not count in her eyes, and she naturally ended her official letters by the humble formulas of a subordinate: "deepest respect" for the dean of the faculty, and "obedient servant" to the rector of the university.

The forty-seven folders did not suffice for the relationship of Mme Curie with the outside world. She was harassed by demands for interviews. On Tuesday and Friday mornings Marie put on her best black dress. "I have to be suitably dressed; it's my day," she would say, her face darkening and her eyebrows lowered. In the laboratory vestibule there would be petitioners waiting for her, as well as journalists, who had been frozen beforehand by Mme Razet's warning: "Madame Curie will'receive you only if you have technical information to ask her for. She does not give personal interviews."

Even though Marie was courtesy itself, nothing encouraged the interviewer to prolong the conversation—neither the little reception room, bare and uncomfortable, the hard chairs, the impatient flicking of the scientist's fingers, nor Mme Curie's sly glances toward the clock.

On Mondays and Wednesdays Marie was nervous and agitated from the time she got up. At five o'clock on these days she lectured. After lunch she shut herself in her study in the Quai de Béthune, prepared the lesson, and wrote the heads of chapters of her lecture on a piece of white paper. Towards half-past four she would go to the laboratory and isolate herself again in a little rest-room. She was tense, anxious, unapproachable. Marie had been teaching for twenty-five years: yet every time she had to appear in the little amphitheatre before the twenty or thirty pupils who rose in unison at her entrance she unquestionably had stage fright.

Tireless and terribly activity! In her "idle moments" Marie composed scientific articles and books: a treatise on Isotropy and the Isotropes, a brief and touching biography of Pierre Curie, a new scientific treatise that would fix in perfect form the lectures of Mme Curie. . . .

These brilliant fertile years were also the years of a dramatic struggle: Mme Curie was threatened with blindness.

The doctor told her in 1920 that a double cataract was going to bring the night upon her little by little. Marie did not allow her despair to appear. She informed her daughters of this misfortune without weakness, and immediately talked of the remedy: the operation, which could be attempted in two years, in three years. . . . From now to then, during the interminable waiting, thicker and thicker crystalline lens were to put between the world and her, between her and her work, a perpetual fog.

Marie to Bronya, November 10th, 1920:

My greatest troubles come from my eyes and ears. My eyes have grown much weaker, and probably very little can be done about them. As for the ears, an almost continuous humming, sometimes very intense, persecutes me. I am very worried about it: my work may be interfered with—or even become impossible. Perhaps radium has something to do with these troubles, but this cannot be affirmed with certainty.

These are my troubles. Above all things, don't speak of them to anybody, as I don't want the thing to be bruited about. And now let's talk of something else. . . .

"Don't speak of them to anybody." . . . Such was the leit-motif of Marie's conversations with Irene and Eve, with her brother and sisters—her only confidants. Her fixed idea was to keep the news from slipping out by indiscretion, lest a newspaper publish some fine day: "Mme Curie is an invalid."

Her relatives and her physicians, Drs. Morax and Petit, became her accomplices. Marie had taken a borrowed name: it was "Mme Carré," an aged, unobtrusive woman, who suffered from a double cataract, and not Mme Curie. It was Mme Carré's glasses that Eve went to get at the oculist's.

If Marie, wandering in a fog which her glance could no longer penetrate, had to cross a street or climb a staircase, one of her daughters took her by the arm and signalled dangers and obstacles to her by an imperceptible pressure of the hand. At table it was necessary to pass objects to her: salt-cellars which she was seeking by touch on the table-cloth with pathetically assumed confidence.

But how was this heroic yet terrible farce to be kept up in the laboratory? Eve suggested taking her mother's most direct collaborators into confidence so that they could manipulate microscopes and instruments of measurement for her. Marie answered dryly: "Nobody needs to know that I have ruined eyes."

For her work, so minute, she invented a "blind-man's technique." She used giant lenses and put coloured signs, very visible, on the dials of her instruments. She wrote the notes she had to consult during lectures in enormous letters, and even in the bad light in the amphitheatre she succeeded in deciphering them.

She concealed her trouble with an infinity of ruses. If a pupil was obliged to submit to Mme Curie an experimental photograph showing fine lines, Marie by hypocritical questioning, prodigiously adroit, first obtained from him the information necessary to reconstruct the aspect of the photograph mentally. Then, and then alone, she would take the glass plate, consider it, and *appear* to observe the lines. . . .

In spite of these precautions, this noble duplicity, the laboratory suspected the drama. And the laboratory was silent, pretending not to understand, playing the game as cleverly as Marie.

Marie Curie to Eve, July 13th, 1923:
Darling,—I think I shall be operated upon Wednesday morning the eighteenth. It would be enough if you arrived here the day before. It is terribly hot and I am afraid you would be very tired.

You must tell our friends at Larcouëst that I have not been able to get through a piece of editing that we were working on together, and that I need you as I have been asked for it in a hurry.

Many kisses.

Tell them as little as possible, darling!   Mé.

Those were torrid days at the clinic, where Eve spoon-fed the motionless, blind "Mme Carré," with her wounded face swathed in bandages. The anxiety of unexpected complications followed: hæmorrhages which destroyed all hope of cure for some weeks. Two other operations followed in March, 1924, and a fourth operation in 1930. Hardly was Marie released from dressings before she began again to use her eyes, although they were badly damaged and no longer capable of focussing.

I am acquiring the habit of going about without glasses and have made some progress [she wrote to Eve from Cavalaire some months after the first operation]. I took part in two walks over awkward, rocky mountain trails. That went off rather well, and I can walk fast without accidents. What bothers me most is double vision; that is what keeps me from recognising persons as they approach. Every day I do some exercises in reading and writing. Up to now it has been more difficult than walking. Certainly you will have to help me write the article for the *Encyclopædia Britannica*. . . .

Little by little she triumphed over her ill fortune. Helped by thick glasses, she acquired almost normal sight, went out alone, even drove her car, and again succeeded in making delicate measurements in the laboratory. As a last miracle in a miraculous life, Marie emerged again from the shadows, and found light enough to work, to work to the end.

A short letter from Mme Curie to Bronya, dated September, 1927, contains the secret of this victory:

Sometimes my courage fails me and I think I ought to stop working, live in the country and devote myself to gardening. But I am held by a thousand bonds, and I don't know when I shall be able to arrange things otherwise. *Nor do I know whether, even by writing scientific books, I could live without the laboratory.*

"I don't know whether I could live without the laboratory."
To understand this cry of confession we must see Marie Curie in front of her apparatus when, having finished her daily tasks, she

could at last give herself over to her passion. No exceptional experiment was necessary to give this hollowed face a sublime expression of absorption and ecstasy. A difficult piece of glass-blower's work that Marie brought off like an artist, a measurement well made, could give her immense joy. An observant and sensitive collaborator, Mlle Chamié, was to describe this everyday Mme Curie, whose enraptured face was never to be caught by photography:

She sat before the apparatus, making measurements in the half-darkness of an unheated room to avoid variations in temperature. The series of operations—opening the apparatus, starting the chronometer, lifting the weight, etc.—was effected by Mme Curie with admirable discipline and harmony of movement. No pianist could accomplish what Mme Curie's hands accomplished with greater virtuosity. It was a perfect technique, which tended to reduce the coefficient of personal error to zero.

After the calculations which Mme Curie made with eagerness, to compare the results, her sincere, undisguised joy could be seen because the margins of difference were much lower than the permitted limit, which assured the precision of the measurements.

When she was at this work the rest of the world was effaced. In 1927, when Irène was seriously ill and Marie was tormented by despair, a friend came to see her in the laboratory to ask for news He received a laconic answer and an icy look. Hardly had he left the room when Marie, indignant, said to her assistant: "Why can't people leave one alone to work?"

Here is Mlle Chamié's description of her, absorbed in an experiment of capital importance: the preparation of actinium X for the spectrum of alpha rays—the last work Marie accomplished before her death·

Actinium X had to be pure and in such a chemical state that it could not disengage its emanation. The working day was not long enough for the separation. Mme Curie remained at the laboratory that evening without dinner. But the separation of this element is slow: one had to pass the night at the laboratory, therefore, so that the intense source being prepared would not have time to "decrease" much.

It was two o'clock in the morning, and the last operation remained to be done: centrifugation of the liquid for an hour above a special support. The centrifuge turned with a tiresome noise, but Mme Curie remained beside it without leaving the room. She contemplated the machine as if her ardent desire to make the experiment succeed could produce the precipitation of actinium X by suggestion. Nothing existed for Mme Curie at this moment outside the centrifuge: neither her life of the morrow nor her fatigue. It was a complete depersonalisation, a concentration of all her soul upon the work she was doing. . . .

If the experiment did not give the hoped-for result, Marie suddenly seemed thunderstruck by some unknown disaster. Seated on a chair, her arms crossed, her back humped, her gaze empty, she suggested some old peasant woman, mute and desolate in a great grief. The collaborators who saw her were vaguely afraid some accident had happened, and inquired. Marie lugubriously pronounced the words that summed up everything: "We haven't been able to precipitate actinium X." Or else, sometimes she openly accused the enemy, thus: "That polonium has a grudge against me."

But success made her light and young, fluttering. She wandered cheerfully in the garden, as if she wanted to tell the rambler roses and the lindens and the sun how happy she was. She was reconciled to science, she was ready to laugh and to marvel.

When a research worker, profiting by her evident good humour, proposed to show her a current experiment, she followed him eagerly, bent over the apparatus where the numeration of atoms took place, and admired the sudden irradiation of a willemite ore by the action of radium.

Before these familiar miracles a supreme happiness was set alight in her ash-grey eyes. One might have said that Marie was gazing at a Botticelli or a Vermeer, the most enchanting picture in the world.

"Ah, what a pretty phenomenon!" she would murmur.

MARIE CURIE IN 1934
Three Years before Her Death

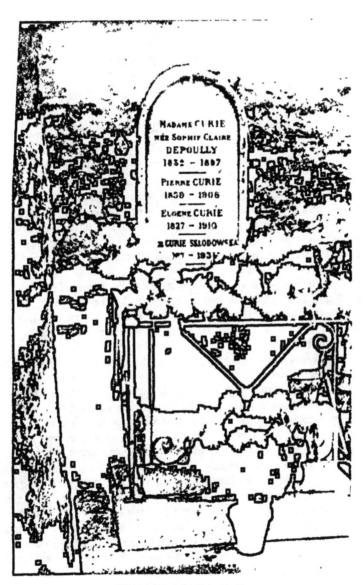

THE CURIE FAMILY TOMB

CHAPTER XXVII

The End of the Mission

MADAME CURIE often spoke of her own death. She commented upon the inevitable event with apparent calm and considered its practical consequences. Without emotion she would pronounce phrases like: "It is evident that I can't live many more years," or else: "I am worried about the fate of the Institute of Radium when I am no longer there."

But there was no serenity, no acceptance, in her. She repulsed with all her instinct the idea of an end. Those who admired her from afar thought she had an incomparable life behind her. In Marie's eyes this life was negligible, without proportion to the work undertaken.

Thirty years before, with a foreboding of death, Pierre Curie had buried himself in work with tragic ardour. Marie, in turn, took up the obscure challenge. Defending herself against the aggression that she feared, she feverishly built round her a rampart of projects and duties. She scorned a fatigue which became more evident every day, and the chronic ills that oppressed her: her bad sight, rheumatism in one shoulder, droning murmurs in her ears.

What did all that amount to? There were other things, more important. Marie had just built a factory at Arcueil for the treatment of ores in mass; she had wanted this factory for a long time and had organised the first tests there with enthusiasm. She was preoccupied by the writing of her book—a monument of science which nobody else could write once Mme Curie had disappeared. And the research work on the actinium family was not advancing rapidly enough. . . . When it was finished she had studies on the "fine structure" of alpha rays to undertake. Marie rose early, hurried to the laboratory, and returned there at night after dinner. . . .

She was working with singular haste—and also with the singular imprudence which was usual with her. She had always scorned the precautions which she so severely imposed on her pupils: to manipulate tubes of radioactive bodies with pincers, never to touch unguarded tubes, to use leaden "bucklers" to ward off the harmful radiations. She barely consented to submit to the blood tests which were the rule at the Institute of Radium. Her blood content was abnormal. What of it? . . . For thirty-five years Mme Curie had handled radium and breathed the emanation of radium. During the four years of the war she had been exposed to the even more dangerous radiation of the Röntgen apparatus. A slight deterioration in the blood, annoying and painful burns on the hands, which sometimes dried up and sometimes suppurated, were not, after all, such very severe punishments for the number of risks she had run!

In December, 1933, a short illness impressed Mme Curie more deeply. The X-ray photographs revealed a rather large stone in the gall bladder. The same disease that had carried off M. Sklodovski[1] . . . To avoid an operation which frightened her, Marie followed a strict regime and took more care of herself.

All at once the scientist who, for years past, had neglected her own comfort, and put off the humble personal plans she had nevertheless set her heart on—building a country house in Sceaux and changing flats in Paris—passed suddenly to action. She examined estimates, conquered her indecision, and unhesitatingly committed herself to heavy expenses. It was settled: the villa at Sceaux would be built during the fine weather, and in October, 1934, Marie would leave the Quai de Béthune for a modern apartment in a new building in the university city.

She felt tired and made a point of proving to herself that she was not in poor health. She went skating at Versailles and joined Irène in the ski fields of Savoy; she was happy to have kept supple and agile limbs. At Easter time, profiting by Bronya's visit to France, she organised a motoring trip in the south with her elder sister.

The expedition was disastrous. Marie had wanted to make a

roundabout journey in order to show her sister some fine landscapes. When she reached her villa at Cavalaire after a journey of
several stages, she was exhausted and had a cold. Her house was
icy when they arrived, and the heat, hastily turned on, did not
warm it fast enough. Marie, shaken by a chill, suddenly abandoned
herself to an attack of despair. She sobbed in Bronya's arms like a
sick child She was obsessed by her book and was afraid that
bronchitis might deprive her of the strength to finish it. Bronya
took care of her and calmed her. On the following morning Marie
had conquered the spiritual despondency, which was never to recur.

A few fine days comforted and consoled her. When she returned
to Paris she felt better. A doctor said she had the flu and—like all
doctors for the past forty years—that she was overworked. Marie
took little account of the light fever which was always with her.
Bronya vaguely worried, went back to Poland. Beside the
Warsaw train, on the platform they had so often trod, the two
sisters embraced for the last time.

Marie was wavering between illness and health. On the days
when she was feeling equal to it she went to the laboratory. When
she was dizzy and weak, she stayed at home and worked on her
book. She was giving several hours a week to her new apartment
and to the plans for the villa at Sceaux.

I feel the need of a house with a garden more and more, and I
ardently hope that this plan will succeed [she wrote to Bronya on
May 8th, 1934]. The price of the building has been brought down
to a sum suitable to my means. Therefore it will be possible soon
to lay the foundations.

But her secret enemy was gaining rapidly on her. The fever
became more insistent and the chills more violent. Eve had to
employ patient diplomacy to make her mother consent to see a
doctor again. On the pretext that men of the medical art were
"boring," and that "it was never possible to pay them"—no
French practitioner had ever accepted a fee from Mme Curie—
Marie constantly abstained from having a regular doctor. This
scientist and friend of progress was as refractory to treatment as
any peasant.

Professor Regaud came to pay Marie a friendly visit, and suggested asking the advice of his friend Dr. Raveau, who himself recommended Professor Boulin, a doctor of the hospitals. His first words, when he saw Marie's bloodless face, were: "You must stay in bed. You must rest."

Mme Curie had heard these exclamations so often before! She paid little attention to them. She went down and up the tiring stairs in the Quai de Béthune, working nearly every day at the Radium Institute. On one sunny day in May, 1934, she stayed until half-past three in the physical laboratory, wearily touched the tubes and the apparatus—her faithful companions. She exchanged a few words with her collaborators: "I have a fever," she murmured, "and must go home."

She made a tour of the garden again, where the new flowers were making brilliant splotches of colour. Suddenly she stopped before a sickly rambler rose and called her mechanic:

"Georges, look at this rose-vine: you must see to it right away!"

A student came up to her and begged her not to remain out-of-doors but to return to the Quai de Béthune. She yielded, but before getting into her car she turned back again:

"Don't forget, Georges: the rose-vine . . ."

This worried glance toward a blighted plant was her farewell to the laboratory.

She did not leave her bed again. The unsatisfactory struggle against an uncertain disease, called grippe and bronchitis by turns, condemned her to a fatiguing regime: she endured it with sudden terrifying docility and consented to be carried to a clinic for a thorough examination. Two radiographies and five or six analyses left the specialists who had been called to her bedside still perplexed. No organ seemed to be attacked, no definite disease declared itself. But as the X-ray pictures of the lung were clouded by the old lesions and a little inflammation, Marie was treated accordingly. When she went back to the Quai de Béthune, neither better nor worse than before, the word "sanatorium" was pronounced for the first time.

Eve fearfully suggested the idea of this exile to her. Here again Marie obeyed and consented to the departure. She had hope in purer air, and imagined that the noise and dust of the city kept her from being cured. Plans were made: Eve would go with her mother and stay at the sanatorium for several weeks, then Marie's brother and sisters would come from Poland to keep her company; Irène would pass the month of August with her, and in the autumn she would be well again.

In the sick woman's room, Irène and Frédéric Joliot talked to Mme Curie about laboratory work, the house at Sceaux, and the proof-reading of the book Marie had just finished. A young collaborator of Professor Regaud's, Georges Gricouroff, who came to get news every day, discoursed in front of Marie on the pleasantness and efficacy of sanatoria. Eve busied herself with the new apartment, chose the colours for wallpapers and hangings.

Several times Marie said, with a little laugh, searching her daughter's eyes:

"We're taking a lot of trouble for nothing, perhaps . . ."

Eve had a reserve store of protests and pleasantries ready for her, and, to solace Mme Curie, she harassed the builders. Even so, she did not hope to avert or conjure fate: though the doctors were not pessimistic, and nobody seemed worried in the house, she had, for no motive that could be expressed, an absolute certainty that the worst was near.

During the bright days of this too radiant spring she passed long hours of intimacy with her mother, condemned to leisure. Marie's intact soul and vulnerable, generous heart appeared to her as they were—and her sweetness without limit, almost unbearable at this moment. She was the "sweet Mé" of other days. She was, above all, the adolescent who had written forty-six years ago in a little letter of youth:

Creatures who feel as keenly as I do, and are unable to change this characteristic of their nature, have to dissimulate it at least as much as possible.

That is the key of a reserved nature, sensitive to excess, fearful and easily wounded: through the whole length of a splendid life Marie constantly forbade herself those spontaneous impulses, confessions of weakness and perhaps those cries for help which rose to her lips.

Now, even now, she did not confide or complain—or, if she did, it was most reticently. She spoke only of the future . . . of the laboratory's future; of the future of the institute in Warsaw; of her children's future: she hoped, felt certain, that Irène and Frédéric Joliot, in a few months' time, would receive the Nobel Prize; and of her own future too, in the apartment that was to wait for her in vain, or in the house at Sceaux that never would be built.

She grew weaker. Before attempting to move her to a sanatorium, Eve asked for a last consultation between four eminent men of the faculty—the best and most celebrated doctors in France. To name them might suggest that I blame them or that I have an unjust ingratitude toward them. For half an hour they examined a woman who was exhausted, inexorably condemned by an incomprehensible disease. In their doubt, they concluded that her old tubercular lesions had awakened. They believed that a visit to the mountains would conquer her fever. They were mistaken

Preparations were made in tragic haste: Marie's strength was spared as much as possible and she no longer saw any but intimate friends. In spite of this she defied orders, secretly summoned her collaborator Mme Cotelle to her room, and made certain recommendations to her: "You must carefully lock up the actinium until my return. I count on you to put everything in order. We shall resume this work after the holiday."

In spite of a sudden turn for the worse, the doctors advised immediate departure. The journey was sheer torture: in the train, arriving at Saint-Gervais, Marie collapsed, fainting, in the arms of Eve and the nurse. When she was at last installed in the best room at the sanatorium of Sancellemoz, new X-ray photographs and examinations were carried out: the lungs were not attacked and the journey had been useless.

Her temperature was above forty degrees.* This could not be hidden from Marie, who always inspected the thermometer with a scientist's attention. She hardly spoke by then, but her paling eyes reflected a great fear. Professor Roch of Geneva, called in at once, compared the blood tests of the last few days, in which the number of white corpuscles and that of red corpuscles were both falling in a

* Forty degrees Centigrade = 104 degrees Fahrenheit.

rapid line. He diagnosed pernicious anæmia in its extreme form. He comforted Marie, who was obsessed by the idea of gallstones. He assured her that no operation would be inflicted upon her and undertook her treatment with desperate energy. But life was in full flight from her tired body.

Then began the harrowing struggle which goes by the name of "an easy death"—in which the body which refuses to perish asserts itself in wild determination. Eve, at her mother's side, was engaged in another struggle: into the brain of Mme Curie, still very lucid, the great idea of death had not penetrated. This miracle must be preserved, to save Marie from an immense pain that could not be appeased by resignation. Above all, the physical suffering had to be attenuated; the body reassured at the same time as the soul. No difficult treatments, no tardy blood transfusions, impressive and useless. No family reunion hastily called at the bedside of a woman who, seeing her relatives assembled, would be suddenly struck to the heart by a terrible certainty.

I shall always cherish the names of those who helped my mother in these days of horror. Dr. Tobé, director of the sanatorium, and Dr. Pierre Lowys brought Marie the benefits of all their knowledge. The life of the sanatorium seemed suspended stricken with immobility by the dreadful fact: Mme Curie was about to die. The house was all respect, silence and fervour. The two doctors alternated in Marie's room. They supported and comforted her. They also took care of Eve, helped her to struggle and to tell lies, and, even without her asking them, they promised to lull Marie's last sufferings by soporifics and injections.

On the morning of July 3rd, for the last time Mme Curie could read the thermometer held in her shaking hand and distinguish the fall in temperature which always precedes the end. She smiled with joy. And as Eve assured her that this was the sign of her cure, and that she was going to be well now, she said, looking at the open window, turning hopefully toward the sun and the motionless mountains: "It wasn't the medicines that made me better. It was the pure air, the altitude . . ."

During her agony she made dreamy, amazed complaints: "I can't express myself any more. I'm absent-minded." She did not pronounce the name of any living person. She did not call on her elder daughter, who had arrived at Sancellemoz the day before with her husband, or Eve or her relations. The great and the little worries of her work wandered aimlessly in her marvellous brain and were expressed by inconsecutive phrases: "The paragraphing of the chapters ought to be done all alike . . . I've been thinking of that publication . . ."

And, staring fixedly at a teacup in which she was trying to stir a spoon—no, not a spoon, but a glass rod or some delicate laboratory instrument:

"Was it done with radium or with mesothorium?"

She had drawn away from human beings; she had joined those beloved "things" to which she had devoted her life, and joined them for ever.

She spoke only indistinctly after that—except when she made a weak cry of exhaustion to the doctor who came to give her an injection: "I don't want it. I want to be let alone."

Her last moments revealed the strength, the remarkable resistance, of a creature whose fragility was only apparent, of her robust heart, trapped in a body from which all heat was departing, which continued to beat tirelessly, implacably. For another sixteen hours Dr. Pierre Lowys and Eve each held one of the icy hands of this woman who was rejected both by life and by nothingness. At dawn, when the sun had set the mountains aglow and was beginning its journey across a beautifully pure sky, when the full light of a glorious morning had filled the room, the bed, and reached the hollow cheeks and expressionless eyes of ashen-grey made stony in death, the heart, at last, beat no more.

Science still had to pronounce its verdict over this body. The abnormal symptoms, the blood tests, differing from those in any known case of pernicious anæmia, accused the true criminal: radium.

"Mme Curie can be counted among the eventual victims of the radioactive bodies which she and her husband discovered," Professor Regaud wrote.

At Sancellemoz, Dr. Tobé drew up the following report:

Mme Pierre Curie died at Sancellemoz on July 4th, 1934.

The disease was an aplastic pernicious anæmia ⟨f rapid, feverish development. The bone marrow did not react, probably because it had been injured by a long accumulation of radiations.

The news escaped from the silent sanatorium and was spread round the world, reaching points of acute suffering here and there: in Warsaw, Hela. In Berlin, in a train that was hurrying toward France, Joseph Sklodovski; and Bronya—Bronya who was to try in vain to get to Sancellemoz in time to see the beloved face again. In Montpellier, Jacques Curie; in London, Mrs. Meloney. In Paris, faithful friends.

The young scientists sobbed before the inert apparatus at the Radium Institute. Georges Fournier, one of Marie's favourite students, wrote: "We have lost everything."

Mme Curie was sheltered from these sorrows, agitations and tributes, on her bed at Sancellemoz, in a house where men of science and devotion, her own kind, had protected her to the end. No stranger was admitted to trouble her rest even by a look. No curious eyes were ever to know with what supernatural grace she invested herself in farewell. All in white, her white hair laying bare the immense forehead, the face at peace, as grave and valiant as a knight in armour, she was, at this moment, the noblest and most beautiful thing on earth.

Her rough hands, calloused, hardened, deeply burned by radium, had lost their familiar nervous movement. They were stretched out on the sheet, stiff and fearfully motionless—those hands which had worked so much.

On Friday, July 6th, 1934, at noon, without speeches or processions, without a politician or an official present, Mme Curie modestly took her place in the realm of the dead. She was buried in the cemetery at Sceaux in the presence of her relatives, her friends, and the co-workers who loved her. Her coffin was placed above that of Pierre Curie. Bronya and Joseph Sklodovski threw into the open grave a handful of earth brought from Poland. The gravestone was enriched by a new line: MARIE CURIE-SKLO-DOVSKA, 1867-1934.

A year later, the book which Marie had finished before

disappearing brought her last message to the young "lovers of physics." At the Radium Institute, where work had been resumed, the enormous volume was added to other scientific works in the light-filled library. On the grey cover was the name of the author: "Mme Pierre Curie, Professor at the Sorbonne. Nobel Prize in Physics Nobel Prize in Chemistry."

The title was one severe and radiant word:

RADIOACTIVITY.

MME CURIE'S PRIZES

Prix Gegner, Académie des Sciences, Paris, December 12th, 1898.
This prize was again awarded on December 11th, 1900, and
on December 14th, 1902.

Nobel Prize for Physics (jointly with Henri Becquerel and Pierre
Curie), 1903.

Prix Osiris, awarded by the Syndicat de la Presse Parisienne,
divided with M. Branly, January 4th, 1904.

Actonian Prize, Royal Institution of Great Britian, May 6th, 1907.

Nobel Prize for Chemistry, 1911.

Ellen Richards Research Prize, April 23rd, 1921.

Grand Prix du Marquis d'Argenteuil for 1923, with bronze medal,
Société d'Encouragement pour l'Industrie Nationale, March
15th, 1924.

Cameron Prize, University of Edinburgh, 1931.

MME CURIE'S MEDALS AND DECORATIONS

Berthelot Medal (with Pierre Curie), 1903.

Medal of Honour of the City of Paris (with Pierre Curie), 1903.

Matteucci Medal, Italian Society of Sciences (with Pierre Curie),
August 8th, 1904.

Davy Medal of the Royal Society of London (with Pierre Curie),
November 5th, 1903.

Kuhlmann Gold Medal, of the Society of Industry of Lille,
January 19th, 1908.

Elliott Cresson Gold Medal, Franklin Institute, January 6th, 1909

Albert Medal, Royal Society of Arts, London, July 4th, 1910.

Grand Cross of the Civil Order of Alphonse XII of Spain, April
28th, 1919.

Benjamin Franklin Medal, American Philosophical Society,
Philadelphia, 1921.

John Scott Medal, American Philosophical Society, Philadelphia, April 13th, 1921.
Gold Medal of the National Institute of Social Sciences, New York, 1921.
Willard Gibbs Medal, American Chemical Society, Chicago, 1921.
Order of Merit of Rumania, first class, with warrant and gold medal, August 4th, 1924.
Gold Medal of the Radiological Society of North America, December 8th, 1922.
Medal of the New York City Federation of Women's Clubs, 1929.
Medal of the American College of Radiology, April 16th, 1931.

MME CURIE'S HONORARY TITLES

Honorary Member of the Société Impériale des Amis des Sciences Naturelle d'Anthropologie et d'Ethnographie, December 1st, 1904.
Honorary Member of the Royal Institution of Great Britain, May 9th, 1904.
Foreign Member of the Chemical Society of London, May 18th, 1904.
Corresponding Member of the Batavian Philosophical Society, September 15th, 1904.
Honorary Member of the Mexican Society of Physics, 1904.
Honorary Member of the Mexican Academy of Sciences, May 4th, 1904.
Honorary Member of the Warsaw Society for the Encouragement of Industry and Commerce, 1904.
Corresponding Member of the Argentine Society of Sciences, November 6th, 1906.
Foreign Member of the Dutch Society of Sciences, May 25th 1907.
Corresponding Member of the Imperial Academy of Sciences, St. Petersburg, January 29th, 1908.
Honorary Member of the Society of Natural Sciences, Brunswick, March 10th, 1908.
Doctor of Medicine, University of Geneva, 1909.

Corresponding Member of the Academy of Sciences, Bologne, March 31st, 1909.

Associate Foreign Member of the Czechish Academy of Sciences, Arts and Letters, 1909.

Active Foreign Member of the Academy of Sciences, Cracow, 1909.

Doctor of Laws, University of Edinburgh, July 23rd, 1909.

Honorary Member of the Philadelphia College of Pharmacy, September 27th, 1909.

Corresponding Member of the Scientific Society of Chili, December 19th, 1910.

Member of the American Philosophical Society, April 23rd, 1910.

Foreign Member of the Swedish Royal Academy of Sciences, 1910.

Honorary Member of the American Chemical Society, March 1st, 1910.

Honorary Member of the London Society of Physics, 1910.

Honorary Member of the Society for Psychical Research of London, February 1st, 1911.

Foreign Corresponding Member of the Portuguese Academy of Sciences, April 19th, 1911.

Doctor of Sciences, University of Manchester, November 24th, 1911.

Honorary Member of the Belgian Chemical Society, April 16th, 1912.

Collaborating Member of the Imperial Institution of Experimental Medicine, St. Petersburg, April 12th, 1912.

Member of the Scientific Society of Warsaw, 1912.

Honorary Member in Philosophy of the University of Lemberg, 1912.

Member of the Warsaw Photographic Society, 1912.

Doctor of the Polytechnic School, Lemberg, 1912.

Honorary Member of the Vilna Society of the Friends of Sciences, July 20th, 1912.

Member Extraordinary of the Royal Academy of Sciences (Mathematics and Physics Section), Amsterdam, May 21st, 1915.

Doctor, University of Birmingham, 1913.

Honorary Member of the Association of Arts and Sciences of Edinburgh, January 15th, 1913.

Honorary Member of the Physico-Medical Society of the University of Moscow, March, 1914.

Honorary Member of the Philosophical Society of Cambridge, May 30th, 1914.

Honorary Member of the Scientific Institution of Moscow, March, 1914.

Honorary Member of the Institution of Hygiene, London, April 15th, 1914

Corresponding Member of the Philadelphia Academy of Natural Sciences, April 22nd, 1914.

Honorary Member of the Royal Spanish Society of Medical Electrology and Radiology, April 1st, 1918

Honorary President of the Royal Spanish Society of Medical Electrology and Radiology, April 25th, 1919.

Honorary Director of the Radium Institute of Madrid, July 5th, 1919.

Honorary Professor of the Warsaw University, 1919.

Member of the Polish Chemical Society, 1919.

Ordinary Member of the Danish Royal Academy of Sciences and Letters, 1920.

Doctor of Sciences of Yale University, June 10th, 1921.

Doctor of Sciences of the University of Chicago, July 18th, 1921.

Doctor of Sciences of the North-western University, June 15th, 1921.

Doctor of Sciences of Smith College, May 13th, 1921.

Doctor of Sciences of Wellesley College, July 12th, 1921.

Doctor of the Women's Medical College of Pennsylvania, May 23rd, 1921.

Doctor of Sciences of Columbia University, June 1st, 1921.

Doctor of Laws of Pittsburgh University, June 7th, 1921.

Doctor of Laws of University of Pennsylvania, May 23rd, 1921.

Honorary Member of the Buffalo Society of Natural Sciences, June 16th, 1921.

Honorary Member of the Mineralogical Club of New York, April 20th, 1921.

Honorary Member of the North American Radiological Society, 1921.

Honorary Member of the New England Association of Chemistry Teachers, April 14th, 1921.

Honorary Member of the American Museum of Natural History, April 20th, 1921.

Honorary Member of the New Jersey Chemical Society, May 16th, 1921.

Honorary Member of the Industrial Chemistry Society, July 13th, 1921.

Member of the Christiania Academy, March 18th, 1921.

Honorary Life Member of the Knox Academy of Arts and Sciences, June 18th, 1921.

Honorary Member of the American Radium Society, July 29th, 1921.

Honorary Member of the Norwegian Society for Medical Radiology, October 15th, 1921.

Honorary Member of Alliance Française of New York, June 10th, 1921.

Associate Member, Académie de Médecine, Paris, February 7th, 1922.

Membre Honoraire du Groupe Académique Russe de Belgique, January 22nd, 1922.

Honorary Member of the Rumania Society of Medical Hydrology and Climatology, January 10th, 1923.

Honorary Member of the Czechoslovakian Union of Mathematicians and Physicists, January 20th, 1923.

Honorary Citizen of the City of Warsaw, 1924.

Honorary Member of the Polish Chemical Society of Warsaw, 1924.

Doctor of Medicine of the University of Cracow, February 25th, 1924.

Doctor of Philosophy of the University of Cracow, February 25th, 1924.

Honorary Citizen of the City of Riga, 1924.

Honorary Member of the Society of Psychic Research of Athens, December 15th, 1924.

Honorary Member of the Medical Society of Lublin, Poland, July 4th, 1925.

Member of the "Pontificia Tiberina" of Rome, March 31st,
    1926.
Honorary Member of the Chemical Society of Sao Paulo Brazil,
    August 12th, 1926.
Corresponding Member of the Brazilian Academy of Sciences,
    August 24th, 1926.
Honorary Member of the Society of Pharmacy and Chemistry of
    Sao Paulo, Brazil, July 17th, 1926.
Honorary Member of the Brazilian Association of Pharmacists,
    July 23rd, 1926.
Doctor of the Chemical Section of the Polytechnic School of
    Warsaw, 1926.
Honorary Member of the Academy of Sciences of Moscow,
    January 4th, 1927.
Foreign Member of the Bohemian Society of Letters and Sciences,
    January 12th, 1927.
Honorary Member of the Academy of Sciences of U.S.S.R.,
    February 2nd, 1927.
Honorary Member of the Interstate Postgraduate Medical
    Association of North America, 1927.
Honorary Member of New Zealand Institute, February 8th, 1927.
Honorary Member of the Society of the Friends and Sciences of
    Poznan, Poland, March 6th, 1929.
Doctor of Law of the University of Glasgow, June, 1929.
Honorary Citizen of the City of Glasgow, 1929.
Doctor of Sciences of the University of St. Laurent, October 26th,
    1929.
Honorary Member of the New York Academy of Medicine,
    January 7th, 1930.
Honorary Member of the Polish Medical and Dental Association
    of America, October, 1929.
Honorary Member of the Société Française des Inventeurs et
    Savants, March 5th, 1930.
Honorary President of the Société Française des Inventeurs et
    Savants, June 16th, 1930.
Honorary Member of the World League for Peace, Geneva, 1931.
Honorary Member of the American College of Radiology, April
    16th, 1931.

Foreign Corresponding Member of the Madrid Academy of Exact Natural Physical Sciences, April 25th, 1931.

Member of the Imperial German Academy of Natural Sciences, Halle, March 18th, 1932.

Honorary Member of the Society of Medicine of Warsaw, June 28th, 1932.

Honorary Member of the Czechoslovakian Chemistry Society, September 24th, 1932.

Honorary Member of the British Institute of Radiology and Rontgen Society, London, 1933.

INDEX